Foundations of
Counseling and Psychotherapy

Evidence-Based Practices for a Diverse Society

Foundations of Counseling and Psychotherapy

Evidence-Based Practices for a Diverse Society

David Sue
Diane M. Sue

BICENTENNIAL
1807
WILEY
2007
BICENTENNIAL

JOHN WILEY & SONS, INC.

We would like to dedicate this book to those who have devoted their lives
to helping others through service in the mental health professions;
our three children, Joel, Jennifer, and Christina;
and our twin grandsons, Joaquín and Adrián, born March 24, 2007.

CONTENTS

Chapter 4 _____

Contextual and Collaborative Assessment   **53**

Chapter 5 _____

Diagnosis and Conceptualization   **69**

Chapter 6 _____

Psychodynamic Theory and Techniques   **85**

Chapter 14 _____

Chapter 15 _____

The goal of *Foundations of Counseling and Psychotherapy: Evidence-Based Practices for a Diverse Society* is to provide students and practitioners with an overview of theories of counseling, as well as the application of such theories within the context of a scientific model that is relevant to diverse populations. We focus on the ability of empirically supported therapies and relationship variables to meet the requirements of private practice, clinical settings, and managed-care systems. Recognizing that this is a period of significant change in the fields of counseling, psychotherapy, and social work, we provide practical information with a focus on evidence-based therapies and techniques that can be used by practitioners from varying backgrounds. Our chapters summarizing treatment packages such as Core Conflict Relationship Theme Therapy, Motivational Enhancement Therapy, Interpersonal Therapy, Beck's Cognitive-Behavioral Therapy, and Dialectic Behavior Therapy provide a unique addition to the current literature and allow readers to become familiar with the way in which each theory is incorporated into therapeutic practices. We discuss how each of the therapies is conducted, how the approach is explained to clients, the development of the therapeutic alliance, its specific strategies and techniques, and the termination process. Throughout this text, we hope not only to supply students and practitioners with a strong sense of the various therapeutic approaches, but also to pique their interest and encourage them to read the original works cited. Consistent with one of the main goals of this book, we discuss the issue of multiculturalism in several chapters specific to the topic and throughout the text. Furthermore, in one of the final chapters, we emphasize specific techniques for clinicians when dealing with emergency situations, such as clients who are suicidal or may be violent toward others. Finally, given the fact that practitioners are increasingly expected to be knowledgeable about psychotropic medications, their effects and side effects, and barriers to compliance with medical recommendations, we have devoted two chapters to these topics.

Many applicants to mental health training programs express interest in evidence-based practice, empirically supported treatments, and multicultural competencies. We are gratified to hear of these interests because of our belief that the mental health profession under-uses the scientific model, and that training has been less than adequate in preparing therapists to work with diverse populations. The call to integrate research into the training curriculum has come from social work (Bledsoe et al., 2007; O'Hare, 1991), psychology (Beutler, Kim, Davison, Karno, & Fisher, 1996; Chwalisz, 2003) and psychiatry (Fenton, James, & Insel, 2004; Halleck, 1996). In all of the mental health fields, there is an increasing emphasis on the use of research-based guidelines for psychotherapy, a shift driven by changes in public policy and managed-care requirements. The President's New Freedom Commission on Mental Health (2003) specifically calls for the dissemination of research findings on treatments both to service providers and to the public. We believe that preparation for the use of "best practices" with clients and for work in a managed-care environment is best accomplished by emphasizing the importance of research, evidence-based practice, and brief models of treatment throughout undergraduate and graduate curriculums and in professional development programs for practitioners. Very few psychotherapy textbooks authors emphasize a scientific framework when presenting theories of counseling. Instead, they present theories in their original form and often do not discuss treatments that have evolved from the theory. Our approach to presenting theories is to demonstrate how the theoretical assumptions are linked to specific therapeutic strategies and to discuss how the techniques can be adapted for diverse populations. Our goal is to effectively prepare students to meet current requirements for accountability in mental health service delivery and to feel confident in the use of empirically supported techniques in the practice of psychotherapy. As such, exposure to research-based treatment paradigms is essential.

Our society is becoming increasingly diverse, and by the year 2050 it is estimated that people of color will constitute the majority of the population (U.S. Census Bureau, 2005). By the year 2030, 20 percent of the population will be 65 and older. There is growing recognition that traditional forms of psychotherapy are not adequately meeting the needs of persons from diverse backgrounds in terms of ethnicity, religion, language, sexual orientation, age, or disability. Currently, training in counseling and psychotherapy is often based on models developed many decades ago and designed for nondiverse populations. Needless to say, these models are insufficient when it comes to meeting the complex needs of various groups. Currently, our means of dealing with diversity and cultural differences in psychotherapy is through classes or texts on cross-cultural therapy. Although this has been a valuable approach, several problems exist with this model, including the potential stereotyping of ethnic groups and the attempt to determine which groups should be considered culturally different.

We believe that this textbook is unique in that it combines a scientist-practitioner model, an emphasis on connecting theory with empirically supported therapies and relationship variables, and a strong diversity and contextual perspective. We cover the major theories of counseling, as well as techniques based on each theory. Each treatment chapter also discusses the theory behind the approach. We believe that the theories of counseling and psychotherapy are easier to understand when seen in the context of a specific theoretical approach. This book is a practical, up-to-date text that will expand the readers' repertoire of therapeutic skills, understanding of evidence-based techniques from various theoretical perspectives, and base of knowledge for meeting the needs of diverse populations. Highlights and themes of this text include:

- Focus on scientific and critical thinking, including an emphasis on the importance of formulating and testing hypotheses, and evaluating process and outcome variables in psychotherapy.
- Use of research findings and evidence-based practice guidelines.
- Consistent consideration of contextual and diversity issues in discussions of assessment, diagnosis, conceptualization, and intervention.
- Assessment procedures consistent with managed-care requirements including intake interviews, the mental status exam, and the *DSM-IV-TR* diagnostic system.
- Presentation of major theories of psychotherapy, with an emphasis on how each has evolved into models that are accepted and competitive within the managed-care system.
- Emphasis on current theories of psychotherapy and evaluation of each theory according to research findings.
- Presentation of brief therapies from the different theoretical perspectives, with sufficient detail for the reader to understand the specifics of the approach.
- An overview of specific considerations related to diversity in areas such as ethnicity, gender, age, religion, sexual orientation, and socioeconomic status.
- Crisis intervention strategies specific to violent or suicidal clients, including research findings and guidelines for best practices.
- Overview on medication with a focus on some basic pharmacological concepts, research findings on effectiveness and side-effects of specific medications, issues related to therapist-client-physician partnerships, and social-cultural influences on medication use.

We believe that this textbook is suitable for use by advanced undergraduates and graduate students in any of the mental health professions including social work, clinical psychology, counseling psychology, psychiatry, and human services. We recommend the text be used for counseling and psychotherapy foundations, theory, and techniques courses or by practitioners in the field. It is our belief that current mental health professionals will benefit from this up-to-date and practical focus on theory linked to psychotherapy, the overview of issues related to medication and crisis interventions, and the discussions of assessment, diagnosis, and conceptualization with a focus on diversity. We believe that this text will provide readers with the knowledge and skills to effectively and confidently work from an evidence-based perspective and with an increasingly diverse population.

Special thanks for this book go to Tracey Belmont, who was strongly supportive of our book proposal and helped guide the beginning of our project; Lisa Gebo, who took over the task and helped us complete the book by furnishing gentle reminders regarding deadlines; Sweta Gupta, who furnished cheerful assistance with manuscript preparation; and Frank Dattilio, Ph.D, for his comprehensive and valuable review of our manuscript.

DAVID and DIANE M. SUE

Science and Diversity in Psychotherapy: Important Perspectives

Whether you are currently in or preparing to enter the mental health profession, you are most likely aware that an important evolution is taking place in the field, significantly changing the practice of counseling and psychotherapy. When we first began to provide mental health services, there were few limitations on practice, such as the number of sessions allowed or the type of therapy provided. Within the last 10 years, enormous changes have occurred in the field. The impetus for change comes primarily from three forces:

1. Managed care, which demands accountability and efficiency in the provision of mental health services.

2. Research and evidence-based practice guidelines, which are becoming the touchstone of psychotherapy.

3. Culture-sensitive or diversity-sensitive therapies, which are promoted to address the needs of ethnic minorities and other diverse populations.

All of these factors have been highly influential in defining appropriate treatment and services for clients. In a survey of 62 psychotherapy experts regarding the future direction of the mental health field (Norcross, Hedges, & Prochaska, 2002), there was a strong belief that almost all systems of psychotherapy will develop short-term therapies to conform with managed-care systems and that efficient therapies will grow in importance. The expert psychotherapists predicted that of the different theoretical orientations, the eclectic and the cognitive-behavioral will assume greater importance because they are amenable to the development of concrete goals and brief treatment strategies. A survey conducted to determine the theoretical orientation of a group of psychologists revealed the following percentages: eclectic (35 percent), psychodynamic (21 percent), cognitive-behavioral (16 percent), Rogerian/Humanistic/Gestalt/Existential (6 percent), Systems/Family Systems (3 percent), and Interpersonal (3 percent) (Norcross, Hedges,

theoretical orientations of a group

1

& Castle, 2002). Allegiance to these orientations may change dramatically in future years depending upon the ability of each theoretical framework to meet changing demands in the mental health field.

Psychotherapies are evolving and beginning to meet demands for accountability by using efficient, research-supported treatment and accommodating diversity issues. For example, from psychoanalysis came the object relations and the self-perspective theories that led to short-term psychoanalytic approaches such as the *core conflictual relationship theme method (CCRT)* and *interpersonal therapy (IPT)*, an empirically supported approach for depression. Additionally, some psychoanalysts are emphasizing the need to examine the cultural values of both the therapist and the client in the therapeutic relationship (Bucci, 2002) and increase the role of research in psychoanalysis (Schachter, 2005). Similarly, person-centered approaches have given rise to *motivational interviewing,* a concrete and goal-oriented therapeutic approach. In addition, some practitioners are calling for humanistic therapies to incorporate aspects of empirically supported treatments and to use quantitative documentation to evaluate treatment outcome (Joiner, Sheldon, Williams, & Pettit, 2003). Both psychodynamic and humanistic approaches are including more action-oriented techniques into their therapies. In contrast, cognitive-behavioral therapies have always stressed the importance of research and technical skills, while placing less emphasis on the quality of the therapeutic relationship in treatment outcome. However, there has been a recent shift within the cognitive-behavioral school of thought and there is now an effort to explore and incorporate relationship variables between the therapist and client in a systematic manner (Lecompte & Lecompte, 2002). These changes, which are occurring across different theoretical orientations, are important not only because they benefit the consumer, but also because they offer therapists more flexibility in the provision of services.

Evidence-based guidelines have been developed for many mental disorders and are now considered the standard of practice from which to determine the appropriateness of a selected treatment. These treatment recommendations are based on outcome research and clinical expertise and are advocated by the American Psychiatric Association, National Association of Social Workers, American Psychological Association, and the American Counseling Association. These guidelines, combined with the identification of research-based relationship variables and therapeutic techniques, will have a great impact regarding the provision of mental health services and the curricula of mental health training programs. Newcomers to the field and experienced practitioners alike will be expected to be familiar with new treatment guidelines.

Although culture-sensitive therapies do not fit under the efficiency or effectiveness models, they are expected to increase in importance as more attention is paid to the needs of our increasingly diverse society. Practitioners face several areas of controversy when dealing with diversity issues in psychotherapy. First, when considering diversity, should the major emphasis be on ethnic groups or do we need to consider additional areas of diversity (gender, age, sexual orientation, disability, religion, social class, etc.)? Second, should we modify existing psychotherapies to incorporate diversity issues, or develop specific therapies for each group? How therapy should be modified to deal with diverse populations is still a matter of debate. The culture-sensitive movement, however, has been instrumental in changing the view that mental health difficulties reside solely within an individual to include consideration of a person-environment interaction. In other words, social context is increasingly recognized as vitally important in the assessment and treatment of psychopathology.

All of these changes are both challenging and exciting. They allow therapists an opportunity to be creative and in the forefront of meeting the new demands of the field. Additional skills needed in the mental health profession are also addressed in this text. In Chapter 16, we cover best practices and specific techniques for dealing with crises confronted by many clinicians, including situations where there is a concern about suicide or violence toward others. There has been increased attention on behavioral medicine and psychopharmacology in the mental health field. Many mental health professions now require courses on and knowledge of psychotropic medications. This has become more important as medical professionals increasingly collaborate with mental health professionals and the integration of services (both mental and physical) becomes an accepted model of treatment. Medication is a topic we cover in depth in Chapters 17 and 18. For the remainder of this chapter, we will focus in greater detail on the changes occurring in the mental health field.

Impact of Managed Care

An observation made by Cohen (2003) regarding social work applies equally to other mental health training programs: "traditional curricula are no longer adequate to prepare students for practice in the era of managed-care. Managed-care's emphasis on the provision of mental health services at contained costs requires specialized practice skills, particularly rapid assessment, brief treatment, and the ability to document treatment outcomes" (Cohen, 2003, p. 41). What are the skills needed to meet the demands of a managed-care environment? In most training programs, a primary focus involves helping students develop interviewing and interactional skills. Bradley and Fiorini (1999) found that, in a survey of mental health programs, the most frequently addressed practicum competencies involved the microskills (listening, reflection of feelings, empathy, and genuineness) emphasized by Rogerian theory.

microskills

Less than one third rated "readiness for employment as an entry level counselor" as an expected competency. As Bradley and Fiorini concluded, ". . . this heavy focus on basic listening skills may need to be questioned in light of the increasingly complex clients who are being seen by practicum students. Competence in basic attending skills may no longer be sufficient for success in practicum or internship courses" (p. 117). This observation is especially true both in terms of the more severe and chronic populations faced by mental health professionals and in meeting the requirements of insurance companies and managed-care systems.

Unfortunately, most psychotherapy textbooks and mental health training programs do not address the need for new skills in a comprehensive manner. This leaves trainees without adequate background preparation. Textbooks have been deficient in providing a bridge between the theories and the current work requirements of mental health professionals. Most texts present the theories of counseling and psychotherapy without much guidance regarding how they can be adapted to meet the challenges posed by managed-care requirements or in work with diverse populations. During internships, especially in managed-care settings, the theories of therapy learned by students are of little help in meeting assessment, therapy, and outcome requirements. Brief models and techniques that have evolved from these theories are not presented, nor is there much focus on the applicability of theory to practice. This leads to a disconnect between what students learn from texts and the skills they are expected to apply under managed care and accountability guidelines. Also, students receive little guidance in working with diverse populations.

In addition to interviewing techniques, what skills are necessary for practitioners working in a managed-care environment? According to a managed-care representative, the following are expected (Anderson, 2000):

[handwritten margin note: necessary skills]

1. Diagnosis. The ability to diagnose using *DSM-IV-TR* and to describe symptoms used to justify the diagnosis is essential; the diagnosis often determines whether the treatment is covered for insurance reimbursement.
2. Treatment plan. An individualized treatment plan must be developed for each client that includes goals, objectives, and interventions for treatment. The plan should include: (1) a clear statement of the client's problems, (2) specific and concrete goals, and (3) measurable criteria to evaluate goal attainment.

An example incorporating these features for a client suffering from depression might include:

[handwritten margin note: Example]

> *The client currently exhibits flat affect, depressed mood and reports disturbed sleep (no more than 4 hours a night for the past month) and decreased appetite*

(has been eating one meal a day for the past 2 weeks), and has not engaged in pleasurable activities for 3 weeks. The goals are (1) to make a list of three pleasurable activities from which client will choose one to perform 3 days out of the week, (2) to eat two well balanced meals a day for one week, and (3) to identify triggers to depression by writing in a journal three times a week. I plan to see the client in weekly individual sessions. I will be using cognitive-behavioral techniques to help identify triggers to depression as well as client-centered therapy to enhance the therapeutic relationship . . . I am requesting 12 sessions. At the end of these sessions, client progress will be reevaluated. (Anderson, 2000, p. 347)

This degree of specificity is not only important for meeting managed-care requirements, but also helps both the client and therapist understand the goals for treatment and planned interventions. Although the above example involves the cognitive-behavioral perspective, other therapeutic approaches can be utilized as long as goals and treatment strategies are clearly specified. In the case of psychodynamic approaches, techniques must be adapted for managed-care. Since there is little time allowed for traditional transference analysis (client reactions to the therapist because of childhood conflicts), psychoanalytically oriented therapists may focus on transferences that exist within the client's current relationships. Instead of analyzing transference reactions to the therapist, insight techniques are employed to help the client understand core conflictual themes from childhood that are responsible for the relationship difficulties. The insight is then explained in behavioral and affective changes as indicated in the follow case:

A retired woman came into therapy complaining of sleeping difficulties, discomfort even at home, and dissatisfaction with her relationship with friends and family. The interpersonal pattern itself was life-long and had roots in her childhood as a result of a dominant and aggressive father and an attentive but passive mother. (Sperling & Sack, 2002)

The woman could have received traditional psychoanalysis with years of weekly or even more frequent sessions. However, because of managed-care constraints, therapy focused on the analysis and interpretation of interactional patterns with two of her closest friends. By understanding current relationship problems as the result of past childhood difficulties, the client was able to "chip away at the repression of negative feeling" (p. 367) and improve her interpersonal relationships. To meet managed-care requirements, psychodynamic therapists can use alternative language to describe their therapy. Instead of referring to positive transference, the process can be described as modeling. Instead of interpretation, terms such as reattribution or reframing are used to describe the process in which the therapist works to relabel the client's perceptions so that problematic situations or behaviors are interpreted in a more positive light. Not all psychoanalytically oriented therapists, or those of other theoretical orientations, agree to these changes. However, therapists of all orientations need to be willing to make modifications in their therapy if they are to participate in current health care plans. We can no longer use global statements such as "develop insight into patterns of behavior" or "help the client improve self-esteem" in our work with clients. We will be expected to describe precisely how the client will be different in terms of behaviors and life choices once the therapeutic goals have been attained.

Some mental health professionals believe that the need for specificity in treatment detracts from the human aspect of psychotherapy. As one client-centered therapist lamented, "Humanistic therapy looked like what graduate students imagined therapy should be: a sensitive, understanding, caring, supportive, and authentic person engaged in a personal encounter with the client in a manner that facilitated personal discovery and learning. Yet, many of these graduate students would eventually embrace cognitive or cognitive-behavioral or some of the 'brief' or 'strategic' approaches emphasizing therapist technique and wizardry" (Cain & Seeman, 2002). The reason for this change is due to the current "therapeutic zeitgeist" of managed-care with its emphasis on diagnosis, treatment planning, and rapid remediation of clients' symptoms. Although many therapists see managed-care as an unwelcome impediment, the positive side is that theories are continuing to evolve and incorporate these requirements. Additionally, as we will illustrate later, the need for rapid assessment and treatment does not preclude the use of empathy and other interpersonal skills when working with clients. It is essential that, as mental health professionals, we develop the ability to perform assessment, define goals, provide brief interventions, and evaluate client progress and outcome within the context of a positive therapeutic relationship.

Evidence-Based Practice and Empirically Supported Therapies

On a videotape, a 10-year-old girl, Candace, was seen begging for her life. She was wrapped tightly in a blanket and pressed upon with pillows by four adults. The girl was undergoing "rebirthing therapy" to treat a purported diagnosis of reactive attachment disorder, a condition thought to prevent the girl from forming loving relationships. The therapy was to enable Candace to be "reborn" and thus, able to bond with her adoptive mother. The session was supposed to be a simulation of birth with the womb represented by the blanket and pillows. Candace underwent this process for 70 minutes and complained about not being able to breathe. After being unwrapped, Candace was no longer breathing. According to the coroner, the cause of death was suffocation. The state of Colorado has since enacted a law specifically outlawing rebirthing therapy. (Kohler, 2001)

As a therapist, how do you decide what form of therapy to apply with specific mental health problems? Should therapists be allowed to choose whatever therapy they believe will be effective? Should therapies be subject to evaluation? If so, what kind of process would this involve? Currently, there are hundreds of different forms of psychotherapy and few restrictions on what can be practiced. Within the court system, the *Frye standard* (Frye v. United States, 1923) is often utilized to determine whether a particular treatment, such as "rebirthing therapy," is effective or appropriate (Beutler, 2000a). It depends upon the principle of *general acceptance* by the appropriate scientific community. Under this principle, therapies frequently practiced by therapists are deemed to be valid and "true" regardless of their effectiveness or potential for harm. In some cases, consideration is given to the principle of the *respectable minority,* in which treatments cannot be considered for malpractice if they are based on a theory and supported by a "respectable minority" of therapists. Again, whether the therapy is effective or responsible for harm to a client is not taken into account. In 1993, the Supreme Court set the *Daubert* Standard (Daubert v. Merrel Dow Pharmaceuticals) regarding the admissibility of expert witness testimony in federal courts. This was done to eliminate "junk science" from the courtroom. Under this standard, theories or techniques must be falsifiable through empirical testing, subjected to peer review and publication, and generally accepted by the appropriate scientific community. This is a welcome move, although judges will now have to serve as gate keepers and deal with controversial issues such as repressed memory and syndromes such as sex abuse accommodation and parental alienation. Unfortunately, many judges do not have the scientific background to understand aspects of the Daubert decision such as falsifiability and still rely on the Frye standard (Dahir et al., 2005).

Evidence-Based Practice

Currently, all mental health professions (psychiatry, social work, clinical psychology, or counseling) are espousing the view that treatments should have a research base. Evidence-based interventions are being increasingly promoted in social work (Bledsoe et al., 2007; Gibbs & Gambrill, 2002), school psychology (Kratochwill, 2002), clinical psychology (Deegear & Lawson, 2003), counseling psychology (Chwalisz, 2003), and psychiatry (Eisendrath et al., 2003). However, research and clinical practice often travel separate paths, with little connection between the two. This is surprising since mental health programs often require a number of courses dealing with scientific methodology. With the advent of managed-care and the need for accountability in health care, the demand for evidence-based practice has increased. This emphasis is reflected in the President's New Freedom Commission on Mental Health (2003), which calls for disseminating research findings on treatment to both service providers and the public. The commission argued for more effective means of identifying, disseminating, and utilizing evidence-based practices in providing mental health care.

Similarly, the American Psychological Association has promoted empirically supported treatments (ESTs) that have been evaluated using specific research criteria. Based on the type and quality of research evidence, certain treatments have been designated as being either "well-established" or "probably efficacious." Empirically supported treatments are available for a number of disorders involving anxiety and stress, depression, chemical abuse and dependence, childhood problems, and marital discord (Chambless & Ollendick, 2001; Woody & Sanderson, 1998). There is an increased expectation for mental health professionals in all disciplines to be aware of current research on effective treatments. Research has also been directed toward discovering empirically supported therapy relationship variables (ESRs) that are related to treatment outcome. In outcome research, therapist variables have demonstrated consistent and robust effects (Norcross, 2000). The conclusion of the Division 29 Psychotherapy Task Force of the American Psychological Association (Ackerman et al, 2001) was that the following therapist qualities were "demonstrably effective": (1) therapeutic alliance, (2) empathy, and (3) goal consensus and collaboration. The "promising and probably effective" variables included: (1) positive regard, (2) congruence/genuineness, (3) feedback, (4) repair of alliance ruptures, (5) self-disclosure, (6) management of countertransference, and (7) quality of relational interpretations. These qualities are discussed in detail in Chapter 3.

Training programs are beginning to incorporate techniques that have received empirical support. Eisendrath et al. (2003) described a research-based treatment program for depression. Before this program was instituted, psychiatric residents treated patients suffering from major depression using long-term psychotherapy, even though there was no strong evidence for the effectiveness of this approach with this disorder. After reviewing the research literature on interventions and medications for depression, Eisendrath and his colleagues identified components recommended for successful treatment and developed a comprehensive, empirically based therapy package that included:

1. Patient/family education classes about depression and its treatment.
2. Patient education information available in written form and on a website.
3. 12 week cognitive group therapy (CBT) model based on the manual by Munoz et al. (1995).
4. 16 week interpersonal psychotherapy (IPT) involving individual treatment as described by Klerman, Weissman, Rounsaville, and Chevron (1984).

5. Booster sessions of CBT or IPT for relapse prevention.

6. Medication management based on guidelines from a review of the literature.

7. Initial and regular follow-up using the Beck Depression Inventory to monitor clinical symptoms, course, and to inform treatment decisions.

Since the program was developed, psychiatric residents are now formally trained in both CBT and IPT, both of which are empirically supported treatments, and in the use of medication guidelines for specific disorders. The residents also learn to analyze objective outcome information to supplement their clinical assessments. Due to the scientific foundations of their training model, Eisendrath and his colleagues believe that they have established an evidence-based ethic among the residents.

Need for a Scientific Framework in Clinical Practice

In a survey of 860 therapists, 51 percent endorsed the belief that memories of actual events as far back as birth can be retrieved through hypnosis (Yapko, 1994).

Bennett Braun, a prominent pioneer in the field of dissociative disorders, and a former president and co-founder of the International Society for the Study of Dissociation, lost several lawsuits filed by former clients who claimed he inappropriately used hypnosis and drugs to convince them that they had hundreds of personalities, and in one case, had a client believe that she was a high priestess in a satanic cult, had sexually abused her own children, and had eaten meatloaf made of human flesh (Associated Press, 1998).

The above examples indicate that, as mental health professionals, we need to develop critical or scientific thinking regarding psychotherapeutic practice. For many mental health programs, the evidence-based approach represents a paradigm shift from training models based primarily on a specific theoretical model or the clinical experience of the practitioner (Belar, 2003). Both are subject to bias. For example, one's theoretical orientation can influence diagnosis even when using objective measures. Although the commonly used *DSM-IV* diagnostic system is thought to be theory-free, many clinicians using this system rely on their own theoretical orientation in deciding if a client belongs in a specific diagnostic category, giving greater weight to symptoms that fit their theoretical model (Kim & Ahn, 2002). Wholesale acceptance of a particular theory is not a part of the scientific method. It prevents the consideration of data that do not fit the theory. For example, social workers in one study showed a clear preference for a confirmatory strategy; that is, they only sought information that supported their hypothesis and disregarded information that was inconsistent with their view (Osmo & Rosen, 2002). Confirmatory strategies are not consistent with a scientific model in which hypotheses are tested and alternative hypotheses are developed and evaluated. Instead of relying only on theory, professionals and trainees need to use a scientific or evidence-based methodology in formulating a diagnosis, providing appropriate treatment strategies, and in evaluating their performance with clients. To do this, therapists must learn the skills to evaluate research findings associated with the various constructs and techniques of each of the psychotherapeutic theories. In clinical work with clients, we need to treat our clinical intuitions as hypotheses to be tested and be willing to formulate alternate hypotheses, if needed. Treatment selection should be based on research findings, and interventions strategies should be continually evaluated for effectiveness as treatment proceeds.

Practice Guidelines

*Practice guidelines
"guidelines
"standard → for care "*

Practice guidelines have been developed for a variety of disorders. These guidelines, together with those developed in the future, are becoming "the standard for care" by which the appropriateness of a selected treatment is evaluated and are based on comprehensive reviews of research and clinical data. For example, guidelines developed by the American Psychiatric Association describe the clinical features that may influence the treatment plan and suggest the use of specific forms of psychotherapy and medication that have been found to be effective for different mental disorders. As might be expected, the guidelines of the American Psychiatric Association tend to emphasize the importance of medications over psychotherapeutic orientations. However, the clinical recommendations are quite useful because they identify possible co-occurring problems and suggest therapeutic strategies for dealing with the specific disorders. For example, the treatment suggestions for clients with borderline personality disorder include the following (American Psychiatric Association, 2001):

ex of treatment suggestions for BPD

1. A safety evaluation should be performed because suicidal ideation and attempts are common.

2. Plans should be developed for responding to crises and monitoring the client's safety.

3. Psychoeducation about the disorder should be provided to the client, particularly with respect to symptoms such as emotional reactivity.

4. Special issues associated with this disorder that one should prepare for include (1) *dichotomous* (black or white/good or bad) thinking on the

part of the client and (2) boundaries issues (e.g., client may attempt to initiate contact outside of sessions).

5. Direct discussion is best with clients who violate boundaries. For example, the therapist might say, "You recall we agreed that if you feel suicidal, then you will go to an emergency room. If you cannot do this, then your treatment may need to be changed" (p. 9).

6. Goals for treatment and strategies should be developed collaboratively with the client and a clear and explicit plan should be agreed upon.

7. Regardless of type of psychotherapy, features found to be important in treatment are a strong *therapeutic alliance,* validating the client's suffering, encouraging clients to take responsibility for their actions, having them learn to manage their feelings, promoting reflective rather than impulsive action, and setting limits on self-destructive behaviors.

8. Families and significant others of the client can benefit from psychoeducation about the disorder, its course, and treatment.

9. Psychopharmacology can be used to treat symptoms associated with the disorder such as depression and anger. SSRIs are the recommended treatment, with low dose neuroleptics added for those with poor behavioral control.

Practice guidelines are based on the research and clinical data that are currently available. If significant new information is obtained, the guidelines are updated. Standards of care have also been developed for specific populations by other organizations and include: gender identity disorder (Levine et al., 1998), older adults (American Psychological Association, 2003c), gay and lesbian clients (Division 44/Committee on Lesbian, Gay, and Bisexual Concerns Joint Task Force, 2000), and other special populations (Sue & Sue, 2008). These guidelines are useful since they alert the clinician to possible problems associated with certain disorders and offer treatment recommendations. Practice guidelines and research-based treatments will gradually become the standard of practice for mental health professionals in the treatment of specific disorders and with specific populations. They can be very helpful since mental health professionals are expected to have research support for their clinical decisions.

Cultural and Diversity Issues

Another major emphasis in the mental health field is acknowledging the influence of cultural and diversity factors on mental health, psychopathology, and therapy. In psychotherapy, culture-sensitive or multicultural therapy is expected to become more important as our society becomes increasingly diverse (Norcross, Hedges, & Prochaska, 2002). Culture-sensitive therapy involves the modification of psychotherapy to take into account cultural values and societal context. However, at this point it is not clear, from an evidence-based perspective, whether culturally-sensitive therapy (CST) is more effective with ethnic minority clients than traditional forms of psychotherapy (Hall, 2001). There is some evidence, however, that the ethnic identity of a client can influence the rated credibility of therapies such as cognitive therapy and time-limited dynamic psychotherapy (Wong, Kim, Zane, Kim, & Huang, 2003).

The emphasis on social and cultural factors is gaining importance as the United States becomes increasingly diverse. When the population reaches an estimated 383 million in the year 2050, people of color will constitute the majority group (U.S. Census Bureau, 2000). Other aspects of our society are also undergoing change. We are an aging population. By the year 2030, those 65 and older will constitute 20 percent of the population. Diversity in the structure and definition of family has also increased. There has been a large increase in married women who are employed, single parent households, blended families, adoptive families, and mixed ethnic families. By the year 2010, married couples will no longer constitute the majority of households (Robinson & Howard-Hamilton, 2000). Can the theories of counseling and psychotherapy developed many decades ago deal with the changing characteristics of our population? Are mental health professionals equipped to meet the complex characteristics of clients that include variations in race, ability, gender, economic status, health status, sexual orientation, and religious beliefs, to name a few?

Population-Specific Approaches

Attempts to develop population-specific approaches for ethnic groups has often led to fragmentation, confusion, and controversy in the field of counseling and psychotherapy. Diversity training has been accused of professionally sanctioned stereotyping in which cultural attributes are given primary consideration, rather than understanding the uniqueness and life circumstances of the individual client (Freitag, Ottens, & Gross, 1999; Sue & Sue, 2003). In our attempt to acknowledge group-specific differences, we are in danger of developing a cookbook approach, in which the characteristics of groups are memorized and suggested counseling techniques are applied (Speight, Myers, Cox, & Highlen, 1991). Weinrach and Thomas (1998) believe that there is no need for diversity sensitive therapy since "widespread assimilation may reduce the urgency for radical modification of existing counseling theories" (p. 117). Should we maintain our traditional training model or do we need an alternative approach to conceptualizing and meeting the diverse needs of our clients?

These conflicting viewpoints on diversity sensitive therapy can be confusing for mental health professionals and students alike. Our current model of multicultural training generally leads one to believe that there are two types of psychotherapy, "regular therapy," which is taught in traditional counseling and psychotherapy courses, and "multicultural therapy," which is often a separate course. In training for regular therapy, trainees spend countless hours practicing microskills (interviewing and communication skills) and other therapy techniques (Ivey, Ivey, & Simek-Morgan, 1993). Students and practitioners are warned, however, that these skills may not be appropriate for individuals from different cultural backgrounds. This admonition results in confusion and feelings of inadequacy in mental health students and professionals when exposed to clients of a different ethnic background. Textbooks on counseling and psychotherapy have attempted to acknowledge diversity issues by devoting small sections of chapters to the discussion of ethnic and cultural influences. Such an approach once again promotes the view that there are two types of counseling and does not address the changing nature of the population and the increasing probability that we will be seeing large numbers of culturally diverse clients. We believe that the diversity considerations should be a standard part of assessment, diagnosis, and treatment. In later chapters, we will illustrate how this can be accomplished, but we will first discuss how the mental health professions are attempting to acknowledge cultural and societal issues.

Current Diversity Guidelines

Recently, specific guidelines have been published by mental health organizations to address sociocultural factors when providing psychotherapy. The *DSM-IV-TR* (American Psychiatric Association, 2000) has taken a step in this direction with Axis IV of the multiaxial assessment. This axis focuses on "psychosocial and environmental problems" as they play "a role in the initiation or exacerbation of a mental disorder" (p. 29). Examples given of such problems are acculturation conflicts, discrimination, and housing and economic difficulties. Also, in Appendix I of the *DSM-IV-TR,* clinicians are asked to be aware of the possible impact of cultural factors on assessment, diagnosis, treatment, and the therapeutic relationship. However, there is little guidance in terms of what to do if cultural factors are judged to be important. Similarly, in the "Guidelines for Providers of Psychological Services to Ethnic, Linguistic, and Culturally Diverse Populations" (American Psychologist, 1993), psychological service providers are asked to consider the impact of issues such as political, social, and economic factors on the sociopsychological development of different populations. If they are found to play a significant role, the psychologist is to: "help clients to understand/maintain/resolve their own sociocultural identification" and to "help a client determine whether a 'problem'

stems from racism or bias in others so that the client does not inappropriately personalize problems" (p. 46). Again, there is no guidance on how sociocultural factors are to be assessed. Although the guidelines from the American Psychological Association are somewhat more specific than those in *DSM-IV-TR*, problems remain. With the exception of the fields of social work and multicultural therapy, mental health theories and therapies have focused primarily on the individual, with little attention to socioenvironmental factors.

Contextual Framework

There has been a call for a "reconstruction" of our mental health training in shifting from the "sole location of client issues in the individual to the recognition of the contexts in which all human behavior is embedded" (McAuliffe & Ericksen, 1999, p. 269). To accomplish this, changes have to be made in the process of assessment and therapy so that therapeutic approaches and techniques are not imposed on the client, but are modified and evaluated in terms of the degree of fit with the client's perspective. We believe that to work successfully with clients, it is necessary to understand how each client experiences the world and that therapy is most successful when adapted to the client's worldview. The recognition of contextual issues necessitates an acknowledgment of potential etiological influences on problems from individual, family, cultural, and situational contexts. It allows societal issues involving gender, disability, aging, and other forms of discrimination to be addressed.

Impact of Worldview and Values on the Therapist

Therapists need to acknowledge and recognize their own set of attitudes, values, and expectations when providing services to diverse populations. For example, several mental health organizations have established the following guidelines:

> *Social workers should obtain education about and seek to understand the nature of social diversity and oppression with respect to race, ethnicity, national origin, color, sex, sexual orientation, age, marital status, political belief religion, and mental or physical disability. (National Association of Social Workers, 1999, p. 6)*

> *Counselors will actively attempt to understand the diverse cultural backgrounds of the clients with whom they work. This includes, but is not limited to, learning how the counselor's own cultural/ethnic/racial identity impacts her/his values and beliefs about the counseling process. (American Counseling Association, 2005, p. 11)*

Guidelines

Psychologists are encouraged to recognize that, as cultural beings, they may hold attitudes and beliefs that can detrimentally influence their perceptions of and interactions with individuals who are ethnically and racially different from themselves. (American Psychological Association, 2003b, p. 17)

Dealing with diversity issues in therapy involves consideration of issues from multiple perspectives. First, diversity issues need to be considered for all clients. Second, as therapists, we must identify how our beliefs, experiences, attitudes, and values influence the way we provide therapy to each client we work with.

Evidence-Based Practice and Diversity Issues in Therapy

Evidence-based practice is the integration of the best available research with clinical expertise in the context of patient characteristics, culture, and preferences. (APA Presidential Task Force on Evidence-Based Practice, 2006, p. 273)

The central theme of this book is the need to prepare students and practitioners for the evolving standards in the mental health profession. In doing so, we are in accord with the definition of evidence-based practice set forth by the APA Presidential Task Force, which considers the importance of research, therapist skills, client characteristics, and cultural factors in the provision of psychotherapy. We believe it is essential to consider each of these areas in assessment, case formulation, intervention, and evaluation of outcome.

The book is organized in the following manner: The current chapter, Chapter 1 (Science and Diversity in Psychotherapy: Important Perspectives), addressed the need for scientific and diversity training in psychotherapy to meet the demands for accountability and effectiveness in treatment. Chapter 2 (Evidence-Based Practice in Psychotherapy: Techniques and Relationships) prepares the reader to use scientific and critical thinking skills in clinical practice. Chapter 3 (Therapist-Client Relationship Skills) presents research-supported therapy skills, and strategies for establishing joint goals and interventions strategies. Chapter 4 (Contextual and Collaborative Assessment) incorporates diversity issues in traditional clinical assessments such as the intake interview and the Mental Status Exam. Chapter 5 (Diagnosis and Conceptualization) covers differential diagnosis, the use of *DSM-IV-TR*, and case conceptualization with an emphasis on diversity considerations. Chapters 6 through 15 cover the major theories that form the foundation of counseling and psychotherapy (Psychodynamic, Humanistic, Cognitive-Behavioral, Multicultural) as well specific techniques and manualized treatment approaches connected to the theories (Interpersonal Therapy, Core Conflictual Relationship Theme Therapy, Motivation Enhancement Therapy, Cognitive-

Behavioral Therapy, Dialectic Behavior Therapy, and multicultural practice guidelines and strategies). Chapter 16 (Assessment and Interventions in Emergency Situations) reviews current research and best practices when dealing with psychological crises, including threats to self or others. Chapter 17 (Understanding Psychopharmacology) and Chapter 18 (Medications Used with Psychological Disorders) cover most common types of medications used in mental health settings, research involving their effectiveness, and the need to consider cultural beliefs regarding medication.

The different theories of counseling and psychotherapy are presented in the following manner:

- An overview of the theory
- Psychotherapy techniques derived from the theory
- Modifications to incorporate diversity issues
- Research findings
- Manualized treatments developed from psychoanalytic, humanistic, and cognitive behavioral theories

We have included examples of manualized therapies so that readers can have a clear understanding of how specific theories are used in practice, and have included the reference for the original sources at the end of each therapy chapter. Books on counseling and psychotherapy rarely show how therapy is conducted from the initial session to termination. For each therapy, we will demonstrate how the therapeutic relationship is established, the types of assessment employed, and treatment strategies. Exposure to the actual process involved in different evidence-based therapies is vital to the education and training of practitioners. We believe this textbook will prepare students and current mental health practitioners to work in the changing field of mental health and to develop the necessary skills to practice in a managed-care environment with increasingly diverse clients.

Evidence-Based Practice in Psychotherapy: Techniques and Relationships

2

Chapter

One can but hope that greater numbers of clinicians will gravitate to broad-based methods of assessment and therapy; understand science and the scientific method; and master specific treatments of choice for particular conditions and disorders . . . an effective therapist needs to know what is being used in clinical practice, why particular methods have been discounted whereas others are viewed with favor; and learn how best to administer experimentally supported treatments of choice. (Lazarus, 2000, p. 155)

These comments emphasizing the importance of science in psychotherapy are from Arnold Lazarus, who has been a practicing therapist and researcher for nearly 50 years. We agree with his perspective on utilizing the scientific framework in psychotherapy and with his view that it is "imperative to devise specific methods of dealing with people of different races and backgrounds" (p. 155). We also believe that it is just as important to consider the potential impact of *any* diversity issues in psychotherapy. A research orientation is especially important since therapists can easily trick themselves into believing that they have special insight into client problems and unusual talents for remedying these problems (Chambliss, 2000). This is especially likely to occur if they do not keep current with research or take time to evaluate the effectiveness of their therapeutic approach. With the emphasis on managed care and evidence-based practice, psychotherapists will be expected to justify their choice of interventions through references to the scientific literature. As Jacobson (1995) states:

> *. . . we can no longer afford to ignore the scientific foundations that . . . distinguish therapists from the ever expanding cadre of self-proclaimed psychics, new-age healers, religious gurus, talk-show hosts and self-help book authors. (p. 40)*

In this chapter, we will discuss the use of scientific methodology to guide clinical practice through a discussion of empirically supported therapies, empirically supported relationships, and how the scientist-practitioner model can be used effectively in the practice of psychotherapy.

Psychotherapy as It Is Often Practiced

> . . . a standard of evidence based on clinical experience and personal beliefs is inadequate, if not actually dangerous. To leave patients' well-being and functioning to the dubious validity of sincere beliefs and appealing clinical theories is to risk patient well-being. (Beutler, 2000a, p. 2)

It is not unusual for well-trained students and fellow professionals to return from psychotherapy workshops with unbridled enthusiasm for new techniques and therapies introduced in the training. The information is often accepted without hesitation. It is as if the ability to think critically has been suspended. What is it about mental health training programs that allow trainees, supervisors, and mental health professionals to show wholesale acceptance of dubious information or ideas? Part of the reason may be the result of common practices during clinical training. For example, you may have been asked to say the first thing that comes to your mind, engage in warm up and trust exercises, state what you are experiencing emotionally, free associate, engage in shame-inducing exercises, or have different parts of your body talk to one another. During family sessions, family members might have been asked to participate in activities such as "sculpting" (asking different members to physically arrange the family to illustrate alliances and other feelings about the family members), instructed to communicate directly with one another, or engage in role-playing. Many of these techniques can be highly effective, so why are we expressing reservations concerning their use? These activities conducted during individual, group, or family sessions are based on specific theoretical approaches; therefore, observed patterns of behaviors tend to be interpreted similarly, with little or no consideration given to possible situational, personality, or diversity influences. Client difficulty or reluctance to perform such tasks may be interpreted as resistance. How can we blithely view these techniques as having universal applicability or effectiveness? In this text, we are advocating that you ask yourself thoughtful questions about the appropriateness of a particular technique or theoretical approach given the unique characteristics of the client.

The problem with psychotherapy, as currently practiced, is that it is based on the following fallible sources: (1) a specific theoretical orientation with its set of assumptions and techniques, (2) "experts" in the field, or (3) "clinical intuition." As such, the scientific perspective is frequently not used. This becomes especially problematic since there are literally hundreds of different schools of psychotherapy, each purporting to be the best therapy for specific

Table 2.1   **Examples of Empirically Supported Treatments**

Well-Established Treatments	Probably Efficacious Treatments
Cognitive behavior therapy for panic disorder	Cognitive therapy for OCD
Exposure/guided mastery for specific phobias	Exposure treatment for PTSD
Cognitive therapy for depression	Brief dynamic therapy, depression
Cognitive-behavior therapy for bulimia	Brief dynamic therapy, opiate dependence
Cognitive-behavioral relapse prevention for cocaine dependence	Interpersonal therapy for bulimia
Behavior therapy for headache	Reminiscence therapy for geriatric patients
Behavioral marital therapy	Emotionally-focused couples therapy

From Chambless et al., 1998

problems. As Melchert (2007) points out, "current scientific evidence no longer supports choosing from a selection of theoretical orientations for guiding one's approach to psychological practice" (p. 41). This view is also echoed by Fenton, James, and Insel (2004) who argue that we need to move away from authority and theory-based practices to those supported by research evidence from clinical trials. What is especially astonishing is that mental health training programs require coursework on research methodology, yet practitioners often fail to apply these analytical skills to psychotherapy. Because of these problems, there has been a move to promote scientific methodology in guiding clinical practice. Beginning in 1993 the American Psychological Association began to identify a list of empirically supported treatments for different disorders. To qualify, treatment studies had to meet certain methodological standards and utilize a manual. In Table 2.1, some of the empirically supported treatments that are either "well-established" or "probably efficacious" are noted. Those in the "well-established" category meet a higher standard of methodological rigor. The following section on empirically supported therapies will provide more detailed information regarding this topic.

Empirically Supported Therapies (ESTs)

Once upon a time, in the dark ages, psychotherapists practiced however they liked, without any scientific data guiding them. Then a group of courageous

warriors . . . embarked upon a campaign of careful scientific testing of thera-
pies under controlled conditions. Along the way, the Knights had to overcome
many obstacles. Among the most formidable were the wealthy Drug Lords who
dwelled in Mercky moats filled with Lilly pads. Equally treacherous were the
fire-breathing clinician-dragons, who roared, without any basis in data, that
their ways of practicing psychotherapy were better. After many years of tireless
efforts, the Knights came upon a set of empirically supported therapies that made
people better. They began to develop guidelines so that patients would receive the
best possible treatments for their specific problems. And in the end, Science would
prevail, and there would be calm (or at least less negative affect) in the land . . .
(Westen, Novotny, & Thompson-Brenner, 2004, p. 631)

Empirically Supported Therapies (ESTs)

Empirically supported therapies (ESTs) are thought to be an answer
to concerns about the use of unsupported techniques and psychotherapies.
Under this research model, clients are viewed as having a problem or specific disorder for which a specific treatment can be developed. Because the
therapist is seen as less important than the specific treatment or technique
and variability among therapists might produce error variance in research
studies, the therapy is conducted using manuals. ESTs have been identified
for anxiety and depressive disorders, couples' problems, severe mental conditions, chemical abuse and dependence, childhood disorders, and psycho-
physiological disorders. As of 2001, there were over 130 different manualized
treatments listed as empirically supported (Chambless & Ollendick, 2001),
with more added each year. Most of the validated treatments are cognitive
or behavioral in orientation, with a few psychodynamic therapies meeting
the criteria. The rationale behind the establishment of ESTs is admirable; we
believe that therapies should be evaluated by the scientific model rather than
based on personal beliefs or sketchy theories. Research findings are becoming increasingly important as managed care is demanding more proof of the
effectiveness of therapies. We owe it to our clients to provide them with care
that has demonstrated efficacy. However, it is our contention that relying
only on ESTs is insufficient with many mental health problems. The shortcomings of the EST approach are summarized below:

- Contextual, cultural, and other environmental influences are not considered.
- The importance of therapist-client relationship variables is not acknowledged.
- The research model uses criteria that strongly favor the cognitive-
  behavioral approaches.
- Problems with external validity exist. The results of therapy with carefully selected subjects who have a single disorder may not transfer to

clients seen in mental health clinics who frequently have concurrent disorders.

- Scripted use of manualized treatment does not truly resemble the work of therapists performed in mental health settings.

- Therapies based on different theoretical models are listed as effective for the same type of disorder (e.g., interpersonal therapy and cognitive therapy for depression).

- Concern over the large number of manuals that would have to be developed since there are over 400 *DSM-IV-TR* disorders.

ESTs are useful in that they provide evidence for therapies that have been found to be effective with specific disorders. We should always be aware of experimentally supported techniques when working with client problems. However, the identification of treatments is only a part of the process; it is vital that we also consider contextual influences and therapist-client relationship factors in treatment outcome. This view (i.e., that contextual and therapist factors are also important in therapy outcome) allows the field to move beyond the traditional medical framework in which an objective illness can be diagnosed and a specific cure recommended, to a greater understanding of the complexities involved in psychological disorders.

Contextual and Empirically Supported Relationships

Interestingly, the medical field is moving beyond a strict medical model and beginning to emphasize the importance of patient-centered communication and the impact of cultural and social issues such as ethnicity, gender roles, structure of the family, views of disease and dying, religion, and spirituality on both clinical care and health outcomes (Cooper et al., 2003; DeAngelis, 2005; Dowdy, 2000; Tervalon, 2003). Medical students are urged to consider the context of treatment by attending to cultural differences in the definition of health and illness. Additionally, collaboration is emphasized in that the "physician and the patient negotiate between their concepts of the etiology of the disease and the most appropriate means of treatment to reach mutually desirable goals" (Kagawa-Singer & Kassim-Lakha, 2003, p. 582). In providing medical treatments, the context, (i.e., the culture of the provider), the culture of the patient/family, and the culture of the organization have to be considered. Thus, the medical establishment is going beyond the traditional medical model by considering belief systems as they affect treatment outcome and moving closer to the perspective now held by many mental health organizations.

Similarly, some psychotherapists believe that, in promoting ESTs, we have neglected other factors impacting treatment outcome, such as the context of the therapeutic relationship, client values and beliefs, and the working alliance between client and therapist (Ahn & Wampold, 2001; DeAngelis, 2005). To remedy this shortcoming, the American Psychological Association Division 29 Psychotherapy Task Force was formed to review research and identify characteristics responsible for effective therapeutic relationships, and to determine means of tailoring therapy to individual clients. A number of studies have found that therapist effects contribute significantly to the outcome of psychotherapy and, in many cases, this factor exceeds that produced by techniques (Wampold, 2001). The quality of the working relationship between the therapist and client (i.e., the therapeutic alliance) has been found to be related to the treatment outcome (Castonguay, Goldfried, Wiser, Raue & Hayes, 1996; Weinberger, 2002), and it is becoming increasingly accepted that adapting intervention strategies according to specific client characteristics enhances the effectiveness of treatment (Messer, 2002).

After review of the research on the therapist-client relationship variables as they relate to treatment outcome, the APA Division 29 Task force reached these conclusions (Ackerman et al., 2001):

1. The therapeutic relationship makes substantial and consistent contributions to psychotherapy outcome, independent of the specific type of treatment.

2. The therapy relationship acts in concert with discrete interventions, patient characteristics, and clinician qualities in determining treatment effectiveness.

3. Adapting or tailoring the therapy relationship to specific patient needs and characteristics (in addition to diagnosis) enhances the effectiveness of treatment.

4. Practice and treatment guidelines should explicitly address therapist behaviors and qualities that promote a facilitative therapy relationship.

Relationship variables that are considered "demonstratively effective" or "promising and probably effective" are listed in Table 2.2.

We do not believe that empirically supported therapies and relationships should be in conflict with one another; both contribute to therapeutic outcome. Mental health practitioners should incorporate both processes in their work with clients. We support the recommendation of the Division 29 Task Force's view that the "concurrent use of empirically supported relationships and empirically supported treatments tailored to the patient's disorder and characteristics is likely to generate the best outcome" (Ackerman et al., 2001, p. 496). Similarly, Lampropoulos (2000) suggests that relationship

Table 2.2   **Empirically Supported Relationship Variables**

Demonstrably Effective	Promising and Probably Effective
Therapeutic alliance	Positive Regard
Cohesion in group therapy	Congruence/Genuineness
Empathy	Feedback
Goal consensus and collaboration	Repair of alliance ruptures
Customizing therapy to deal with resistance or functional impairment	Self-disclosure
Management of countertransference	Quality of relational interpretations
	Customizing therapy for coping style, stages of change, expectations

From Ackerman et al. (2001)

variables provide a broad guiding structure, whereas ESTs provide specific interventions.

Selection of specific techniques is informed by research; similarly, research informs considerations for the enhancement of the therapist/client relationship. We believe that there are other important variables associated with therapeutic outcome, in addition to the therapist-client relationship or specific therapy techniques. These factors are sometimes neglected by therapists, but should be considered since they affect therapy. As outlined below, Lambert and Barley (2001) have identified four factors and estimated the percentage of the variance each contributes to treatment outcome. Of course, the importance of each of these factors and their relative contribution may differ from client to client and depend on the specific issues involved. Although there is agreement that each of these factors does contribute to outcome, there is some disagreement over the specific percentages cited (Beutler, 2004).

Factors Related to Treatment Outcome

In counseling and therapy, it is not unusual for us to believe that the outcome for our clients is primarily dependent upon our skills as a therapist. However, an unrecognized truth is that, together with social, cultural, and environmental factors, client characteristics often play a key role in outcome, as seen in the following discussion.

Client Resources and External Factors

Client resources are the characteristics or conditions, both internal and external, that the client brings to therapy; these resources can have a strong impact on the recovery process. Inner resources include the client's readiness for change, level of coping, personal/social skills, motivation, ego-strength, intelligence, psychological mindedness, and past successes in change efforts. *External factors* include environmental variables such as social supports, financial and community resources, and fortuitous events. We would also include sociocultural and diversity issues that may influence the course of therapy. These are thought to account for up to 40 percent of the variance in treatment outcome.

Implications

We tend to assume that clients are coming in for treatment ready to work on their problems and able to understand the purpose and need for therapeutic processes such as emotional exploration. We must make certain our clients are "on the same page" with us by determining their motivational level, their level of commitment to change, and their beliefs about the helpfulness of therapy. Clients vary in their degree of motivation and psychological mindedness. In many cases, a client's level of motivation for change can be increased and therapeutic effectiveness enhanced by addressing beliefs or questions regarding therapy. Clients may not respond positively to a therapy, even ones that are empirically supported, if they have questions about the approach or if it doesn't make sense to them. Outside situations, such as need for employment, losing friendships, or changes in community support, can also affect outcome. During therapy, changes in external factors should be assessed on a continual basis. Unless we understand the potential impact of these variables, the therapeutic process can be hampered.

Therapist-Client Relationship

The outcome of therapy depends a great deal on how the therapist and client relate to one another. Both individuals have their own set of beliefs, expectations, and values that impact how they view one another. Research on empirically supported relationships has identified the importance of the therapeutic alliance, which includes the core conditions of effective treatment described by Rogers (1957): empathy, respect, genuineness, and warmth. These dynamics typify a therapeutic relationship in which a client feels understood, safe, and encouraged to disclose intimate material. These characteristics, often referred to as *common factors* (relationship variables associated with a positive outcome), transcend the therapist's orientation. The therapeutic relationship, or working alliance, is an important factor common to all psychotherapies. This quality is emphasized a great deal with psychodynamic and experiential-humanistic therapies, but not as much with cognitive-behavioral techniques (Weinberger, 2002). The therapeutic alliance also includes the agreement on goals and techniques used in the therapy. The therapist-client relationship accounts for up to 30 percent of the variance in treatment outcome.

Implications

To have a successful working relationship with a client, it is important for the therapist to identify and use interpersonal qualities that enhance therapist-client interactions. In doing so, the clinician should be aware of his or her own set of values and beliefs, as well as assessing those of the client, especially as they influence the therapeutic relationship. It may be helpful to acknowledge and discuss differences. Clients may differ in the types of therapist behaviors that they consider empathetic or genuine. That is why the scientific approach is helpful. Instead of assuming that the techniques we have learned to enhance therapist-client relationships will work in this manner, we need to evaluate whether specific skills are actually enhancing the therapeutic relationship with a particular client.

Intervention Strategies and Tactics

Intervention strategies and tactics include techniques that are unique to specific theoretical approaches such as free association, confrontation, interpretation, desensitization, reframing, empty chair, and miracle questions (these strategies will be covered in the theoretical chapters). Not all of these techniques have received research support. Complete treatment packages that have met specific research standards are represented by empirically supported therapies (ESTs). Specific theoretical techniques are thought to account for up to 15 percent of the treatment variance.

Implications

The mental health professional should be aware of different treatment techniques that have been found to be effective for specific disorders, including specific research-supported treatment packages. Other techniques used by the therapist should be evaluated in terms of their potential effectiveness in use with specific clients.

Faith, Hope, and Expectancy

The provision of a rationale or theoretical justification for treatment can produce hope in "demoralized" clients by providing an explanation for their difficulties and the means for obtaining relief. The "objective truth" may be less important than the clients' belief in the treatment (Weinberger, 2002). The client's belief in their therapist or in the efficacy of their treatment can affect treatment outcome and is estimated to account for up to 15 percent of the treatment variance.

Implications

Client beliefs and expectations should be assessed and addressed by the therapist. The therapist needs to be certain that the client understands and accepts the treatment rationale. This can best be done with a collaborative approach in which the client's perspectives and explanation of the problem are shared with the therapist. A client whose belief about their mental health issue differs from that of the therapist may not respond well to treatment. Many therapists employ psychoeducation as part of the therapy process to instill hope and to increase the expectancy of a positive outcome. We will give examples of this process in later chapters.

4
factors

Because these four factors can influence treatment outcome, it is important to move beyond simple reliance on traditional therapy models and also consider beliefs, values, and external influences on client issues. How can we accomplish this complex task? As we mentioned earlier, there is greater emphasis being placed on the importance of collaboration and understanding of the context of behaviors. We believe that therapy involves a collaborative effort in which therapeutic approaches and techniques are not imposed on the client, but are modified and evaluated in terms of the degree of fit they have with the client's perspective. To work successfully with clients, we need to understand how they experience the world and then adapt the therapy process accordingly. We take a *coconstructionist stance* in working with clients. In other words, the client's perspective of the issues and solutions are of critical importance when deciding upon appropriate goals and interventions. We now turn to the use of the scientific model as a means to guide clinical practice.

Conducting Therapy Using a Scientific Model

> Mental health professionals "are poor observers of themselves. They are not, by nature, self-correcting, and the nature of clinical practice does not ordinarily allow either the feedback or the opportunity for disproof that is so necessary to correct one's perspective and approach." (Cohen, 2003, p. 2)

As suggested by the APA Presidential Task Force on Evidence-Based Practice (2006), it is important for clinicians to act as scientists, formulating and testing hypotheses in our work with clients, revising conceptualizations as treatment proceeds, with a focus on both confirming and disconfirming evi-

ESTs
&
ESRs

dence. We should also understand biases that can affect clinical judgment, engage in continual self-reflection, and acknowledge the influence of individual and cultural differences on treatment. Although the vast majority of therapists agree on the importance of research and science in the conduct of psychotherapy, many of us have been negligent in infusing scientific methodology into our clinical practice. The use of research findings regarding ESTs (Empirically Supported Therapies) and ESRs (Empirically Supported Relationships) has been helpful in identifying treatment and relationship variables that influence outcome. However, there has been little incorporation of scientific methodology into the here-and-now practice of psychotherapy. Part of the problem involves the manner in which we have been trained to become therapists. In most mental health training programs, students study the different theories of psychotherapy and are typically asked to employ a specific theoretical approach when working with clients. Similarly, students may be asked to conceptualize problems based on a particular theoretical model during case presentations. Adopting these theoretical blinders leads one to collect data and information consistent with that theoretical perspective, preventing the consideration of alternative explanations. In other words, we learn to seek information that confirms our approach, ignoring other potentially important information.

Another potentially faulty training method involves case interpretation and supervision based primarily on the instructor's own experience and background rather than approaches grounded in research. Supervisors guide trainees to behave in the ways consistent with their own theoretical orientation rather than providing them with the scientific foundation of hypotheses formation and evaluation. An extreme form of this type of guidance is the use of the bug in the ear approach in which instructions are conveyed to trainees during actual counseling sessions. Such a process conveys the notion that there is a right way to deal with a specific issue or event, and also takes away the opportunity for students to develop the skills to formulate and test hypotheses about the client. It is of critical importance to be aware of potential biases that can influence our observations and inferences, as seen in the following example of errors that have the potential to affect clinical practice (Spengler, Strohmer, Dixon, & Shivey, 1995):

1. *Confirmatory strategy* involves the search for evidence or information supporting our hypothesis and ignoring that which is inconsistent with our perspective. Mental health professionals have been found to use a *confirmatory strategy* when working with clients (Osmo & Rosen, 2002). This is, in part, a result of the earlier mentioned single theoretical perspective or "expert" analysis and instruction by trainers. Unfortunately, neither of these methods teaches a scientific attitude for clinical work, nor do they include "disciplined inquiry, critical thinking, rigor, skepticism, and openness to change in the face of evidence" (Stricker, 2003, p. 552).

Instead of developing a theoretical or expert driven model of clinical practice, we should use the scientific methodology learned in our research courses. In other words, we should learn to formulate clinical hypotheses, and be open to both confirmatory and disconfirmatory information when working with and evaluating the responses of a client.

2. *Attribution errors* occur when the therapist holds a different perspective of the problem than that of the client. For example, the therapist might see a problem as stemming from a personal characteristic or trait rather than considering possible environmental or sociocultural explanations. Following the lead of the social work field and the multicultural therapy movement, the professions of counseling, psychology, and psychiatry are increasingly acknowledging the need to consider sociocultural or contextual factors in work with clients. Attribution error can be reduced by performing a thorough assessment that includes sociocultural and environmental factors, and testing hypotheses about the importance of intrapsychic versus extrapsychic influences.

3. *Judgmental heuristics* are commonly used quick decision rules. They can be problematic because they short-circuit our ability to engage in a self-correcting scientific process. For example, if we quickly identify our client as "needy" or having a borderline personality, these characterizations will reduce our attempt to gather additional or contradictory information. In one study (Stewart, 2004), 308 clinicians received identical vignettes regarding hypothetical clients, with the only difference being the client's stated birth order. Birth order influenced the judgment of the clinicians, including the expected prognosis for the client, even though there is little research support for personality differences associated with birth order. These kinds of beliefs or associations occur automatically and need to be identified and addressed. This tendency can be reduced by acknowledging the existence of judgmental heuristics, questioning the basis for quick decisions, assessing additional factors, and evaluating the accuracy of opinions regarding clients.

4. *Diagnostic overshadowing* can occur when the presence of a problem is minimized because attention is diverted to a more salient characteristic. For example, individuals who are gay can have a number of psychological issues that have nothing to do with their sexual orientation. In diagnostic overshadowing, a therapist may perceive the presenting problem as having to do with conflicts over sexual orientation and not address other critical issues. We must be aware of our beliefs and values as we work with clients and their specific presenting problems.

Additional errors in clinical judgment can occur in therapy, illustrating the need to adopt a tentative stance and to test out our observations. It is again important for us to be aware of possible errors in clinical judgment and to reduce their effect by using a self-corrective model. How can this be accomplished in therapy? An example of some of the steps used with the scientific approach in clinical practice is seen in the following situation:

> *Janet was a 48 year-old-woman with a severe case of Crohn's disease (a chronic inflammatory disorder affecting the intestines) who complained of constant pain, sleep disturbances and depression over her inability to manage her disease. She had been married to her husband, Jerry, for 20 years. Currently, one of her two grown children, having separated from her husband, was living in Janet's home with her infant daughter. This served as an additional stressor.*
>
> *During therapy, several relationship issues came to the fore. Janet described her husband as alternating between neglect and care regardless of her physical condition. She also expressed high stress and "unremitting distress" over any contact with her mother who had briefly abandoned her when Janet was in her preteen years. Janet was especially distressed that her mother could not even remember the name of her illness. In the initial session, the hurt and anger she felt in relationship to her mother was apparent. In the session, Janet frequently mentioned that Jerry was in "total and absolute agreement" with her portrayal of her mother (Gershon, 2002).*

A scientific approach was used by the therapist, who conducted a literature review of the disorder and entertained several hypotheses about etiological factors in the client's physical condition. The therapist noted that traditional psychoanalytic theory viewed Crohn's disease as a *psychosomatic illness* (a physical disorder thought to be due to intrapsychic conflict). Specifically, from this perspective, the disorder is described as the inability of an individual to express rage when threatened by separation from an important person. The rage is turned inward, resulting in irritation and damage to the intestinal lining. In utilizing the scientific framework, Gershon considered the psychoanalytic perspective as a hypothesis rather than fact, and examined current empirical research on the relationship between emotional states and Crohn's syndrome, finding minimal or inconsistent support for an emotional connection. Gershon also reasoned that even if a relationship had been reported, the identified emotional or personality characteristics may be a consequence of, rather than the cause of, the serious and debilitating illness. The therapist considered contextual elements in the illness and the possibility that "its meaning is co-constructed between the 'sick' patient and significant others, who come to share a culture of illness beliefs and expectations . . ." (p. 383). To determine if contextual elements were involved, the relationship system of the patient was assessed.

The therapist was interested to see if the "mother hating" had a contextual as well as individual meaning, and asked to see both Janet and Jerry in

Use of the scientific approach

Consider psychoanalytic perspective as a hypothesis and then research

a joint session to discuss an impending visit by Janet's mother. The therapist noted that Jerry appeared to inflame Janet's rage toward her mother and asked herself, "Why would he do this?" A distinct possibility was that Jerry was using the anger toward the mother to deflect anger that might be directed toward him. Instead of directly confronting Jerry, the therapist approached this possibility indirectly. She asked Jerry how he might increase his personal support for Janet. This led to a discussion of care-taking responsibilities and resulted in a dramatic decrease in criticism of the mother from both of them. The therapist observed that Janet appeared to need to take care of everyone and formulated several hypotheses: (1) Janet could be responding to a compensatory wish to experience nurturance not available from childhood; (2) her care-taking may be a means to disparage her mother's performance by comparison; and (3) Janet's problems may be due to current relationship issues. Gershon decided not to follow up on the first two hypotheses, but to determine what would happen if she continued to focus on the here-and-now experiences of the client and directly address self-care issues. The discussion of these topics led to several changes. First, Janet set limits on the demands of her adult children. Second, she established a pattern of self-care that resulted in reduced complaints about her mother. The relationship also changed with her husband. Jerry began to focus on their relationship and his role in caring for Janet. Although Janet's physical symptoms remained, she became more self-assertive and took charge of her own treatment. She confronted her doctor about the lack of progress and the physician sent Janet for a second medical opinion.

[handwritten margin note: What the therapist did]

Gershon followed the strategy that we hope all practitioners in the mental health field would employ. She considered different theoretical explanations for the client's problem, performed a literature review, formulated and tested hypotheses, and examined contextual and relationship factors in therapy. Although Gershon had a psychodynamic perspective, she adopted neither theoretical blinders nor a confirmatory strategy. Additionally, she did not commit the error of attributing the client's problems to strictly intrapsychic factors. Gershon skillfully used a self-correcting model.

Self-Correcting Strategies

[handwritten margin note: Self-correcting process]

To reduce the chance of error, it is important to focus on the reciprocal interaction between assessment and intervention decisions or judgments. This self-correcting process involves the counselor listening to the client, observing nonverbal communication, collecting data, and testing the validity of assumptions, impressions, or hypotheses. In turn, client reactions to the counselor and feedback regarding the intervention allow the counselor to further assess the validity of formulations. This process continues in a reciprocal fashion, with the therapist open to new sources of confirmatory or disconfirmatory data. This model is advocated by Spengler and collegues (1995), who offer the additional suggestions:

- Adopt a scientific attitude by being open to alternative explanations. Consider judgments to be tentative and subject to proof or disconfirmation.

- Consider base rate data. Research findings indicate that up to 20 percent of women were sexually abused as children, whereas about 10 percent of men were similarly abused. For certain diagnoses, these base rates may increase. This information allows the therapist to consider a sexual abuse hypothesis for certain types of problems.

- Perform assessment and evaluation of the processes that occur during interactions between the counselor and the client. Therapists should ask themselves questions such as, "How am I responding to this individual?" Conversely, "How is the client responding to me?" "Am I or the client responding to stereotypes of each other?" "Is my use of empathy increasing or decreasing the responsiveness of my client?" "From my observations of the client, do I need to change my technique or style?"

- Perform an evaluation of each session with the client. "Were the goals that were identified accomplished during the session?" "With the number of sessions that we have had, are we meeting the specific goals?" At termination, it is important to ask "What was the treatment outcome?"

- Adopt the prerequisite attitudes of therapist self-awareness, openness, and curiosity. Be aware of values, biases, and theoretical assumptions and their possible impact on work with a client. Be tentative in putting forth ideas, and be open to new explanations.

Although we consider the Spengler and colleagues' (1995) scientist-practitioner model to be highly useful, especially with its added focus on examining the therapist's values and personal perspectives, we do have a concern that therapist-client collaboration is missing from this framework. We believe it is very important for the client to be a participant in defining the problem, assisting with the formulation of hypotheses regarding origins of the concern, and testing these hypotheses. We suggest modifying the Spengler scientific model in the following manner (modifications are in italics):

(1) Obtain clinical data obtained through observations of and interactions with the client. *Determine the client's perception and perspective of the problem. Combine therapist and client input regarding the disorder.*

(2) *Through collaboration with the client,* develop inferences about possible internal or external causal factors associated with the presenting problem.

(3) *With the client,* formulate a tentative hypothesis about the problem.

Figure 2.1	**Prerequisite Attitudes**
Scientific-Practitioner Collaborative Model	

Prerequisite Attitudes

Counselor Self-Awareness
Values, Biases, Preferences,
Theoretical Assumptions

Counselor Openness
Search for New Explanations
Tentativeness

Scientific Attitude

Data Source
Therapist Assessment of Client
Client Perspective

Inference and Problem Definition
Therapist Inference Regarding Client and Problem
Client Definition of the Problem
Comparing and Collaborating on Problem Definition

Develop Hypotheses with the Client Regarding Problem

Both Client and Therapist Test the Hypotheses

If Hypothesis Is Correct, Continue

*If Hypothesis Is Incorrect, Collect Additional Data and Formulate New
  Hypotheses*

From Spengler et al. (1995) modified to include client involvement

---

(4) Test the hypothesis with *both the client and therapist* serving as scientists. If the hypothesis is not supported, a new formulation must be developed *with the assistance of the client.* (See Figure 2.1 for the scientist-practitioner collaborative model.)

Although we advocate the scientific model, we do not believe that clients are merely objects to be observed by the therapist. A client's perspective of the problem can provide valuable information and needs to be taken into consideration. Unless the client agrees with the therapist regarding the problem, little therapeutic progress can be achieved.

In summary, the thesis of this text is that mental health professionals need to adopt a scientific framework in their work with clients. They need to move beyond the use of theoretical blinders and employ methodology from their research foundation courses. Instead of just focusing on the development of microskills, students and professionals can learn to articulate and evaluate hypotheses regarding the disorder, the goals, and appropriate

[handwritten margin note:] Client needs to be involved and ultimately agree

interventions. This should be done in a collaborative manner with the client. Therapists should engage in the following type of internal dialogue. "Is this approach consistent with the client's perspective of the problem?" "If I focus on emotions in the session, how do I expect the client to respond?" "What is my rationale for using this approach?" "If I don't get the expected response, what will I do next?" "Would it be more helpful to work on the cognitive level with the client?" "What are other possible explanations for the client's reaction?" By focusing on scientific strategies, mental health professionals can develop their analytical skills through the use of a self-correcting internal dialogue. We will be following the scientific and collaborative model throughout the book.

Therapist–Client Relationship Skills

In the most recently published book I've read, a doctor writes that psychotherapy is useless with schizophrenia. How could he even suggest that, without knowing me, the one over here in this corner, who finds a lot of support, understanding, and acceptance by my therapist? Marianne is not afraid to travel with me in my fearful times. She listens when I need to release some of the "poisons" in my mind. She offers advice when I'm having difficulty with just daily living. She sees me as a human being and not only a body to shovel pills into or a cerebral mass in some laboratory. Psychotherapy is important to me, and it does help. (McGrath, 1987, p. 37)

This response is from Mary McGrath, an individual with schizophrenia who talks about her personal experience with psychotherapy. Clients with severe mental disorders identified friendship, giving practical advice, and helping them understand how the past affects current behavior as the most important contributions from a therapist. Nearly three-fourths believed that individual psychotherapy was helpful (Coursey, Keller, & Farrell, 1995). One former client with schizophrenia who had seen a number of different therapists recommended the following when working with clients with severe mental disorders (Bassman, 2000): (1) Decrease the power imbalance between the therapist and client, (2) work together in a collaborative manner, (3) be honest and engage in genuine interactions, and (4) identify strengths and abilities, not just deficits. Understanding clients' perspectives and reactions to therapy is important, but is often neglected in the conduct of psychotherapy. As part of a collaborative and interactive process, we must examine clients' experience of the therapist-client relationship and identify elements that assist or hamper therapy.

In a study of clients with depression who were treated with either cognitive-behavioral therapy (CBT) or interpersonal therapy (IPT), two very different forms of psychotherapy, the factor associated with *relationship is constant factor*

"collaborative emotional exploration"

positive therapeutic outcome was "collaborative emotional exploration" (Coombs, Coleman, & Jones, 2002). This factor included characteristics or behaviors exhibited by both therapists and clients. The process of collaborative emotional exploration was associated with clients' feelings of being understood and supported by the therapist and having trust in the therapy sessions. Clients who displayed qualities of "being introspective and insightful about their problem," "understanding the therapy process," "having positive expectations of the therapy," and "having emotional catharsis" were likely to benefit from therapy. Therapist behaviors of "being nonjudgmental and accepting of the clients," "displaying empathy and sensitivity," "being attuned to the client's feelings," and "accurately perceiving the client's experience in therapy" also contributed to a positive outcome.

The importance of the therapist-client relationship on outcome was found in another study in which clients, who were specifically asked about what contributed to the success of treatment, pointed to a sense of connection with the therapist. Connectedness was described as having feelings of closeness with the therapist, working together in an enabling atmosphere, receiving support for change, and being provided an equality of status within the working relationship (Ribner & Knei-Paz, 2002). Similarly, clients undergoing psychoanalysis reported that therapist behaviors such as "being open to my ideas, experiences, and feelings," "was nonjudgmental and noncritical," "was genuine," "showed warmth," and "validated my experiences" were helpful in therapy (Curtis, Field, Knann-Kostmas, & Mannix, 2004). Thus, clients believe that it is important to feel accepted by their therapist on an emotional and cognitive level. In addition, it is important for the therapist to help the client understand the process of therapy and to work together on mutually agreed upon goals. As you can see, the therapist-client relationship is very important to treatment, regardless of the theoretical approach used in therapy, and contributes as much as 30 percent to the outcome variance (Lambert & Barley, 2001).

working together

In this chapter, we will consider research findings regarding relational variables in therapy, beginning with the therapeutic alliance and later focusing on relational skills, goal consensus, and intervention selection. We will also discuss therapeutic ruptures, obstacles in forming a strong therapist-client relationship, and how to deal with therapeutic failure.

The Therapeutic Alliance

. . . one of the more robust findings from psychotherapy research has been that the quality of the therapeutic alliance—as measured in different ways from different perspectives, and in different therapeutic traditions—is the best predic-

tor of outcome in psychotherapy. (Muran, Segal, Samstag, & Crawford, 1994, p. 185)

According to the conclusions of the APA Division 29 Task Force (Ackerman et al., 2001), the *therapeutic alliance* (including empathy, goal consensus, and collaboration) consists of "demonstratively effective" therapeutic qualities that are associated with positive outcome in therapy. Positive regard, congruence/genuineness, feedback, repair of alliance ruptures, self-disclosure, and management of countertransference are considered "promising and probably effective" characteristics. Although the aforementioned qualities are listed separately, many overlap with one another. For example, the therapeutic alliance includes the elements of empathy, positive regard, and genuineness as well as goal consensus. For this reason, we will include all of these variables within the discussion of therapeutic alliance.

The therapeutic alliance was originally described by Freud (1912, 1958) as an attachment of the patient to the analyst and the analyst's "sympathetic understanding" of the client. More recent conceptualizations of the therapeutic alliance includes three elements: (1) an emotional or interpersonal bond between the therapist and the client, (2) mutual agreement on appropriate goals with an emphasis on changes valued by the client, and (3) intervention strategies or tasks that are viewed as important and relevant by the client and therapist (Garber, 2004). Defined in this manner, the therapeutic alliance has been shown to have a significant effect on outcome that transcends different psychotherapies, psychopharmacology, and even placebo conditions (Krupnick et al., 1996). In other words, the therapeutic alliance appears to exert positive influences on outcome across different treatment modalities, accounting for a substantial proportion of outcome variance (Brown & O'Leary, 2000; Conners, Carroll, DiClemente, Longabaugh, & Donovan, 1997; Whiston & Coker, 2000; Zuroff & Blatt, 2006). Generally, more attention is paid to this quality by psychodynamic and humanistic therapists than cognitive-behavioral therapists. However, fostering a therapeutic relationship is receiving greater emphasis in cognitive-behavior therapy (Beck, Rush, Shaw, & Emery, 1979; Holtforth & Castonguay, 2005; Linehan, 1993a). It is important to remember that there is no set formula or response that will ensure the formation of a therapeutic alliance with a particular client. Therapists must maintain a scientific stance by testing out the effectiveness of different relational skills with a particular client, assessing their impact ("Have I succeeded in developing a collaborative and supportive relationship with the client?" "How is the client responding to me?"), and modifying the approach when necessary. This self-assessment or evaluation is important with respect to each of the following components of the therapeutic alliance.

Emotional or Interpersonal Bond

The formation of a bond between the therapist and client is a very important aspect of the therapeutic relationship and is defined as a collaborative partnership based on empathy, positive regard, genuineness, respect, warmth, and self-disclosure. For an optimal outcome, the client must feel connected with, respected by, and understood by the therapist. In addition, the therapist must identify issues that may detract from the relationship, such as countertransference (reactions to the client based on the therapist's own personal issues). These qualities are described in detail below; their importance may vary according to the type of mental health issue being addressed and characteristics of the client (gender, socioeconomic status, ethnicity, cultural background).

be aware of counter-transference

Collaborative Relationship

Collaboration is a shared process in which the views of the client are respected and his or her participation is encouraged in all phases of the therapy. An egalitarian stance, encouraging sharing and self-disclosure, facilitates the development of empathy (Dyche & Zayas, 2001) and reduces the power differential between therapist and client. The potential for a positive therapeutic outcome is increased when the client is on board regarding the definition of the problem, identification of goals, and choice of interventions. When differences exist between a client's view of a problem and the therapist's theoretical conceptualization, negative dynamics are likely to occur. Collaboration regarding definition of the problem reduces this possibility and is most effective when employed consistently throughout therapy. In the initial sessions, a collaborative set can be developed by making statements such as,

important when client is on board

> "Therapy is a collaborative effort. We will work together so that I can understand how you see the problem and how it is affecting you. To do this, I will need your explanation of the difficulties that you face. I know that some problems may be difficult to talk about, but it is important to discuss them so we can understand how they are affecting your thoughts, feelings, and behaviors. After we understand the problem, we will think of and develop solutions together. Do have questions about why it is important to work together on your problem? Is this something you are willing to do?"

This statement (which may vary depending upon the theoretical orientation of the therapist) conveys to clients the importance of their participation, sets up expectations for client input, and defines therapy as a joint venture between the therapist and client. The degree of collaboration can vary depending upon the characteristics of the client and the specific therapy employed. Some clients expect direction and structure in therapy. In these cases, the therapist can take a more active role but still seek the input of

client
input

the client within this structure. Client input is also sought in the definition of the problem and suitable interventions. We have found that clients who expect the therapist to take a directive role are still very much interested in making choices and participating in the process once they understand the options available to them. Theoretical approaches also differ in terms of the degree of collaboration expected. Some therapeutic approaches are much more prescriptive in their definition of the client's role. In interpersonal therapy, for example, therapy is structured by defining the client's problem with depression as an illness and focusing on the involvement of interpersonal issues:

> *We've just diagnosed you as having an episode of major depression, which is a common and treatable medical illness. It seems to me that your depression has a lot to do with what's been happening in your life lately. Your symptoms seem to have started shortly after your husband died and you had trouble dealing with his death. This is not an uncommon way for depression to present—we call it complicated bereavement—and it's treatable. (Markowitz, 1998, p. 44)*

Similarly, cognitive-behavioral therapists define the disorder for a client. The following is an explanation for acute stress disorder given by a cognitive-behavior therapist:

> *After a trauma, people often experience the sorts of problems you have told me about. We call this posttraumatic stress. It means that after you have been through a traumatic experience, you tend to feel very scared, on edge, and uncertain about things. This happens because when you go through trauma, you learn that things around you can be harmful and you tend to be on the lookout for other things that might hurt you again. (Bryant & Harvey, 2000, p. 90).*

Providing an explanation for a client's problems can offer relief by giving a name to the difficulties being experienced. However, these explanations should only occur after a careful assessment and by obtaining the client's description of the problem. We also believe that you should have the client evaluate the therapist's explanation of the problem by asking "Does this seem to make sense to you?" Clients should also be asked if they have a different explanation for their problem. (Ideally, this should be done early in the assessment phase.) Even when using structured approaches, you can seek input from clients to determine what they consider to be the best method of achieving targeted goals. For example, when developing positive or rational thoughts to replace negative or irrational ones with the cognitive-behavioral approach, clients can be asked to generate different possibilities. They may also be asked to evaluate the effectiveness of using the thoughts that were generated. Collaboration often increases the client's self-efficacy and motivation in performing tasks and can be used even with very structured and prescriptive therapies.

Empathy

Empathy is defined as the ability to place oneself in the client's world, to feel or think from the client's perspective or to be attuned to the client. Empathy allows therapists to form an emotional bond with clients, helping them feel understood. It is not enough for the therapist to simply communicate this understanding; the client must perceive the responses from the therapist as empathetic. This is why it is vital for the therapist to be aware of client receptivity by evaluating both verbal and nonverbal responses ("How is the client responding to what I am saying?" "What are the verbal and bodily cues communicating?"). Empathy can be demonstrated in several different ways—having an emotional understanding or connection with a client (*emotional empathy*) or understanding the client's predicament cognitively, whether on an individual, familial, or societal level (*cognitive empathy*). An illustration of emotional empathy is provided below:

> *A White male therapist in his late twenties is beginning therapy with a recently immigrated, 39-year-old West Indian woman. The client expresses concern about her adolescent daughter who she describes as behaving in an angry, hostile way toward her fiancé. The woman is well dressed and is somewhat abrupt, seeming to be impatient with the therapist. Though not a parent himself, the therapist recognizes the distress behind his client's sternness, and thinking of the struggles he had with his own father, responds to the woman's obvious discomfort with "I imagine that must hurt you." This intuitive response from the therapist reduces the woman's embarrassment, and she pauses from the angry story of her daughter's ungratefulness to wipe a tear. (Dyche & Zayas, 2001, p. 249)*

Many therapists are trained to be very direct with emotional responses, using statements such as "You feel hurt" or "You sound hurt" in an effort to demonstrate empathy. The response "I imagine that must hurt you" would be rated a more intermediate response. Statements that are even less direct might include, "Some people might feel hurt by that," or "If I was in the same situation, I would feel hurt." We have found that people differ in their reaction to the directness of emotional empathy, depending on factors such as the degree of comfort and emotional bonding with the therapist, the specific issue involved, and the gender, ethnic, or cultural background of the therapist or the client. When working with international students, we found most preferred a less direct style of emotional empathy, although there were individual differences in preference. In general, recognition of emotional issues through either indirect or direct empathy increases the client's feeling of being understood. As therapists, we must continually evaluate and determine if the degree of emotional empathy we are using with a client is achieving the desired effect.

Cognitive empathy involves an understanding or an attempt by the therapist to understand the issues facing the client. For example, in the case just described, the therapist might explore the possibility that the daughter's anger is related to the immigration to the United States by saying, "Sometimes moving to a new country can be difficult." A similar statement could be made regarding changes in the mother-daughter relationship with the addition of a fiancé. The degree of directness can vary by making the observation tentative or prefacing statements with, "I wonder if . . . ?" or "Is it possible that . . . ?" Cognitive empathy can also be demonstrated by communicating an understanding of the client's worldview such as the influences of family issues, or discriminatory experiences such as classism, ageism, or sexism. By exploring or including these elements for diverse populations, a therapist is able to incorporate diversity or cross-cultural perspectives regarding the client's problem. Communicating an understanding of different worldviews and acknowledging the possibility of cultural influence can increase the therapist's credibility with the client. When working with diverse clients, we believe that empathy must include the ability to accept and be open to multiple perspectives of personal, societal, and cultural realities. This can be achieved by exploring the impact of cultural differences or diversity issues on client problems, goals, and solutions (Dyche & Zayas, 2001; Chung & Bernak, 2002). We must also be sensitive to the possible impact of societal issues such as discrimination, classism, ageism, and sexism through cognitive statements such as:

> *"Sometimes it's difficult to meet the societal demands of being a man (woman). Could this be this related to your difficulty expressing your emotions?"*

> *"Some people believe that family members should be involved in making decisions for individuals in the family. Is this true in your family?"*

> *"Being or feeling different can be related to messages we receive from our family, or society, or messages based on our religious background. Have you considered whether these are related to your feelings of isolation?"*

> *"How families function has changed over time. What are some of the standards you learned as a young child or adolescent? I wonder if the conflicts in your family are related to differences in expectations between you and your parents."*

These examples are stated in a very tentative manner. If a therapist has sufficient information, more direct statements of cognitive empathy can be made. We believe that the perception of and response to empathy varies from individual to individual. There are no set responses that will convey empathy and understanding to all clients. In general, therapists must learn to evaluate their use of both cognitive and emotional empathy to determine if it is improving the emotional bond with the client and to make modifications, if needed, to enhance the client's perception of empathy within the relationship.

Positive Regard, Respect, Warmth, and Genuineness

The characteristics of positive regard, respect, warmth, and genuineness are important qualities in establishing an emotional bond. *Positive regard* is the demonstration by the therapist that he or she sees positive aspects in the client as a person. There is an appreciation for the values and differences displayed by the client. One method of showing this is by identifying and focusing on the strengths and assets of the individual rather than attending only to the deficits or problems. *Respect* is shown by being attentive, and by demonstrating that you view the client as an important person. Behaviors such as asking clients how they would like to be addressed, showing that their comments are valuable, and tailoring your interaction according to their needs or values communicate respect. *Warmth* is the emotional feeling received by the client from the therapist that conveys verbal and nonverbal signs of appreciation and acceptance. Smiling, the use of humor, or showing interest in the client can convey this feeling. *Genuineness* can be displayed in many different ways. It generally means a therapist is responding to a client in a real manner rather than through a role and is expressing how she or he actually feels without hiding behind a facade. These interpersonal attributes can strengthen the therapist-client alliance and increase the client's trust, cooperation, and motivation to participate in therapy.

Self-Disclosure

The revealing of thoughts or personal issues by a therapist remains controversial, although self-disclosure by therapists is considered to be a "promising and probably effective" technique (Ackerman et al., 2001). In one study, limited and brief therapist self-disclosures in response to comparable self-disclosures by the client were associated with reductions in symptom distress and greater liking for the therapist (Barrett & Berman, 2001). Counselor disclosure in cross-cultural situations (sharing reactions to clients' experiences of racism or oppression) may also enhance the therapy relationship (Burkard, Knox, Groen, Perez, & Hess, 2006; Cashwell, Shcherbakova, & Cashwell, 2003). Self-disclosures may show the therapist's human qualities and lead to the development of closer ties with the client. This may be especially important in work with Hispanic Americans and African Americans. Research to determine the impact of therapist self-disclosure is difficult since it depends on many variables such as the type of disclosure, its timing and frequency, and client characteristics. Some therapists feel that self-disclosures are not appropriate in therapy and will either not answer personal questions or will bounce the question back to the client. However, some clients who ask, "Has this ever happened to you?" may be doing so in an attempt to normalize their experience. Bouncing the question back to the client by saying, "Let's find out why you want to know this" can be perceived as patronizing rather than helpful (Hays, 2001). Should you make self-disclosures to a client? The answer is, "It depends." Sharing experiences or reactions can strengthen the emotional bond between the therapist and client. However, such self-disclosure should be limited and aimed at helping the client with his or her issues. If the requests for self-disclosure become frequent or too personal, the therapist should explore with the client the reason for the inquiries.

Management of Countertransference

Countertransference involves the therapist's emotional reaction to the client based on the therapist's own set of attitudes, beliefs, values, or experiences. These emotional reactions, whether negative or positive, can bias a therapist's judgment when working with a client. Multicultural therapists have been in the forefront in stressing the importance of acknowledging the influence of values, preferences, and worldviews on psychotherapy and the psychotherapist. We need to be self-aware and recognize when personal needs or values are being activated in the therapeutic relationship and not project these onto our clients (Brems, 2000). For example, in one study, gender role expectations held by therapists were associated with how much they liked or had empathy for clients with a different sexual orientation (Wisch & Mahalik, 1999). In a national study, liberal clinicians demonstrated less empathy and personal regard toward clients who affirmed conservative values (Gartner, Harmatz, Hohmann, Larson, & Gartner, 1990).

The opposite can also occur when clients are in accord with our values and perspectives; we may not be able to be objective and may view the problem through our own set of lenses. We may identify with these clients and underestimate their role in problems. These unconscious reactions can interfere with the formation of a healthy therapeutic emotional bond with the client. Because of the negative impact of countertransference, clinicians should examine their experiences, values, and beliefs when experiencing an emotional reaction to a client that is beyond what is expected from the therapy session. A scientific frame of mind necessitates the examination of one's own values and beliefs in order to anticipate the impact of possible differences and similarities in worldviews on therapy when working with clients.

Goal Consensus

An agreement on goals between the therapist and client (i.e., goal consensus) is another important aspect of the therapeutic alliance. Unless the client agrees on what the goals should be, little progress will be made. As therapists, we too easily envision what the appropriate outcome should be when working with a client and become dismayed or discouraged when a client does not feel the same way, or if they seem satisfied with more limited solutions. Goals should be determined in a collaborative manner with input from both client and therapist. Although it is very important to get the client's response in regard to the problem and goals, the therapist has the important task of clarifying the client statements and providing tentative suggestions. It frequently happens that the client will make a global statement such as, "wanting to improve self-esteem." The therapist's job is to help the client define the goal more specifically and to foster alternative ways of interpreting situations (Hilsenroth & Cromer, 2007). Concrete goals enhance the ability to measure progress in therapy and are a necessity for meeting the expectations of managed health care programs. To obtain more specificity regarding a global goal, therapists can ask questions such as such as: "What does your low self-esteem prevent you from doing?" "How would your life be different if you had high self-esteem?" "What would you be able to do if you had more self-esteem?" or "How would you know if you are improving in self-esteem?" The answer to these questions, such as "being able to hold a job or ask for a raise," "feeling more comfortable in group situations," or "standing up for myself," can help identify aspects of self-esteem that are more concrete. Each of these responses can be used to define sub-goals. A client might be asked, "What are small steps that you can make that will show you are moving in the direction of higher self-esteem?"

In determining goals, the therapist can also have the client define changes in thoughts, emotions, behaviors, interpersonal reactions, or in family and societal relationships as a result of higher self-esteem. Final questions might include, "Are these goals important enough for you to work together with me to make changes in your life?" "Would you be willing to try ideas we come up with outside of our sessions?" These last questions help determine if the goals are important to the client. If not, the client should be asked to describe goals they would be interested in working on both within and outside of therapy. In defining goals, diversity aspects can also be considered with questions such as, "How would a higher self-esteem help you in issues with your family?" ". . . in adjusting to societal expectations?" ". . . in feeling more comfortable with your religious beliefs?" or ". . . in coping with prejudice and discrimination?" From the information obtained from these types of questions, concrete goals can be identified and culturally appropriate interventions taking into account the worldview of the client can be developed.

Choosing Relevant Interventions

Interventions are strategies and techniques that the therapist employs to help the client achieve the stated goals. In order for the interventions to be useful they need to make sense to the client. Within a therapeutic alliance, the focus is on agreed upon interventions to achieve the goals that were mutually defined by the therapist and client. In addition, a belief on the part of the client that they can be helped by the therapy is important. In a study by Coombs and colleagues (2002), clients who reported "understanding the therapy process" and "having positive expectations of the therapy" were more likely to improve. Because specific intervention strategies will be discussed in the theory chapters, we will now only focus only on the generic aspects of intervention strategies. These include providing psychoeducation, therapy rationale, selecting interventions, and evaluating the effectiveness of the intervention.

Psychoeducation

Psychoeducation involves giving information about the disorder to a client. The information can provide some relief since clients may not be aware of the cause for their discomfort. In doing so, we must be correct in our diagnosis and reach a conclusion only after a careful assessment of the problem. In conveying information about a diagnosis, you might begin in the following manner: "The symptoms that you are talking about seem to be similar to those found in obsessive-compulsive disorder. Have you heard of this before? I'd like to go through some of the symptoms and would like you to let me know if they apply to you." This style of presentation encourages participation by the client. As part of the psychoeducational process, you would also discuss different ways of managing the symptoms. Providing information about disorders to clients requires that mental health professionals be knowledgeable about these conditions. *DSM-IV-TR* and different practice guidelines can provide useful information. Except in situations where there may be cultural prohibitions against acknowledging a disorder or when it may be detrimental to a client, providing information regarding disorders is important. For example, the American Psychiatric Association practice guidelines for schizophrenia and borderline personality disorder recommend psychoeducation about the disorder, not only for the client, but also for family members. When a client is not psychologically ready for a specific diagnosis or in situations in which psychoeducation may be contraindicated (e.g., agitation, confusion, defensiveness, social or cultural factors), the therapist can use a more general term such as anxiety and define it this way, "Sometimes when people are anxious or under stress, they may feel or behave in the following manner . . . Does this apply to you?" Using this approach, symptoms can still be presented and discussed. The use of a general term such as anxiety or stress may be more acceptable to certain individuals than a specific diagnosis.

Providing a Rationale for Therapy

It is important for the therapist to provide a rationale for therapy because doing so can set up an expectation for improvement. As we mentioned earlier, when clients feel they understand the therapy and believe it can improve their condition, the outcome is more positive. The following is an example of providing a rationale for cognitive-behavioral therapy with an anxiety disorder:

> *"There are several ways of treating anxiety disorders, ranging from medications to behavioral treatments. The approach that we use is exposure, which involves a gradual introduction to situations that produce anxiety. You will be asked to do things that produce some anxiety, but we will move slowly in this process and only go to the next step when you feel more comfortable. This will be repeated over the next 12 sessions until the situations no longer produce as much anxiety for you. In many research studies, exposure has been found to be a highly effective treatment. There are other treatments available but this seems the best for us to try. How does that sound to you? Do you have any questions about the problem or treatment?"*

Selecting Intervention Strategies

Your selection of interventions will depend upon the diagnosis, the specific issues experienced by the client, sociocultural factors, and your theoretical orientation. In different chapters of the text, we present psychodynamic, cognitive-behavioral, humanistic, and multicultural intervention strategies. The approach that is chosen by a therapist should have a research foundation for the specific disorder. However, although therapists endorsed the use of ESTs, most rated experience and theory as more important when selecting interventions (Riley et al., 2007). The American Psychological Association has developed a list of empirically supported treatments and the American Psychiatric Association has practice guidelines for specific disorders. In addition, specialty guidelines or treatment suggestions exist for older adults (APA Working Group, 1998), women (DeVoe, 1998), individuals with disabilities (Olkin, 1999), sexual minorities (Division 44, 2000), and ethnic minorities (Sue & Sue, 2007).

Treatment Manuals

Treatment manuals for different disorders are becoming more prevalent and can be quite useful for the therapist. They spell out in detail the steps involved in specific forms of therapy, beginning with a pre-therapy address to the client and continuing through the termination sessions. What is the reaction of practicing therapists to treatment manuals? In one study, 891 psychotherapists were surveyed about their attitude toward treatment manuals. Of this group, 47 percent never used treatment manuals; only 6 percent used manuals often or almost exclusively. Of those who tried manuals, 34 percent had a positive reaction, 21 percent had a negative reaction, and 45 percent were neutral. Most indicated a belief that manualized therapy had a dehumanizing effect because techniques were emphasized over the need for flexibility or the development of a strong therapeutic relationship (Addis & Krasnow, 2000). Therapists in another study were trained to use manuals in providing either cognitive, supportive-expressive, individual, or group counseling for substance abuse. In general, the therapists were positive about the treatment protocol contained in the manuals, but indicated a low likelihood of using them in the future without modification (Najavits et al., 2004).

In evaluating the use of manuals, we agree with the statement by Stuart and Robertson (2003) that, "Requiring strict adherence to a manual outside of a research protocol is likely to diminish the effectiveness of the treatment because it discourages therapists from exercising their clinical judgment. The data that a therapist obtains from a client during the course of therapy, such as the degree of insight the patient is developing, the degree to which he or she is motivated to change, or the effect of transference on their interaction should assist the therapist to better decide whether the patient might benefit from a homework assignment, might develop more insight with a well-timed therapist self-disclosure, or might improve more with twenty as opposed to sixteen sessions of therapy" (p. 23). We agree that although treatment manuals may offer excellent guidelines in the treatment of specific disorders, therapist-client relationship variables are essential components of effective treatment and that flexibility in one's approach is needed in order optimize the therapeutic alliance throughout treatment.

Homework
Homework (i.e., having clients reflect on behavior or practice behavioral activities out of session) is an intervention used across different theoretical approaches that has been found to be significantly correlated with positive outcome (Scheel, Hanson, & Razzhavaikina, 2004). It is employed by the majority of practicing psychologists (Kazantzis, Lampropoulos, & Deane, 2005). Because the client's difficulties involve circumstances outside of the therapy sessions, progress is enhanced when the client practices skills and makes changes in behavior in real-life situations. Therapists often find, however, that clients may not complete homework assignments due to a lack of motivation, confusion about the activity, belief that the task is unimportant, or discouragement from others regarding homework. Greater participation in homework assignments can be achieved by using a collaborative approach —that is, clients help to identify tasks that they believe are both important and practical. Motivational problems can be assessed by asking the client,

"What is the likelihood that you will be able to perform this activity?" "What might get in the way of doing it this week?" Additional suggestions for improving compliance (Kazantzis & Deane, 1999) include:

1. Clarify how the task is relevant to the client's goal. The assignment should be developed collaboratively with the client and not just dictated to them. The client should identity assignments they believe are relevant.

2. Consider the client's ability to perform assigned tasks. Some clients will agree to perform tasks even when they consider them to be too difficult. It is important to ask clients if the task needs to be modified to make it easier for them to perform.

3. Provide the client with different choices for homework activities or other ways to complete the assignment. It is often helpful for clients to generate the activities themselves.

4. Determine the client's confidence about completing the assignment. You might ask if there are events occurring that might prevent completion of the homework.

5. Give the client a brief note or form describing the homework and when it is to be practiced, or ask the client to write down the assignment.

6. Make certain you discuss the completion of the assignment at the next session and give positive feedback and encouragement for task completion.

7. If the assignment is not performed, determine the reason by going back to Step 1.

Use of Client Metaphors

Using the client's language or paying attention to *metaphors* used by clients can be helpful in designing interventions. Babits (2001) gives several examples of this process. One client described her depression as a pool in which she was drowning. This led to a discussion of how a lifeline to safety might look. In another case, a client described the sense of being lost, wandering aimlessly. The therapist responded, "You're wandering and it seems that, for now, you're out of touch with your internal compass" (p. 22). In both examples, discussions led to interventions based on the clients' metaphors. Attempts to devise strategies that do not fit into the client's beliefs may lead to negative dynamics. In one case, a depressed man was treated with a cognitive-behavioral approach. He dutifully filled out the homework sheets of the situations and thoughts that were associated with increases in depressive mood. However, his response when the connection was pointed out was,

"So what?" The interesting aspect of this case was that the client would bring in a proverb every session. When the therapist began to focus on the proverbs as metaphors, the client began to see the applicability of cognitions and their influence on moods. This illustrates the importance of tailoring homework assignments to the client's belief system.

Evaluating the Effectiveness of the Intervention

As much as possible, it is important for the client to be an active participant in the treatment program by helping with problem definition and goal setting, experimenting with the recommended interventions, generating alternative solutions, and evaluating their effectiveness. It is essential that the client learn to evaluate treatment strategies. The client can be taught to give direct feedback regarding the success of interventions and to behave in a scientific manner. Assignments can be reviewed before implementation as to what would constitute success or failure. Clients can also offer suggestions on what would lead to greater improvement with different homework assignments. By being encouraged to generate and evaluate interventions, self-efficacy is encouraged and there is less dependence on the therapist.

Preventing Treatment Failure

Regardless of how motivated or skilled a therapist is, treatment failures (i.e., clients who refuse treatment, drop out prematurely, fail to respond to treatment, deteriorate during treatment, relapse after successful treatment) will occur. This is not just a temporary backslide that often occurs during therapy, but the failure of the client to benefit from treatment. In some cases, it is due to the characteristics or the approach of the therapist; in other cases, it is due to client variables, or the therapist-client combination. Therapists, especially those who are less experienced, will tend to blame themselves for the lack of improvement in the client. Others will place the responsibility on the client. To reduce treatment failure, we must be alert to cues regarding client dissatisfaction with therapy and develop appropriate intervention strategies. We must also remember that no matter what we do, unresolved termination of therapy will sometimes occur.

Ruptures in the Therapeutic Alliance

Because of the importance of the therapeutic alliance to outcome, the therapist must be vigilant about indications of impairment to the therapeutic process. Even relatively minor conflicts between the therapist and client may have a negative impact on outcome (Castonguay et al., 2004). Anything that causes deterioration in the quality of the therapist-client relationship should be identified and addressed by the therapist (Hilsenroth & Cromer, 2007; Safran, Muran, Samstag, & Stevens, 2001). For example, clients may have questions or negative feelings about the therapy or the therapist, but are afraid to bring them up. The therapist should be alert to verbal or nonverbal indications of dissatisfaction or disapproval by the client. In general, developing a collaborative relationship will decrease this possibility. It is important for the therapist to allow clients to have the opportunity to express negative feelings about the therapy should such feelings emerge. This can be done as part of an evaluation procedure to determine progress from the viewpoint of the client. Obtaining the client's perspective is a way of checking the degree of congruence with the therapist's assessment.

If a difference in perspective becomes apparent, the therapist should respond in an open and nondefensive manner and accept responsibility for his or her part in the problem. The client may feel criticized, unsupported, or not helped by the therapist. Exploring clients' dissatisfactions and allowing them to express negative feelings about the treatment can contribute to resolving the alliance rupture. Although most of the attention has been directed to therapist-client interactions, external forces such as criticism of the therapy by family members, friends, colleagues, or organizations can also interfere with the therapeutic bond. The latter issue can be handled by asking the client how therapy is viewed by family and friends. In this way, the possibility of disapproval by others can be directly discussed. This may be especially important in collectivistic families where family members have an important role in decision-making processes.

If the therapist notices indications of dissatisfaction or disapproval from the client, it is recommended that the therapist respond with "techniques of acceptance" through the use of empathy and validation of the client's response (Linehan, 1993a, b). The therapist should be open and nondefensive when client dissatisfaction is expressed and respond by (1) paraphrasing the client's criticisms and feelings of disappointment or anger about the therapist or the therapy; (2) attempting to find some truth in the client's criticisms even when they seem unfair or extreme; (3) exploring the therapist's contribution to the problem, such as not explaining the treatment rationale clearly, misunderstanding the client's experience, or having a negative attitude toward the client; and (4) expressing respect for the feedback from the client (Burns & Auerbach, 1996). These listening skills and strategies can help repair the therapeutic alliance through openness to concerns or negative comments from clients, validating their experiences, and thus, disarming the emotional reaction.

Strategies for Dealing with Treatment Failures

Therapists, regardless of their efforts to maintain a strong therapeutic alliance and use validated intervention practices, will sometimes have treatment failures, which unfortunately are a relatively common occurrence in psychotherapy. In a review of studies of clients with generalized anxiety disorder, less than 40 percent recovered after therapy (Fisher & Durham, 1999). In a comprehensive treatment program for depression sponsored by the NIMH Collaborative Research Program, between 36 percent and 56 percent of clients recovered during treatment, while up to 5 percent showed deterioration (Elkin et al., 1989). Although we tend to take client failures personally, (and sometimes we *are* responsible), success is dependent not only on our skills as a therapist but also on client characteristics, such as their readiness and motivation for change, intelligence, interpersonal skills, and overall ability to cope. External factors such as the loss of a job, a lack of support from family members, and other negative external events can also lead to treatment failure. The following suggestions were made by Persons and Mikami (2002) to reduce treatment failure:

- Perform a comprehensive and accurate assessment of the client and the issues involved.
- Use therapies based on empirically supported and research-based treatments.
- Determine that you have the requisite skills for the specific problem or intervention.
- Set realistic treatment goals that are mutually agreed upon.
- Describe in detail the treatment plan and explicitly ask the client whether he or she wishes to carry it out.
- Monitor progress at each session and adherence to treatment plan.

These authors also suggest that the therapists ask themselves questions such as: "Are there additional issues that I am not attending to?" "Is my hypothesis regarding the present problem faulty?" "Are there unidentified reinforcements that prevent the client from improving, such as welfare or disability payments?" "Are there external factors, including family or friends, undermining the treatment plan?" "Does my case formulation suggest any reasons the treatment is not working?" or "How might a different conceptualization lead to a different treatment?" The approach suggested here leads to therapist self-assessment regarding the therapeutic procedure, along with an evaluation of client contributions to problems during treatment. It may also be helpful to ask diversity sensitive questions such as "Am I forgetting to consider the impact of societal issues such as discrimination?" or "Have I remembered to assess the client's background and worldview with respect to my conceptualization and intervention?"

In summary, scientific thinking is promoted through generating hypotheses about problematic influences involving the therapist-client relationship, taking into consideration external factors, and identifying inaccurate case conceptualizations. Evaluation can occur at each step of the therapeutic process. Working jointly with the client to identify and deal effectively with problematic concerns can reduce treatment failure. In the next chapter, we will discuss how intake assessments can be conducted in a contextual and collaborative manner.

Contextual and Collaborative Assessment

Psychological practice is, at root, an interpersonal relationship between psychologist and patient. Each participant in the treatment relationship exerts influence on its process and outcome, and the compatibility of psychologist and patients(s) is particularly important. (APA Presidential Task Force on Evidence-Based Practice, 2006, p. 277)

4

Chapter

Accurate assessment, diagnosis, and conceptualization are essential prerequisites for providing appropriate treatment. The stance of the APA Presidential Task Force on Evidence-Based Practice (2006) is that these components of the therapeutic endeavor are dependent upon the characteristics, values, and worldviews of both the therapist and client. Unfortunately, our current methods of assessment and diagnosis often do not take these factors into account, especially in regard to therapist variables. A major point to understand is that, as clinicians, we are not objective observers of clients, but instead have our own set of beliefs, values, and theoretical assumptions. To reduce error, a clinician must be aware of potential biases that may affect judgment. In addition, client variables such as gender, racial or cultural background, and socioeconomic status can also affect the complexity of assessment, diagnosis, and conceptualization. In general, many of our instruments for assessment and diagnosis do not cover these important variables in a meaningful manner. If the evidence-based practice guidelines are to be followed, such background factors *must* be considered. In this chapter on assessment, we will first cover: (1) the impact of therapist variables on assessment and diagnosis, (2) contextual and collaborative assessment, and (3) intake forms and assessment. Each of these will be presented with evidence-based guidelines taken into consideration. Diagnosis and conceptualization will be covered in the next chapter.

Clinical Assessment

There is some evidence that clinicians may have a tendency to overdiagnose schizophrenia in some ethnic groups. Studies conducted in the United Kingdom and the United States suggest that schizophrenia may be diagnosed more often in individuals who are African American and Asian American than in other racial groups. (DSM-IV-TR, p. 307)

Even though recent editions of the Diagnostic and Statistical Manual have been formulated to be atheoretical (neutral in respect to theory), experienced clinicians have been found to employ their own theoretical orientation when deciding whether a client belongs to a specific diagnostic category. (Kim & Ahn, 2002)

Clinical assessment involves the collection of client data such as demographic information, specifics about the presenting problem, psychosocial history, family background, and medical history. This information is used to help form a diagnosis and aid in the conceptualization and development of a treatment plan for the client. Traditionally, assessments are thought to be objective with the client's problems seen as a phenomenon to be studied and categorized. Little consideration is given to the influence of the characteristics, values, and beliefs of the clinician or the client on the process. However, errors in clinical judgment do occur because of clinician or client attributes. Clinicians may have a theoretical orientation or sets of beliefs that strongly influence the assessment process. As mentioned earlier, even diagnoses based on the commonly used *DSM-IV-TR* diagnostic system (American Psychiatric Association, 2000) have been found to be influenced by the clinician's theoretical orientation (Kim & Ahn, 2002). What is particularly problematic is that diagnostic judgments may be made unconsciously and automatically. Because of this, it is important that decision-making processes be brought into consciousness. We can safeguard against or reduce clinical errors by identifying our beliefs and biases, deliberately working to avoid quick judgments, and using research, whenever possible, to support clinical conclusions.

Errors can also be reduced by encouraging active participation by the client during the assessment process. Unless clients feel free to describe their symptoms and situation in detail, it is difficult to form an accurate and complete picture of the problem. We need to get away from the view that clients are merely objects to be studied, and understand that their beliefs, expectations, and experiences are critical to the assessment process. Assessment is best thought of as a two-way street, influenced by both client and therapist variables. Therapists filter all observations through their own set of values and beliefs. Therefore, we will begin our discussion with a focus on therapist self-assessment.

Assessment of the Therapist

A treatment team observing a clinical interview erupted in laughter when a foreign-born psychiatric resident attempted to find out what caused or precipitated the client's problem. In poor and halting English, the resident asked, "How brought you to the hospital?" The patient responded, "I came by car." (Chambliss, 2000, p. 186)

Later, during the case conference, the psychiatric resident attributed the patient's response to concrete thinking, an attribute that is sometimes displayed by people with schizophrenia. The rest of the treatment team, however, believed the response was due to a poorly worded question. This example illustrates what can occur with a focus solely on the client without considering the impact of therapist responses or qualities. Our own set of characteristics, attitudes, and beliefs can influence how and what we assess and our interpretation of data from clients. Therapists have been said to respond more favorably to clients who are more similar to them or have YA-VIS (young, attractive, verbal, intelligent, successful) attributes (Schofield, 1964). This observation led Sundberg (1981) to facetiously point out that individuals who are QUOID (quiet, ugly, old, indigent, and dissimilar culturally) need not apply.

Therapists may be unaware of the impact of differences between themselves and their clients, or that they may be responding in a stereotypical way to clients. For example, studies have found that mental health professionals judge older clients as significantly less competent and less likely to improve than younger clients, and female clients as less competent than males (Danzinger & Welfel, 2000). Gender bias from both male and female counseling trainees has been found for clients who display nontraditional gender role behavior (Seem & Johnson, 1998). Reactions by clinicians are also influenced by the degree of ideological congruence between themselves and the client (J. Gartner, Harmatz, Hohmann, Larson, & A. Gartner, 1990). The personal values and beliefs of therapists can influence clinical judgment. These judgments or inferential errors constitute deviations from the scientific model of gathering information and using a self-correcting model of hypothesis testing.

What are some steps that can be taken to reduce errors in clinical judgment due to our own belief system? We need to develop self-awareness regarding our assessment process and identify our values, theoretical orientation, and beliefs about different groups whose social, cultural, or ethnic backgrounds differ from our own. Do we hold assumptions about gender roles, sexual orientation, older individuals, political philosophy, and healthy family structure that may influence our clinical judgment? Mental health professionals have been encouraged to recognize that they are cultural beings who hold attitudes and beliefs.

> *Psychologists are encouraged to recognize that, as cultural beings, they may hold attitudes and beliefs that can detrimentally influence their perceptions of and interactions with individuals who are ethnically and racially different from themselves. (American Psychological Association, 2003b, p. 382)*

> *Social workers should obtain education about and seek to understand the nature of social diversity and oppression with respect to race, ethnicity, national origin, color, sex, sexual orientation, age, marital status, political belief, religion, and mental or physical disability. (National Association of Social Workers, 1999)*

> *Counselors will actively attempt to understand the diverse cultural backgrounds of the clients with whom they work. This includes, but is not limited to, learning how the counselor's own cultural/ethnic/racial identity impacts her/his values and beliefs about the counseling process. (American Counseling Association, 1997)*

Leung, Cheung, and Stevenson (1994) have identified questions a clinician can use for self-assessment in the areas of awareness, knowledge, and skills when dealing with an ethnically different client. We strongly believe, however, that this type of self-assessment for therapists is important for all clients.

Attitude Toward Client

- Are there ways the client and I differ in background or beliefs? Do I have political or social beliefs or values that may influence my responses during our sessions?

- How might feelings I have about the client influence the way I provide therapy?

- Do I view clients of a different gender, age, class, ability, religion, ethnic group, political stance, or sexual orientation as having values and behaviors that are inferior to mine?

- Am I willing to alter my treatment techniques and approaches to fit the client's perspective and understand that therapy is also culture-bound?

- Am I willing to collaborate with the client to determine appropriate intervention strategies and in evaluating treatment effectiveness?

Knowledge of Client

- Have I attempted to determine the extent that social, family, or contextual issues are involved in the presenting problem?
- Are the treatment goals sensitive to social, cultural, and diversity issues?
- Should I consider involving family, clergy, or other individuals in providing appropriate services for the individual?
- Have I assessed the possible influence of environmental factors such as living condition, prejudice, and discrimination on the problem presented by the client?

Skills

- Am I aware of my own helping style and its appropriateness for different types of clients?
- Do I possess the skills to provide a broad range of support such as advocacy, problem solving, or concrete approaches?
- Can I tailor the intervention to the diversity context or the specific needs of this individual or family?
- Knowing the diversity issues associated with this individual, am I able to be alert to characteristics that may impact the effectiveness of therapy?

Clinician self-assessment is a necessary step in working with clients who differ from them in some aspect. Although most of the suggestions regarding attitudes, knowledge, and skills involve majority culture therapists working with minority clients, ethnic minority therapists should also consider these suggestions when working with majority culture clients, or even those of the same ethnic background. Sociocultural errors are reduced when we make clients partners in the assessment process and allow them to provide feedback and correction, as needed, as we generate hypotheses. We will now consider how the intake interview, mental status exam, and the use of *DSM-IV-TR* can be expanded to include these contextual elements—a step that can be valuable with all clients. Before discussing assessment, however, we will first summarize the rationale for emphasizing contextualism and collaboration in this process.

Contextual and Collaborative Assessment of the Presenting Problem

What we are going to do today is gather information about you and the problem that brings you in for counseling. In doing so, I will need your help. In therapy we will work together to decide what the problem is and what solutions you feel comfortable with. Some of the questions I will ask may seem very personal, but they are necessary to get a clear picture of what may be going on in your life. As I mentioned earlier, all the information that you give me is confidential with the exceptions that we discussed earlier. I will also ask about your family and other relationships, and about your values and beliefs as they might be related to your concerns. Sometimes our difficulties are not just due to personal issues but are also due to expectations from our parents, friends, or society. The questions will help me obtain a more complete picture of what might be happening with you. When we get to that point, we can talk together to see if my ideas about what is going on seem to be on the right track. Do you have any questions before we begin?

Assessment and diagnosis are critical elements in devising a treatment plan. An introduction such as the one just presented helps set the stage for a collaborative and contextual intake interview. Clients are informed that family, environmental, and socio-cultural influences will be explored. Many clinical assessments and interviews do not consider these factors when collecting data, and therefore must be modified (Eriksen et al., 1997). To remedy this shortcoming, we stress the importance of both the collaborative approach, in which the client and therapist work together to construct the definition of the problem, and the *contextual viewpoint,* which acknowledges that both the client and therapist are embedded in systems such as family, work, and culture. These perspectives are gaining support within various mental health professions. For example, ethical principles regarding informed consent to therapy emphasize the need to give clients information necessary to make sound decisions and, thus, be collaborators in the therapy process (Behnke, 2004). The importance of collaboration is also stressed in the report of the President's New Freedom Commission on Mental Health (2003), in which clients are described as "consumers" and "partners" in the planning, selection, and evaluation of services. Contextualism is also important in recognizing that both therapist and client operate from their own experiences and worldviews. Clients may have socialization experiences, mental health concerns, and experiences with prejudice or discrimination that play a role in the presenting concerns (American Psychological Association, 2003a, b).

Many interview forms and diagnostic systems place little emphasis on collaboration or contextualism. Instead, the traditional medical model is usually followed with diagnosis made primarily through the identification of symptoms without attempts to validate impressions or determine the meaning of the symptoms for the client. Problems are seen to reside in the individual with little attention being given to family, community, or environmental influences. If a therapist recognizes and values the importance of a collaborative and contextual approach, modifications in standard assessment intake forms, the mental status exam, and diagnosis with the use of *DSM-IV-TR* can be made to address these concerns.

Intake Interviews

Nearly everyone in the mental health field will conduct intake interviews. Intake interviews are generally conducted over a one and one-half to two hour session. The client should be informed that the assessment session is not a therapy session but a time to gather information in order get to know the client and understand the problem more fully. During an intake interview, it is important for therapists to ask questions in a supportive and empathetic manner. "The ability . . . to connect with the patient, establish rapport, and demonstrate empathy is an important ingredient in the assessment process" (American Psychiatric Association, 2003a, p. 7). Specific therapist relationship building skills were addressed in Chapter 3; these skills can be extremely important in the context of assessment as well as therapy.

Intake forms generally include questions concerning demographic information about the client, the presenting problem, history of the problem, previous therapy, psychosocial history, educational and occupational experiences, family and social supports, medical and medication history, mental status exam, risk assessment, *DSM-IV-TR* diagnosis, and goals for treatment (see Appendix A for a sample intake form). Many of the questions are focused primarily on the individual with little consideration of situational, family, sociocultural, or environmental issues. We realize that it is difficult to modify standard intake forms used by clinics and other mental health agencies, but consideration can be given to these contextual factors when gathering data or making a diagnosis. Common areas of inquiry found in standard diagnostic evaluations and the rationale for each are presented below (Rivas-Vazquez, Blais, Rey, & Rivas-Vazquez, 2001), together with suggestions for specific contextual queries that can be used to supplement the standard interview:

- **Identifying Information** (to gain an immediate sense of the client and reason for the evaluation). Information gathered includes age, gender, ethnicity, marital status, the reason for the visit, and referral source. If appropriate, such as with immigrants or children of immigrants, ask about the primary language used in the home or the degree of language proficiency of the client or family members. Determine if an interpreter is needed. (It is important not to rely on family members to translate when assessing clinical matters.)

- **Presenting Problem** (to understand the source of distress in the client's own words, obtain his or her perception of the problem, and assess the degree of insight the client has regarding the problem and the chronicity of the problem). Some of the questions that clinicians can ask themselves include: Why is the client seeking therapy at this time? Is the problem chronic or recent? Is it always present or does it occur only in some situations? Does the problem stem from social or environmental factors? What is the explanation for the problem according to the client, family members, or friends? What does the client perceive are possible solutions to the problem?

- **History of the Presenting Problem** (to assist diagnostic formulation by providing a chronological account of and perceived reasons for the problem; to determine levels of functioning since and prior to the problem; to explore social and environmental influences). When did the present problem first occur and what was going on when this happened? Has the client had similar problems before? How was the client functioning before the problem occurred? What changes have happened since the advent of the problem? Are there any family issues, value conflicts, or societal issues involving factors such as gender, ability, class, ethnicity, or sexual orientation that may be related to the problem?

- **Psychosocial History** (to gather perceptions of past and current functioning in different areas of living and understand early socialization and life experiences including expectations, values, and beliefs from the family that may play a role in the problem). How does the client describe his or her level of social, academic, or family functioning during childhood and adolescence? Were there any traumas during this period? Were there any past experiences or problems in socialization with the family or community that may be related to the current problem? McAuliffe and Eriksen (1999) describe some questions that can be used, when appropriate, to assess social background, values, and beliefs: "How has your gender role or social class influenced your expectations and life plans?" "Do religious or spiritual beliefs play a role in your life?" "How would you describe your ethnic heritage; how has it affected your life?" "What was considered to be appropriate behavior in childhood, adolescence, and as an adult?" "How does your family respond to differences in beliefs about gender, acculturation, and other diversity issues?" "What changes would you make in the way your family functions?" Specific questioning related to current or prior abuse issues is also an important component of the psychosocial history (refer to Box 4.1 for additional ideas on gathering such information).

- **Strengths** (identifying strengths often helps put a problem in context and defines support systems or positive individual characteristics that may help deal with the problem). What are some attributes that they are proud of? How have they successfully handled problems in the past?

Box 4.1   **Discussing Abuse Histories with Clients**

Despite the potential importance of the information, many mental health professionals do not routinely inquire about abuse histories. In one study, even though the intake form included a section on abuse, less than one-third of those conducting intake interviews inquired about abuse (Young, Read, Barker-Collo, & Harrison, 2001). It is extremely important to address this issue since background information such as a history of sexual or physical abuse can have important implications for diagnosis, treatment, and safety planning for the victim. The following questions involve domestic violence for women (Stevens, 2003, p. 6), but can and should be expanded for use with other groups, including men and older adults:

> Have you ever been touched in a way that made you feel uncomfortable?
> Have you ever been forced or pressured to have sex?
> Do you feel you have control over your social and sexual relationships?
> Have you been ever been threatened by a (caretaker, relative, or partner?)
> Have you ever been hit, punched, or beaten by a (caretaker, relative, or partner?)
> Do you feel safe where you live?
> Have you ever been scared to go home? Are you scared now?

If a client discloses a history of having been abused, particularly during the intake process and if there are no current safety issues, the therapist can briefly and empathetically respond to the disclosure and return to the issue at a later time. Of course, abuse issues may need to be reported to protective services or to the police if children, adolescents, or dependent adults are involved. In addition, developing a safety plan and obtaining social and law enforcement support may be necessary when a client discloses current abuse issues.

What are some strengths of the client's family or community? What are sources of pride such as school or work performance, parenting, or connection with the community? How can these strengths be used as part of the treatment plan?

- **Medical History** (determination of medical, physical conditions, or limitations that may be related to the psychological problem and important for treatment planning). Did the client suffer any major illnesses or physical problems that might have affected their psychological state? How does the client perceive these conditions? Are they engaging in appropriate self-care? If there is some type of physical limitation or disability, how has this influenced their life? What are responses to this condition by family members, friends, or society?

- **Substance Abuse History** (substance abuse or dependence impacts diagnosis and treatment; substance abuse is often underemphasized in clinical assessment). Assessment in this area is important because substance abuse often occurs concurrently with a number of mental disorders (American Psychiatric Association, 2000). What is the client's current and past use of alcohol, prescription medications, and illegal substances including age of use, duration, and intensity? If the client drinks alcohol, how much is consumed? Does the client (or family members) have concerns about substance abuse or dependence? Has drinking or substance use ever affected the social or occupational functioning of the client? What are the alcohol and substance use patterns of the client's family and closest friends?

- **Risk of Harm to Self or Others** (clients may share information about suicidal or violent thoughts; it is necessary to consider risk of potential for self-harm or harm to others). What is the client's current emotional state? Are there strong feelings of anger, hopelessness, or depression? Is the client expressing intentions of self-harm? Does there appear to be the potential to harm others? Have there been previous situations involving dangerous thoughts or behaviors? Sample questions are presented in Box 4.2; an in-depth discussion of intervention with individuals experiencing suicidal or violent ideation is presented in Chapter 16.

Diversity Considerations

Although these questions are typically not included on intake forms, we believe that they can be quite useful in obtaining the client's perspective on the issues involved. Questions that might give a fuller account might include (Dowdy, 2000):

- *"What do you think is causing your problem?"* This helps the therapist to understand the client's perception of the factors involved. In some cases, the client will not have an answer or may present an explanation that may not be plausible. The task of the therapist is to help the client examine different possible aspects related to the problem such as physical, intrapsychic, interpersonal, social, or cultural influences. However, one must be careful not to impose an explanation on the client.

- *"Why is this happening to you?"* This would tap into the issue of causality and possible spiritual or cultural explanations of the problem. Some may believe the problem is due to fate, "bad behavior" on their part, or as a punishment. If this question does not elicit a direct answer or if you want to obtain a broader perspective, you can also inquire, "What does your mother (husband, family members, or friends) believe is happening to you?"

BOX 4.2 Assessing Risk of Harm to Self or Others

Many interns and therapists are apprehensive about discussing suicidal or violent thoughts or behavior with clients. This may occur for several reasons. First, therapists may be fearful that raising issues of harm or violence may cause clients to develop these ideas. Second, identifying thoughts of suicidal or violent ideation increases the responsibility of the therapist to assess and monitor these conditions. Documentation is required in progress notes for actions and plans to deal with suicide or violence potential. There is no research support for the view that discussing suicidal or violent thoughts precipitates these behaviors. In fact, acknowledging and addressing these issues may help alleviate the sense of hopelessness and anxiety produced by avoidance. Some intake assessment forms include a brief lethality risk rating ("none," "low," "medium," and "high"). In general, if the rating is "medium" or "high," a lethality assessment should be immediately performed and consultation obtained. The following are suggestions taken from the Practice Guidelines for the Assessment of Patients with Suicidal Behaviors (American Psychiatric Association, 2003, p. 10b):

Suicidal Ideation or Plan:

Begin with questions that address the patient's feelings about living.

> Have you ever felt that life was not worth living?
> Do you ever wish you could go to sleep and just not wake up?

Follow up with specific questions that ask about thoughts of death, self-harm, or suicide.

> When did you first notice such thoughts?
> What led up to the thoughts?
> How often have those thoughts occurred?
> How close have you come to acting on those thoughts?
> How likely do you think it is that you will act on them in the future?
> Have you ever started to harm yourself?
> Have you made a specific plan to harm or kill yourself? (If so, what does the plan include?)
> Have you made any other plans about harming yourself?
> Do you have guns or other weapons available to you?
> Have you made any particular preparations for suicide (purchasing items, writing a note, steps to avoid discovery, rehearsing the plan)?

Current Risk of Suicide*

_____ None   _____ Low   _____ Medium   _____ High

*If it is determined that suicide potential is medium or high, a plan must be developed to deal with this possibility, including further risk assessment, professional consultation, developing a supportive plan of action for the client, and/or mobilization of social support. In cases of very high risk, voluntary or involuntary hospitalization may be necessary.

Another area that may need to be addressed during the initial assessment interview or during the course of therapy is possible violence against others, which can be addressed with some of the following questions:

(continued)

Box 4.2 **Continued**

Ideation or Plan for Violence:

    Have you ever had thoughts of violence against others?
    Have you committed violent acts in the past?
    How close have they come to violence against others?
    Have you ever used a weapon or thought of getting a weapon to injure another?
    What caused the violence/violent thoughts?
    Are you currently angry with a specific individual or individuals?
    What is the likelihood that you will act on this feeling?

Current Risk of Violence*

____ None   ____ Low   ____ Medium   ____High

*If medium or high risk, perform more thorough assessment and obtain consultation. Therapists should be familiar with "duty to warn" issues when there is the specific potential for harm to others (see Chapter 16 for additional information).

- *"What have you done to treat this condition?" "Where else have you sought treatment?"* These questions can lead to a discussion of previous interventions, the possible use of home remedies, and the client's evaluation of the usefulness of these treatments. It could also give information on additional individuals who have provided treatment.

- *"How has this condition affected your life?"* This question helps identify individual, interpersonal, health, and social issues related to the concern. Again, if the response is limited, the clinician can inquire about the impact the concern is having on these different areas.

- *"How can I help you?"* This addresses the reason for the visit and expectations of therapy from the client. Clients can have different ideas of what they want to achieve. We have had clients who wanted to engage in age regression activities or hypnotherapy. Unclear or clashing expectations between the client and therapist can hamper therapy.

Mental Status Exam

Most intake forms include a mental status exam that involves the clinician's estimation of the emotional and cognitive functioning of clients through the observation of their verbal and nonverbal characteristics. However, because this exam is not conducted in a collaborative manner, mistakes can occur as a result of the therapist's interpretation of client responses. Therefore, consideration should always be given to the potential influence of situational, contextual, cultural, and other diversity issues. With these cautions in mind, valuable information regarding client functioning in the following areas can be gained with this assessment:

Physical Appearance and Behavior—While conducting the intake interview, the clinician makes mental note of observations about the client, indicating any atypical behavioral or physical characteristics. Is the manner of dress, self-care, behavior, cooperation, and activity level appropriate for the individual's age, social class, and cultural background? Are there situational variables that may be involved with observed characteristics such as anxiety, drug use, long work hours, or lack of sleep? Could the responses observed be due to anxiety over participating in an intake process or discomfort with the person doing the assessment?

Mood and Affect—Mood and affect provide important diagnostic clues. For example, individuals with borderline personality disorder or mania may exhibit behavior described as *emotionally labile* (i.e., rapid fluctuations and changes in emotions). *Blunt affect* or *flat affect* indicates a lack of emotional response to topics that would tend to evoke emotion; this can be symptomatic of schizophrenia, depression, or brain damage. However, it is important to keep in mind that demonstrative expression of emotion can be influenced by cultural differences, medication, or situational factors. What is the overall emotional state of the client? Does he or she appear to be depressed, irritable, anxious, restless, hostile, and so on? Are there moment to moment emotional changes? Is their emotion or affect appropriate to the content that they are describing? Does it appear that emotional expression is influenced by cultural factors?

Speech—A client's speech pattern can lead to clues related to possible mental and organic disorders. Is the speech slurred, slowed, or pressured? Is the communication logical, organized, fluent, and easy to understand? Does the client respond quickly to questions or require a period of time to process information? Does the client appear to have racing thoughts or frequent shifts from topic to topic? What is the volume of the client's speech? Does the client perseverate (i.e., say the same thing over and over again)? Is the communication unusually vague or overly detailed? Does it appear that age, cultural factors, or inexperience with English are affecting communication?

Motor Activity—Observation of the client's activity level (hyperactivity or very slow, deliberate movements), degree of restlessness or motoric agitation, tremors, compulsive behaviors, facial or tic behaviors, throat-clearing or excessive eye-blinking, atypical gait or posturing, closing of the eyes, staring episodes, or fluttering of the eyelids can provide important diagnostic information.

Thought Processes—Any signs of illogical thinking involving the use of language or thought processes such as suicidal or homicidal themes, paranoia, suspiciousness, feelings of unreality, ideas of reference or influence, preoccupations, or obsessions are important to note. It is important to be aware that "ideas that may appear delusional in one culture . . . may be commonly held in another" (*DSM-IV-TR*, pp. 306) and that paranoid-like thinking may be displayed by members of oppressed groups. There are also cultural variations in beliefs that must also be considered. In addition, it is important to note cognitive functioning in the following areas:

Attention—Does the client display appropriate attention or seem easily distracted? Is the client responsive to the therapist?

Fund of Knowledge—Does the client possess accurate knowledge of basic information such as historical or current events? Be alert for cultural or experiential influences. For example, immigrants often have difficulty identifying the current or past presidents and Native Americans may be more attuned to the beginning of hunting and fishing season rather than months of the year or dates (Hays, 2001).

Orientation—Does the client know who he or she is, the day of the week, who she or he is talking to and why? Does the client appear to be confused?

Abstract Ability—Can the client think abstractly? This may be apparent through conversation or with questions such as "In what ways are a table and chair similar?" "In what ways are an apple and banana alike?" or proverbs such as "What do people mean when they say 'Don't judge a book by its cover' or 'Rolling stones gather no moss'?" These items are not in themselves diagnostic; however, difficulty in responding may lead to a decision to conduct further assessment. Be aware that many individuals have difficulty with proverbs but can display abstract reasoning in other areas. In addition, individuals with limited English language skills or limited exposure to proverbs may struggle with this task.

Memory—Does the client experience or report problems with short, intermediate, or long-term memory? Does the client remember what was just discussed or what happened several hours or days ago? Are childhood experiences easily recalled?

Insight—Does the client have an understanding of the nature of their problem?

Level of Intelligence—What is the therapist's estimation of the client's intelligence? Is there any evidence of specific learning problems?

The mental status exam helps to give a more complete picture of the client and can be conducted informally during the intake process. If it is clear that the client has good abstract thinking ability, it is not necessary to perform that part of the exam. The mental status exam reviews areas that are important to assess in working with clients. As mentioned earlier, client characteristics such as cultural, educational, and linguistic background should be considered with each area assessed. From the information gathered, the clinician can begin to formulate an understanding of how earlier experiences, social and environmental factors, and patterns of behavior relate to the presenting problem. The next step is the formulation of a provisional diagnosis and the conceptualization of the disorder, which are both covered in the next chapter.

Diagnosis and Conceptualization

5

As mentioned in the previous chapter, accurate assessment, diagnosis, and conceptualization are essential components in providing quality mental health treatment. In the mental health field, *diagnosis* (the categorization of an individual's problem as a specific disorder) is based on the medical model, in which certain clusters or patterns of symptoms signify a specific illness. A diagnosis is required in most clinics and mental health facilities since the specific diagnosis determines the level of care authorized and the type of reimbursement allowed by managed care organizations. Regardless of your own beliefs about the validity of diagnostic systems or the value of diagnosing clients, it is important to be knowledgeable about the symptoms and prognosis for different mental disorders. Additionally, diagnosis has significant implications in terms of the most appropriate interventions or treatments for a client. For example, a diagnosis of schizophrenia as compared to major depression has consequences for treatment options. The skill of *conceptualization,* making a tentative determination of what caused or is maintaining a client's difficulties, is linked closely with the diagnostic process. This chapter will first present an overview of diagnostic considerations from *DSM-IV-TR,* the most commonly used diagnostic manual for mental disorders, followed by a discussion of case conceptualization. Both discussions will strongly emphasize the importance of therapist-client collaboration and the consideration of situational and diversity issues.

Diagnosis Using DSM-IV-TR

The *DSM-IV-TR* is a widely accepted diagnostic manual (published by the American Psychiatric Association in 2000) that identifies different domains used in the diagnosis and treatment of mental disorders. It contains the diagnostic criteria for various mental disorders and medical conditions, includes the consideration of psychosocial and environmental influences, and provides an assessment of the level of functioning of the individual. To make a diagnosis, the clinician determines if certain symptoms are present in the client. The diagnostic manual depends a great deal on clinical expertise and is not to be used in a cookbook fashion. The *DSM-IV-TR* is an evolving and changing diagnostic manual that offers guidelines on making specific diagnoses. In our opinion, it is used most effectively when there is strong therapist-client collaboration, with the therapist carefully considering the background and perspective of each client.

The specific criteria for disorders in the manual and reliability considerations were determined through reviews of research literature. Symptoms of each disorder are described in detail so that clinicians can more easily make a diagnosis. As an example, the symptoms necessary to make a diagnosis for obsessive-compulsive disorder from *DSM-IV-TR* include:

A. Either obsessions or compulsions

Obsessions as defined by (1), (2), (3), and (4):
1. recurrent and persistent thoughts, impulses, or images that are experienced, at some time during the disturbance, as intrusive and inappropriate and that cause marked anxiety or distress.
2. the thoughts, impulses, or images are not simply excessive worries about real-life problems.
3. the person attempts to ignore or suppress such thoughts, impulses, or images, or to neutralize them with some other thought or action.
4. the person recognizes that the obsessive thoughts, impulses, or images are a product of his or her own mind.

Compulsions as defined by (1) and (2):
1. repetitive behaviors (e.g., hand washing, ordering, checking) or mental acts (e.g., praying, counting, repeating words silently) that the person feels driven to perform in response to an obsession, or according to rules that must be applied rigidly.
2. the behaviors or mental acts are aimed at preventing or reducing distress or preventing some dreaded event or situation; however, these behaviors or mental acts are either not connected in a realistic way with what they are designed to neutralize or prevent or are clearly excessive.

B. At some point during the course of the disorder, the person has recognized that the obsessions or compulsions are excessive or unreasonable. Note: This does not apply to children.

C. The obsessions or compulsions cause marked distress, are time consuming, or sufficiently interfere with the person's normal routine, occupational (or academic) functioning, or usual social activities or relationships.

In addition to specific symptoms, *DSM-IV-TR* contains information on other aspects of the disorders. For obsessive-compulsive disorder, this includes:

- Associated Features—frequent avoidance of situations involving the content of the obsessions such as avoiding public restrooms, if obsessions about germs are present
- Associated Laboratory Findings—none have been found that are diagnostic
- Specific Cultural, Age, and Gender Features—more common in boys than girls, but equally common in adults
- Prevalence—lifetime prevalence of 2.5%
- Course—usually begins in adolescence and waxes and wanes, often because of stress
- Familial Pattern—some evidence for genetic contribution

This additional information is useful in gaining a more complete understanding of the disorder. With obsessive-compulsive disorder, for example, we find that hypochondriacal concerns may be common, as well as feelings of guilt, depression, and the excessive use of alcohol or medications. In addition, other anxiety disorders may also be associated with this disorder. These comorbid symptoms or disorders may also have to be treated during psychotherapy.

Although the *Diagnostic and Statistical Manual* (*DSM*) has been criticized for its reliance on the medical model (i.e., disorders are seen to reside in the individual with a diagnosis made according to a set of symptoms) we have chosen to focus on this diagnostic system because it is widely used, and required by many managed care and mental health systems. In addition, the *DSM* has increasingly recognized sociocultural and diversity issues as illustrated by the addition of the subheading "Specific culture, age, and gender features" attached to each disorder. The manual cautions that, "A clinician who is unfamiliar with the nuances of an individual's cultural frame of reference may incorrectly judge as psychopathology those normal variations in behavior, beliefs, or experience that are particular to the individual's culture" (*DSM-IV-TR*, p. XXXIV).

Also, Appendix I of *DSM-IV-TR* includes an "Outline for Cultural Formulation" that "is meant to supplement the multiaxial diagnostic assessment . . . The cultural formulation provides a systematic review of the individual's cultural background, the role of the cultural context in the expression and evaluation of the symptoms and dysfunction, and the effect that cultural differences may have on the relationship between the individual and the clinician" (p. 897). It is suggested that the clinician take these factors into consideration on each of the *DSM-IV* axes before making a diagnosis. (See Box 5.1

Box 5.1 Cultural and Diversity Considerations When Using *DSM-IV-TR*

Social/Cultural Identity of the Individual

What is the reference group for the client? Do they have a traditional or an acculturated perspective? Among immigrants and ethnic minorities, what is their degree of involvement with their culture of origin or with the host culture? For other areas of diversity such as religion, sexual orientation, age, gender, or physical disability: Are any of these factors important in understanding the client or any of the difficulties the client is facing?

Social/Cultural Explanations of the Individual's Difficulties

What is the individual's explanation for their problem? For ethnic group members, does the explanation involve somatic, spiritual, or culture-specific causes? Among all groups potentially affected by disadvantage, prejudice, or oppression: does the client's own explanation involve internalized causes (such as internalized homophobia among gay males or lesbians, or a woman blaming herself for a sexual assault) rather than external, social, or cultural explanations?

Social/Cultural Factors Related to Psychosocial Environment and Level of Functioning

How does the client describe both social stressors and social support networks? How important are systems such as the family, the community, or the role of religion in providing emotional and other forms of support? Are there additional supports that should be considered in formulating a treatment plan?

Social/Cultural Elements of the Relationship between the Individual and the Clinician

Are there differences in values, beliefs, culture, or social status that exist between the clinician and the client? Is it possible that these factors will affect conceptualization and treatment? How might these differences be understood and negotiated in a way that would be most beneficial for the client?

Overall Social/Cultural Assessment for Diagnosis and Care

Are there cultural, diversity, family, or relational variables associated with the complaint? Have social and cultural factors been considered consistently in diagnosis, conceptualization, and the design of a treatment plan? How will the client's life change from an individual, family, sociocultural perspective if the problem is resolved?

for a summary of cultural and diversity considerations to keep in mind when using *DSM-IV-TR*.) These kinds of modifications increase clinician awareness regarding the possible impact of cultural beliefs and values on diagnosis, as well as emphasizing other diversity considerations that may impact diagnosis and treatment, such as age, gender, or sexual orientation. In addition, medical or physical reasons for symptoms should always be considered when making a diagnosis; many clinicians neglect to assess for medical conditions or medication use that may produce or exacerbate psychological symptoms.

From *DSM-IV-TR*

In order to present an overview of the *DSM-IV-TR* system, we will review each of the five major axes and demonstrate how to consistently incorporate diversity issues. A multiaxial assessment system is used to facilitate comprehensive evaluation of the presenting problems of each client. The five axes used with *DSM-IV-TR* include:

Axis 1: Clinical Disorders
Other conditions that may be the focus of clinical attention (including V codes)

Axis II: Personality Disorders and Mental Retardation

Axis III: General Medical Conditions

Axis IV: Psychosocial and Environmental Problems

Axis V: Global Assessment of Functioning

We suggest that all clinicians carefully attend to Axis IV, Psychosocial and Environmental Problems, since these issues can influence notations on the first three axes and have a strong impact on diagnosis, treatment, and prognosis. V codes, which are "other conditions that may be a focus of clinical attention," are also important to consider since they do not pathologize the individual. For example, there are V codes for a wide variety of issues including bereavement, relational problems, issues related to abuse or neglect, concerns with adjustment to a new culture or problems over issues such as sexual orientation, uncertainty about career choices, or questions about faith or spiritual values. Hays (2001) recommends considering the V codes and Axis IV before beginning with Axis I. Her point is that doing so enables one to consider the context for the behavior and reduces the chance of making an error on Axis I and II. It is important to be aware, however, that many insurance companies will not cover the V codes for reimbursement when these are the primary diagnostic concern. Refer to Box 5.2 for an example of a completed diagnostic section of a typical intake form. We will now go into a more complete discussion of each of the five axes.

Box 5.2 **Diagnosis Using the *DSM-IV-TR***

The therapist, following assessment and conceptualization, often completes an intake form with a summary of the diagnosis based on the *DSM-IV-TR* multiaxial system. This information is generally required under managed care programs and is considered the official diagnosis for the purpose of treatment and insurance reimbursement decisions. The following is an example of a completed diagnostic section of an intake form that relies on the *DSM-IV-TR*. The case involves a 27-year-old woman, Laci, who displays anxiety and near panic in social situations, especially when she feels someone might be observing her. She reports always being shy, but remembers that she became increasingly anxious during high school. Her social anxiety is present in nearly all situations and is limiting her work opportunities. Laci finds it difficult to interact with colleagues and is employed doing data input, a job that allows her to work by herself. Laci's social anxiety has limited her opportunities for dating, and she relies on alcohol to reduce her fear in social situations. In fact, she has been drinking to excess for the last year, even though it is worsening her recently diagnosed stomach ulcers.

Axis I (Clinical Disorders and Other Conditions That Are the Focus of Clinical Attention)

	Diagnostic Code	*DSM-IV-TR* Name
Primary	300.23	Social Phobia
Secondary	305.00	Alcohol Abuse

Axis II (Personality Disorders and Mental Retardation)

	Diagnostic Code	*DSM-IV-TR* Name
Primary	301.82	Avoidant Personality Disorder (Provisional)

Axis III (General Medication Conditions Potentially Relevant to Understanding of Mental Disorder)

ICD Code (or physician exam)	ICD Name (or condition)
Stomach Ulcers	Stomach Ulcers

Axis IV (Psychosocial and Environmental Problems)

Has little social support, other than from parents. Desires more social contact, but because of anxiety has limited opportunities. Lives an isolated life and spends most of her time when not working inside her apartment. Occupation level is below what is expected for Laci's educational level and is a source of dissatisfaction for her.

Axis V (Global Assessment of Functioning)

Score 55
Time Frame this week
Laci has a score of 55, which reflects moderate to severe symptoms in terms of impairment in social and occupational functioning. She has had occasional panic attacks and is relatively socially isolated. She is drinking to excess, which is aggravating her ulcers. She reports some occasional suicidal thinking.

Axis I: Clinical Disorders and Other Conditions That May Be a Focus of Clinical Attention

Any disorder listed in the manual, other than a personality disorder or mental retardation, is noted on Axis I. This axis also includes "other conditions that may be a focus of clinical attention" such as relational problems between parent-child, partners, siblings, or coworkers, problems involving abuse or neglect, identity concerns, religious or spirituality issues, phase of life issues, acculturation difficulties, psychological factors affecting medical conditions, medication-induced movement disorders, noncompliance with treatment, and malingering. These concerns are all listed on Axis I, together with the corresponding V code number, meaning that the problem is a primary focus of clinical attention, but does not represent a discrete diagnostic category.

Axis II: Personality Disorders and Mental Retardation

Personality disorders and mental retardation are listed on Axis II. These may occur either as the only mental health issue or in combination with a mental disorder from Axis I. An individual may have more than one personality disorder noted on Axis II. Again, cultural and societal factors need to be considered. A personality disorder diagnosis, "should not be confused with problems associated with acculturation following immigration or with the expression of habits, customs, or religious or political values professed by the individual's culture of origin . . . and clinicians must be cautious not to over diagnose or under diagnose certain personality disorders in females or in males because of social stereotypes about typical gender roles and behaviors" (*DSM-IV-TR*, pp. 687–688). The diagnosis of paranoid personality disorder may be especially problematic since individuals who are subjected to neglect or discrimination may develop mistrust of the establishment and display behaviors that could be labeled as paranoid.

Axis III: General Medical Conditions

Any medical condition that is potentially relevant to the understanding and management of the individual's mental disorder is noted on Axis III. If the medical condition is directly related to the mental disorder in terms of the cause, development, or worsening of mental symptoms, it is listed in Axis I as a "Mental disorder due to a general medical condition," with the specific medical condition noted on Axis III. For example, if depression is judged to be directly due to the effects of hypothyroidism, it would be listed as a mental disorder due to a general medical condition on Axis I and the hypothyroidism would be recorded on Axis III. If the physical problem is not directly related to the Axis I disorder, it is only noted in Axis III.

Axis IV: Psychosocial and Environmental Problems

This axis is very important since it may affect diagnosis and significantly influence the treatment plan. This would include issues such as reactions to the social environment (e.g., acculturation, discrimination,), changes in social or emotional support systems (e.g., a recent move, negative reactions as a result of "coming out," retirement, loss of a close family member), academic difficulties, occupational stress (e.g., loss of a job, harassment in the workplace), or economic stressors such as inadequate housing, health care, or finances. When psychosocial or environmental problems are the primary focus of clinical attention they should be recorded on Axis I, with a V code from the list of "Other Conditions That May be a Focus of Clinical Attention." If psychosocial or environmental problems are not the primary focus, the problem is listed on Axis IV. Thus, Axis IV allows for the possibility that mental conditions involving anxiety and depression can have an external cause, which subsequently becomes the focus of treatment. For example, studies have found that perceived sexism is related to psychological stress symptoms in women (Moradi and Subich, 2004) and workplace heterosexualism functions as a stressor for lesbians, gay males, and bisexual individuals (Smith & Ingram, 2004).

Axis V: Global Assessment of Functioning

The clinician rates the client on a 100-point scale based on assessment of psychological, social, and occupational (or academic) functioning. This rating, called the Global Assessment of Functioning (GAF), is a clinical judgment of the current overall functioning of the client based on a full 1–100 continuum. The scoring, combining the clinician's assessment of the client's impairment, psychological symptoms, and social and occupational functioning, ranges from 1–100. For example, ratings might include no symptoms and superior functioning in all areas (rating of 100); mild symptoms or some difficulty in social or occupational functioning, but with adequate overall functioning (rating of 70); serious symptoms such as suicidality or serious impairment in social or occupational functioning (rating of 50); serious impairment in communication or judgment, behavior considerably influenced by hallucinations or delusions, or inability to function in almost all areas (rating of 30); or persistent danger of severe self-harm or assaulting others, a serious suicidal act or inability to maintain minimal personal hygiene (rating of 10). Impairments due to physical or environmental limitations such as someone whose occupational functioning is affected by a physical disability or whose social functioning is limited due to lack of transportation are not included in the ratings. Axis V is used in treatment planning to measure the effectiveness of treatment and to predict outcome.

Although the *DSM-IV-TR* diagnostic system is now placing more emphasis on diversity and cultural concerns, problems remain. For example, Appendix A of the *DSM-IV-TR* contains a variety of "Decision Trees for Differential Diagnosis." These are flow charts used with the diagnostic criteria specified in the disorders section of the manual. Within the model of differential diagnosis, physical and medical conditions that may result in symptoms of a mental disorder are considered. For example, mood disorder symptoms may result from a medical condition or may be substance-induced. We strongly believe that psychosocial and environmental issues should also be included at the beginning of the decision tree because, in our view, the implications for diagnosis and treatment are as important as medical factors.

From the information obtained through the intake interview, mental status exam, and other assessments, the mental health professional makes a diagnosis, or provisional diagnosis, and continues to the next step, a more detailed focus on case conceptualization. As we discuss in the next section, consideration of specific cultural and diversity factors is once again essential for an accurate understanding of the client's presenting problems.

Conceptualization and Development of Treatment Goals

> *[Case conceptualization is] . . . a set of "hypotheses about the causes, precipitants, and maintaining influences of a person's psychological, interpersonal, and behavioral problems" . . . [It involves] the extent to which the therapist elicits relevant data and integrates the information into a conceptualization of the patient's main problem . . . the extent to which the interventions are in the sequence or context specified by the theory. (Eells, Lombart, Kendjelic, Turner, & Lucas, 2005, p. 580)*

Conceptualization is an ongoing process that begins with the initial intake interview, assessment, and diagnosis, and continues throughout the course of therapy. It involves the cognitive skill of making sense of what the client is saying, connecting information obtained during assessment and therapy sessions, and determining the influence of present and past events on the client's problem. In other words, it is an attempt to determine what caused or is maintaining the client's problem. How to conceptualize accurately can be challenging given the quantity of information obtained during the intake interview and therapy sessions. You may ask yourself, "What do I focus on?" "How do I know if the information shared by the client is important to the understanding of the problem?" "What data are relevant?" "What follow-up questions should I ask?" "What are the important historical and present causes of the person's problem?" "Is it primarily an intrapsychic or internal issue?" "Do environmental, social, or cultural factors play a role?" Conceptualization is critical because it attempts to link the symptoms reported by the client to hypothesized causal factors, producing a road map that guides the therapist in deciding the best route for treatment.

In general, therapists have used theories as a guide when developing inferences and hypotheses about causal factors involved in specific disorders. However, the use of theories to guide case conceptualization has some major shortcomings. First, adopting a set of theoretical lenses can lead to a confirmatory bias, that is, a tendency to look only for data that fit the theoretical perspective. Depending on theoretical orientation, the same problem can be conceptualized quite differently. For example, social anxiety in a client may be viewed as resulting from: (1) deficits in social skills or conditioned anxiety associated with social situations (cognitive-behavioral theory); (2) an unconscious conflict involving either sexual impulses or early relationship difficulties with parental figures (psychodynamic theory); (3) conditional regard—that is, the client is only accepted if behaving according to parental standards (client-centered theory); (4) external societal influences such as prejudice or discrimination shown to disadvantaged groups (i.e., ethnic or religious minorities, lesbians, gay men or bisexual individuals, older adults, women, or individuals with disabilities) (Multicultural or feminist theory); or (5) biochemical or neurological variables (medical model).

Another concern with the over-reliance on theory is that clients' perspectives regarding their problem may receive little attention. Because clinicians often use a specific theoretical framework when collecting data or formulating conceptualizations, there may be little evaluation of the degree of fit between the client's perception regarding the problem and the therapist's theory. This problem can be reduced by using intake forms that include client perspectives, together with information regarding possible family and societal influences. Additionally, as mentioned in previous chapters, therapists are cultural beings who may hold attitudes, stereotypes, and prejudices regarding those who are different from them in terms of age, gender, sexual orientation, religious background, ethnicity, or race. Differences in these areas may lead to errors in the conceptualization of problems experienced by the client.

Mental health programs currently encourage recognition of the fact that therapists and clients are cultural beings whose values, assumptions, and beliefs must be considered in the process of conceptualizing and treating mental disorders. Fortunately, this multicultural and diversity perspective is becoming more and more infused throughout the training of mental health professionals. However, is the message getting across to mental health practitioners? Hansen and colleagues (2006) conducted a random sample survey of 149 clinicians regarding the importance of multicultural competencies and, more importantly, whether they practiced these recommendations. Although the participants rated competencies such as "using *DSM-TR* cultural formulations," "prepare a cultural formulation," "use racially/ethnically sensitive data gathering techniques," and "evaluating one's own multicultural competence" as very important, they were much less likely to actually use these competencies in their practice. What accounts for this discrepancy between the ratings of importance of and the actual use of multicultural competencies? We believe that a contributing factor is the reliance on theories of counseling and psychotherapy that were developed without consideration of diversity issues or the impact of therapist qualities on assessment and conceptualization. The following case demonstrates the effective use of a cultural framework in the conceptualization of a mental health issue with a client:

> *Diane was a 21-year-old woman who was born on the island of Samoa and immigrated to the United States with her family when she was in her teens. Diane sought treatment when she began to feel emotionally destabilized by the psychological problems of an acquaintance. Diane worked off-campus as the assistant manager of a bookstore. One of the employees had developed a severe eating disorder, and Diane had become increasingly distressed as she witnessed her employee's deterioration. In addition, Diane began to experience a loss of appetite and became convinced that she, too, was developing an eating disorder. In the intake interview, Diane did not present significant anorexic symptoms. At first glance, she seemed to need help differentiating herself from others. (Seeley, 2004, p. 126)*

During the second session, Diane expressed even more emotional distress because her employee had announced that she would be leaving her job to receive treatment for anorexia. Diane shared that she felt responsible for her employee's condition, and explained how she had tried very hard to get her to eat. She expressed a great sense of failure when she was unable to do so. In conceptualizing the case, Seeley needed to determine if the client's symptoms were the result of obsessive tendencies or possible identity and boundary issues that resulted in an unhealthy relationship with her employee. In other words, was the presenting problem an internal or intrapsychic phenomenon? Because Diane was an immigrant from Samoa, Seeley entertained the possibility of cultural involvement in Diane's behavior and emotional distress. Seeley conducted an ethnographic inquiry by asking Diane about work relationships in Samoa, especially between supervisors and employees. Diane mentioned that the work relationship was "like a family" and that supervisors assume responsibility for the well-being of their employees. When asked how she viewed the relationship with her current employee in Samoan terms, she described it as being like a "mother-daughter" relationship.

In addition, Diane explained how eating and food are a very important part of social relationships in Samoa, describing how a good host is responsible to make sure that everyone eats and has enough to eat. With this additional information, Seeley hypothesized that Diane's feelings of "excessive responsibility" were probably the result of cultural influences rather than obsessive tendencies or boundary issues. When Seely presented this hypothesis to Diane, she agreed that this could be the cause of her distress regarding the employee's welfare. After discovering the roots of the "excessive" responsibility for her employee, Diane began an exploration of the differences in expectations in employer-employee relationships in the United States compared to Samoa. This process helped Diane reduce her feelings of responsibility and distress, which resulted in a reduction of depressive symptoms. Seeley's use of a cultural inquiry allowed her to conceptualize the problem accurately. This example illustrates the importance of obtaining clients' input regarding possible social and cultural elements that may be associated with their difficulty. We believe it is important to assess for possible environmental, social, or cultural factors with all clients.

Is there a means to accurately evaluate the adequacy of a case conceptualization? One group of researchers attempted to do so. In a study regarding the quality of case formulations, Eells and his colleagues (2005) found that "experts" (therapists who had written about or had led workshops on case conceptualization) presented with clinical vignettes had case formulations that were of "higher quality" (more comprehensive, greater elaboration of ideas, and more systematic use of reasoning) compared to novices (clinical psychology graduate students with less than 1,500 hours of supervised psychotherapy experience) and experienced therapists (10 or more years of clinical experience). There are several interesting aspects to this study.

First, approximately half of the therapists that participated had a cognitive-behavioral orientation and half had a psychodynamic orientation, which, of course, resulted in significantly differing conceptualizations of the vignettes. However, theoretical orientation was not related to "conceptual quality"; that is, two extremely different conceptualizations of the same case could both be rated "high quality" because they were comprehensive, elaborate, and used systematic reasoning. Second, the novices did better on certain aspects of case formulation than did the experienced therapists. Novices may do better on case formulation because of exposure to the same guidelines used by the "expert" therapists. Of the findings, what seems especially problematic is that conceptualizations of the same vignettes based on different theoretical models (i.e., very different conceptualizations of the same case) were deemed to be of equally high quality. How can strikingly different conceptualizations of the same case receive similar ratings? This is an excellent example of problematic results when different theoretical lenses are applied.

The missing element in the study is the client's perspective. Isn't it essential to obtain the client's input regarding the accuracy of a conceptualization? We believe that a case conceptualization produced jointly by the therapist and client is far superior to one in which the therapist imposes an "expert" formulation.

Collaborative Conceptualization Model

Gambrill (2005) believes that there are several aspects critical to accurate conceptualization and treatment of mental health disorders. First, as we have emphasized previously, therapists need to be aware of the impact of their own values, worldview, and beliefs on their practice. Similarly, clients' unique characteristics, values, and circumstances should be considered. Additionally, clients should be encouraged to actively participate in the assessment and conceptualization process. In this manner, the therapist and client can choose intervention strategies that involve the integration of the best research studies, clinical expertise, and client input. How can this be accomplished? We believe that conceptualization, as well as assessment, is best done in a collaborative manner in which therapist self-awareness, client involvement, and the scientific method are utilized.

A collaborative conceptualization model that includes client perception and input includes the following steps (modified from Spengler et al., 1995, to include client involvement):

1. **Use clinician observation and client perspective to understand the problem.** Clinical expertise is essential in assessment, developing hypotheses, eliciting client participation, and guiding conceptualization. Therapists bring experience, knowledge, and clinical skills into this process; clients bring an understanding of their own background and their perspective of the problem. Therapists should be aware of values, biases, preferences, and theoretical assumptions that may influence their work with clients.

2. **Collaborate and jointly define the problem.** Within this framework, the clinician and client, either jointly or independently, formulate conceptualizations of the problem. A joint process generally leads to more accurate conceptualization. In cases where definitions of the problem differ, these differences are discussed and the agreed upon aspects of the problem can receive the primary focus. In some cases, the therapist can reframe the client's conceptualization in a manner that results in mutual agreement.

3. **Jointly formulate a hypothesis regarding the cause of the problem.** The therapist can tentatively address possibilities regarding what is

causing or maintaining the problems with questions such as "Could being alone all of the time be contributing to your feelings of depression?" or "Do you think your depression might be due to the way you criticize yourself so much?" or "You mentioned before that you get really down on yourself when you feel you aren't living up to your parents' expectations. Do you think that might have anything to do with how you've been feeling lately?" or "I remember you saying that it's been hard to be so far away from others who share your religious background. Do you think that has anything to do with your depression?" When perceptions or explanations of the problem differ, these differences can be acknowledged and an attempt made to identify and focus on similarities.

4. **Jointly develop ways to confirm or disconfirm the hypothesis regarding the problem, continuing to consider alternative hypotheses.** The therapist might say "If your feeling depressed is due, in part, to a lack of activity, how would we determine if this is the case?" or "How can we figure out if your parents wanting you to get all As in college is part of what is going on?" or "What else might be involved in your feeling depressed?"

5. **Test out the hypothesis using both the client and the therapist as evaluators.** The therapist might ask, "You engaged in more activities this week. Did that reduce your depressive feelings?" or "You mentioned you felt more depressed this week when you were mainly eating a lot of junk food. Do you think that your eating habits might be contributing to your depression?" or "It sounds like you were really feeling down after you talked to your parents this week and you shared you had gotten a B- on your calculus exam. What do you think that means in terms of what is going on with your depression?"

6. **If the conceptualization appears to be valid, develop a treatment plan.** The therapist might say "It sounds like your hypothesis that being alone is really contributing to your depression was really confirmed this week, when you noticed you felt better when you spent some time with friends. You also noticed that you tend to spend less time thinking negative thoughts about yourself when you're with others. Let's talk about how that important information can be used when we decide on how to best treat your depression."

7. **If the hypothesis is not borne out, the therapist and client collect additional data and formulate new, testable hypotheses.** The therapist might say "It's good we checked out that idea that there is a connection between your activity level and your depression. You mentioned that when you went out walking by yourself, your depression seemed to get even worse. Can I ask you to share some of the thoughts that were going through your head when you were walking?"

We believe it is of critical importance to go through a collaborative process in which the therapist and client adopt the scientific framework as they work to conceptualize the problem, and that they both have an equal voice in evaluating the problem definition. Unless there is substantial agreement on the definition of the problem, client and therapist motivation is likely to be less than optimal, resulting in less productive sessions. The following case illustrates how a therapist and client might have differing perspectives on a problem, and how a therapist can use hypothesis testing, combined with a collaborative conceptual and treatment process:

A graduate student, Sarah, came in for counseling complaining of a depression that was interfering with her social life and her academic studies. She indicated that she was uncomfortable talking about her problem. The therapist noticed that Sarah was sitting as far away from him as possible. He knew that there were many possible reasons for this behavior, such as being embarrassed or having negative feelings about seeking therapy. He decided to test out a hypothesis that her discomfort had to do with his being male. He stated that many female clients have a right to be distrustful of men. Sarah's response to this statement was to burst out in tears and describe being sexually assaulted after a student party. Later, she expressed the view that she was responsible for the assault because she had left the party with the man.

After providing emotional support regarding the situation and allowing Sarah an opportunity to talk about her feelings, the therapist gently asked the client to reconsider her belief about being responsible for the assault. The supportive therapy allowed Sarah to gradually understand that she was not responsible for the attack. They collaboratively discussed different possibilities (suggestions provided by both the therapist and the client) for dealing with her situation and developed a joint plan of action. The therapist had Sarah consider all possible areas, such as interpersonal and community support, as part of their plan. The agreed upon action included meetings with a women's support group, a meeting with Sarah and selected friends and family to share what happened and to help her confront feelings of shame and isolation, judicial action against the offender, and participation in community action to educate students about the impact of sexual assault. (Steenbarger, 1993)

This case demonstrates several key elements in the assessment, conceptualization, and treatment process. First, the therapist tested out his observation that the presenting problem might be related to some type of issue involving men. Second, he reframed the problem from one of personal responsibility to one that included mistaken beliefs about her role in the sexual assault, understanding that the belief was causing her distress. He also identified other aspects of the environment that might maintain or create further distress, such as reactions from her family or friends. Third, the therapist and client developed the therapy plan collaboratively, with both taking active roles in deciding the course of action. This allowed the client to feel empowered by being part of the decision-making process. Fourth, multiple sources were mobilized for support (individual, family, friends, school, and other students) and action was taken to address the assault. Instead of only focusing on intrapsychic variables, the therapy also involved identifying and responding to external influences. Traditional assessment, conceptualization, and treatment might only have involved therapy for reducing the anxiety and emotional reactions to the sexual assault, without including a focus on contextual or environmental contributors.

Collaborating on Intervention Strategies

There is a movement away from relying on "practitioners' ideology or preferences" for treatment options to interventions that have received research support (Edmond, Megivern, Williams, Rochman, & Howard, 2006). We believe intervention strategies should be based on research on facilitating qualities possessed by therapists (empathy, warmth, and genuineness), client characteristics (motivation, personality, and support systems), and techniques. Interventions should not be rigidly applied to a client's problem, but instead should be modified according to client characteristics and feedback. Consensus between the therapist and client regarding the course of therapy allows the therapeutic relationship to strengthen. In addition, using a collaborative approach allows clients to develop confidence that the therapist is using methods that that are likely to achieve desired goals. Thus, collaboration improves treatment outcome by enhancing clients' hope and optimism.

This chapter has focused on the importance of the use of a collaborative approach in diagnosis and conceptualization. Because of our contextual approach, the characteristics and perspectives of the therapist as well as the client are seen as integral parts of these processes. We have also infused contextual elements into the intake interview process, suggesting the use of specific questions to obtain the client's input or perspective, taking into consideration social and cultural influences.

In the following chapters, we present psychodynamic, humanistic, cognitive-behavioral, and multicultural perspectives on therapy, followed by examples of therapy formats based on these different models. These theoretical intervention guides are not how-to manuals, but rather are distillations of the strategies and techniques used in each approach. They are meant to familiarize individuals with different empirically based therapies and concrete examples of how theory links with treatment interventions. We will continue to infuse social, cultural, and diversity perspectives throughout these chapters and the concluding chapters that focus on crisis intervention and psychopharmacology.

Psychodynamic Theory and Techniques

6

Chapter

The focus of psychoanalytic inquiry has become too narrow, addressing certain sources of human misery but largely ignoring others that are equally important . . . Social inequality and injustice represent another source of unnecessary suffering that, in principle, can be modified and diminished. . . . How can we make psychoanalytic treatment available to a broader range of patients. . . . (Wachtel, 2002, p. 199)

In 2001, a survey reported that 21 percent of psychologists practicing psychotherapy endorsed a psychodynamic orientation. It was second only to the 35 percent indicating an eclectic orientation (Norcross, Hedges, & Castle, 2002). However, the therapy being practiced is generally not traditional psychoanalysis, but instead modified approaches based upon relational psychoanalytic theories. Within the field, attempts to incorporate more contextual and diversity issues into the therapy and promote the importance of research are becoming more common. When reading about psychoanalysis, students are given the impression that therapists with this theoretical approach spend most of their time using free association or dream analysis. This perspective occurs because most texts focus primarily on traditional psychoanalytic theory, leaving students with a mummified version of the approach. Readers are left with the impression that the theory has not evolved over time and is not amenable to the scientific approach, diversity issues, or managed care requirements. Such a view is not correct. The psychodynamic approach has, in fact, produced many different offshoots such as object relations therapy, self-psychology therapy, brief focused psychodynamic therapy, psychodynamic-interpersonal psychotherapy, interpersonal psychotherapy, and supportive psychodynamic therapy.

Manualized forms of some of these briefer therapies have been developed and some have even made it onto the list of empirically supported therapies for certain mental disorders. To address current modifications, we will focus more on psychoanalysis as it is practiced today.

We will use the terms, *psychodynamic* or *psychoanalytic,* to designate modified forms of psychoanalysis. In this chapter, we will first present the different models of psychodynamic theory and discuss how they have evolved over time. Second, we will consider the different techniques used in psychodynamic therapy and the research findings associated with each. Third, we will consider effectiveness studies with the more recent psychodynamic therapies. Finally, we will indicate how the diversity perspective can be incorporated within the psychodynamic framework. In Chapter 7, we will also describe in detail the steps involved in Core Conflictual Relationship Theme Therapy, a brief manualized 16 session treatment, with the goal of giving readers an understanding of the process and assumptions involved in this type of therapy. Interpersonal Therapy (IPT), an empirically supported therapy for depression, which is often described as a form of psychodynamic therapy, will be covered in Chapter 8.

The Evolution of Psychodynamic Theory

Psychodynamic theory has evolved over time as indicated by five distinct models (Hansen, 2000; Robbins, 1989; and Todd & Bohart, 1999). The first two, drive and structural/ego models, are traditional models characterized by positing human behavior as attempts to express, gratify, or defend against instinctual drives. Human behavior and interpersonal relationships are said to derive primarily from sexual or aggressive impulses. This *intrapsychic* (i.e., within the individual) orientation also influenced the tenets of the therapy. The therapist is not considered to be part of the "field" in psychotherapy with a client but exists merely as an observer. Under the drive and ego/structural models, the therapist is neutral and objective, functioning as a blank screen onto which clients project their instinctual conflicts. With the therapist seen as a neutral observer, every behavior exhibited by a client is presumed to come only from internal processes occurring within the client; thus, these models are characterized as being "one person" or client-only theories.

Some psychoanalytic theorists (Kernberg, 1976; Kohut, 1971; Mahler, 1968) were unhappy with the prominence given to instinctual drives. These theorists believed childhood development is not merely determined by sexual and aggressive drives, but that early relationships with primary caretakers, usually the mother, are of primary importance. This need for human relations was proposed to be as innate as drives and impulses. In the relational theories, the emphasis is on the importance of love and support from primary caretakers in the development of self-identity in a child. Deprivation of appropriate nurturance in childhood is believed to result in relationship problems in adulthood. The focus on interpersonal needs produced a change in the way the analytic relationship was conceptualized. Psychoanalysis was now seen as a two-person (therapist and client) enterprise in which the characteristics or responses of the therapist become part of the context of therapy. It is within object relations, self-psychology, supportive-expressive, and other contemporary psychodynamic theories that relational and collaborative elements in the therapeutic relationship are acknowledged. These changes have also influenced how psychoanalytic techniques are conceptualized and utilized. In considering the evolution of psychoanalytic theory, we will first begin with the one-person approaches (drive and structural), then with the relational, or two-person theories (object, self, and interpersonal).

Traditional One-Person Psychoanalytic Theories

The earliest psychoanalytic approaches to psychological development and psychopathology involved a focus on instinctual drives and forces within the individual (one-person), with little attention paid to the impact of relationships. These one-person theories are represented by drive theory and structural/ego psychology.

Drive Theory

Freud's (1915, 1957) initial theory revolved around the sexual and aggressive motivation of human beings and the conflicts between these drives and the demands of society. These sexual and aggressive drives operate at an unconscious level, continually seeking expression. Mechanisms such as repression are employed to defend against the conscious recognition of drive-laden fantasies. In many cases, these processes are not entirely successful, resulting in psychological symptoms. Anxiety is believed to be the result of undischarged drive energy (Hansen, 2000). To be functioning at an optimal level, these instinctive impulses needed to be discharged through processes such as catharsis (release of pent-up emotional energy). Human development is seen to revolve around the manner in which these instinctive drives are expressed or how they are defended against. For example, an individual may become an artist or writer as an unconscious means to *sublimate* (turn an instinctive impulse into a more socially acceptable form). Relationships with other people are, therefore, influenced primarily by the manner in which the different drives are expressed or inhibited. In drive theory, the psyche is divided up into three parts—the conscious, the preconscious, and the unconscious. Therapy involves analyzing and working through the unconscious causes for symptoms. Later psychoanalytic thinkers expanded the theory, arguing that emotions can result from reactions from the ego rather than just unconscious impulses (Greenberg, 2002).

Structural/Ego Psychology

The drive model was unable to account for certain symptoms shown by clients, such as internalized guilt. Because of this, Freud modified drive theory and developed a model that divided mental functioning into three structures: id, ego, and superego. The *ego* is the part of personality structure that is in contact with reality, the *superego* is the personality structure representing the internalized moral standard from the child's experiences with parents and society, and the *id* is the repository of unconscious drives. Instead of focusing only on drives and impulses, the concept of the ego and superego offered greater complexity, involving conflicts between these three structures of personality. Psychological symptoms occur when unconscious impulses from the id seek expression and are incompletely blocked by defense mechanisms that are contained in a portion of the ego that is unconscious. This model remedied the theoretical problems of drive theory by accounting for internalized guilt, by making provisions for the defense mechanisms to be unconscious and identifying a self-punitive part of the personality. Anxiety is conceptualized as a signal that mobilizes defenses. When unconscious, ego-alien impulses push for expression, a person experiences anxiety, which initiates activation of the defense mechanisms.

Psychological symptoms are viewed as a means of preventing awareness of underlying, unconscious conflicts. Phobias, for example, represent unacceptable sexual or aggressive fears or fantasies that have been repressed and then displaced onto an external object or situation. A fear of knives may represent an unresolved *Oedipal conflict* (conflict in male child over sexual feelings toward mother and fear of retribution through castration from the father; female children who have sexual feelings toward the father and jealousy and anger toward the mother suffer from the *Electra complex*). Having a phobia over knives is much less threatening to the ego than the recognition of sexual and aggressive wishes against the parents. Especially critical to the theory are these conflicts during the Oedipal stage and how they are resolved (Freud, 1923, 1961). Incomplete resolution can lead to symptoms such as phobias, other anxiety disorders, or sexual dysfunction. However, the role of parent-child relationships is still based only on the manner in which the child deals with sexual and aggressive impulses toward the parents. Other aspects of the parent-child relationship, such as the need for love or emotional support, receive little attention. As the theory continued to evolve, theorists such as Adler (1929, 1964), Erickson (1968), and Hartmann (1964) suggested that the ego was not totally dominated by impulses but also had adaptive abilities. This perspective launched the ego psychology movement and much literature devoted to conceptualizing the precise functions of the ego. Under this approach, it is still important to bring unconscious impulses into awareness and interpret fantasies during therapy, but because the ego is perceived to be adaptive, strengthening its abilities to deal with problems is also a major goal (Robbins, 1989).

Therapy Based on Traditional Psychoanalysis

Because psychological symptoms are seen as the result of unconscious impulses and drives seeking expression, little emphasis is placed on environmental causes. Instead, the focus is on the internal world of clients, identifying central themes in their lives, bringing unconscious conflicts to consciousness, and developing healthier behaviors. Some of these elements are present in the following case:

> *A 45-year-old man came to therapy with reports of depression and anxiety after being fired from his job as a medical technician, a position he had held for the last five years. The loss of income was very stressful since he was the primary source of financial support for his family. He was angry about being fired and expressed pessimism about finding a new job. The client was allowed to ventilate his emotional feelings during the initial sessions. Later, instead of focusing on present life circumstances or investigating possible social or occupational factors as contributors to the depression, the therapist directed her attention to the internalized experience of the client. This was done to see if there was any association between depression, the client's loss of a job, and childhood or early life experiences. In recounting the past, the client shared that when he was eight years old, his father had died unexpectedly. Further exploration of this event led to the memory that the father had been laid off of work, a source of anxiety for the entire family. The therapist believed that the client's current reaction to his own job loss had its roots in childhood and probed the concept of loss of a job and death with the client. As the client began to understand these connections as contributing to his current depression, he began to work through these issues. This led to a more adaptive outlook on life and he was able to seek and obtain new employment. (Wheelock, 2000)*

In traditional psychoanalysis, little attention is paid to current life situations except as a means to identify earlier developmental issues. Once insight is obtained and the formerly unconscious issue is worked through, it is assumed that healthy behavior patterns will develop. In the case above, the man was able to find a new job after discovering the reason behind his depression. In traditional psychoanalysis, the therapist remains remote in terms of a therapeutic relationship, merely observes the client, and interprets current behavior as reflecting underlying conflicts. Because of this therapeutic stance, the relationship between the therapist and client is unequal, with the therapist occupying the position of power. In traditional psychoanalysis, the therapy is structured for client exploration and can involve up to five or six hourly sessions per week for years.

Two-Person or Relational Psychoanalytic Theories

Object relations, self-psychology, and relational theories arose because of dissatisfaction over the mechanistic view of human nature and the focus on drives in determining human behavior. Although the role of drives in human motivation was accepted, these psychoanalytic theorists believed in the importance of relationship needs in the developmental process. Instead of just viewing other people as means to reduce drives, relational theorists (Bowlby, 1969; Klein, 1932, 1975; Mahler, 1968) believe that social needs (to be loved, accepted, and receive emotional support) are critical factors in early childhood development and identity. When a child does not receive empathy or emotional support from caregivers, it may be difficult to achieve a healthy self-identity. Problem behaviors may develop because the individual attempts to seek interpersonal experiences that were lacking in childhood. The emphasis on early relationship needs led to three offshoots of psychoanalytic theory—object relations, self-theory, and relational approaches. (see Table 6.1 for a comparison of the different psychoanalytic approaches.)

Object Relations Theory

In object relations theory, the role of attachment to others and the development of self-identity become areas of emphasis rather than the influence of sexual and aggressive drives. According to this perspective, problems can occur during the attachment, separation, and individuation process of a child if the parents do not provide appropriate emotional support (Bowlby, 1969; Mahler, 1968). In object relations theory, a child is initially in a state of fusion with the mother and is unable to distinguish him or herself from the mother. Later, the child begins to gain a sense of self, moving to develop a separate self. It is the process of attachment-separation with the mother and the development of a separate identity that can result in either healthy or troubled development. This process is determined by the mother's reaction during this stage. If the mother resists or is unable to assist the child's move toward autonomy and separateness, the self may become fragmented. During this developmental process, objects (the intrapsychic or mental representation of aspects of the mother or other people), both good and bad, are incorporated by the child through introjection, a process in which attributes of primary caretakers and significant others are taken into the mind, resulting in an internal representation of each person. The amount and type of love and emotional support determine the type of objects that are incorporated. These

Table 6.1 **Models of Psychoanalysis**

Drive Theory Model

- Sexual and aggressive urges conflict with societal rules.
- Drive-laden fantasies continually seek expression.
- Symptoms occur when repression cannot effectively contain drive.
- Unconscious drive fantasies express themselves as psychological symptoms.
- Relationships with others are determined by the expression of drives and impulses.
- Therapy involves analyzing and working through unconscious causes of the symptoms.

Structural or Ego Model

- Mental functioning is divided into id (repository of the drives), superego (repository of internalized feeling of guilt), and ego (structure that attempts to accommodate and mediate between id and superego).
- Unconscious defense mechanisms originate from the ego.
- Unconscious impulses push for expression, anxiety develops and activates defenses.
- Ego is not totally subsumed by id demands and can be adaptive.
- Not all behavior is viewed as the result of dynamic conflict with aggressive or sexual impulses.
- Therapy involves not just uncovering unconscious fantasies but also modification and bolstering of ego and superego.

Relational Model (Object Relations and Self Psychology)

- Interpersonal relationship needs are innate and are as important as drives.
- Attachment and relationships in human functioning are important.
- Perceptions of others are taken into the mind and become represented psychically.
- Children internalize templates based on relationships with primary caretakers.
- Presenting problems with others may be due to the imposition of these early life templates onto current relationships.
- Therapy involves exploration of patterns to see if the client is distorting perceptions of current relationships based upon early relationship experiences.

From Hansen, 2000; Robbins, 1989; Todd & Bohart, 1999

objects form a template or mental imagery of others that are not reality based, but nevertheless may impact the way relationships with others are perceived. Current relationships are viewed through childhood lenses; the failure to establish healthy object relations early in life results in an inability to form stable, enduring relationships.

Crises involving separation and individualization carry over to future relationships and behavior patterns. Mahler (1968) believed that an individual with separation conflicts will search for relationships that match unsatisfactory patterns learned early in life. Because a stable inner self has not developed, the individual may need constant emotional stimulation from outside to feel alive and engage in behaviors such as promiscuous sex or use of drugs. If the individual continues to feel fused with the mother, he or she may continually seek the fusion experience, but because this is not possible, will feel alone and empty (Todd & Bohart, 1999). Conflicts with the mother during the attachment-separation process can also lead to problems such as eating disorders in females. In this case, the lack of maternal support leads to a desire on the part of the maturing girl to remain separated from their mother (a negative, maternal object). The maturation of the woman's body produces fear because it is as if the mother's body is being imposed on her and she is becoming the "bad" mother. To prevent this, the woman may engage in anorexia, keeping her body in a prepubertal state in an attempt to triumph over the body as mother (Sands, 2003). An example of a case analysis and conceptualization from the object relations perspective follows:

> *A 29 year-old-woman, Ms. A., sought therapy after the breakup of a relationship with a boyfriend. She stated that she wanted to work on "letting go" so that she could move onto new relationships. She was preoccupied with thoughts about the reasons for the end of the relationship. She had met the man through a singles club and the relationship had gone well for about four months until they had sexual intercourse, resulting in feelings of insecurity (the woman indicated that this was a recurring pattern after sexual intimacy with males). The client reported that she became demanding, seeking reassurance of their relationship after having sex with the man. She felt that his response was inadequate and sent him an "impulsive, angry e-mail." In response, the boyfriend effectively ended the relationship by refusing to communicate with her. Further attempts to reestablish the relationship were unsuccessful. The woman sought therapy to deal with this repetitive and self-destructive behavior pattern with males. She reported that she had seen other therapists but had ended treatment because the sessions were not particularly helpful. (Kassaw & Gabbard, 2002)*

In object relations theory, the premise is that internalized object relations determined by childhood experiences repeat themselves in adult relationships. To explore past relationship issues, historical relationship patterns are the focus of therapy. Ms. A. revealed a significant event that occurred when she was 5 years old; she and her three-year-old sister were in a bedroom when an uncle who was intoxicated entered the room and touched the girls in a sexual manner. Ms. A. recounted that she crawled under the bed, leaving her younger sister behind. After the uncle left, she told her mother who responded by saying "That wasn't so bad." Her father also refused to take any action since he claimed that he "might become violent toward the uncle." Ms. A. believed that her parents had failed her. During her childhood and adolescence, she felt closer to her father than her mother, who she described as being very critical. The mother gave mixed messages to Ms. A. regarding relationships. She was critical of her daughter's interest in boys and encouraged her to have a career before marrying, but later criticized her for still being single. The mother threatened not to finance Ms. A.'s graduate school expenses if she moved away.

In a later session, Ms. A. related the following dream that occurred after a cousin's wedding:

> *We were on the roof of the church. The bride, the groom, we each had big lavender balloons, which were taking us to a city. My cousin and her new husband were already floating away. I was about to go as well, but my mother insisted on taking more pictures of me. Mother started to back up with the camera. I saw what was going to happen, but I couldn't do anything. Mother fell off the roof of the church. I ran down to the ground, but I already knew she was dead. (p. 723)*

In making sense of the dream and current relationship problems, several early experiences were considered. It seems plausible that the molestation event contributed to Ms. A.'s problematic relationship pattern. She might have felt unprotected and vulnerable because of the lack of action by her parents. Because the child was unable to process her experiences with the parents, a significant scar developed. In addition, separation conflicts developed with the mother, who seemed to encourage independence yet refused to let Ms. A become independent. The early experience of sexual abuse led to anger because of its link with exploitation. Relationships also produced conflict since they symbolized "separation from mother," something that she had learned was not acceptable. The dream could be interpreted as a warning that separation from the mother would be catastrophic (resulting in the mother's death). On an unconscious level, the dream may also be a wish for her mother to die so that Ms. A. could become free from control. These are all hypotheses that need to be tested during therapy sessions. Kassaw and Gabbard (2002) offer these suggestions when using the object relations approach:

- Focus on only one or two key themes believed to be at the core of the patient's problems. Don't try to deal with all difficulties.
- Bring out the possible relationship between early experiences and current difficulties.
- Identify precipitating stressors that may have triggered the symptoms.

- Use transference and countertransference to link the past to current problems.
- Remember that the formulated hypothesis needs to be evaluated and revised as you get more information.

Self-Psychology

Self-psychology was the last major psychoanalytic movement to emerge and was developed specifically to account for symptoms such as the feelings of emptiness, affective instability, or exaggerated self-importance seen in the narcissistic and borderline personality disorders. It is similar to the object relations approach in that the quality of parent-child interactions during certain periods is believed to determine adult functioning. According to Kohut (1971), the mother or primary caretaker is critical in providing the environment necessary for the development of healthy self-identity. Children have an innate need to idealize others and to have their experiences empathetically mirrored by caretakers. Idealizing is the need of a child to admire and look up to the caretaker as a source of strength. During the period when a child shows attention-seeking behavior, the provision of empathetic support or mirroring by the mother (experiencing and accepting the child's behavior) will enable the development of a sense of self-worth. The child will then be able to engage in self-nurturing. If this support or acceptance is not provided, however, the self can never fully develop a separate identity and the child will remain dependent on others for approval and be unable to soothe him or herself. People who have not received empathetic mirroring or have not moved beyond idealizing others will have disturbed relationships with others. In some cases, the person constantly looks for a person to idealize. They may show symptoms such as chronic feelings of emptiness, affective instability, unstable self-identity, or, as a defense, portray a false sense of self-importance. These characteristics of narcissistic or borderline personality disorders are seen as an attempt to get the kind of emotional support needed to resume growing (Todd & Bohart, 1999).

From the self-psychology perspective, the use of *transference interpretation* (i.e., interpreting client reaction to the therapist as a projection of parental figure issues) with clients who have narcissistic or borderline personality is considered too threatening. It is believed that due to their fragile self-identity, the use of this technique may lead to extreme hostility and self-destructive behaviors (Ogrodniczuk & Piper, 1999). Instead, Kohut (1971) suggested that a more effective intervention involves the therapist providing the empathy that the client was missing in childhood as the means to heal the fragmented self. Empathy allows the client to gain control of and manage disruptive emotions, gradually integrating them within the personality. In therapy, faulty early childhood experiences are revived and reworked. Although insight into the relationship between current problematic behaviors and parenting deficits is important, the focus is on the therapeutic relationship providing corrective experiences. Both the importance of empathy in the therapeutic relationship and a belief in the self-growth potential of the client are commonalities between self-psychology and humanistic psychology, which will be discussed in later chapters.

Other Relational Models

Additional relational models are represented by the interpersonal therapies. They share similarities with one another in that they: (1) focus on and evoke client emotions, (2) explore resistance or factors that inhibit the progress of therapy, (3) connect current patterns of behavior with past experiences, (4) attend to the client's interpersonal experiences, and (5) emphasize the therapist-client relationship (Barkham & Hardy, 2001). These therapies deal specifically with depression and are based on the view that depression occurs in a social and interpersonal context. It is this context that needs to be understood for improvement to occur. As with self-psychology and object relations theory, depression is hypothesized to be due to problematic relationships. However, the emphasis is on changing current interpersonal relationships. Several interpersonal structured therapies have been developed and researched. Both *Core Conflictual Relationship Theme Therapy* (CCRT) and *Psychodynamic Interpersonal Psychotherapy* (PDIPT) encourage a focus on past relationship issues, here-and-now experiences, and emotional and relationship experiences. *Short-Term Psychodynamic Psychotherapy* (STPDT) emphasizes understanding the early cause of depression. *Interpersonal Psychotherapy* (IPT) provides some focus on childhood experiences; however, the primary focus is on current rather than past relationships, and on the client's social issues rather than enduring personality characteristics. In the next two chapters, the CCRT and the ITP models will be presented in detail.

Therapy Based on Relational or Two-Person Theories

The emphasis on interpersonal needs and the acceptance of the here-and-now relationship between therapist and client led to modifications in traditional psychoanalytic procedures (Frosch, 2002). First, external reality and an emphasis on modifying current relationship patterns were given a more prominent role. Second, *transference* and *countertransference* (emotional reactions of the client toward the therapist and the therapist toward the client) were seen as joint creations of both the therapist and the client. Third, it became accepted that reactions of both the client and therapist may be due to current interaction patterns rather than reflecting past unconscious conflicts. Countertransference was no longer seen merely as the therapist's unresolved issues but perhaps due to unconscious therapist bias as a result of personal values, beliefs, or situational events. In addition, current characteristics such as the client's communication style, dress, or mannerisms were also seen as possible influences on therapist reaction. As a move away from theoretical bias, some psychodynamic therapists began to suggest that interpretations made by the therapist regarding the client behaviors are hypotheses that needed to be tested (Safran, 2002). Such a suggestion could lead to greater use of the scientific method in psychoanalytic therapies. Similarly, transference by the client could indicate unresolved, unconscious conflicts or could be client reaction to the current responses or characteristics of the therapist. The move to the bidirectional relational model (therapist and client both influence each other) has had a large impact on the way psychodynamic techniques are currently conceptualized and utilized.

Psychodynamic Concepts and Techniques

We will present some of the concepts and techniques used by psychodynamic therapists and indicate how they have evolved with the different theoretical orientations. Therapists from other theoretical orientations sometimes employ these same techniques, although perhaps with a different purpose in mind. Research findings regarding these techniques will be presented later in the chapter.

Blank Screen

Although this is not a specific technique, this concept does support the tenets of traditional psychoanalysis. The analyst functions as a "blank screen" so that the unconscious conflicts of the client can come to the surface without being influenced by the therapist. Freud (1912, 1958) argued that "the doctor should be opaque to his patient and, like a mirror, should show nothing but what is shown to him" (p. 118). By keeping the therapist's thoughts, day-to-day reactions, and feelings unrevealed, associations and reactions by the client can come to the surface without being contaminated. These conflicts and *transferences* (client's reaction to therapist that is triggered by unconscious conflicts) can be projected onto the therapist who can then "objectively" analyze the unconscious meanings of the associations and transferences. Current psychodynamic theorists reject the blank screen notion and consider therapy to be a two-person enterprise. The therapist is seen as a full participant in the psychoanalytic process and both direct and indirect influences of the therapist on the therapeutic process are recognized.

Self-Disclosure

In traditional psychoanalysis, self-disclosures by the therapist are completely discouraged as they are considered to be a "countertransference temptation" and believed to contaminate the client's ability to access unconscious experiences (Davis, 2002). Currently, some relational psychodynamic therapists do use selective self-disclosure to give feedback to the client. Its use varies depending upon the rationale for self-disclosure. If a client requests a self-disclosure, the therapist may decide to answer but may also investigate the reason for the request. When one therapist was asked about her husband by an 83-year-old client who observed the therapist wore a wedding band, the therapist responded, "I think it might be more interesting and helpful to you if we could talk about why you want to know that about me, rather than hearing my answer" (Hillman & Stricker, 2002, pp. 398). This is a gentle way for both the therapist and client to understand the reason for the question and facilitate self-exploration on the part of the client. It is important to respond to personal questions in a sensitive manner and also realize that in some cultural groups, a more relational manner is expected between therapist and client. These expectations should be discussed during initial sessions.

Free Association

In this process the client is asked to report their thoughts and feelings as they occur spontaneously, and to do so without monitoring or evaluating them. At the beginning of a session, the client may be asked, "What comes to your mind?" "What do you associate with those thoughts?" "As you think about that, what are you feeling?" A variant of this approach is the word association test in which the clients are asked to give an association to specific words. An example might be, "Can you tell me the first word you think about when I say 'happiness'?" To see if there is a connection between reported thoughts, feelings, and associations, the therapist may ask, "Do these thoughts remind you of anything that is happening to you currently?" With these association tasks, it is believed that repressed material may slip out and allow the client and therapist to examine its meaning and perhaps identify themes or patterns of reactions. Therapists of other theoretical orientations sometimes use this technique as a means to help a client focus on the here and now, move clients away from scripted verbalizations, focus on internal thoughts and feelings, identify conflict areas that are just outside of current awareness, or change the structure of the counseling session.

Dream Analysis

Dream analysis is also employed to understand the nature of the conflict underlying the presenting symptoms. Freud believed dreams were the "royal road to the unconscious" (Freud, 1900). During dreams, the ego becomes less aware or vigilant and allows some drive content to "leak" through, but only in a disguised form. The altered content represents the manifest content of the dream as reported by the individual. What is more important in psychoanalysis is the latent content or the "true" meaning of the dream. To understand the real meaning of the dream, the client may be asked to free associate with aspects of the dream or to concentrate on emotions involved in the dream. Interpretation of dreams can sometimes lead to an understanding of unconscious conflicts. Clients may also report dreams to nonpsychodynamic therapists. It can be valuable to explore feelings and concerns about dreams and to examine the possibility that they may reveal some conflict. This can be done without accepting psychoanalytic symbols or interpretations, but instead finding the meaning of the dream for the specific individual.

Analysis of Resistance

During sessions, clients may display behaviors such as blocking during associations, arriving late or missing sessions, or canceling therapy entirely. These behaviors are typically seen by traditional psychoanalysts as attempts by the client to prevent further probing into unconscious conflicts. They are considered to be escape behaviors. A therapist may address these by having the client free associate to these problematic behaviors. We believe that disengagement behaviors should be addressed directly by the therapist by making comments such as, "I notice that you are arriving late to the sessions. Has something changed?" There are many possible reasons for client resistance behaviors including: (1) a defense against revealing or confronting difficult issues, (2) a belief that the sessions are not helpful, (3) a change in work schedule, (4) a lack of support for therapy by a spouse or family members, or (5) the client may not like the therapist or the therapeutic style. It is important for the therapist to recognize the multitude of factors that can result in resistant behaviors and to address them in an open and nondefensive manner.

Transference

Traditional psychoanalysts believe that client reactions such as anger, love, or disappointment toward the therapist are projections of earlier relationship issues, usually involving the parents; they refer to this process as *transference*. One therapist reported that a client described him as "sometimes like her mother" and "other times like her father" (Frosch, 2002). The concept of transference has been broadened by relational therapists to also include here-and-now relationship issues between a therapist and client. During therapy, clients may display a variety of emotional reactions to the therapist. Transference issues from past relationships is certainly one possible explanation, but the client may also be having a bad day, doesn't like the therapy style, may feel misunderstood by the therapist, or is troubled because the therapist reminds them of someone they don't like. Broadening the meaning of transference allows diversity differences to be considered. Emotional reactions to the therapist by the client can be due to value, belief, class, or gender differences and must be explored because they can interfere with therapy. To reduce the chances that we are imposing our interpretations on the client, transference interpretations should be made in a tentative manner and client feedback about their perceptions of what is going on in the relationship should be obtained.

Transference interpretations can be made on different levels. At a personal level a therapist may state the following, "You told me about your colleague doing less than her share of the job, which gives you a headache. This may be an allusion to a feeling you have that I don't do my share of analytic work. It may be difficult for you to say this directly to me" (Hoglend, 2003, p. 272). A transference interpretation could also be directed to *extratransference situations* (a client's contemporary relationships or past relationships rather than the relationship with the therapist), for example, "You feel that your colleague is exploiting you, which may be difficult to say to her directly, so your headache builds up" (p. 272). In the second case, an interpretation can be made regarding the same material without referring to the therapist, but instead referring directly to the current relationship. Transference is a valuable concept, especially with this broadened meaning. As therapists, we need to be aware of possible reactions that our clients have to us, our therapy, or to our personal characteristics.

Countertransference

Freud (1910, 1957) believed that *countertransference* (emotional reactions of the therapist toward the client) represented unresolved issues of the therapist that were triggered by the client's transference. Under this framework, therapists are not seen as objective, but rather as responding based on their own unconscious conflicts. Freud believed that countertransference negatively impacts the progress of the client and gratifies the therapist's needs. Countertransference is believed to affect the working relationship and undermine the therapeutic alliance (Rosenberger & Hayes, 2002). As a precaution, it is believed that analysts should undergo personal analysis to identify possible countertransference issues. (See Box 6.1.) Shonfeld-Ringel (2001) gave an example of a countertransference issue involving cultural differences. A therapist was working with a female Asian immigrant who reported feelings of alienation and estrangement in the American culture. The therapist was a large woman from a religious minority who also felt stared at and marginalized, and unconsciously began to identify with the client. She became increasingly angry at the client's need for family approval and wanted to shake her—to make her more assertive. During supervision the therapist reflected on her own countertransference issues, revealing the source of her emotional

Box 6.1   **Reactions of 75 Psychoanalysts to Their Own Analysis**

Psychoanalysts completed questionnaires regarding their personal experiences after undergoing analysis. Most believed that positive changes occurred as a result of the process. Qualities and interventions that were identified as helpful were relationship variables such as the provision of rapport and support. Interestingly, therapist interpretations were considered to be "nonhelpful." Specific characteristics of their therapy that were judged to be helpful are listed below together with a summary of treatment outcome.

Helpful Analyst Behaviors

Analyst characteristics of support, acceptance, genuineness, and warmth ("open to my ideas, experiences, and feelings," "being nonjudgmental and noncritical") were responded to positively by the psychoanalysts undergoing analysis. These therapist qualities could easily fit the humanistic model and would certainly differ from the traditional psychoanalytic therapist functioning as a "blank screen." Gaining new perspectives on experiences was also considered helpful such as "asking questions to help me think and feel in new ways," "encouraging me to discuss experiences and feelings," "validating my experiences," and "helping to provide for new meanings for my experiences." Although interpretations are a cornerstone of the psychoanalytic approach, they were considered less helpful than supportive qualities. Rated lower were transference interpretations such as "provided interpretation of my interactions with others" and "provided interpretation of our interactions."

External Influences on Treatment Outcome versus Changes Attributed to Treatment

Most participants (85 percent) attributed psychological changes they had experienced to undergoing analysis. Some, however, believed that the positive changes were due to factors such as professional achievement, ongoing or new relationships, or simply "getting older."

Positive changes that the participants attributed to the analysis included increased capacity for emotional intimacy and closeness; the ability to experience a range of emotions; the ability to link past and present experiences; recognition of a wider range of options in behaviors with others; comfort with one's own power; ability to put feelings and thoughts into words; development of realistic thoughts, feelings, or perceptions of oneself; recognition of feelings of self-doubt and inadequacy; and the ability to recognize and experience what others feel.

Interventions Associated with Change

Successful interventions involved the probing of avoided experiences, assistance in becoming open to experiences, increased ability to tolerate anger and sadness, developing the ability to link past with present, and providing new meaning for current experiences. Therapist behaviors that were mentioned as "helpful" included genuineness and self-disclosure of feelings.

From Curtis et al. (2004)

reaction. Her frustration stemmed from her preference for egalitarian relationships, self-autonomy, and independence, qualities that were foreign to the Asian woman's culture.

Understanding countertransference can also lend itself to acknowledging diversity issues. In some cases our emotional reactions to the client could be due to earlier childhood conflicts that are brought to our consciousness by the client. However, we believe that the concept of countertransference should be broadened to include unconscious reactions to a client that are generated because of experiences, beliefs, values, or stereotypes held by the therapist. This conceptualization of countertransference easily allows for the consideration of diversity issues. The need to examine one's reaction to a client is a very important contribution of psychoanalytic theory. In fact, as we stated earlier, being self-aware and evaluating our reactions to clients is an important part of the scientific model.

Insight

Insight is the degree to which the client accurately understands the material being explored. It is an important process in psychoanalytic theory. By being consciously aware of the wishes, defenses, and impulses that have produced emotional symptoms, a more integrated and mature ego can develop (Kivlighan, Multon, & Patton, 2000). Understanding a connection between current emotional issues and past or present experiences can be important to clients. Helping them make sense of their symptoms can reduce anxiety. Because clients may be seeking an explanation for their difficulties, it is important for interpretations to be made tentatively and also to recognize that insights by either the client or therapist may be incorrect. Questions that help clients explore connections could be: "Is there an earlier time when you remember having the same feeling?" "Do you see any connection between your need for me to provide answers and what you wanted from your parents or other important relationships?" Questions in this format allow the client an opportunity to reflect.

With the relational models, insight has been extended from unconscious impulses to the understanding of current problematic relationship issues. It is also important to consider the possible impact of diversity issues on psychological symptoms. For example, for members of diverse groups, insight about intrapsychic conflicts may be less important than the insight that societal norms, expectations, or reactions may be factors contributing to the problem. If this is the case, the therapist may have to address issues relating to oppressive societal norms rather than allow the client to blame themselves for their difficulties. Some clients may not realize that prejudice, discrimination, or other societal issues may be contributing to their problem. Therefore, a focus on insight should not neglect the possible impact of class or cultural differences.

Other Techniques

Current psychodynamic therapists employ a variety of techniques that are commonly used within other theoretical perspectives and also believe in the value of the *therapeutic alliance* (i.e., the importance of establishing a bond with the client, working together with the client to define goals, appropriate solutions, and interventions). Collaboration with the client as an equal partner, the provision of empathy (experiencing the world through the viewpoint of the client) and focusing on behavioral change are accepted techniques for relational therapists and are increasingly seen as important for all psychodynamic therapists.

Research on Psychodynamic Therapy and Techniques

There are fewer outcome studies evaluating psychodynamic therapy compared to the large number of studies conducted on cognitive-behavioral therapy. This is, in part, due to the difficulty in finding outcome measures that tap into the changes produced by psychodynamic approaches. Compounding this problem are the many derivations of psychodynamic therapy. For example, supportive psychodynamic therapy differs from more traditional interpretative therapy in that the former places greater pressure on the client to talk, emphasizes the client's immediate adaptation to life situations rather than the past, uses structured problem-solving, and focuses on current external relationships. Earlier meta-analysis of therapies of different therapeutic orientations has indicated that the outcome of treatment by psychodynamic therapies is somewhat better than placebo treatment, but not as effective as cognitive-behavioral approaches (Glass & Kliegl, 1983). In contrast, recent studies based on more rigorously designed research involving brief psychodynamic therapies have found them to be as effective as comparison treatments (Archer, Forbes, Metcalfe, & Winter, 2000; Gabbard, Gunderson, & Fonagy, 2002). In some studies, psychodynamic therapies and cognitive-behavioral therapy are equally effective in the treatment of depression (Barkham & Hardy, 2001; Shapiro et al., 1995) and personality disorders (Leischsenring & Leibing, 2003; Fonagy, Roth, & Higgitt, 2005). Recent outcome studies involving manualized psychodynamic approaches have also found them to be effective treatments (Magnavita, 1994). Within psychodynamic approaches, interpretative and supportive psychodynamic therapies have been found to be equally successful treatments. However, there was four times more client drop-out with interpretive therapy (Piper, Joyce, McCallum, & Azim, 1998). This may be due to the fact that supportive psychodynamic therapies place much less emphasis on interpretation with clients. The researchers of this study caution that the use of interpretations during short-term therapy may produce high levels of anxiety in clients. Also, therapists should be attentive to client reactions when using this technique.

Client characteristics may also be important in transference interpretations. It was found that those with low object relations (i.e., resulting in difficulty reflecting on their interpersonal relationships) respond to interpretation as a rejection by the object (therapist). Therefore, interpretation, at least in brief therapies, should be reserved for clients who have high or mature object relations and, even in those cases, be used sparingly (Hoglend, 2003; Ogrodniczuk, Piper, Joyce, & McCallum, 1999). In addition, for transference interpretations to be successful, the therapeutic alliance must be strong and a series of supportive interventions should be used to pave the way for this process (Ogrodniczuk & Piper, 1999). Advances are being made in the psychodynamic therapies, with practitioners of many of the different therapies participating in comparative studies. Recently, a randomized, controlled clinical trial for panic disorder was conducted comparing the effectiveness of a manualized form of psychoanalytic therapy with applied relaxation. A significantly greater reduction in panic symptoms was found among those treated with psychodynamic therapy (Milrod et al., 2007). More research of this nature must be done before different forms of psychodynamic approach can be considered to be empirically supported.

Diversity Issues with Psychoanalytic Intervention

In the context of the imprint of diverse cultures and acute social needs, it is not only the classical drive model that must be questioned but also the relational formulations on which the two-person psychologies are based. Some concepts of attachment theory and object relations may themselves be Western ideas and perhaps middle-class Western ones. The emphasis on a single nurturing figure and on marital intimacy reflects cultural values of individualism over the importance of extended family ties. (Ogrodniczuk & Piper, 1999, p. 216)

Ogrodniczuk and Piper stress the importance of understanding the "crucial impact of culture and society on personality organization"(p. 216). Similarly, Kaplan (2004) argues for the inclusion of cultural and environmental considerations in psychodynamic theory, suggesting that we need to be attuned to characteristics of both therapist and client, such as communication and personality style, class, and ethnicity. Traditional psychoanalysis has been characterized as being too narrow and failing to address external issues such as social inequality, race, class, gender, and culture. Psychoanalysis was developed primarily for middle- and upper-class White individuals within a culture in which the values of these groups were held as the standard for human behavior (Wachtel, 2002). For example, Freud (1896, 1962) believed that hysteria was rarer in the lower classes because the moral character of people in these classes was less developed. The view that traditional psychoanalytic and even relational theories may be culturally bound or tied into specific values has led to questions regarding assumptions of individuality, appropriate parent-child relations, single attachment figures rather than more communal relationships, and the culture-specific nature of psychoanalysis.

We agree with the perspective that internal and external influences on the therapist-client relationship should be assessed, particularly when the therapist and client are of different backgrounds. In addition, it must be determined if psychodynamic constructs have universal application, or if they are specific to western civilization. As mentioned earlier in the chapter, broader conceptualization of certain techniques such as transference and countertransference do allow for the examination of diversity issues as they impact the client-therapist relationship and therapeutic outcome. In examining unconscious determinants for behavior, we can include cultural values, norms, and beliefs that are shaping behavior, and also societal issues such as oppression or dominance. Countertransference may be based on the therapist's reactions to a variety of factors including cultural values, stereotypes, or specific client characteristics. Transference issues from a client may result from experiences of being oppressed; a therapist from a different religious, ethnic, or social group may be seen as supporting the oppression. Questioning the effectiveness and universality of the psychodynamic framework for certain individuals or populations is important and has resulted in important changes within this theoretical model. We believe these changes have resulted in greater applicability of the model and techniques to diverse populations. In the Chapters 7 and 8, we will discuss in detail Core Conflictual Relationship Theme Therapy and Interpersonal Psychotherapy, both manualized and research-based psychodynamic therapies that illustrate the continuing evolution and contribution of the psychodynamic model.

Core Conflictual Relationship Theme Therapy

As a psychoanalytically oriented psychotherapist accustomed to treating patients once to thrice a week for a duration of years, I was not curious about brief psychodynamic psychotherapy (BPP). Although aware of this modality, I had regarded BPP as a second-class "Band-Aid" therapy—a lesser and poorer relative to the more aristocratic, longer-term treatments. (Book, 1998, p. xv)

As can be seen in the above quote, Howard E. Book, a therapist coming from a traditional psychoanalytic framework, had serious reservations about the prospect of effective treatment using brief forms of psychodynamic therapy. However, Book changed his mind about brief psychodynamic psychotherapy for several reasons. First, traditional long-term psychodynamic psychotherapy was receiving less attention than other forms of therapy in training programs and was in danger of becoming obsolete. Second, therapists from all theoretical backgrounds were feeling the impact of managed care with its cost-effective perspective, requiring short-term treatments and demonstrations of therapeutic effectiveness. Third, Book found that brief psychodynamic psychotherapy could, in fact, retain some of the psychodynamic concepts and techniques that he valued. Realizing that psychodynamic therapy needed to evolve, Book began to review different types of brief psychodynamic therapies. He became impressed with the work of Lester Luborsky, who in 1975 had developed the Core Conflictual Relationship Theme (CCRT) method, a brief psychodynamic approach. CCRT, now a manualized treatment, is presented in this chapter as an example of a brief psychodynamic model that has received research support.

CCRT therapy is a form of supportive-expressive psychodynamic therapy. In common with other psychodynamic therapies, it emphasizes the "lasting effects of early childhood experiences on adult functioning; the power of unconscious motivation in directing behavior; the tendency toward *repetition compulsion*, that is, the need to repeat, reexperience, and reenact traumatic memories, often in an effort to master them; and the ubiquity of the transference phenomenon" (Liem & Pressler, 2005, pp. 186–187). This therapy employs two main classes of techniques—supportive and expressive. As an interpersonal form of psychodynamic therapy (as opposed to traditional psychoanalytic therapy where the analyst functions as a blank screen and minimizes any relationship with the client), the therapist takes a supportive stance, demonstrating qualities such as empathy, respect, and support. A collaborative relationship is established as the therapist and client work together to identify the problem and develop treatment goals. These supportive aspects have been included in CCRT because they contribute to the therapeutic alliance and are associated with successful treatment outcome (Luborsky, 1984). The supportive techniques pave the way for the use of more psychodynamic, expressive techniques by creating an atmosphere in which clients can more freely express their thoughts and feelings. The expressive techniques include interpretation, confrontation, and clarification, which are used with the purpose of allowing repressed or unconscious material to surface. An important aspect of CCRT therapy is the identification of transference issues involved with the client's current relationship problems; once clients understand the underlying reasons for their discomfort or unhappiness, they can begin to exert more control over their behaviors.

Although CCRT therapy is not an empirically supported therapy, we are using it as a representative of the brief psychodynamic therapies because there have been a number of research studies on the constructs of the CCRT method and their reliability (Luborsky & Crits-Christoph, 1997b), and because there has been empirical support for the effectiveness of supportive-expressive psychodynamic psychotherapy (Crits-Christoph & Connolly, 1998). We are also impressed with the fact that Luborsky (1984) uses the scientific method in his approach and that he has based some of his methodology on research findings about strengthening the therapeutic alliance. Especially noteworthy is the use of therapist-client relationship enhancement through collaboration and support—aspects that we have emphasized as being critically important in therapy. The description of the CCRT method that follows relies on the treatment manuals developed by Luborsky (1984) and Book (1998), and on the work of Luborsky and Crits-Christoph (1997b).

Theoretical Basis of the CCRT Method

CCRT therapy is a brief psychodynamic method based on the hypothesis that current adult relationship problems are the result of repressed and unresolved negative childhood experiences. A specific maladaptive pattern of response occurs when an interaction with another individual triggers these unconscious conflicts. Luborsky (1984) believes that identification of these patterns in problematic relationships provides for an understanding of the specific unconscious underlying parent-child conflict. Once the "core conflictual relationship theme" is identified, the problem is then interpreted as resulting from a *transference reaction* (transferring these childhood-based issues onto current situations). This transference reaction impacts current relationships, including the client-therapist relationship, and resembles patterns of behavior learned with parents or other caretakers. Once the unconscious pattern is identified, the therapist can assist the client in becoming aware of the original childhood relationship issues that have led to problems in current relationships. With this approach, it is first necessary for the therapist and client to identify the *Core Conflictual Relationship Theme* (CCRT), the unconscious pattern or schema that the client uses in certain relationships or in interpersonal situations. To accomplish this, the therapist must carefully listen to the client's description of interactions with other people, called *relationship episodes* (REs), and from these generate possible core themes. An example of a relationship episode follows:

> *Well, actually the first night we saw each other was last Monday night. It was the first time we've seen each other in two weeks. . . . We went out to eat and then went back to the apartment and started talking. He didn't have a car that night so I said "Are you going to stay here? Do you need to go home? Let me know because I don't want to be driving that late." He said at first, "I want to stay here. . . ." Then we decided he had stuff to do in the morning and maybe he should go. All of a sudden I was like, "NO." I didn't want him to go. . . . Driving him home my eyes were welling up. Like, "Why can't you do something? You know I'm upset." He said, "This is exactly the reason that I need to fix myself. . . I'm sorry." (Liem & Pressler, 2005, pp. 188–189)*

According to Luborsky, the CCRT can be determined by examining three aspects of the *relationship episode* (the conflicted interpersonal communication) including "what the patient wanted from the other people, how the other people reacted, and how the patient reacted to their reactions" (Luborsky & Crits-Cristoph, 1998, pp. 3–4). What the individual wanted from the interaction is termed a *Wish* (W), such as wanting to speak up, to be close, or to be the center of attention. The second aspect is the *response from the other person* (RO). The RO can be anticipated or imagined (such as fearing rejection) or an actual event (such as receiving rejection from someone). What is critical is the subjective evaluation of the interaction from the perspective of the client, rather than whether or not the rejection actually occurred. The third component to the CCRT is the *response of the self* (RS). This includes both a behavioral element (i.e., what the client does in the situation) and an emotional reaction (i.e., how they felt). In the case discussed previously, the relation episode from the female graduate student contained the following elements:

Wish—To be in a close relationship with a male who is "there for her."

RO—Boyfriend said he needed to "fix himself" before he could be "there for her."

RS—To cry and be upset and then to feel bad about being "needy."

In keeping with the brief model, the goal of the CCRT method is on symptom relief with a primary focus on the one aspect of the patient's maladaptive style most clearly associated with the presenting problem. Because of the short-term nature of this therapy, clients appropriate for CCRT therapy must have good ego strength demonstrated by adequate reality testing, impulse control, and frustration tolerance coupled with adaptive defenses. In addition, it is best if clients are insightful and motivated, and have the ability to readily engage in therapy and see the connection between present and past events. This approach would not be appropriate for situations such as borderline personality disorder that require lengthier treatment. In the next section, we present a more detailed explanation of the components of the CCRT method.

Supportive Elements Necessary for a Strong Therapist-Client Bond

Both Luborsky and Book emphasize the importance of establishing a strong therapist-client bond and consider this task to be of primary importance in utilizing the CCRT method. This relationship-building sets the groundwork by enabling the client to more easily deal with anxiety-provoking or threatening material, and opens a path for the use of expressive techniques. A good working relationship involves the therapist:

- establishing a collaborative relationship with the client
- working with the client so they both have a similar understanding of the problem
- encouraging the client to believe that the intervention will be helpful
- ensuring that the client feels understood by the therapist
- helping the client maintain optimism that the therapy will work
- acknowledging the positive changes occurring during therapy

How can a therapist display the specific supportive elements encouraged in CCRT therapy? Luborsky (1984) recommends that the therapist verbally and nonverbally convey respect and support for the client's desire to accomplish identified goals, as well as understanding and acceptance of the client. It is important for the therapist to communicate a belief that treatment goals are achievable, providing genuine affirmation as the client gains skills in the use of insights and strategies learned in treatment and makes progress toward goals. A strong therapist-client bond is a critical first step, allowing for deeper exploration of problematic relationship issues in the client's life using expressive techniques as the therapy proceeds. The amount of energy the therapist devotes to the formation of the therapeutic alliance depends upon the specific issues involved and characteristics of the client. Individuals who are highly anxious or defensive may require extra time and attention to increase the level of support.

Expressive Techniques: Listening and Identifying the Relationship Episodes

Listening in a supportive and empathetic manner sets the stage for clients to express their thoughts and feeling about interpersonal issues. It also allows for the emergence and expression of repressed thoughts and feelings. In tapping the repressed material, the therapist initially addresses aspects of the main relationship problem that are closer to awareness. As mentioned earlier, the task of the therapist is to identify the *core conflict relationship theme* that underlies the client's problematic relationships. To do so, the therapist listens and attends to the client's verbalizations with a focus on identifying problematic interactions with others, *relationship episodes* (REs). Not all relationship issues presented are REs. The therapist is looking for episodes that represent a conflict between what the client hopes or wishes for in a relationship and what the client is experiencing. In determining the components of the CCRT for a particular client, Luborsky advocates adopting a scientific attitude in which the therapist avoids imposing a specific dynamic or perspective on the client's problem when gathering information. Instead, the therapist formulates and shares hypotheses with the client, listens to the client's response, and evaluates for accuracy.

After collecting a number of REs, the therapist reviews each with the help of the client with an emphasis on identifying: (1) The client's wish (W)—what he or she wanted to say or do in a specific interaction with another; (2) the response from others (RO)—the actual or anticipated response from the other individual (RO) (remember, ROs are based on the client's subjective reaction and may not be based in reality); and (3) the response to the self (RS)—how the client behaves and feels at the end of the relationship episode. The therapist can write down the RE and its components as they are discussed in the session with a client. After a review of multiple relationship episodes, a common or overarching theme often emerges. This theme identified is at the "core" since it lies at the heart of the client's symptoms and interpersonal difficulties, and represents the repetitive, interpersonal concern that brings the client in for treatment. In summary, the three components of the CCRT are:

Client Wish   →   Response   →   Response to Self   =   CCRT
                      from others

(what the client   (real or   (how client reacts,
wants to say or do)   imagined)   behaves, or feels)

In general, wishes are positive; however, therapists should be alert for the possibility of unhealthy or destructive wishes. They should have a plan to deal with a wish that is harmful to the client or to others, such as wanting to isolate oneself, be overly dependent, or to retaliate against or injure someone. In CCRT, unhealthy or destructive wishes are referred to as *regressive wishes*. In such cases, the therapist would not want to assist the client in actualizing the wish. Instead, the wish is interpreted as a response from the self (RS) and the therapist searches for a *progressive wish*, a wish that involves appropriate adult behaviors.

Book (1998) gave an illustration of man who mentioned that arguments with his wife produced fantasies of "punching her in the face" (W). He did not do it, because of the possibility of being put in jail (RO); he held back, while still feeling very angry (RS). Because physical violence is harmful, it is considered a regressive wish. Regressive wishes are reinterpreted as a response from the self (RS), and a search is conducted to determine the progressive wish. In the case of the client who had this wish to be violent with his wife, Book looked for the progressive wish. Further questioning revealed that the actual wish (W) involved being treated as an equal and with respect. The response from the wife (RO) was "to dominate," and "to belittle." The client's reaction (RS) was to act in a polite and compliant manner, while silently enraged. Through this process, the actual wish was identified and the therapist was able to help the client work toward a more equal and respectful relationship with his partner. It is always necessary to identify and reinterpret regressive wishes before therapy proceeds.

Steps in Identifying the CCRT

Correct identification of the CCRT is an essential step in the therapy process. As previously mentioned, there may be multiple themes occurring simultaneously. It is important to evaluate multiple episodes presented by the client and identify the one overriding theme. In a sample of 33 clients (Luborsky, Barber, Schaffler, & Cacciola, 1997), the most frequent wishes expressed were "to be close," "to assert myself," and "to be independent." The most frequent

Table 7.1 **Examples of Common Wishes (W), Response from Others (RO), and Response of Self (RS)**

Common Wishes (Ws)

To be close and accepted	To oppose, hurt, and control others
To be loved and understood	To be controlled, hurt, and not responsible
To feel good and comfortable	To be distant and avoid conflicts
To achieve and help others	
To assert self and be independent	

Response from Others (RO)

Helpful	Controlling
Likes me	Upset
Understanding	Anger
Strong	Rejecting and opposing

Responses of Self (RS)

Helpful	Helpless
Respected and accepted	Wanting to oppose, hurt, and control
Self-controlled and self-confident	Anxious and ashamed
	Disappointed and depressed
	Unreceptive

From Barber, Crits-Christoph, & Luborsky (1997)

responses from others were "rejection" and "control," while the most frequent responses from the client were "disappointment and depressed," "unreceptive," and "helpless." You will find some common wishes (both progressive and regressive) and reactions of self and others presented in Table 7.1.

Those who use the CCRT method generally go through the following process as they listen for and identify core themes (Luborsky, 1984; Book, 1998):

1. The therapist listens for and writes down each relationship episode expressed by the client.

2. The therapist analyzes each episode for an understanding of the wishes, responses of others, and responses of self. If the client does not describe the interaction sufficiently to note all three components, the following clarifying questions can be used:

   a. Unclear Wishes (Ws). "What did you want to do?" "What did you wish would happen?" "It seems that you wanted to . . ."

   b. Unclear Actual or Anticipated Response from Others (ROs). "How did the other person behave?" "How did you think they would respond?"

   c. Unclear Response from Self (RSs). "What did you do?" "How did you feel?"

3. The therapist evaluates the set of narratives to determine a possible core conflict relationship theme (CCRT), and then presents part or all of this CCRT to the client for his or her consideration and feedback. In work with clients, it is important to obtain at least five to ten REs and their corresponding Ws, ROs, and RSs, before the CCRT is identified. Never attempt to identify the CCRT with only one or two REs.

4. The therapist and client work together to determine if the identified theme is, in fact, an important theme to emphasize throughout treatment. If confirmed by the client, this focus usually becomes a treatment goal. If not confirmed, the therapist works with the client to explore other possible themes.

The following case presented by Book (1998) illustrates some of the steps in discovering the CCRT:

> Mr. Black was a 31-year-old accountant who complained about feeling depressed during the previous weeks, no longer enjoying work nor engaging in any other activities. Although the client brought up a number of different issues, the therapist listened specifically for relationship events (REs), problems regarding interactions with others. An episode that the client mentioned that was a possible RE involved his description of being cut off during a road trip by an individual driving a Porsche. The therapist wanted to determine if the wish, response from others, and response of self could be obtained. When asked about what he did and how he felt, Mr. Black indicated that he took no action because of the possibility that the other driver may have had a gun. Further questioning revealed that Mr. Black felt "deflated" after the incident. From this information, the therapist was able to tease out the elements of the RE. The wish (W) for Mr. Black was to be able to express his feeling of anger to the other driver. His (RO), an imagined response from the other, was anger and retaliation. Due to the concern that the other person might harm him, his (RS) response to the self was fear, a decision to do nothing and then to feel irritated and shamed.

Because of the collaborative nature of the CCRT method and importance of checking the accuracy of the therapist's conceptualization, Book (1998) presented his view to the client in the following manner:

> We've talked about a number of issues and concerns that go on in your life. . . . But I've been struck by one that seems to me really crucial to the difficulties we've

Box 7.1 **Self-Analyzing Your Own CCRTs**

In order to determine what interpersonal patterns occur in your own behavior with others, it is helpful to consider and reflect on some of your typical behavior patterns. In this exercise, after finishing the tasks below, you can attempt to identify a CCRT.

First, think of about ten events involving another person that occurred either recently or in the past. These events may be either positive or negative. Write down each event in the following manner: (1) Describe the event. It can involve parents, relatives, friends, fellow students, or colleagues at work. (2) Indicate when it occurred. (3) Describe what the other person said or how they responded. (4) Describe how you responded.

For each episode, write down the following:

W (Wish) What did you need or wish in terms of the interaction with the other person?

RO (Response from others) How did the other person respond or how did you think they would respond? Is this response one that you imagined might happen or one that actually occurred?

RS (Response from self) How did you react to the response you received (or imagined you would receive) from the other individual? What did you do? How did you feel?

From these ten events, try to identify an overarching pattern in terms of the Ws, ROs, and RSs that occurred. Do you see a pattern? How is this pattern similar to interactions you displayed as a child with your parents or caregiver? Are there any social or cultural influences involved in the theme?

From Luborsky & Crits Cristoph (1997b)

discussed. And it's an issue that seems to occur and recur over and over again. And this is what I've been struck by: It seems to me that in relationships you want to be able to speak up forcefully, especially when you feel wronged. But, for some reason you fear that if you do so, the other person will really get back at you. So, to guard against this, you bite your tongue, swallow your words, remain silent; but you pay the price of feeling frustrated, silently resentful, and very down on yourself. And I think this is why you feel so fed-up and irritable at work. . . . (pp. 30–31)

The therapist then gives the client the opportunity to reflect and give his or her reaction to the conceptualization. In general, clients accept the explanation given by the therapist since the CCRT comes from the client's own description of different relationship episodes presented during therapy sessions. You may be interested in practicing self-observation and analysis to gain a better understanding of the steps and concepts involved in deducing a core conflictual relationship theme; if so, refer to Box 7.1 for a self-analysis activity.

Therapeutic Goals with CCRT

The goal of CCRT therapy is to help the client obtain symptom relief by actualizing the wish; that is, behaving in a manner that results in the need being met. For Mr. Black, this would involve being able to speak up in situations where he is treated unfairly. In doing so, his response to self (RS) would change and he would no longer feel belittled as a consequence of doing nothing. The actualization of a wish can occur when a client begins to understand the response from other (RO) as either a *transference* phenomenon or a *repetition disorder.* Transference interpretations focus on allowing clients to see that the anticipated response from others is due to expectations developed during childhood. The CCRT may also be due to a *repetition disorder,* a maladaptive behavior pattern in which a client behaves in a manner that actually elicits negative responses from others. In this case, the focus of therapy is on how the client has learned to behave in certain ways with others as a means of mastering early childhood experiences. Although the focus of therapy varies, both transference and repetition response patterns are seen to stem from early childhood experiences with parents or caregivers.

Before they can master early childhood experiences, clients must understand how the CCRT relates to their unhappiness or "psychic pain." As Luborsky explains,

> *Both the therapist and patient continually understand more and more about two facets of the patient's communications: (1) the most interfering symptoms and psychic pain and (2) their interpersonal context. This context is composed of both inner and outer conditions precipitating and continuing the symptoms and psychic pain. The inner conditions are versions of core conflictual relationships; the outer ones are the behaviors of others that appear to the patient to fit into the core conflictual relationship template. (Luborsky, 1984, p. 94)*

Clients are generally unaware of the source of their conflict, partly because of defense mechanisms operating to keep this from their awareness or due to the pain of the past memories. For this reason, it is necessary to continue to emphasize the problematic relationship issues that are resulting in dissatisfying interactions with others. Only through increased understanding and awareness can clients begin to understand the pattern and learn to establish greater conscious control over their situation. This process involves learning more about how often the CCRT is present in problematic interactions with: (1) current family members, friends, coworkers, or others; (2) past relationships with early caregivers, such as parents; and (3) the relationship between the therapist and the client. Of the three areas, attention to the current relationship between the client and therapist has the greatest therapeutic potential because it involves a here-and-now experience.

To reduce client resistance and discomfort, the therapy first focuses on issues that are closest to conscious awareness and the least anxiety provoking. Therefore, the therapist first explores patterns of current relationships rather than those from childhood. Similarities across relationships involving Wishes (W), Response from Others (RO), and Response from Self (RS) are identified and discussed with the client. As the client becomes more aware of the CCRT in current relationships, the therapist gradually explores the historical roots of the problematic behavior patterns and, in a gentle fashion, begins to point out the connection with early childhood experiences. For example, when exploring the roots of a client's depression, a therapist offered this interpretation:

> . . . *You described wanting a deeper connection and more support from your mother, but instead experienced her as rejecting and neglectful of you. This led you to withdraw from her, feeling sad, hopeless that she will ever be concerned about your needs.* . . . *(Hilsenroth & Cromer, 2007, p. 208)*

Additionally, problematic patterns that appear in the client-therapist relationship provide an opportunity for exploration of the CCRT. Maladaptive behaviors are interpreted as coping attempts; once clients understand this, they can begin generating alternative and more productive responses.

When clients have moved to this point, the real work of CCRT begins, which is to concretely demonstrate how the current attitudes and behaviors toward others are produced by unresolved childhood experiences. Because this pattern of behavior is so ingrained, the therapist and client often need to repeatedly examine problematic relationships, until the client understands and accepts the influence of the CCRT, and develops new ways of responding. Successful understanding of the CCRT in current relationship problems is demonstrated when the client shows increased (Book, 1998; Luborsky, 1984):

1. ability to see current relationship problems as aspects of the CCRT.

2. understanding of how he or she contributes to relationship problems rather than blaming communication problems on others.

3. recognition of the power of the core relationship theme and its association with other relationship issues.

4. insight into how the CCRT originated from early childhood experiences.

5. understanding of how the behavior produced by the CCRT can also result in reinforcement as a secondary gain, such as receiving sympathy or attention from other people.

6. skill in generating alternative behaviors when confronted with situations that reflexively bring up the CCRT.

Understanding Transference

In the case of Mr. Black, his restraint in speaking up because of a fear of negative consequences was determined to originate from his relationship with his father. He described his father as a violent individual who did not tolerate any dissention in the family and who was abusive to his mother. This led him to conclude it was better not to speak up in situations that might produce conflict. His wish (W) (to be able to speak up) was inhibited by his fear of retribution (RO) from his father, producing the behavior of holding his tongue and feeling helpless (RS). Insight into his current behavior problems occurred by working through the response from others (RO) issue as a *transference* phenomenon. In other words, he had transferred the childhood relationship pattern with his father to current interactions with others. When Mr. Black was able to understand and work through this issue, he became able to act more assertively in situations rather than feeling helpless and doing nothing (Book, 1998).

Transference issues involving the client and therapist, referred to as *enactments,* can be the most therapeutic because they involve a here-and-now interaction. During therapy, the client may begin to respond unconsciously to the therapist in a manner reflective of the CCRT. This is not surprising since the core conflict is easily aroused. In these circumstances, the therapist should be alert to its expression by noting dramatic or unusual changes in the client's behavior. The therapeutic relationship can be assessed through statements such as, "You know we've talked a lot about the issue of _____ today, and I wonder how that might play out in here between the two of us?" (Hilsenroth & Cromer, 2007, p. 206). Book (1998) recalls an incident in a session with a client, during which he received an unexpected call. Although he terminated it quickly by reminding the receptionist that he was in session, the client, who had been very engaged in therapy, suddenly became silent and nonresponsive. Attempts by the therapist to return to the earlier discussion were unsuccessful. The client seemed stuck. As Book noted, "Initially unaware that an enactment was occurring between us, I attempted to be helpful by encouraging the patient to return to describing what had happened . . . But in doing so I was overlooking an unfolding of an enactment . . ." (p. 69). The therapist began to consider the possibility that an episode based on the CCRT was occurring. The client's problem revolved around wanting to have her ideas taken seriously by others (W), and withdrawing and feeling sad (RS) when feeling dismissed by others (RO). To check the accuracy of this hypothesis, Book asked the client if it was possible that her core conflict was being played out with the incident regarding the phone call. After discussing the event in relationship to elements of the CCRT, the client agreed with the interpretation and gained further understanding of the pervasiveness of the pattern.

Understanding Repetition Compulsion

In some cases, the negative response from others (RO) does, in fact, occur and is not just imagined or expected. The client may be slighted, ignored, or encounter hostility from others. This tendency to elicit negative responses from others is called a *repetition compulsion*. For example, Book (1998) discussed the case of a woman who talked about the behavior of her boss as being curt and dismissive when she attempted to bring up her ideas. Her wish (W) was to be taken seriously as a competent individual. The actual response from others (RO) was dismissive, which produced withdrawal and feelings of sadness (RS). Further questions involving this and other incidents supported the view that colleagues and other individuals at her work did not appear to take her seriously. When the RO actually exists, the client's behavior is analyzed to determine what he or she is doing to provoke the responses. Again, the childhood roots are examined. In this case, the woman's behavior was a result of an early relationship pattern with her mother. The client wanted to be seen as valuable and competent to her mother, but also relied on her in an overly dependent fashion. In evaluating her current work situation, the client acknowledged that she displayed helplessness and disorganization with her coworkers, but wanted to be taken seriously. She was repeating this unproductive pattern of behavior in an attempt to master the ambivalent relationship with her mother.

The Three Phases of CCRT Therapy

CCRT therapy is conducted over 16 fifty-minute sessions. Book (1998) divides the 16 sessions into three phases. The first phase (sessions 1 to 4) involves assessment, identifying the CCRT with the client, determining the goals for therapy, and providing the treatment rationale. During the second phase (sessions 5 to 12), the primary focus is working through the RO by examining the childhood roots of this pattern. The response from others is interpreted as the transference of unconscious attitudes and behaviors derived from past relationships with parents or other caregivers. The transference perspective is offered every time the clients bring up a problematic relationship issue. The therapist weaves current problems with similar issues from the past. *Enactments,* the transference displayed to the therapist, are especially valuable for learning during this phase. The third phase (sessions 13 to 16) deals with termination issues. We will now describe in detail the components involved in the three phases:

1. First Phase (sessions 1–4)
   (a) The assessment interview, mental status exam, and diagnosis are conducted to determine if the situation is appropriate for a brief

therapy such as CCRT therapy. The client needs to have sufficient ego strength, motivation, and insight into their problem to benefit from this treatment. Those who appear to require longer-term therapy are referred for a different form of therapy.

(b) During this assessment, the therapist listens carefully for relationship episodes and notes the wishes (Ws), response from others (ROs), and response from the self (RSs). If some components of the relationship episode are unclear or not stated, the therapist uses questioning to clarify. The core conflict or overarching theme is identified from about 10 relationship events described by the client. If there are several themes, the one that seems to be involved in the greatest number of relationship episodes becomes the focus.

(c) The CCRT is presented to the client for their feedback. Clients usually accept the theme since it is based on their own description of relationship problems. If the client does not accept it, several possibilities exist. First, the therapist may have been inaccurate in his or her formulation of the CCRT. In this case, the therapist works with the client to determine if it is the W, RO, or the RS that needs to be better understood. This usually results in an acceptable CCRT. The second possibility is that the client may be resistant to the process and perhaps not appropriate for brief therapy.

(d) The therapist relays expectations regarding the tasks of the therapist and client during therapy; this is referred to as the "socialization address" (Book, 1998) and is presented in the following manner:

"Our therapy sessions will be different from what we did during the assessment process where I asked specific questions and you answered. In therapy, a more active role from you will be the most helpful. Your part will be to talk about any issue that comes to your mind, even if it seems to be irrelevant. My job will be to listen carefully to what you are saying and try to determine if it is related to the focus of the therapy. We will work together to learn more about your current relationship issues, especially in regards to what you do and how you feel about it. In doing so, we will also talk about your childhood experiences and how they may relate to current problems. During therapy, you may also develop reactions to me. This can also provide useful information regarding relationship difficulties. We are going to determine what is the 'core' or central aspect that is producing repetitive interpersonal difficulties. This understanding will allow you to change what you do in problematic social interactions and to feel better about yourself.

"During therapy, you may be tempted to make major changes in your life. Please do not do so before having a chance to discuss them in our sessions. This is not for the purpose of receiving advice from me, but for you to

understand the motivation for considering changes. Do you have any questions about the tasks of therapy as I have described them?"

(e) The therapist repeatedly confronts the client regarding the frequency with which the CCRT is present in interpersonal interactions and the power it has in producing problems in relationships with friends, coworkers, peers, family members, and even the therapist. Again and again, the therapist points out how the client's wish is blocked and frustrated by an unconscious fear or anxiety about the others' responses, and how this results in avoidance behavior and negative emotions.

2. Second Phase (sessions 5–12)

It is in this phase where most of the real therapy occurs. The childhood roots that fuel the client's RO are uncovered. The therapist, through confrontation, clarification, and interpretation, helps the client identify, understand, and resolve the early experiences that give rise to the RO, which represents a reliving in the present of unresolved childhood feelings. Working through these transferences constitutes the heart of the CCRT method. Transference interpretations are made connecting present interpersonal difficulties with past childhood experiences. The interpretation involves explaining and demonstrating that the client is unconsciously and inappropriately reliving past attitudes and issues, but with people in the present. The therapist repeatedly discusses interactional episodes until the client understands the connection and is able to perform the transference analysis on current interactions.

At some point during therapy, it is presumed that the client will demonstrate an *enactment* by responding to the therapist with a CCRT. When this occurs, two types of therapeutic responses from the therapist are helpful (Book, 1998). First, the therapist can point out the client's CCRT and help the client realize that a *transference reaction* involving the two of them has occurred. This can be very powerful for the client since it involves a here-and-now exchange with the therapist. Thus, the power and ever-present nature of the CCRT is directly demonstrated through direct feedback from the therapist. Second, the therapist, by using empathy and by being nonpunitive during the enactment, allows the CCRT to be expressed, experienced, understood, and worked through. As a result, the negative childhood experiences will lose their power to affect current relationships. This same process is used whether the episode is due to *transference* (imagined responses from others) or to *repetition compulsion* (actual response from others). In repetition compulsion, the focus is on how the client chooses to interact with people who behave a certain way, or how the client elicits certain responses from others, both of which reflect attempts to master patterns learned in childhood. The same working-through process occurs within this mid-phase of therapy whether the patient's RO is an expected or actual response from the other. In the latter case, the focus is on understanding the way that early childhood relationships influence the client to choose to be around people who behave in a certain way, or to provoke people to behave in an expected manner.

Once the influence of unconscious issues is identified, clients are encouraged to apply their understanding to future interactions and to bring up for discussion situations where the CCRT is occurring. The therapist supports the client's effort to adaptively activate their wishes, demonstrating how the RS (response to the self) consequently changes. Eventually, the client's goal of being able to adaptively activate the wish is reached.

3. Third Phase (Sessions 13–16)

The third and last phase of the therapy involves dealing with termination issues (Book, 1998; Luborsky, 1984). The therapist should be alert for separation anxiety or any regression on the part of the client. Fantasies from the client regarding why treatment is ending should be explored. Enactments may also occur, with themes such as abandonment or rejection. These issues are often related to the CCRT and provide another opportunity for the therapist and client to work though the CCRT pattern. Even if enactments do not occur during these last sessions, the therapist should bring up the possible impact of the CCRT on the remaining sessions. In some cases, clients may be concerned about whether they can maintain gains by themselves without the help of therapy. The therapist handles this concern by expressing confidence in the client, reassuring them that they will retain what they learned in therapy about the CCRT, and that they will carry the change with them. In the final session, the therapist summarizes and reinforces accomplishments and gains.

Evaluation of CCRT Therapy: Scientific Basis, Contextual and Diversity Issues

The CCRT method developed by Luborsky is a relational form of brief psychodynamic therapy that has a scientific foundation. The supportive and expressive elements suggested in the approach are based on research findings regarding effective components of the therapeutic alliance—a factor that has been found to have an evidence-based association with therapy outcome. Consistent with a collaborative philosophy, therapists are tentative in formulating hypotheses concerning the CCRT and careful to determine their accuracy by checking with the client. The constructs of CCRT have been examined for their reliability, with the findings published in the book, *Understanding Transference: The Core Conflictual Relationship Theme Method* (Fried, Crits-Christoph, & Luborsky, 1997). Research supports some aspects of the CCRT method—that the relationship with the therapist may parallel that of the client's relationship with other people and that an individual's relationship patterns appear to be consistent (Fried, Crits-Christoph, & Luborsky, 1997). However, more research is needed to determine the effectiveness of CCRT therapy compared to other therapeutic approaches.

CCRT therapy espouses the hypothesis that the current needs or wishes of the individual, the response from others, and the response by the self are determined by early childhood experiences with parents or caretakers. In many cases, this may be accurate. However, consideration of the possible impact of social or cultural influences is lacking. We would encourage that this be accomplished during the assessment phases. The consideration of social or cultural effects may be important for some clients when identifying and analyzing core themes. Instead of viewing the RO (either real or imagined) as only due to parent-child interactions, social and cultural factors should be assessed as possible influences. For example, individuals with a different sexual orientation, who have a disability, or who are of an ethnic minority background may have an RO that is due to prejudice and discrimination rather than parenting experiences. Thus, current problems in relationships can be due to the impact of social and cultural issues, including prejudice and discrimination or societal expectations. The goal of activating the wish or need may also be affected by diversity or societal issues.

As we mentioned in the chapter on psychodynamic theory (Chapter 6), concepts and techniques such as transference can be broadened to incorporate the possibility that the client's behavior pattern toward the therapist may be due to experiences of being oppressed or reacted to in a certain manner based on specific characteristics. A client's enactment with the therapist may involve reacting to the therapist as being part of the oppressing environment. This may be particularly true when the client lives, works, or grew up in a setting where their diversity was very central to negative interactions with others. Luborsky's model of therapy may be even more useful if societal and cultural issues are incorporated in devising the CCRT. For instance, the clients' wishes (W) can be assessed to determine the degree to which they are influenced by social or cultural factors. The response from others (RO), either real or imagined, could also consider social or cultural factors in determining appropriate interventions. Additionally, the response to self (RS) can be influenced by cultural factors. Certainly, the identification of core themes and patterns in relational conflict can be critical. Including social and cultural diversity perspectives should strengthen the use of CCRT therapy with diverse populations.

Recommended Readings

Book, H. E. (1998). *How to practice brief psychodynamic psychotherapy.* Washington, DC: American Psychological Association.

This book provides an excellent introduction to the CCRT method with chapters on: Identifying the CCRT Focus, Making the Unspoken Components of the CCRT Explicit, The Goal of Brief Psychodynamic Psychotherapy, How to Present the CCRT to the Patient, and The Three Phases of Treatment. In addition, a specific case study is presented beginning with assessment and continuing through the three phases of treatment. Common questions regarded CCRT are answered. The content will give readers a solid grounding for conducting CCRT.

Luborsky, L. (1984). *Principles of psychoanalytic psychotherapy: A manual for Supportive-Expressive treatment.* New York: Basic Books.

This book contains Luborsky's manual for the CCRT method. The concepts are clearly explained with an emphasis on both scientific methodology and the therapist skills required to engage the client in therapy. Topics in the book include: Beginning and Explaining Treatment, Supportive Relationships, Expressive Techniques of Listening and Understanding, Formulating the CCRT, Principles of Responding, and Ending Treatment. In addition, he shares a method for determining the CCRT and gives a summary of the research on CCRT.

Interpersonal Therapy

8

Chapter

In IPT, we focus on the patient's problems of depression and interpersonal distress. Psychiatric illness occurs in a social context with interpersonal antecedents and consequences. While recognizing the role of biological and psychological factors in the causation of and vulnerability to psychiatric problems, IPT focuses on social factors and current interpersonal problems. (Ravitz, 2004, p. 15)

Interpersonal psychotherapy (IPT) is a time-limited, dynamically informed psychotherapy which aims to alleviate patients' suffering . . . IPT focuses specifically on interpersonal relationships as a means of bringing about change, with the goal of helping patients to either improve their interpersonal relationships or change their expectations about them. (Stuart & Robertson, 2003, p. 3)

Interpersonal Psychotherapy (IPT) shares with CCRT and other brief psychodynamic approaches the view that experiences with attachment figures early in life affect current interpersonal relationships. Negative experiences are believed to produce enduring personality or character problems, resulting from factors such as guilt, low self-esteem, or inhibited expression of anger. Thus, the concept of attachment bonds provides a strong theoretical basis for therapists to understand the interpersonal context of depression. To a large extent, psychodynamic approaches such as CCRT direct their therapy toward correcting maladaptive childhood patterns and changing adult personality patterns. IPT, in contrast, focuses primarily on contemporary interpersonal and romantic relationships, although childhood or past relationships may be analyzed within the context of presenting problems. IPT attempts to alter current relationship patterns rather than changing personality features that have their origin in early experiences and employs action-oriented or behavioral strategies. In this chapter, we will use IPT as an example of a research-based psychodynamic approach, describing in detail the introductory, intervention, and termination stages of IPT and the steps involved with each. IPT was selected as one of the representative psychodynamic therapies for this text because it does meet the criteria for a well-established treatment for depression (Crits-Christoph, Frank, Chambless, Brody, & Karp, 1995) and was one of the therapies considered to be effective in the National Institute of Mental Health Treatment of Depression Collaborative Research Program (NIMH-TDCRP, Elkin et al., 1989). Before we begin with the therapy itself, the research behind this approach will be presented.

The NIMH-TDCRP research project involved a methodologically sound, multisite, clinical trial that compared Interpersonal Therapy (IPT), Cognitive-Behavioral Therapy (CBT), and imipramine (an antidepressant) against a placebo control group for the treatment of major depression. Because of the methodological rigor involved, the project is considered to be the gold standard for psychotherapy research. All treatments were found to produce significant improvement in depressive symptoms. In a later analysis, IPT was found to be marginally superior to CBT for more severely depressed clients (Elkin, 1994). We will be describing the IPT treatment model (Klerman et al., 1984) utilized in the NIMH-TDCRP study. A wealth of data was available for analysis, including pre- and post-measures, videotapes, transcripts of sessions, and ratings by raters, clients, and therapists. We will incorporate findings from the NIMH-TDCRP study as we illustrate specific components of IPT therapy.

Theory of Interpersonal Therapy

IPT is based on a *biopsychosocial diathesis model* in which genetic predisposition (vulnerability to stress and temperament) interacts with early life experiences (attachment style) to produce mental conditions such as depression (Stuart & Robertson, 2003). IPT has a relational perspective and roots in psychodynamic attachment theory. Childhood experiences with parental figures can result in secure or insecure attachment. During childhood, templates are forged that color an individual's views regarding relationships and expectations of others. Those who have a "secure" attachment are able to develop trust in others because of the early positive experiences. If childhood relationships with parents are negative, an insecure attachment develops and maladaptive patterns of communication and interpersonal relationships can result (Ravitz, 2004). From a psychodynamic perspective, depression can be the result of any of three factors: (1) psychodynamic mechanisms, such as attachment style, that involve affective or emotional issues or states, (2) social and interpersonal relationship conflicts, and (3) enduring personality characteristics. Because IPT has a session limit of 16 sessions, changes in personality traits are not expected, nor are they addressed directly during therapy. Rather than attempting to modify psychodynamic mechanisms such as attachment style, IPT adopts a here-and-now analysis of the client's current interpersonal relationships with a focus on developing a social support system that functions more effectively (Stuart & Robertson, 2003). The therapy is intended to help clients communicate needs and emotions in a manner that results in interpersonal mastery and differentiation.

IPT posits that a certain level of positive social interaction is necessary for the maintenance of psychological health; below this level, the risk of a psychiatric disorder such as depression is increased. Current relationship events that are influencing the client negatively are discussed in therapy, with a focus on the client's emotions. The exploration of current situations as they affect the client emotionally is central to the process. Clients are encouraged to ventilate painful emotions, clarify internal emotional states, and talk about interpersonal situations that evoke feelings such as shame, guilt, and resentment. In therapy, they learn to correct misinformation and explore alternative ways to improve current interpersonal functioning (Coombs et al., 2002). A reduction of negative emotions through self-understanding and insight is expected to result in increasingly positive and satisfying social interactions, thus reducing feelings of depression.

The specific components of ITP include:

1. Depressive emotional symptoms resulting from psychodynamic mechanisms are targeted for treatment. Emotions are brought to the surface for discussion and exploration, especially as they relate to current interpersonal problems.

2. Interpersonal relationship patterns related to childhood experiences, social competence, or current social relationships are worked on at the conscious or preconscious levels with an emphasis on helping the client develop better strategies for dealing with current problematic relationships.

An analysis of the transcripts of IPT sessions from the NIMH-TDCRP showed that both of these components were present throughout the therapy (Ablon & Jones, 1999). Specifically, in therapy sessions it was found that:

- Interpersonal relationships were a major theme of the therapy.
- Love and romantic relationships were topics of discussion.
- Clients' feelings were emphasized, allowing them to experience the feelings more deeply.
- Sexual experiences and feelings were discussed.
- Inner thoughts and feelings were explored.
- Memories of childhood were topics of discussion.

Therapist Role and Strategies in IPT

How does the therapist conduct therapy using this approach? The role and stance of the IPT therapist have some similarities with and differences from traditional psychoanalytic approaches. The following are strategies and roles of the therapist seen in the ITP therapy process (Klerman et al., 1984):

1. In contrast with the therapist neutrality seen in traditional psychoanalysis, the IPT therapist works initially as a client advocate and may even help the client with practical concerns such as finding transportation, housing, or financial support. In line with the more recent psychodynamic interpersonal approaches, therapist relationship qualities such as warmth, unconditional positive regard, and being nonjudgmental are emphasized. This is done to help solidify the therapeutic alliance, which is viewed as very important. When confrontation is necessary, it is gentle. The relationship skills discussed in Chapter 3 are consistent with IPT; however, there is less emphasis on collaboration and the therapist takes more of a doctor-patient stance, at least during the initial sessions.

2. The therapist encourages the client to talk about present concerns in interpersonal relationships, particularly those that are associated with depression, and to explore the emotions associated with these relationships.

3. The therapist helps clients acknowledge and accept painful feelings for situations that cannot be changed, making statements like "Of course that would make you angry," or "Most people would feel that way in the same circumstance." These statements also offer support to the client, strengthening the therapist-client relationship. Emotional expression within the session is only the starting point; the therapist also encourages the client to learn to manage their emotions in interpersonal situations.

4. As opposed to most psychodynamic therapies, client responses to the therapist are not interpreted as a transference phenomenon, but rather as a realistic and current reaction to the therapist. However, the relationship of the client to the therapist may be considered and used as a way of analyzing the client's current relationship difficulties.

5. In dealing with problematic relationships or interactions, the client is taught to consider different options, evaluating the possible consequences of different choices. It is emphasized that action should not be taken until this process has been completed. Clients are encouraged to ask themselves, "What alternatives do I have in this situation?" "What

will happen if I make this choice?" and "Is this an outcome that I would want?"

6. The therapist may make selective self-disclosures to the client as a means of educating the client, illustrating communication patterns, or providing feedback about the client's communication style.

Do IPT therapists actually show fidelity in the use of these role characteristics and strategies? According to the transcript analysis from the NIMH-TDCRP study (Ablon & Jones, 1999), raters determined that IPT therapists:

- Demonstrated empathy and were attuned to the feelings of the client.
- Displayed nonjudgmental acceptance.
- Asked clients for more information or elaboration of feelings about events.
- Placed attention on "unacceptable feelings."
- Clarified, restated, or rephrased client communication.
- Facilitated client speech.
- Linked feelings and perceptions to current or past situations.
- Pointed out the use of defensive mechanisms such as denial.
- Identified themes in client relationships.
- Interpreted unconscious feelings, wishes, or ideas.
- Drew connections between the therapeutic relationship and other relationships.

IPT therapists were active in directing clients to interpersonal issues, displayed warmth and empathy, and focused on emotional reactions to relationship issues. Psychodynamic aspects such as interpreting unconscious feelings and identifying the use of defense mechanisms were also employed. We will now begin our discussion of the stages and steps involved in treating depression with IPT. This information is based on the treatment manual developed by Klerman and colleagues (1984), with further elaboration by Markowitz (1998) and Stuart and Robertson (2003).

IPT Treatment of Depression

As previously noted, ITP therapists view depression as a result of emotional states that affect relationships and as a response to situations or events (death or loss of a loved one, current relationship conflicts, role transition difficulties, or interpersonal isolation) that result in reductions in positive social interactions. The treatment protocol typically involves 16 therapy sessions and uses the following strategies to address identified goals:

1. Exploration of the issues related to depression and the response of the client to these circumstances.
2. Encouragement of emotional expression in the discussion of relationship problems.
3. Clarification of issues to gain further understanding of the problem.
4. Analysis of current communication patterns in relationships.
5. Use of the therapy relationship to encourage changes in behavior.
6. Education regarding behavior change techniques such as modeling and role-playing.

IPT for the treatment of depression is divided into three stages. During the first stage, a careful diagnostic interview is performed with particular attention to the client's current interpersonal relationships and pattern of social functioning. Changes in relationships are examined with a particular interest to those that preceded the depressive episode. In IPT, links are drawn from relationship issues to depression. During this initial stage, the problem areas are identified, the diagnosis and client role are explained, the IPT therapeutic process is discussed, and a contract is developed. In the intermediate phase, the intervention techniques described earlier are applied, focusing on one of the following interpersonal areas associated with depression:

- Grief (the death or loss of a loved one)
- Interpersonal Dispute (current relationship conflicts)
- Role Transitions (e.g., job change, marriage, retirement)
- Interpersonal Isolation (minimal social contacts or support)

In the termination phase, feelings about termination are discussed, progress is reviewed, and any remaining work is outlined. We will now present in more detail the different components involved in the treatment of depression using IPT (Klerman et al., 1984).

Stage I: The Initial Sessions

The initial stage involves assessment, giving a name to the disorder, psychoeducation, connecting depression with interpersonal difficulties, and developing goals and interventions. It can last from one to three sessions.

A. Assessing Depression, Naming the Disorder, and Defining the Role of the Client

1. Ask if the client has had a physical exam within the last 6 months. If not, request a comprehensive medical exam. Explain to the client that depression is sometimes caused by medications, use of herbs, or physical conditions, and that it is important to eliminate these as possible causes.

2. Assess for depressive symptoms by asking questions such as, "How have you been feeling?" "Have you lost interest in activities?" "Are you feeling hopeless?" and "Do you blame yourself for things that have happened?" These questions help to assess for depressive symptoms. Also, determine the presence of other symptoms related to depression, such as a lack of interest in life, social isolation, or complaints of fatigue. During this time it is also important to be alert for suicidal ideation with questions such as, "Do you think that life is not worth living?" "Do you have thoughts of taking your life?" "Have you made any plans to do so?" If there appears to be possible suicide risk, a complete suicide assessment must be performed (see Chapters 14 and 15 on suicide assessment and crisis intervention), including determining if hospitalization is necessary. If immediate protective intervention is not needed, explore the circumstances associated with the onset of suicidal thoughts or actions and the meaning of the suicidal thoughts or actions with the assumption that they represent attempts at interpersonal communication. Ask the client what they imagine would be the reaction of other people to his or her death, what they would hope to achieve through suicide, and have them consider other ways of obtaining those results.

3. If the client meets the criteria for a depressive disorder, educate the client about depression by reviewing the symptoms obtained during assessment and give it the name of "depression." You might present it to the client in the following manner: "What you have described to me does not appear to have a physical cause, but it is a real illness called depression. The thoughts and feelings you reported are consistent with this disorder. You are currently suffering from a depressive episode." In addition, a positive expectation for therapy is achieved by adding, "Although the symptoms are quite unpleasant, the outcome with treatment is very good. There are a number of therapies that have been shown to be effective with depression, so don't feel discouraged if the therapy you try first does not seem to work. The treatment I will

be describing is a type of psychotherapy that has been found to be effective in a number of research studies. If, after explaining the therapy, you decide you want a different approach, I can help you get connected with another therapist who has a different specialization. The therapy I am referring to is called interpersonal therapy. Would you like to hear more about it?"

4. An effort is made to have the client adopt the "sick role" by saying, "Because you are in a depressive episode, you may not feel like engaging in social activities. This is part of the depression. You may want to explain to your (spouse, family, or friends) that you will be actively involved in therapy and, because of the depression, will engage in only limited social activities." The sick role allows certain changes to occur: (1) pressure is removed from the client to perform normal social activities, (2) expectations from others regarding the performance of tasks by the client are reduced, (3) being in the state of depression is considered to be undesirable, and (4) the role of patient carries the obligation of getting well (Klerman et al., 1984).

5. Determine if medication is necessary. In cases where the client is suicidal, extremely agitated, unable to sleep, or having other severe symptoms, a referral to a physician for consideration of a medication trial might be appropriate.

B. Connecting Depression to the Interpersonal Context

In IPT, interpersonal interactions are considered critical both as the cause of and as the means to reduce depressive states. Current and past relationship problems are explored and related to current symptoms. Areas of dissatisfaction are identified and the client is asked to state the specific changes being sought. Questions that you might ask include,

"Sometimes our feeling of depression is related to our relationships. Can you think of something happening with your relationships with others (spouse, parents, family, friends, coworkers), either currently or in the past, that is related to your feelings of depression? What expectations did you have of the relationship? Were these fulfilled? What are satisfying and unsatisfying aspects in the relationship? What are changes that you are hoping will occur in your relationships? If these changes occur, how will that impact your current problem?"

The emphasis is on promoting changes in current relationships.

C. Identification of Problem Areas and Development of Goals

From the information gathered from the questions above, problem areas are defined. Because of the short-term nature of the treatment, the focus is on only one or two of the more significant problems. The most common interpersonal problems involve: (1) Grief or loss issues, (2) interpersonal conflicts with others, (3) feelings of loneliness or isolation because of the lack of social contact, and (4) role transitions through changes such as divorce, marriage, living together, retirement, or moving away from friends and family. The specific type of interpersonal problem would dictate the types of questions to ask or statements to make. For interpersonal conflicts, the therapist might say,

"From what you are saying, your conflictual relationship with your husband and feelings of isolation are related to feeling depressed. This is something we can work on together during our sessions. You say that much of your interaction with your husband involves arguments. What are changes that you hope will occur through therapy? What are some different ways of responding that may reduce conflict? If these changes happen, how will it impact your relationship?"

The therapist helps the client identify changes that are attainable within the number of sessions allotted or that could be seen as small steps in improving functioning. For each problem area identified, the client is asked to indicate what would be the "best outcome," "expected outcome," or "worst outcome." This allows the client to become aware of different possibilities when undergoing treatment and for the clinician to understand the possible consequences from the client's perspective. In a collaborative manner, realistic goals are developed.

D. IPT Treatment Is Explained and the Contract Is Discussed

Explain the rationale for IPT and its emphasis on interpersonal functioning and jointly develop a contract. The rationale helps set the expectation for therapy and defines the role for the client. You might say the following:

"As I mentioned earlier, IPT is a therapy that has been found to be effective in treating problems such as yours. We identified some of the problems you are having with other people and discussed how they are related to the feelings of hopelessness and the depression that you have." (As part of this explanation, the clinician uses the information gathered from the major problem areas and connects it to interpersonal functioning). *"In IPT we will be spending most of our time talking about your current relationships, although we might look at your past relationships for clues as to what is happening with you now. We will also focus on your emotions during the sessions. Sometimes we are affected by emotional reactions that we are not aware of. Working through emotions involved in these situations can lead*

to a healthier adjustment. What will be helpful in our work together would be your willingness to openly discuss painful issues, to help come up with different ideas that you might try to improve the relationship problems you are experiencing, and to practice these ideas outside of the session. Therapy is a joint process where your contribution is very important. Do you have any questions?"

Address the questions, if any, and then discuss the contract. This may include:

1. A discussion of practical concerns such as the frequency and length of the sessions, the fees, policy for late arrival or missed appointments.

2. Agreement on the interpersonal context for the intervention—an understanding that current stresses and relationships are contributing to the depression.

3. Agreement on client contributions during therapy (openly discussing sensitive material, addressing emotional issues, collaborating in developing strategies to improve interpersonal functioning, and practicing new behaviors outside of session).

4. Agreement on the problem areas and goals.

Stage II: Intervention Strategies and Focus

The second stage involves the use of specific intervention strategies and techniques to treat problem areas and can last up to about the 12th session.

A. Intervention Techniques

1. Each session is started by asking the client, "How have things been since our last meeting?" or "How have things been with your (parents, spouse) since we last met?" If the client mentions a mood, the therapist can inquire about, "What was happening to produce this feeling?" If instead, the client reports an event, the therapist can ask, "How did that make you feel?" The opening question serves the purpose of having the client focus on the immediate past and link the mood to events associated with the problem area.

2. The therapist uses nondirective exploration, open-ended questions, and encouragement for client verbalizations. Self-disclosure by the client is encouraged.

3. The therapist is directive, especially during initial sessions, and may use advice, suggestions, educating, or modeling to help the client find solutions for the interpersonal problems. To ensure

that the client is discussing topics dealing with identified goals, the therapist may use questions such as, "Tell me more about your conflict with your wife." "What do you get from your current relationship?" or "Is it possible that you are angry with Jim?" Questions should be asked for a specific purpose such as having the client examine the relationship in a realistic manner or allowing the therapist to test a hypothesis. The therapist may initially give the client advice regarding how to deal with specific situations when the client is unable to make an independent decision. However, the goal is to allow clients to develop the skills to analyze interpersonal situations themselves and to make appropriate choices.

4. The client's emotional feelings are explored so that they can be more freely expressed, allowing for the development of insight with an increased ability to manage emotions. Often, clients have excessive guilt or anxiety but are only somewhat aware of these emotions. Emotional learning is considered an essential ingredient for producing change.

5. The therapist-client relationship is used as a means of understanding relationships with other people in the client's life. "You appear to be very cautious when you talk to me. Is this how you are when you are talking to your coworkers?" Also, the therapist can share with clients the way he or she might have handled different situations.

6. Direct analysis is used to help clients consider a range of actions they can take and consider the consequences of each. Clients are taught to explore options before taking action by asking themselves, "What alternatives do I have in this situation?" "If I react this way, what consequences do I expect?" "With this information, what is the best response?" After practicing direct analysis in session, clients are asked to try this process outside of the therapy session.

7. Role playing can be used to help the client learn to interact with others in a different manner. The therapist can play the role of the client's friend, spouse, or other individual and ask the client to act out an event. Role reversal can also be employed where the therapist role-plays the client, modeling different ways of interacting that the client can observe (Markowitz, 1998).

B. Specific Problem Areas

Although the focus is on relationship issues, there are slightly different strategies depending upon the specific interpersonal problem and whether or not it is related to the depression. Below are different problem areas associated with depression that are specified in IPT (Klerman et al., 1984).

1. **Grief.** With this problem, the goals are to help facilitate the mourning process and to assist the client in reestablishing relationships while coping with his or her loss.

   Strategies: Depressive symptoms are reviewed and related to the death or loss of a significant other. The relationship is reconstructed; events prior, during, and after the death or separation are described and both positive and negative emotions during this period are explored. A focus is placed on learning to manage negative emotions and reestablishing relationships with others.

2. **Interpersonal Conflicts.** The goals for this problem area involve the identification of factors involved in the conflict, development of a plan of action, and modifying expectations or faulty communication to achieve a successful resolution to the dispute.

   Strategies: Depressive symptoms are reviewed and the symptoms are related to conflicts with significant others. The therapist helps the client identify the specific interpersonal dispute, develop a plan of action that encourages better patterns of communication, and evaluate the outcome of this plan. The specifics of the conflict need to be determined with the help of the client. What are the issues involved? How much of the conflict is caused by differences in values or expectations from the individuals? What options are open to the client and what is the likelihood of finding alternatives? What are the consequences of changes that would occur if action is taken? Are there additional resources available to the client? Are there gains for the client in having the dispute perpetuated? It may be necessary to modify a client's expectations to achieve a successful resolution. The stage of the conflict is determined. If the individuals are in negotiation, effort is placed toward reducing conflict so that a resolution can occur. If the people involved are at an impasse, an increase in conflict may be attempted to produce a move toward negotiation. If the conflict has moved to the dissolution stage, strategies similar to those of the grief process are utilized. In a situation where it appears that the relationship conflict cannot be resolved, the possibility of ending the relationship is considered.

3. **Role Transitions.** The goal in dealing with relationship transitions produced by events such as divorce, separation, immigration, or change in employment is to mourn and accept the loss of

the old role, develop a positive view of the new role, and improve self-esteem through the mastery of the new role.

Strategies: The connection between depressive symptoms, the loss of the previous role, and grieving the loss is addressed. Feelings about loss and the change process itself are explored and discharge of emotions is encouraged. The client is asked to determine "realistically, what was lost?" The client reviews the positive and negative aspects of both the old and new roles, and feelings about the change. Encouragement is given to exploring opportunities in the new role, developing a new social support system, and learning the various skills necessary for the new role. The therapist helps the client consider the opportunities with the new role with the goal of improving self-esteem through mastering the new role.

4. **Interpersonal Deficits.** The goal is to reduce the sense of social isolation of the client and encourage the formation of new relationships. The problem may be due to interpersonal sensitivity (fear of rejection) or a lack of social skills.

Strategies: Depressive feelings are explored and related to feelings of social isolation and loneliness. Past relationships are explored for their positive and negative features and repetitive harmful patterns are explored. Therapeutic relations or transference are used as an example of a relationship and parallels with other relationships are discussed. Interpersonal functioning is reinforced and social skill development through role-playing is employed.

Stage III: Termination Phase

During the remaining sessions of treatment several tasks are accomplished (Markowitz, 1998). Issues about termination are brought up and openly discussed. Feelings of sadness can be acknowledged. Lessons learned from the other sessions can be used to discuss healthy ways of ending relationships; this process can be framed as an opportunity to develop more outside relationships. Termination can also be viewed as a graduation or the acknowledgment of the gains in therapy. The symptoms of depression are reviewed and the risk of reoccurrence is discussed. To reduce the chances for relapse, means of maintaining the gains are considered and alternative action regarding possible future problems are evaluated. Any future work that needs to be done is addressed. For individuals who have made little or no progress, the issue of self-blame for the lack of progress is addressed and other therapeutic options can be considered.

Evaluation of Interpersonal Therapy: Scientific Basis, Contextual and Diversity Issues

Although IPT has not been evaluated as extensively as cognitive behavior therapy, it is still considered a well-established treatment. In an analysis of the NIMH-TDCRP study, certain theoretical assumptions of IPT were supported. IPT therapy holds that affectively involved treatment is more effective in bringing about enduring change than just addressing cognitive processes. By increasing awareness of underlying emotions, clients can clarify their experiences and come to terms with problematic interpersonal situations. IPT reinforces the importance of emotions and the value of eliciting, understanding, and working through emotions. "Collaborative emotional exploration" requires clients to be introspective, insightful, understanding of the process of therapy, and positive in expectations; all of these factors relate to positive outcome in therapy. Other qualities advocated by IPT that have been found to have a significant impact on outcome include: (1) the presence of emotional expression and catharsis in therapy sessions, (2) nonjudgmental acceptance of the client, (3) therapist empathy and sensitivity, and (4) close attunement to client feelings and experiences (Coombs et al., 2002). Thus, some of the underlying assumptions of IPT have been supported in the NIMH-TDCRP study. In a research study utilizing PET scans before and after treatment, IPT produced normalization of metabolic brain activity similar to that produced by antidepressants in regions of the brain associated with major depressive disorder (Brody et al., 2001). IPT has a sufficient and increasing research base to be a treatment of choice for depressive disorders (Ellen et al., 2007; Weissman, 2007). IPT has also been adapted for use with other disorders such as social anxiety, bipolar disorder, and eating disorders (Ravitz, 2004).

Can IPT be used to deal with diverse populations? We need to be able to adapt, develop, and evaluate treatment approaches that show empirical effectiveness with diverse populations. For many groups, depression may be related to prejudice, discrimination, or societal conditions. For both males and females, role constrictions and expectations may be the source of problematic relationship issues. We believe that IPT can be used effectively with diverse populations with the following changes and emphasis:

1. During the assessment phase, determine the degree that the problem is due to social or cultural issues. Allow the client to explain the problem according to their perspective. Remember that the link between interpersonal issues and depression is a hypothesis to be tested rather than a fact. Situational, cultural, or societal issues may be involved.

2. Collaborate with the client in terms of problem definition, goals, and interventions. The degree of collaboration may need to differ from cli-

ent to client. Some may feel comfortable being given the diagnosis of depression and the associated focus on the "sick role"; others may prefer not to be labeled as being ill. As we mentioned in Chapter 2, a scientific framework requires that we observe the effects of our approach on the client and modify it if the feedback we receive is negative.

3. Goals and problem definition should be tentative and tested with the help of the client. A possible issue that may exist for some individuals is the procedure of bringing up and focusing on painful emotions. Emotional issues are important to address, but the depth and manner of emotional expression should be evaluated with each client. In some cultural groups, there may be discomfort with emotional exploration, or such a focus may not be viewed as helpful. It is important to remember that techniques and theories are to be tested and may have varying applicability depending upon the particular client and the influence of diversity issues.

4. In IPT, potential changes in relationships or interaction patterns are identified, as well as possible consequences for any action. We believe that this approach is both helpful and respectful of diversity since it allows the client to anticipate the reaction of significant others. In some cultural groups, there is a family or group identity and individual changes should be considered within this context.

5. Remember that the role of a scientist-practitioner is to test out different hypotheses, be alert to therapist-client interaction variables and processes, and to avoid a confirmatory bias.

There is preliminary evidence that IPT can be effectively employed with ethnically diverse populations. Rossello and Bernal (1999) modified IPT in treating Puerto Rican adolescents experiencing depression by incorporating Latino cultural values such as *respecto* (respect), *personalismo* (personal contact in social situations), and *familismo* (family orientation) in the therapy. The positive aspects of these cultural values were identified, strengthened, and used in the design of treatment strategies. Because of the importance of family relations, parents of the adolescents in the study were interviewed in a climate of utmost respect to gain their participation. The results are promising regarding the impact of cultural modification of IPT, but should be interpreted cautiously since the sample size was small.

IPT, with its emphasis on interpersonal relationships, has been found to be an effective therapy for depression. Because it is manualized, the techniques and strategies are relatively easy to learn, although clinical skills are also required. The therapy has both psychodynamic and behavioral aspects, as well as a strong focus on the therapeutic alliance. IPT is a brief treatment and, as such, may not be appropriate for individuals with personality disorders or more complicated psychiatric histories.

Recommended Readings

Klerman, G. L., Weissman, M., Rounsaville, B. J., & Chevron, E. S. (1984). *Interpersonal psychotherapy of depression.* New York: Basic Books.

> This book contains the manual used in the NIMH study. Contents include an overview of IPT, background on interpersonal approaches to depression, the steps involved in conducting IPT, tasks of both the therapist and the client during therapy, examples of techniques utilized, and the components of each of the three stages in IPT. This book clearly explains how to conduct IPT.

Markowitz, J. C. (1998). *Interpersonal psychotherapy for dysthymic disorder.* Washington, DC: American Psychiatric Press.

> The book contains a treatment manual with a focus on the treatment of dysthymic disorder. The author includes many specific examples of statements that a therapist can make when using IPT. Content includes a discussion of dysthymic disorder and an overview of IPT and its use with dysthymic disorder. There are step-by-step illustrations on how to conduct IPT that are elucidated through the use of case examples.

Stuart, S., & Robertson, M. (2003). *Interpersonal psychotherapy: A clinician's guide.* New York: Oxford University Press.

> This guide contains a very complete explanation of the theory underlying IPT and clear examples of the techniques employed. Various disorders that can be treated with the IPT approach are presented. Case studies are used to illustrate concepts, as are diagrams and flow charts that are helpful for therapists new to this approach. There is also an evaluation of the research on IPT. Forms that can be used for assessment and gathering client information are also included.

Humanistic Theories and Techniques

The individual and not the problem is the focus. The aim is not to solve one particular problem, but to assist the individual to grow, so that he can cope with the present problem and with later problems in a better integrated fashion. To accomplish this, nondirective therapy . . . places greater stress upon the emotional elements, the feeling aspects of the situation than upon the intellectual aspects . . . places greater stress upon the immediate situation than upon the individual's past . . . lays stress upon the therapeutic relationship itself as a growth experience. (Rogers, 1942, pp. 28–30)

9

Chapter

Humanistic theories are a group of theories (client-centered, existential, gestalt, and others) that espouse the importance of the whole person rather than looking at parts of the personality such as the ego, superego, and id (psychoanalysis), or in terms of specific behavior patterns or thoughts (cognitive-behavioral therapy). There is a strong belief that people must be viewed holistically and that they are greater than the sum of the parts. Rather than being driven by instincts or affected by stimuli in a mechanistic manner, humans have the freedom to consider life circumstances and choose new directions. They strive to make sense of their experiences. Although there are differences in emphasis among the different humanistic therapies (creating the conditions for therapy in client-centered therapy, searching for meaning in existential therapy, and enhancing awareness in Gestalt), there is a common belief in the freedom and capacity for humans to choose, in our uniqueness and individuality rather than universal processes or mechanisms, and in the importance of subjective reality rather than objective reality (Hansen, 2000). Other common assumptions of the humanistic theories and therapies are presented in Box 9.1.

In this chapter, we will briefly cover the existential and Gestalt theories and techniques, but will focus primarily on Carl Rogers and his client-centered therapy because of its impact on the therapist-client relationship and the therapeutic alliance, both of which are critical to therapy

BOX 9.1   **Common Assumptions of Humanistic Theories and Therapies**

1. **View of the Person**—People have an innate tendency toward self-actualization or developing to their fullest potential. All humans are born with this natural inclination toward self-growth. Humanistic therapies are optimistic in terms of the potential for individuals to make changes and to develop their own resources. People strive to make sense of their experiences and must be viewed holistically. People are social beings who are best understood in terms of their relationships with others. It is through a social relationship, the therapist-client relationship, that constructive change can occur.

2. **Freedom to Choose**—Individuals can become more fully self-aware. This awareness allows for more freedom in making choices about how to live their lives. Because of the potential for self-growth, therapists do not direct or try to persuade the client, but instead provide an environment conducive to clients finding their own direction. Humanistic therapists believe individuals have the right and the capacity to decide what is best for them. Therefore, humanistic therapists adopt a collaborative relationship in which clients are offered great freedom to make their own choices about their lives.

3. **Focus on Subjective Reality**—The emphasis is on the subjective experiences of the individual. Everyone interprets events in an individual manner and it is the subjective experience that is the important focus for therapy. It is the task of the therapist to understand the subjective world of the client.

4. **Therapist Qualities**—Because clients have the potential for self-growth, therapists demonstrate qualities that will enhance this process. These characteristics include being nonjudgmental and demonstrating empathy, genuineness, and acceptance. These qualities furnish the environment in which client self-exploration can occur. In addition, therapists monitor their own reactions to the client to make sure that personal biases or beliefs are not interfering with the therapy.

5. **Emotions**—Emphasis is placed on emotion rather than cognition. The humanistic therapies focus on the importance of emotional and experiential dimensions of human functioning and attempt to take clients to deeper levels of feeling and thinking.

6. **Freedom-Choice-Responsibility**—These aspects are inevitably intertwined. If one makes a choice, there are consequences, good or bad, that follow. A specific choice often precludes other choices. Clients need to understand that with all behavior, they are making choices. It is within this framework that clients begin to realize the importance of actively choosing rather than reacting to their experiences. Once this realization occurs, others paths become available to them. Thus, the existential questions of "How are you living?" and "Are you becoming the person you wish to be?" are addressed.

7. **Meaning**—Clients need to comprehend their behaviors and lives in terms of the larger meanings and patterns of their lives. Only by doing so can they gain a greater sense of clarity and direction in their lives.

From Cain, 2002a; Cain & Seeman, 2002

outcome as discussed in Chapter 3. Client-centered therapy is also important because many of the assumptions regarding congruence, unconditional positive regard, and empathy have been incorporated into cognitive-behavioral and psychodynamic therapies, such as Beck's cognitive-behavioral therapy for depression (Beck, Rush, Shaw, & Emery, 1979), Linehan's dialectic behavior therapy (1993a), and Luborsky's core conflictual relationship therapy (1984). These three approaches are discussed in depth in separate chapters. Several current therapeutic approaches (motivational enhancement therapy and focused expressive therapy) are also based primarily on the principles of client-centered therapy. In our next chapter, we will discuss motivational enhancement therapy, showing how client-centered strategies have been incorporated in a treatment approach for substance abuse issues.

Humanistic therapies, with their focus on the client-therapist relationship and collaborative work with clients, have had a profound effect on the way therapy is conducted. Consistent with the humanistic philosophy, Hubble, Duncan, and Miller (1999) and Duncan and Miller (2000) believe that psychotherapy should be individualized and client directed. They believe that therapy is most effective when therapists:

1. Work in a collaborative manner with clients

2. View the change process as self-change

3. Assess the client's perspective regarding problems and their causes

4. Tailor therapy to the client's goals and solutions

5. Utilize client competencies in therapy and credit them for making constructive changes

6. Openly ask clients to give feedback regarding the therapist's performance

Although client-centered techniques continue to influence therapist-client relationship variables emphasized in many manualized, evidence-based therapies, the humanistic therapies are threatened by experimental designs that stress objective measures. The advent of managed care—with its emphasis on clearly defined goals—along with the movement toward the use of empirically supported techniques, has greatly reduced the number of individuals who identify themselves as humanistic therapists. In a randomly selected group of psychotherapists, less than 6 percent identified themselves as having a primarily humanistic orientation (existential, Gestalt, client-centered) while the percentage was 14 percent in 1981 (Norcross, Hedges, & Castle, 2002). Although the pure forms of humanistic therapies are no longer widely practiced, many other therapeutic approaches incorporate their techniques and assumptions.

The Client-Centered Approach

The form of psychotherapy introduced by Carl Rogers (1942) was revolutionary because of its contrast to the two main schools of therapy at the time—psychoanalytic therapy, with its emphasis on unconscious intrapsychic conflicts, and behavioral therapy, with the focus on stimulus and response. While humans were viewed as either "evil" or impulse driven in psychoanalysis or "neutral" in behavioral therapy, Rogers perceived human nature as "good" and humans as having the potential for *self-actualization*—that is, to move toward growth and development. Rogers considered the question "What prevents individuals from becoming fully self-actualized?" He hypothesized that anxiety, depression, and other problems occur when this innate tendency for growth is somehow blocked. Problems begin when a child's self-growth tendency is subverted by conditional regard. Instead of being valued as a child with infinite potential, messages might be given that "good" is conforming to the expectations of others, such as obeying rules or getting good grades.

Conditional acceptance produces a limited or distorted self-concept in the individual and can lead to a lack of awareness of the factors underlying unhappiness or dissatisfaction (Brodley, 2006). Rogers believed that a therapist, providing the appropriate attitude and accepting therapeutic environment, could reactivate the tendency for self-actualization. The provision of unconditional positive regard to clients allows them to become aware of their true feelings, leading to the ability to make constructive changes. As self-awareness increases, clients can learn to accept themselves as they are, including imperfections. Roger's belief in the growth tendency of individuals is reflected in his therapeutic approach, in which therapist responses focus primarily on reflection and are nondirective. This process results in growth and an opportunity for the client to become open to new experiences (Cepeda & Davenport, 2006).

As mentioned in the quote at the beginning of this chapter, Rogers believed that therapy should not be directed toward correcting a particular problem, but toward helping the individual achieve self-growth, thereby learning to cope with present and future problems. He also felt that the emotional elements involved with issues were more important than the individual's thoughts about what was happening. Much of his therapy focuses on helping clients become aware of their emotions in problem situations. Current events and feelings are deemed much more important to treatment than events in the past. In keeping with his view of therapy, Rogers believed that therapists should possess certain qualities and demonstrate specific behaviors in order to enhance the process of self-actualization.

Core Therapist Qualities

Roger believed that when the therapist is able to furnish three conditions (congruence, unconditional positive regard, and empathy), "the client will experience and understand aspects of the self previously not expressed; become better integrated and more able to function effectively; become more similar to the person he or she would like to be, including becoming more unique and self-expressive; be more understanding and more accepting of others; be more self-directing and self-confident; and be able to cope with the problems of life more adequately and more comfortably" (Rogers, 1961, pp. 37–38).

Rogers believed these three core qualities are necessary and sufficient for positive change to occur. We will present an abbreviated discussion of the necessary and sufficient conditions because we discussed them previously in the therapeutic alliance section of Chapter 3.

1. *Congruence* is the therapist quality of being integrated, self-accepting, self-aware, and whole. This quality allows a therapist to be genuine and authentic when responding to their clients. Rogers saw congruence as the most fundamental condition in therapy (Rogers & Sanford, 1985). Congruence involves therapist self-awareness of values and attitudes that may influence their work with a client. Incongruence in a therapist may involve unconscious biases regarding class, gender, ethnicity, sexual orientation, religiosity, or age. To become aware of possible barriers to congruence, therapists should ask themselves questions such as, "Are my responses (from my own frame of reference) appropriate for the client?" and "Am I committed to protecting my client's autonomy and self-direction?" (Brodley, 2006). In the quote that follows, you will see how a female therapist realized that she and other women may feel conflicted when providing therapy to men, given both the privilege men have in our society and women's tendency to comfort individuals in distress:

   My challenge and change has been in my work with men. I have always felt somewhat constrained with my male clients and did not like the impact it had on our therapy. I had talked to other women therapists about my difficulties and found that they had similar experiences. My problems became most evident to me when issues around privilege, gender and power needed to be discussed. I found myself caught between being too adversarial and challenging on one hand and the "all giving" protector trained to soothe pain on the other. (Kort, 1997, p. 97)

   Issues such as these can influence congruence and affect the relationship between the therapist and client. The situation discussed below, in which a therapist perceived that a change had occurred in interactions with a client, but was unsure as to why, demonstrates a way of dealing with a possible rupture in the therapeutic relationship. If a therapist perceives tension in the relationship, it should be addressed directly, since not doing so could lead to incongruence and questions such as, "Why is the client behaving differently than in previous sessions?" and

"Should I inquire about the tension I feel between us?" Distractions such as these, if not addressed, can hamper therapy. In this case, the therapist decided that self-disclosure might be helpful, combined with asking the client for feedback. By checking with the client, the therapist's internal state of incongruence was resolved.

> THERAPIST: *We have been working together for a few sessions now and I am keenly aware of an uncomfortable distance between us. I am wondering how you are feeling about our working relationship?*
> CLIENT: *Well, now that you mention it, it does feel pretty tense.*
> THERAPIST: *Maybe by talking about it, we can figure out the problem and go from there. (Gonzalez, 2002, p. 573)*

2. *Unconditional positive regard* involves the nonjudgmental caring and acceptance of clients, regardless of the actions of the client or difference between the client and the counselor. It involves the prizing of clients regardless of their beliefs, characteristics, or actions. The therapist demonstrates unconditional positive regard by valuing and respecting the individual through verbal and nonverbal communication. Unconditional positive regard is critical for client self-growth to occur since it combats the conditional regard that produced the problem in the first place. This may sometimes be difficult for a therapist working with a client where there are significant differences between them (such as a religious therapist working with a client who is an atheist) or in cases that are personally repulsive to the therapist (such as a client who has committed abuse against children). In client-centered therapy, the provision of unconditional positive regard is necessary for successful therapy. As Brodley (2006) states, "The client-centered therapist must develop a capacity for a mindset that is free of diagnostic categories, expectations, and prejudices regarding the client" (p. 142). If you are unable to do this, it is best to refer the client to another therapist.

3. *Empathy* involves demonstrating understanding of the subjective experience of the client. Understanding can occur at the emotional or at the cognitive level. In order for empathy to occur, the therapist must listen carefully to the client and attempt to understand the experiential reality of the client. The therapist then communicates empathy, which can then be confirmed or clarified by the client. Statements can be made in a tentative manner or by asking questions such as "Do I understand you correctly?" or "Is this what you are telling me?" This allows the client an opportunity to confirm, reject, or qualify empathetic statements. Statements such as "I sense you are feeling . . ." or "You sound like you . . ." are usually avoided in client-centered therapy since they have the quality of trying to interpret the client or trying find deeper meaning in the client's verbalizations (Brodley, 1991). Although empathy

is generally directed toward the individual and his or her thoughts or emotions, empathy regarding diversity issues can be communicated in a similar manner.

Nondirective and Client-Centered Emphases

Rogers believed therapists should simply provide the environment for the self-actualization tendency to occur; therefore, client responses should not be directed or influenced. Roger's focus was on having the therapist furnish the appropriate attitude or qualities for client self-growth to occur. While adhering to this original belief, Rogers did eventually make several changes in the emphasis of his approach. Rogers initially went through a nondirective phase that emphasized listening to the client and clarifying their statements through reflection. The goal was the creation of an accepting environment through which clients could gain further understanding of the issues involved in their problem. There was little active involvement on the part of the therapist other than providing the conditions of congruence, unconditional positive regard, and empathy. The following is an example of the original nondirective approach. It involves material from the second session meeting with an 18-year-old college senior. Note the use of reflection, warmth, and empathy from the therapist to encourage emotional expression and to help the client gain emotional awareness of his issue:

> CLIENT: *All the things my parents want me to do. Like getting good grades, being president of the service club, planning the youth activities at church . . . all of it! All of this crap!*
>
> THERAPIST: *You try to please your parents by doing all of these things, but you end up feeling very tired and resentful about it.*
>
> CLIENT: *(crying) They expect this stuff! They expect me to do it, they expect me to do it all right, they expect perfection!*
>
> THERAPIST: *They expect so much from you that maybe it just doesn't seem fair.*
>
> CLIENT: *It's not fair! I try real hard and it is never enough. I get an award for having good grades and when I told my dad about it he said, "Yes, but your chemistry grade was too low."*
>
> THERAPIST: *You try your hardest but instead of recognizing your achievement your dad criticizes you. That must have really felt bad.*
>
> CLIENT: *It hurts me so much. It made me wonder if I even want to try to do what they want.*
>
> THERAPIST: *Sometimes it just doesn't seem worth it. (Asay & Lambert, 2002, p. 542)*

During this session, the therapist is attempting to understand the emotional experience of the client and to convey this understanding to the client. In doing so, it is hoped that the client will also become aware of his own needs and the reasons for his unhappiness. In line with Roger's approach, the therapist's responses to the client are tentative and based on the client's comments. Typically, the focus of nondirective therapy is on understanding the client and providing empathy. This allows the client to increase his awareness of emotions involved in the situation. There is no attempt to obtain information regarding the history of the problem, make interpretations, or generate solutions. According to the nondirective perspective, any attempt to problem solve or reduce symptoms, "may serve to erode the therapist's capacity to understand and empathize with the client's internal experience and consequently, inhibit his or her affective expression and processing" (Assay & Lambert, 2002, p. 542) and hamper the therapeutic relationship.

Later, Rogers adopted the client-centered stance—emphasizing accurate empathy. This was characterized by more therapist involvement in terms of self-disclosure and focus on client themes. This reflected Roger's view that clients may be unaware of factors associated with their unhappiness. *Accurate empathy* involves helping clients attend to critical elements associated with their problem and involves a deeper level of reflection. The following is an example:

> CLIENT: *My mother left a message on my machine on Friday saying she couldn't make it in on Saturday. Something about my father wanting to fix something on the farm . . . (sigh) . . . there is always something more important to do . . . I feel so angry with her.*
>
> THERAPIST: *I noticed you sighed when you were talking about it . . . am I right in getting a sense you felt disappointed, what, pushed aside?*
>
> CLIENT: *Yes! I hadn't been so aware of that 'til now, but I did feel . . . well . . . jilted almost. I always had to sacrifice what I wanted for the farm and, of course, mother was always trying to keep the peace with dad so he always got his way. (Watson, 2002, p. 456)*

This empathetic response was more than just a reflection of the client's comments, but it focused on the heart of the problem and allowed the client to connect a meaning to the episode, resulting in a new understanding. In the client-centered phase, the therapist is more active and uses accurate empathy to allow the client to view his or her problem in a different manner. Note that the therapist remains cautious and presents his response to the client in a tentative fashion, "am I right . . . ?" Tentativeness allows the client to reflect on the accuracy of the therapist's response and reduces the chances that the therapist's views are being imposed. (Of course, we still have to entertain the possibility that a client may not actually agree with the therapist comment, and is just politely agreeing.) In this more active stance, the therapist's comment allowed the client to consider his own emotional reaction to his mother's decision not to visit as possibly involving a feeling of being "pushed aside."

Modifications to Client-Centered Therapy

Many client-centered therapists are continuing to adopt a more active stance, believing that clients may not spontaneously attend to or process elements related to their problem. Because of conditional acceptance, clients are unable to see reality. Therapists, therefore, use empathy in a manner that helps clients process and work through these experiences. In this more active approach, directive comments are more likely to be utilized such as, "Can we stay there for a minute?" and "Can we go into this further to see if I understood you?" This allows the client to more thoroughly process and access their emotions. More directive comments may be needed if clients repeatedly describe the same episode, make judgmental statements, talk about emotional reactions but seem hazy on the detail, or describe an emotional experience intellectually (Watson, 2002). In addition to advocating for a more active role in helping clients process emotional issues, many practitioners question the power of the self-actualizing tendency and wonder if the therapist relationship in and of itself is sufficient to promote change. As mentioned earlier, there are few pure client-centered therapists. Other therapies have integrated the client-centered assumptions into their own theoretical structure. Motivational interviewing, for example, a manualized treatment program that will be presented in the next chapter, describes itself as "a client-centered, directive method for enhancing intrinsic motivation to change by exploring and resolving ambivalence" (Miller & Rollnick, 2002, p. 25). Aspects of the client-centered approach, especially in regards to the provision of congruence, unconditional positive regard, and empathy, will remain important in all forms of therapy.

Existential Therapy

Existential counseling is a philosophical discussion about life tailored to a client's issues. It is a talk about living and dying . . . it uses the grim reality of life to spur the search for its wondrous aspects of love and meaning. . . . Mystery, uncertainty, and suffering are our constant eternal companions. . . . The Existential counselor is a companion in reviewing one's life in it's totality, not merely one's pattern of thoughts, feeling, or unconscious conflicts. (Vontress, 1998, p. 2)

Vontress is an African American therapist who was drawn to existential philosophy as a result of the discrimination that he faced. He found that certain universal principles applied to all living creatures—that the human species was only one of many on the planet and that all species face similar issues, such as life and death. As Vontress puts it, ". . . life, however much we may deny it to ourselves, is just a voyage to death, no matter what one's race or social standing" (Vontress, 1998, p. 2). This realization of a shared fate (death) and similar issues faced by all (love, suffering, and meaning) produces a feeling of equality among other men.

Existential therapy has its roots in philosophy, focusing on the universal challenges of existence faced by all humans. These issues and the way one avoids dealing with them are responsible for human unhappiness and psychopathology. For many, life is directionless and without meaning. People need to make sense of their lives. Paradoxically, many individuals are responsible for their own unhappiness in that they have unconsciously chosen their life direction. Many individuals are unaware of choices that are available to them or believe that they are unable to choose. Viktor Frankl's (1963) book, *Man's Search for Meaning,* demonstrated that choice is possible even in the worst environmental situation (in the Auschwitz concentration camp). "Ultimately, man should not ask what the meaning of his life is, but rather must recognize that it is *he* who is asked. In a word, each man is questioned by life; and he can only answer to life by *answering for* his own life; to life he can only respond by being responsible" (p. 172). Frankl believed that humans can strive for meaning and purpose and must come up with their individual answer. Unhappiness results when this is not recognized or acknowledged. As with other humanistic therapies, the therapeutic-client relationship is especially important. It is through this relationship that a client can acknowledge or deal with universal challenges. However, existential therapists are more likely to interpret what the client is saying and challenge clients to examine their lives. Increasing one's awareness of choices allows an individual a greater sense of freedom in choosing new behaviors to replace behaviors that are primarily reactions to external forces. The goal is to help people become intentional in directing their lives. Existential therapists work to have clients consider ways in which their freedom is impaired, and to remove the obstacles to freedom, thus increasing the sense of choice. According to existential theory, problems occur when an individual is faced with four interrelated life concerns (Yalom, 1980):

> **Death**—Underlying human existence is the recognition that life has a limit and that humans must face the fact that life ends. Irvin Yalom, a psychiatrist and existential psychotherapist, describes death in these terms: "one of life's most self-evident truths is that everything fades, that we fear the fading, and that we must live, none the less, in the face of fading" (p. 30). Acknowledging death results in anxiety; many individuals erect defenses against this awareness, resulting in denial and clinical symptoms. Only by accepting this reality can an individual begin to make choices to live life fully and in a meaningful way. Questions

such as "What would you do with you life if you had only one month to live? or one week? or one day?" force individuals to rate the priorities in their lives and to identify what they value. Blocking consideration of death and the limited time available in the lifetime of each individual can prevent people from living meaningful lives.

Isolation—No matter how close a relationship a person has with others, they are still separate entities. Everyone has their own thoughts, values, and beliefs. People live in their own cocoons and are not directly connected to others. Being alone, they defend against feelings of isolation by not thinking about it, or by trying to tie their existence with that of other individuals.

Meaninglessness—Because life is finite, how do people know if they are living their lives in a meaningful manner? No template exists on how this is to be accomplished. Everyone must define what is meaningful in their own way since there is no inherent meaning to life. They must ask themselves questions such as "What is important to me?" and "Am I accomplishing tasks that are important to my values and beliefs?" The failure to address questions like these can lead to despair and feelings of emptiness.

Freedom—Many of us engage in behaviors and activities without acknowledging or recognizing that we have the freedom to choose to do things differently. This freedom brings with it responsibility and knowledge that we are living the life that we have chosen. Clients often blame circumstances or others for their problems, failing to acknowledge personal responsibility. Existential therapists often have clients use the phrasing "I choose . . ." when describing problematic situations. When situations are presented in this manner, clients realize that they do have a choice and learn to take personal responsibility for their actions.

After the traumatic events that occurred on September 11, 2001, David J. Cain (2002b) reflected on the existential themes of life and death, meaningfulness, freedom of choice, and aloneness. Cain, a middle-aged man, considered himself to be at the midpoint of life. He ruminated on the signs of aging such as wrinkles and the loss of physical ability, reminders of being on the journey to the end of life. The events of September 11, 2001 demonstrated that life can end unpredictably. Since life span is limited or can suddenly end, a question arises, "Have I made the choices in my life that are meaningful?" Cain believed that life is often lived in a habitual pattern in which "real living" is promised to begin after the person accomplishes some type of task such as graduating from school, raising a family, or entering retirement. A person may realize too late that "postponed living" prevented living a fulfilling life. One should live in and for the moment. Habitual patterns of behavior such as going to work, watching television, and working on the computer limit our freedom of choice by hiding from awareness choices that are available. We begin to forget that we do have freedom of choice and can choose to spend our time doing something else. In terms of meaningfulness, some of the questions we may ask ourselves are: "Do I have a sense of purpose, mission or calling?" "Do I feel that my life makes a difference, even if only in small ways?" "Am I invested and committed to something that matters to me?" "Am I becoming the kind of person I wish to be?" "Does my life seem empty? Wasteful? Without direction?" "Do I have a chronic sense of dissatisfaction?" (Cain, 2002b, p. 13). Meaning in life is defined in an individual manner. Everyone needs to find what life means for them and then make the choice to move in that direction.

Viktor Frankl (1905–1997), an Austrian neurologist and psychiatrist who faced some of the greatest constraints to freedom when he was confined in a Nazi concentration camp, found that he could still have choice within this environment and find meaning regarding his existence. On a march to the camp, amidst the orders and shouts of the guards, Frankl turned his thoughts to his wife and discovered "A thought transfixed me: for the first time in my life I saw the truth as it is set into song by so many poets. . . . The truth—that love is the ultimate and the highest goal to which man can aspire. . . . The salvation of man is through love and in love. . . ." Later his thoughts were interrupted by a man who stumbled and a guard who used a whip on all who had fallen. . . "But soon my soul found its way back from the prisoner's existence to another world, and I resumed talk with my loved one: I asked her questions, and she answered; she questioned me in return, and I answered" (Frankl, 1959, pp. 58–60). Frankl's philosophy, strongly influenced by experiences in the German concentration camp, emphasized a person's freedom to choose and to find meaning in even the most restrictive and inhumane circumstances, and the belief that love produces the ultimate meaning in life. In *logotherapy,* the therapy developed by Frankl, the purpose is to help clients contemplate the meaning of their existence and to understand that no matter what the environment or circumstances, they retain the ability to choose their attitude.

Existential therapy uses listening skills, but the therapist participates more actively than in client-centered therapy. They use interpretation and other means to help the client wrestle with existential themes and confront the anxiety associated with the search for meaning, purpose, and authenticity. The following is an example of existential therapy:

> *Mr. A was a 45-year-old man who was married and had four children. He had a successful career in engineering and had come into treatment for panic attacks that now averaged about four times per week. His first attack occurred at a gym where he exercised regularly. During one workout session, he had a premonition of impending death, which was accompanied by symptoms of heart*

palpitation, shortness of breath, and dizziness. He was taken to the emergency room where an examination found no physical basis for his symptoms. His physician recommended anti-anxiety medications. These were effective for a while, but lost their effectiveness over time. The physician then recommended psychological treatment. (Randall, 2001)

The therapist, Elizabeth Randall, had initially considered cognitive-behavioral therapy and relaxation to treat the panic attacks. However, she had recently reread Yalom's (1980) book on existential psychotherapy and noted that many of the themes related to existential anxiety appeared to parallel Mr. A.'s descriptions of anxiety episodes. Initially, Mr. A. had a fulfilling relationship with his wife. They shared interest in outdoor activities consistent with his interest in physical fitness. His career was in an upward progression. However, his wife had always wanted a large family and had convinced him of the importance of children; four children were born in rapid succession. Mr. A. loved his children, but they prevented the freedom he once had to explore the outdoors with his wife. To provide for the large family, he began to work an extra 15 hours a week. His wife gave him conflicting messages about the need for more money and a desire for him to spend more time with the children. He attempted to continue his interest in physical fitness by working out at the gym. Feeling pulled in different directions, Mr. A. indicated his life felt repetitive and "duty-bound" and that he was on a treadmill. The therapist hypothesized that it was the loss of freedom and meaning in Mr. A's life that had led to the panic attacks. During a therapy session with him, she stated "Each time you panic, you're overwhelmed with a fear that you might die right then, and the panic seems like a cry of protest that you're not ready to die, because deep inside it seems like such a long time since you really lived" (Randall, 2001, p. 264).

Mr. A. contemplated this for about 30 seconds and then began to weep, which turned to anguished sobbing. This lasted for about 10 minutes, after which Mr. A. stated, "there might be something" to this interpretation. The next sessions dealt with the themes of isolation, meaning, and freedom; he became determined to change his life. He acknowledged his pain, but worried about sharing his feelings with his wife, fearing a negative response from her. In a joint session with his wife, the therapist presented the idea of stress management for Mr. A. They developed a plan where he could periodically "recharge" by leaving the children with relatives and engaging in recreational activities with his wife. He missed participating in outdoor activities with her, having assumed that the two were "soul mates" in their enjoyment of nature. He recognized now that no matter how much accord or intimacy shared between people, separateness is a part of human existence that can never be fully bridged. Mr. A. joined a local biking group, requested that his wife and children go on camping trips without relatives, and that the family discuss budget limitations so he could curtail overtime work. The latter allowed him to spend more time with the children in a meaningful way and he continued to exercise at the gym. After the fourth week of existential therapy, Mr. A. was panic-free. The existential themes of death anxiety, freedom, isolation, and meaninglessness appeared to be the cause of the panic attacks. Becoming aware of these issues and facing them resulted in Mr. A. taking the time to reevaluate his life and make choices to live a more authentic life.

Gestalt Therapy

We have not a liver or a heart. We are liver and heart and brain and yet, even this is wrong—we are not a summation of parts, but a coordination of the whole. We do not have a body, we are a body, we are somebody. (Perls, 1969, p. 6)

In Gestalt therapy, awareness of behavioral and emotional experiences occurring in the present is seen as the keystone to a client's personal interactions with the world and the process of healing. The focus is always on the present rather than on the past or the future ("nothing exists but the here and now. The past is no more, the future is not yet," Perls, 1969, p. 41). Indeed, preoccupation regarding the past or the future prevents people from facing present concerns. When past problems interfere with the present (unfinished business), Gestalt therapists use various techniques to bring them to the present. Problems are seen as resulting from a split between experiences and feelings. This occurs when individuals behave in a manner that has been dictated by rules of behavior, learned as children, regarding how to feel. Gradually, people disown certain feelings and experiences because they are not acceptable. Thus, splits occur without conscious awareness, and these splits, in turn, influence behavior and functioning.

Humans can only become integrated through experiencing life in the here and now and this is best accomplished through *awareness*. Awareness allows an individual to make meaningful choices and to live fully, and includes areas such as contact with the environment, responsibility for choices, and self-understanding. A focus on awareness in the present is promoted by asking questions such as "Are you aware that you are trembling?" "What are you experiencing?" and "Where in your body is the anxiety located?" Questions such as these force an individual to attend to the present, with a focus on bodily sensations and their own style of verbal and nonverbal expression. Gestalt therapy attempts to allow splits in an individual's experience to come to consciousness so that individual becomes whole. The goal is to have clients be aware of their present behavior and its impact, and then to develop an understanding of how they interact. Such awareness improves the ability of an individual to interact in a more authentic manner, and to be effective in the present (Cain, 2002a). To accomplish this task, emotional rather than intellectual processing is critical (Strumpfel & Goldman, 2002). Gestalt therapy developed techniques that are still used in many forms of therapy including:

The Empty Chair—This technique allows a past or present problem with another individual to be dealt with in the therapy session by having the client imagine that the other person is sitting in the other chair. The client is asked to speak aloud, in the present tense, as if the other person were actually there. After the client makes a statement, he or she is asked to switch chairs, assume the other person's identity, and then give a response. In doing so, clients bring a problem with another into the present and become more aware of their feelings and the feelings of the other person. This technique is also used for processing internal conflict, where two sides of a different perspective can be asked to interact with one another.

Use of Language—Gestalt therapy focuses on how individuals may reduce responsibility or awareness though the use of language. Clients may be asked to change their typical way of responding to situations. Instead of saying "You never know how others will react," an individual might say "I don't know how you will react" or by changing from "I can't" to "I won't" or from "I should" to "I choose." An awareness of how language can increase or decrease the perception of personal responsibility can lead to more active involvement in life choices.

Exaggeration—In the classic training film, *Three Approaches to Psychotherapy,* Fritz Perls, cofounder of Gestalt therapy, asked the client, Gloria, to exaggerate nonverbal responses, including her sigh and the movement of her leg. She was asked to repeat these. With her sigh, Gloria became aware of an emotional feeling. The request to repeat or exaggerate a behavior allows the client to become aware of unconscious emotions.

Research on Client-Centered Therapy

> *In general, humanistic and transpersonal psychotherapies have eschewed the use of objective tests, formalized assessment, and conventional empirical research methodologies on the grounds that they are reductionistic and unable to do justice to the inherent richness, complexity, and often ineffability of subjective human experience. (MacDonald & Friedman, 2002, p. 104)*

Many humanistic therapists believe that quantifiable research, the use of tests, and the focus on techniques do not capture the essence of humanistic therapy, which is holistic, discovery-oriented, and client-directed (Cain, 2002a). Humanistic therapists believe that the criteria used to determine the effectiveness of specific therapeutic approaches are not the kinds of changes promoted by their theories and therapies. They argue that the importance of relationship variables has, in fact, been supported by research on the therapeutic alliance and common factors in therapy. They point out that when clients are asked to describe what was helpful in therapy, they do not refer to specific techniques, but instead describe therapist qualities such as feelings of friendship, warmth, acceptance, and being treated as an equal (Ribner & Knei-Paz, 2002). The importance of the therapeutic relationship has been reported by the Task Force on Empirically Supported Therapy Relationships (Cornelius-White, 2002) and therapist contribution to outcome has been found to be greater than that from techniques (Asay & Lambert, 2002).

Carl Rogers did engage in process research specific to his client-centered approach to therapy (Rogers & Dymond, 1954) and even attempted to measure its effectiveness with clients with more severe forms of mental illness, such as schizophrenia. He was among the first to quantify and report details from complete case studies of therapy. Unfortunately, the research on client-centered therapy has decreased since the 1960s, and the existential and Gestalt therapies never developed a research tradition (Elliott, 2002). Currently, there is little research done on the client-centered condition of empathy—partly because the construct is difficult to define and measure, and because of the change in focus to the more broadly defined "therapeutic relationship." Past studies on the impact of empathy have supported the view that therapist empathy is related to client progress in therapy and that it is the client's perception, rather than that of the therapist or raters, that links empathy with positive outcome (Watson, 2002). Of the process-oriented research that does exist, the findings indicate that although empathy, genuineness, and congruence are related to outcome, they are not equally important to all clients. For many clients, outcome is enhanced when the therapist plays an active role, such as through clarification of issues discussed, encouraging self-exploration on the part of the client, and utilizing targeted interventions (Sachse & Elliott, 2002). In other words, many clients do better with active involvement and direct input from the therapist. A few studies have directly compared client-centered therapy with other approaches. For example, Teusch, Bohme, Finke, and Gastpar (2001) compared client-centered therapy alone or in combination with an antidepressant in treating personality disorders. Client-centered therapy produced significant improvements in reported depression, self-esteem, and social adjustment. The addition of antidepressants did not increase effectiveness or affect outcome.

Meta-analytic research on humanistic therapy does exist. One study (Elliott, 2002) found that clients who received humanistic therapies showed large gains, including more change than individuals in the control groups and equivalent changes compared with other forms of psychotherapy; additionally, gains were maintained in follow-up studies. However, the research reviewed included a large percentage of uncontrolled studies. Additionally, few studies used treatment manuals or provided clear diagnoses of the clients—that is, the research did not meet the standards required for consideration as an empirically supported therapy. Even so, Elliott believes there is sufficient research support for humanistic therapies to be considered as "probably efficacious" in the treatment of problems such as depression, anxiety, adjustment disorders, and relationship issues.

Diversity Issues with Client-Centered Therapy

> . . . *our cultural patterns are more often than not invisible to us, because we often take them to be simply "just the way things are"* . . . *we don't look at our own cultural patterns, or the way we think and do things, as an external observer might. We remain unaware of patterns that are deeply embedded in ourselves and in our social environments.* . . . *(Montuori & Fahim, 2004, p. 245)*

In accord with the humanistic focus on self-growth and self-awareness, Montuori and Fahim (2004) believe that cross-cultural therapy provides the opportunity for personal growth through examining our own set of values and beliefs, allowing us to better understand ourselves. Through self-understanding, individuals begin to realize that there are different cultural realities and that everyone is the product of culture. Cross-cultural encounter opportunities can offer a positive opportunity for personal growth by helping individuals to examine beliefs and improve self-understanding.

Acknowledging and understanding that therapists with a more individualistic orientation may experience difficulty understanding clients from a collectivistic background can enhance clinical skills and self-development. Traditionally, humanistic therapies promote clients' independence in making choices and defining meaningfulness at the individual level. Such an approach may not be appropriate for clients who have a collectivistic orientation, and whose decision-making processes are shared with family or other group members. Cross-cultural encounters do allow us to gain a wider perspective and, as discussed in Chapter 2, there are means of modifying therapeutic approaches, such as empathy, to encompass varied cultural groups.

How might attitudes regarding race or ethnicity affect a therapist's perceptions? A vignette presented to therapists involved "an 18-year-old male, first-year college student living for the first time in a residence hall. The client indicated that he was seeking counseling services because of the isolation he felt from other students in his residence hall. He described experiencing symptoms of depression . . . and overall feeling of homesickness. . . . The client indicated he was seeking help because he was considering leaving or transferring from the college" (Burkard & Knox, 2004, p. 392). Under one condition, the client described these feelings as due to feelings of depression and social isolation. In the other condition, he claimed his feelings were due to active exclusion by other students because of his race. Therapists with a color-blind attitude (a belief that race is unimportant in understanding someone's life) reported significantly less empathy for the client than did those who scored low for color-blindness (more likely to acknowledge that race matters). The implication of this study is that some therapists will need to actively develop sensitivity to possible racial issues in order to increase overall capacity for empathy.

Roger's belief in providing clients with unconditional positive regard, genuineness, and empathetic understanding can be applied in cross-cultural therapy with the proviso that the client must perceive these qualities. In other words, the therapist must evaluate his or her means of conveying these conditions by assessing their impact on the therapeutic alliance. Glauser and Bozarth (2001) believe that client-centered therapy has advantages for multicultural counseling, but warn against the danger of adopting a group or specificity guideline. ". . . A 'specificity myth' is endorsed purporting that there are specific treatments for groups of people. . . . This myth is a direct result of a shift in focus from the client to the counselor as the expert who focuses on 'doing' counseling rather than 'being' a counselor" (p. 142). There is certainly a need to attend to a client's cultural identity, but this is achieved through listening to the individual rather than responding to stereotypic knowledge. It is the client's perception of cultural influences that is important. In conducting therapy, it is important to identify environmental variables, such as family support and friends, through the client's frame of reference.

Existential therapy and Gestalt therapies may be especially problematic in working with certain ethnic groups. Vontress, the African American existential therapist, believes that the themes of death, freedom, and meaning apply to all humans. "Existential counseling is probably the most useful approach to helping clients of all cultures find meaning and harmony in their lives, because it focuses on the sober issues each of us must inevitably face: love, anxiety, suffering, and death" (Vontress, Johnson, & Epp, 1999, p. 32). However, there is little acknowledgment of social factors such as prejudice and discrimination. It may, in fact, be important for clients to learn to alter social forces related to their problems. Clients' failure to fulfill basic needs, such as housing, food, and safety, may play a large role in their unhappiness. Addressing basic needs may make more sense to clients than existential themes. The use of the confrontive and emotion-based techniques of Gestalt therapy may be inappropriate for individuals or cultures in which the open expression of emotions is discouraged. If employing these techniques, we suggest explaining the purpose to the client, and evaluating the approach from the client's perspective.

Motivational Enhancement Therapy

A client-centered and empathetic counseling style is one fundamental and defining characteristic of motivational interviewing. We regard the therapeutic skill of reflective listening or accurate empathy . . . to be the foundation on which skillfulness in motivational interviewing is built . . . Through skillful reflective listening, the counselor seeks to understand the client's feelings and perspectives without judging, criticizing, or blaming . . . The crucial attitude is a respectful listening to the person with a desire to understand his or her perspective. (Miller & Rollnick, 2002, p. 37)

Motivational Enhancement Therapy (MET), originally focused on the treatment of substance abuse, is now used to treat a variety of mental health and health related issues. We decided to include MET as an example of a client-centered approach because it is an evidence-based treatment for substance abuse, available in manualized form, and an "evolved" client-centered therapy. This approach, which emphasizes the importance of determining the stage of client motivation before conducting any form of therapy, was first described by W. R. Miller (1983) and further developed and updated in the book, *Motivational Interviewing* (W. R. Miller & Rollnick, 2002). *Motivational interviewing* refers to an interpersonal counseling or communication style rather than a specific therapy or set of techniques (Rollnick & Miller, 1995). This style is evident in the process of MET therapy, with its focus on helping clients overcome reluctance or ambivalence, which then allows them to make positive changes in their lives. While most therapies assume that clients want to change, motivational interviewing assumes that ambivalence is a normal part of human nature; unless a client considers and resolves this ambivalence, change will be slow and short-lived. An important goal of the therapy is to work through the ambivalence by having the client think about and consider the advantages and disadvantages of making a change. The approach promotes the use of self-motivating talk to address the advantages and disadvantages of the status quo and the advantages of change versus not changing. In motivational interviewing, the therapist uses an empathetic manner to help clients resolve their ambivalence.

Motivational Interviewing Theory

Motivational interviewing is best described as a directive client-centered approach. Although this might seem to be a contradictory description, the key assumptions of MET and motivational interviewing clearly fit within the client-centered model. For example, the responsibility and capacity for change is assumed to lie within the client; change can only occur when the client decides to make a change. Given a strong belief that the resources and motivation for change reside within the individual, the therapist focuses on the client's own perceptions, goals, and values throughout the therapy. The client is considered autonomous, with the capacity for self-direction. These views, along with the empathetic, nonjudgmental attitude of the therapist, fit into the client-centered model. The directive aspect of motivational interviewing involves the therapist working to increase the client's motivation to change. In contrast to the traditional client-centered approach, the therapist uses empathy and other supportive responses to reinforce self-motivational statements rather than using supportive, noncontingent techniques in a global, noncontingent manner. Using questioning, the therapist attempts to enhance motivation for change by encouraging consideration of the discrepancy between the client's substance abuse behavior and more adaptive goals. Another contrast with traditional client-centered approaches is that MET has a specific direction for the treatment, using strategies that direct the client toward specific goals rather than simply following the lead of the client. The therapist actively seeks to bring discrepancies to the client's attention, thus creating motivation for behavior change. MET is a directive and persuasive approach, rather than a nondirective and passive approach. The therapist gives advice and feedback, when appropriate. These more directive aspects of the approach are not consistent with the traditional client-centered perspective. (See Table 10.1 for the differences between client-centered therapy and motivational enhancement therapy.)

Understanding Stages of Change

While most therapies assume that clients want to change, MET believes that assessing and increasing motivation are essential for effective treatment. A major part of this assessment involves determining where the client is in terms of readiness for change. This approach comes from the pioneering work of Prochaska and DiClemente (1984). Advocates of this approach posit six separate stages that occur during the process of making changes. These stages are

Table 10.1 **Differences between the Client-Centered and Motivational Enhancement Approach**

Client-Centered

Client determines the content and direction of counseling

Therapist avoids influencing client with advice and feedback

Therapist provides unconditional empathetic reflection

Therapist explores conflicts and emotions presented by the client

Motivational Enhancement

Therapist directs the client toward motivation for change

Therapist willing to offer advice and feedback when appropriate

Empathic reflection is used selectively to reinforce client comments that increase motivation for change

Therapist enhances motivation for change by deliberately creating and amplifying dissonance in the client

Adapted from W. R. Miller et al., 1995

important in that each requires the accomplishment of certain tasks in order to move to the next stage and ultimately achieve change. The stages typically seen in any change process include:

- **Precontemplation**—The individual is not yet considering any changes.
- **Contemplative**—The individual is beginning to consider that they have a problem or that they would like to make a change in their life.
- **Preparation or Determination**—The individual has made a decision to make a change and begins to prepare for action.
- **Action**—The individual begins to make changes in their life or to modify a problem behavior.
- **Maintenance**—There is evidence of sustained change as the individual works to consolidate the changes made during the action phase.
- **Termination**—The individual has successfully maintained a change and has exited the cycle of change; this is the goal of all change efforts.

The stages of change model is important because it guides the clinician regarding which issues to address with the client and helps determine the most effective intervention strategies. Many individuals have several slips, or relapses, as they move forward through the stages. Some individuals need several cycles before learning how to maintain change successfully. Many go through the cycle multiple times. In order to help prevent relapse, MET puts a lot of focus on the contemplation and preparation/determination stages. In the treatment of substance abuse, the objective during these stages is to have clients consider two basic issues: First, "How much of a problem does my drinking pose for me?" "In what ways is my drinking affecting my life?" Both positive as well as negative aspects of drinking are considered. Second, "What are the costs and benefits of changing my drinking behavior?" "Will I be able to make the change?" "How would the change affect my life?" The therapist uses subtle reinforcement and questioning to help tip the balance toward the cons of drinking and help move the individual from contemplation to the preparation or determination stage, in which the client makes a firm commitment to take action in making a change.

Five Basic Motivational Principles Underlying MET

There are five basic motivational principles that form the foundation for MET. Each principle is consistent with the underlying philosophy that the responsibility and capacity for change reside within the individual. This perspective requires the therapist to create a set of conditions that will enhance the client's own motivation for and commitment to change. To accomplish this, clinicians follow the motivational principles throughout the therapeutic process (Miller, Zweben, DiClemente, & Rychtarik, 1995).

Expressing Empathy

The therapist's ability to demonstrate caring for and understanding of the client is critical to the therapy process. Continued emphasis on the client's freedom of choice and self-direction and the idea that only the client can make the decision for change is an ongoing theme of discussion. Empathy allows clients to examine their behavior in a nonjudgmental atmosphere and consider change possibilities. Careful listening by the therapist communicates respect for the client and a belief that the client is an equal partner in the therapy process. Such an approach is much less likely to produce resistance on the part of the client. Empathy involves more than simple reflective listening; often the therapist will reflect the content back to the client in a slightly modified, enhanced, or reframed form.

In one case, for example, a client seemed undecided about whether drinking was a problem, but also stated that sometimes difficulties in "thinking straight" occurred and expressed concern about alcohol "pickling my brain." The therapist restated the client's verbalization in the following manner, "You don't think you're that bad off, but you do wonder if maybe you're overdoing it and damaging yourself in the process" (Miller et al., 1995, p.17).

Reflective listening is used in a selective manner to allow the client to consider the benefits and costs of substance use. Other examples of statements a MET clinician might make would be, "You don't think that alcohol is harming you seriously now, and at the same time you are concerned that it might get out of hand for you later," and "You really enjoy drinking and would hate to give it up, and you can also see that it is causing serious problems for your family and your job" (Miller et al., 1995, p. 19). When reflection and empathy are used in this manner, clients are more able to consider all sides of the situation. Empathy or reflections can reinforce positive aspects of the client's thinking, while unhelpful comments may be deliberately ignored. If used at all, persuasion is gentle, with the assumption that only the client can choose to change.

Developing a Discrepancy

Underlying MET is the belief that motivation for change occurs only when individuals perceive a discrepancy between where they are currently and where they want to be in terms of their maladaptive behavior. Therefore, the therapist's task is to focus on and enhance the client's attention to these discrepancies. This might be accomplished by exploring health issues associated with alcohol consumption or considering its negative impact on relationships, work, or other activities. By bringing to awareness the personal consequences of the behavior, it is hoped that a "crisis" will be precipitated, producing motivation for change.

Avoiding Argumentation

In MET, direct confrontation is viewed as counterproductive because the therapist would be taking on the role of judging behavior, a role that would likely increase client defensiveness. This is in stark contrast to approaches sometimes used in the field of substance abuse that describe alcoholism as a disease over which the victim has little personal choice and where resistance is expected and met with argumentation and correction. With MET, the task is to allow the client to perceive a problem with their drinking and subsequently begin to make their own statements about a need for change.

Roll with Resistance

Resistance is a serious problem since it can have a negative impact on treatment outcome. Client behaviors such as interrupting, arguing with the therapist, changing the subject, or blaming others for the problem are indicators of resistance. In MET, resistance is not viewed primarily as the client's problem, but is considered the result of the therapist's style or approach. Instead of meeting resistance head on, therapists who encounter resistance use reflection and empathy to try to understand what the client is thinking or feeling. The therapist avoids a power struggle and disarms the client not only by listening, but also by acknowledging their point of view. The goal is to reduce defensiveness and allow the client to make self-motivational statements such as "I have a problem," or "I do have to make a change." Ambivalence in therapy should be expected and viewed as a normal reaction; supportive exploration of the ambivalence can ultimately lead to much greater motivation for change.

Supporting Self-Efficacy

Even when individuals admit to having a drinking problem, movement toward change is most likely to occur if the client believes that success is possible. It is essential that clients have optimism about the possibility of changing their behavior. In MET, *self-efficacy,* the belief that the individual can perform the behaviors required for change, is crucial. Unless this occurs, there is little hope for a change in behavior. However, in contrast to therapies that teach specific coping strategies or behaviors, MET builds motivation and elicits change strategies and problem-solving processes from the client. The assumption is that the key to lasting change is the motivation and commitment of the individual to the change.

The Motivational Enhancement Therapy Program for Alcohol Abuse and Dependence

According to the Motivational Enhancement Therapy Manual (Miller et al., 1995), the program for treating individuals with alcohol abuse or dependence consists of four treatment sessions that occur over a 12-week period. As described earlier, the focus of MET is to use strategies to enhance the client's own change resources. The therapy includes six elements believed to be effective with problem drinkers. They are:

- Therapist empathy
- Facilitation of client self-efficacy or optimism
- Feedback regarding degree of impairment or personal risk of dependence
- Emphasis on personal responsibility for change
- Clear advice regarding the importance of change
- A menu of alternative change options

In their treatment manual, Miller and his colleagues (1995) provide detailed information regarding the process of motivational enhancement therapy. We have summarized some specific details of the approach in the following sections. As you will see, a critical aspect of the first MET sessions is to begin building the client's motivation for change. To begin this process, the client is provided with results from pretreatment assessments regarding alcohol use. The client's reaction to the information and plans for the future are discussed using motivational enhancement strategies, with the goal of consolidating the client's commitment to change. The third and fourth sessions occur at weeks 6 and 12, during which the therapist monitors and encourages continued progress, continuing to focus on increasing motivation for change and strengthening commitment to change. The third and final phase of the intervention program involves reviewing progress and renewing motivation and commitment.

Phase 1: Building Motivation for Change

When contacting clients for the first appointment, the therapist emphasizes the importance of bringing in a significant other, someone who can be supportive during the therapy period. This is usually a family member or a close friend. The significant other should be someone who is an important person to the client, spends significant time with the client, and is willing to be involved in the therapy. The therapist mentions that the significant other will participate in the intake and initial planning process, attending one or two sessions. (See Box 10.1 for a discussion of involving a significant other). The therapist also informs the client that being sober is a condition of treatment, and to expect a breath test to be administered prior to each session. Any significant level of alcohol (greater than .05) requires rescheduling of the session.

Building motivation begins in the first session and may continue into the second session. As discussed earlier, clients begin the process in different stages of change. A precontemplator may have been referred by others and not feel the need to change. Other clients may have already decided that a change is necessary. For all clients, building motivation for change is part of the therapy process, although the amount of time spent on this task will depend on the client's readiness to commit to change. In all cases, the positive aspects of drinking and the feared consequences of making a change are weighed against the benefits of reducing alcohol consumption or abstaining from drinking, and the consequences of not making changes.

At the beginning of the first session, the therapist provides the rationale for and information regarding the treatment approach in the following manner:

> *Before we begin, let me just explain a little about how we will be working together. You have already spent time completing the tests that we need, and we appreciate the effort you put into that process. We'll make good use of the information from those tests today. This is the first of four sessions that we will be spending together, during which we'll take a close look together at your situation.*

Box 10.1 **Strategies When Involving a Significant Other**

MET allows for a significant other (partner, family member, or friend) to attend the first two sessions (although the invitation is originally extended to only the first session, allowing the therapist flexibility in deciding whether to include this individual in another session). A significant other often has a strong impact on the client's motivation to change, can provide input regarding the drinking problem, and offer feedback about the development and implementation of the treatment plan. The goal is not to prescribe specific activities for the significant other or provide specific interventions such as couples training in communication. In MET, the idea is for the significant others to demonstrate support and encouragement as the client generates possible solutions. When a significant other does attend a session, the therapist should:

- Reinforce their attendance at the session and their value in giving input and feedback in developing goals and treatment strategies.
- Indicate that the changes or commitment to change will have a positive impact.
- Establish rapport so there can be comfort in sharing concerns and information. Some questions to enhance the relation could be, "What has it been like for you?" "What has encouraged you or discouraged you from trying to help?" "What do you think will happen if drinking continues?" These types of questions tend to show empathy for the situation. It is important for the therapist to take care not to reinforce complaints and to reframe responses that may make the client defensive. If a significant other says, "I've been trying to tell you all along that you were drinking too much. Now maybe you'll believe me," the therapist can reframe the concern in a gentle manner; for example, "You've been worrying about this for a long time, and I guess you're hoping now he'll see why you've been so concerned?" In this example, a criticism was reframed into concern and worry. Most significant others respond well to the empathetic, supportive stance in MET. However, if their presence is counterproductive and the clinician decides not to invite them for the second session, their involvement during the first session can be limited by focusing more on the client.
- Ask questions to elicit affirming and supportive comments: "What are the things you like most about the client when he/she is not drinking?" "What positive signs of change have you noticed that indicate he/she wants to make a change?" "What gives you hope that things can change for the better?"
- Continue to emphasize that responsibility for change remains with the client but that the others close to the client can be helpful and supportive. The therapist can ask questions such as: "In what ways do you think you could be helpful to _____?" or "What has been helpful to _____ in the past?"
- Emphasize positive attempts to deal with the problem. Reframe negative experiences such as stresses to the family or employment in a normative fashion—as events that are common in families with alcohol problems.

Be careful not to create a situation where the client feels the therapist and the significant other are "ganging up" on the client. It is helpful to reframe negative comments, whenever possible, and ask the client for his or her response to information shared by the significant other.

From Miller et al., 1995

I hope that you'll find these four sessions interesting and helpful. I should also explain right up front that I'm not going to be changing you. I hope that I can help you think about your present situation and consider what, if anything, you might want to do, but if there is any changing, you will be the one who does it. Nobody can tell you what to do; nobody can make you change. I'll be giving you a lot of information about yourself and maybe some advice, but what you do with all of that after our four sessions together is completely up to you. How does that sound to you? (Miller et al., 1995, p. 50)

Clients often find this explanation comforting, especially hearing that they will not be coerced and they are in control of making the decision for change. There may be questions about the limited number of sessions. If this occurs, the therapist summarizes the research findings regarding the effectiveness of MET and the belief that, regardless of the type of therapy chosen, it is the client who makes the decision about what to do about their drinking.

In the first session, the therapist informs the client (and the significant other, if present) that there will be feedback regarding the pretreatment assessment, but before this occurs, it is helpful to hear how they see the client's situation. During this discussion, frequently used strategies for eliciting self-motivational statements include the use of empathy, reflection, affirming the client, and reframing comments. A therapist's summary statement that might reflect this balance is, "You really enjoy drinking and would hate to give it up, and you can also see that it is causing serious problems for your family and your job" (p. 19). In MET, strategies are used to tip the balance in favor of change, including open-ended questions or statements that allow for a balanced and open discussion of the issues involved in drinking:

- I assume, from the fact that you are here, that you have been having some concerns or difficulties related to your drinking. Tell me about your concerns.

- Tell me a little about your drinking. What do you like about drinking? And what is the other side? What are your worries about drinking?

- What have other people told you about your drinking? What are other people worried about?

- What makes you think that perhaps you need to make a change in your drinking? (p.19)

If the client has difficulty identifying concerns regarding drinking, the therapist can gently explore areas such as tolerance (drinking large amounts without showing much effect), memory lapses, health concerns, legal or financial problems related to drinking, or relationship changes due to the drinking. Again, the therapist explores these areas with the client and does not blame or confront the client. Reframing is a useful strategy for turning a vague or minimizing comment into a more specific issue. The goal is to have the client make statements that indicate a need for change. Following this discussion, the therapist offers a summary of the major points made by the client and significant other.

The therapist next shares the pretreatment assessment report, which includes a summary of the client's drinking pattern, the severity of the drinking, risk factors, and the results of blood and neurological tests. The scores are compared to normative data. During the feedback portion, the therapist monitors and responds to the client's statements and uses empathy and reflection to encourage self-motivating statements. After sharing specific data from the assessments, the therapist asks for a response with questions such as, "I've given you quite a bit of information here, and at this point, I wonder what you make of all of this and what you're thinking?" The therapist continues to use strategies to elicit self-motivational statements from the client. If the client has difficulty believing the results of the report, the therapist mirrors this reaction back to the client rather than arguing and may repeat the question, "So, what do you make of these results?" Careful listening and finding ways to affirm, support, or reinforce the client are quite important in MET and help strengthen the therapeutic alliance, support the client's self-esteem, and enhance self-efficacy. During the feedback session, the therapist looks for opportunities to respond supportively, "I appreciate your sincere attention to this information, even though it must have been difficult to hear" (p. 21).

The underlying goal of the feedback session is to have the client admit having a problem and indicate there is a need to change. Using cues from the client and significant other, the therapist will also begin to elicit thoughts, ideas, and plans for dealing with problem drinking and the perceived positives and negatives of continuing drinking. At this point, the therapist might summarize the ideas using a decision-making balance sheet. (See Box 10.2.) The potential value of abstinence is discussed at this time. As the therapist proceeds toward the development and confirmation of a plan for change, specific steps and goals are written. The therapist is careful not to press prematurely for a commitment. The client signs the plan only after making a firm decision to follow the plan.

The therapist ends the first session by summarizing what has transpired in the session. At the end of this session, a therapist may find that the client has moved quickly through the tasks and is ready to take action. However, it is important to remember that some clients require a great deal of time to work on the motivational aspect. In the first session, therapists always try to elicit at least a few self-motivational statements from ambivalent clients and begin to take some steps toward discussing a plan for change, even if it is tentative. With all clients, the therapist discusses what the client agrees to do or to change between the first and second sessions. It is important to remember

Box 10.2   **Decision-Making Balance Sheet**

If I continue with (current behavior or concern):	
Benefits of Not Making a Change	Costs of Not Making a Change
1.	1.
2.	2.
3.	3.

If I change (current behavior or concern):	
Benefits of Making a Change	Costs of Making a Change
1.	1.
2.	2.
3.	3.

If I continue with drinking:	
Benefits of Making a Change	Costs of Not Making a Change
1. Helps me relax	1. Husband always upset with me
2. I enjoy drinking	2. Kids seem worried about me
3. I can forget my worries	3. I might have another accident

If I change my drinking:	
Benefits of Making a Change	Costs of Making a Change
1. No more blackouts	1. Can't go out with friends
2. Better health	2. How can I relax?
3. Everyone will be off my back	3. I'm too shy when I'm sober

Adapted from Miller & Rollnick, 2002

that clients must be ready for change and that pressuring a client into taking action before they are ready is contrary to the philosophy of MET.

After the first session, the therapist mails a handwritten note to the client that includes: (1) a statement of appreciation for the client's (and significant other's) attendance at the first session, (2) affirmations of their commitment to the process and understanding of the seriousness of the problem, (3) a summary of the first session with emphasis on specific self-motivational statements made by the client, (4) a statement indicating hope and optimism, and (5) a reminder regarding the next session. The following is a sample letter:

> *This is just a note to say that I'm glad you came in today. I agree with you that there are some serious concerns for you to deal with, and I appreciate how openly*

you are exploring them. You are already seeing some ways in which you might make a healthy change, and your wife seems very caring and willing to help. I think that together you will be able to find a way through these problems. I look forward to seeing you again on Tuesday the 24th at 2:00. (p. 53)

The second session occurs 1 or 2 weeks after the first session, and begins with a summary of what transpired during the first session. At that point, the therapist continues with the tasks outlined for the first session. At the end of the second session, the therapist offers a closing summary of the client's reasons for concern about the drinking, the main themes discussed, and the plan that has been negotiated. If the client has not yet made a commitment for change, the therapist indicates that there will be a check-in to see how the client is doing at the follow-up session in about 4 weeks. If a significant other was involved in the second session, the therapist offers thanks and appreciation for their participation during the initial sessions and gives a reminder that the next two sessions will involve only the client.

Phase 2: Strengthening Commitment to Change

After the client begins to accept the need for change and demonstrates sufficient motivation, the therapist begins the process of consolidating the commitment for change. The timing of this shift is important, because if it is done too early the client may move back to an earlier stage. Some of the signs that a client has moved into the determination stage and that a decision has truly been made to take action include observations that the client appears more settled and resolved, stops resisting and raising objections, and asks fewer questions. Also, the client may be making self-motivational statements such as, "I need to deal with my drinking problem," or "What can I do to change my drinking habit?" Signs that a client may not be ready for a commitment for change include missing appointments, indecision about scheduling future appointments, guardedness in responding to therapist suggestions, and continuing to feel coerced into treatment. Even when a client demonstrates a commitment to change, ambivalence is likely to remain. The therapist must continue to assess where the client falls within the stages of change and continue to use the strategies of empathy, reflection, and reframing to reinforce motivation. Therapists sometimes use a Measuring Readiness to Change worksheet, in which clients list the areas for possible change (e.g., drinking, smoking, relationships with friends) and give each a rating of either "not ready," "considering," "ready," or "very ready." Once the commitment to change is consolidated, treatment moves forward to the planning stage where the commitment to change is further strengthened.

Developing a Plan

The commitment for change is followed by a focus on developing a plan for change. This may involve the client asking what they can do about their drinking problem, or the therapist may ask transitional question such as (p. 29):

- What do you make of all this? What are you thinking you'll do about it?
- Where does this leave you in terms of your drinking? What's your plan?
- I wonder what you're thinking about your drinking at this point.
- Now that you're this far, I wonder what you might do about these concerns.

During this process, the therapist elicits the client's ideas about dealing with his or her drinking, along with plans for specific changes. In MET, the therapist does not prescribe a plan for how the client should change or to teach specific skills, but instead emphasizes that the change in drinking is up to the client. However, inquiries such as, "How are you going to accomplish that?" or "What do you think you need to do?" are acceptable since it is the client's responsibility to make that decision; they have the freedom of choice regarding how to proceed.

Consequences of Action and Inaction

To strengthen the commitment to change, the client is asked to anticipate what would happen if drinking continued unabated. The therapist might have the client write down the possible negative consequences of not changing. Conversely, they would be asked to list the benefits of changing. To obtain a complete picture, the therapist might ask the client about fears regarding change and the possible negative consequences of stopping drinking. Are there any advantages to continuing to drink as before? Use of a decision-making balance sheet (as seen in Box 10.2) allows for a summary of the pros and cons of making a change, the positive and negative consequences of drinking as before, and the positive and negative consequences of making a change. Using this method, the therapist can discuss any reluctance or issues that might affect motivation.

Emphasizing Abstinence

During this phase, it is important to discuss the issue of abstinence. Abstinence is not an expectation imposed on the client—rather, the rationale for abstinence is presented to the client with the understanding that the client will make the choices involved in their plan for change. The therapist may say to the client: "Abstinence is a safe choice since it ensures that there will be no problems because of drinking." "Even a trial period of abstinence can be beneficial since you can learn to live without alcohol, break old habits, and experience positive changes in your life" (p. 31), or "Safe drinking levels have not been determined so some researchers in the field feel that abstinence is the safest way to proceed" (p. 32).

A goal of moderation is discouraged for clients who have had severe problems related to the use of alcohol. The therapist can use persuasion by indicating his or her concern over moderation, but still allowing the client to make the choice. "It's your choice. However, I'm worried about what you are considering and if you are willing to listen, I'd like to tell you my concerns. Some of the situations where I advise against a goal of moderation include when there is a history of severe addiction, pregnancy or medical conditions that are worsened by drinking, use or abuse of medications that in combination with alcohol can be very hazardous or mental health issues that are made worse by drinking" (p. 32). If the client is resistant, the therapist can attempt to defuse the resistance by making statements such as, "So you think you will decide that it is worth it to you to continue drinking, even though you've said that it is costing you in a lot of ways?" or "I wonder if it is possible for you to continue drinking and still do well (in school, at work, with your partner, with your friends, with your family)?"(p. 34)

Change Plan Worksheet
After the client has clearly communicated willingness and motivation to change, a change plan worksheet is used. Change plan worksheets can be useful in many counseling or therapy situations. The specific guidelines regarding use of the worksheet from the MET manual (pp. 34–35) include:

1. *The changes I want to make are:* Specifically, in what ways or areas does the client want to make a change? It is a good idea to include goals that are positive (to begin to . . . to increase . . . to improve . . . do more of) and not just negative goals (to stop . . . avoid . . . or decrease).

2. *The most important reason why I want to make these changes are:* What are the likely consequences of action and inaction? Which reasons for change seem most compelling for the client? This information may come from discussions that occurred earlier in the change process.

3. *The steps I plan to take in changing are:* How does the client plan to achieve the goals? How could the desired change be accomplished? Within the general plan and strategies described, what are some specific, concrete first steps that the client can take? When, where, and how will these steps be taken?

4. *The ways other people can help me are:* In what other ways could other people (including the significant other, if present) help the client in tak-

ing these steps toward change? How will the client arrange such support?

5. *I will know my plan is working if:* What does the client hope will happen because of this plan? What benefits will occur as a result of this change?

6. *Some things that could interfere with my plan are:* Help the client to anticipate situations or obstacles that could undermine the plan. What could go wrong? How could the client stick with the plan despite these problems or setbacks?

The steps and issues covered by the change plan worksheet are comprehensive. There is a focus on renewal of the client's commitment for change, reinforcing the decision and reasons for desiring change, deciding how to go about making changes, how to seek support from others during the change process, and how the client can monitor the effectiveness of the plan and be aware of and work around obstacles for change. With considerable input from the client and supportive assistance from the therapist, the change plan worksheet is completed, thus solidifying the plan. The client is asked if he or she is willing to make the commitments specified. If so, the client signs the plan, taking home the original and leaving a copy with the therapist.

In some cases, the client is ambivalent or unwilling to sign the worksheet. If this occurs, the therapist asks if the client would like to defer a commitment until there is an opportunity to further consider the decision. The therapist never coerces a client into taking action, but instead allows for further exploration of ambivalence and the consequences of making or not making a change. If a client is clearly not ready to commit to a plan, the therapist might say,

> *It sounds like you're not really quite ready to make this decision yet. That's perfectly understandable. This is a very tough choice for you. It might be better not to rush things here, not to try to make a decision right now. Why don't you think about it between now and our next visit, consider the benefits of making a change and of staying the same. We can explore this further next time, and sooner or later I'm sure it will become clear to you what you want to do. Okay? (p. 39)*

Phase 3: Follow-Through Strategies

The three processes that occur during Phase 3 sessions include:

1. **Reviewing progress**—The therapist and client review what has occurred since the last session, exploring progress made and the extent to which the goals and plans have been implemented. The therapist con-

tinues to use reflection, empathy, reframing, and supportive guidance as before.

2. **Renewing motivation**—Depending on the client's level of motivation and commitment to change, the therapist asks questions that allow the client to remember their reasons for wanting to change their drinking. This may lead to a discussion of both the negative consequences of drinking and the positive aspects of change.

3. **Redoing commitment**—This may simply involve an affirmation of the commitment made earlier. If there are significant problems or doubts, the focus is on reevaluation of the plan and developing a new plan or commitment. The therapist continues to reinforce the client's sense of autonomy and self-efficacy, particularly any statements that indicate movement toward the client's goals.

The last two sessions (scheduled for weeks 6 and 12) are booster sessions used to reinforce the motivational processes begun in the initial sessions. During each of the final two sessions, the therapist and client work to: (1) review progress and (2) renew motivation and commitment. The therapist remains alert to the possibility that client ambivalence has returned or has not been fully resolved, and continues to use motivation building and commitment strengthening strategies.

Along with the motivational and commitment focus, the therapist explores situations in which the client recently used alcohol, together with situations where the client avoided drinking. If drinking occurred since the last session, the therapist explores how it occurred, remaining nonjudgmental and empathetic. The therapist focuses again on enhancing motivation and eliciting self-motivational statements from the client rather than teaching coping strategies. Questions to renew commitment might be, "I wonder what you will need to do differently next time?" or "So what does this mean for the future?" (p. 55). If drinking did not occur, self-efficacy is reinforced by asking the client how they coped successfully in these situations. "How were you able to resist drinking?" Clients are encouraged for even small steps toward change.

In the last session, the therapist discusses termination of therapy and provides the client with a final summary of presenting concerns and progress through the sessions. The final summary and discussion include:

- Review of the most important reasons the client cited for making a change
- Summary and positive discussion of the commitments and changes the client has made so far
- Exploration of additional changes the client may wish to make in the future

- Questioning the client regarding the worst thing that could happen if there were a return to drinking as before

- Discussion of upcoming events that could threaten sobriety or other potential obstacles to continued sobriety

- Elicitation of self-motivational statements that will help the client maintain change and prepare for further changes

- Support for client self-efficacy and expression of optimism regarding change, emphasizing the client's ability to change

Evaluation of Motivational Interviewing: Scientific Basis, Contextual and Diversity Issues

Motivational enhancement therapy was originally developed to treat drug addiction, but is now also successfully used with other health issues and mental disorders (Resnicow et al., 2002). It is also used in work with adolescents and young adults (Baer & Peterson, 2002) and adjudicated populations (Ginsburg, Mann, Rotgers, & Weekes, 2002). Studies have found the approach to be effective in treating alcohol abuse (Bombardier & Rimmele, 1999; LaBrie, Lamb, Pedersen, & Quinlan, 2006) and with other situations in which resistance plays an important role. For example, motivational enhancement therapy has been found to be more acceptable to individuals with eating disorders than more directive approaches (Geller et al., 2003) and appears to enhance their readiness to change (Dunn, Neighbors, & Larimer, 2006). Similarly, there is some research evidence that the motivational enhancement approach is more effective than more directive approaches when working with clients in alcohol treatment programs who display *psychological reactance* (a tendency to resist control) during therapy (Karno & Longabaugh, 2005).

Motivational enhancement therapy was one of three therapies evaluated for effectiveness by the National Institute on Alcohol Abuse and Alcoholism (NIAAA) in its Project MATCH program. The other two therapies were cognitive-behavioral therapy (CBT) and Twelve Step Facilitation Therapy (TSF), based on the philosophy and principles of Alcoholics Anonymous. The study involved 1,726 alcohol dependent individuals who were randomly assigned to one of the three manualized, individual therapies for a 12-week period, and who had follow-up assessments performed at 1 and 3 years after treatment. All three therapies produced similar positive results. The participants in the programs showed increases in abstinent days and decreased number of drinks during drinking days. They also reported less depression, and showed decreased use of other substances and improved liver functioning (Project Match Group, 1997). These gains were sustained over a 3-year follow-up period (Project Match Group, 1998a). Of the eleven client attributes examined in this study, the most consistent finding was that the client's pretreatment level of outpatient anger affected response to specific types of therapy. Those high in anger did slightly better with MET, while those who were low in anger did slightly better with CBT and TSF (Project Match Group, 1998b). In a recent meta-analytic review of nine studies, motivational interviewing was concluded to be effective as a brief treatment for excessive drinking (Vasilaki, Hosier, & Cox, 2006). Therapist interpersonal skills have been found to be very important in MET and are associated with client cooperation, disclosure, and expression of affect (Moyers, Miller, & Hendrickson, 2005).

As with many forms of therapy, the approach has not been evaluated for use as a treatment for alcohol or substance abuse with ethnic minorities. There is one study using motivational interviewing to promote HIV testing at an American Indian substance abuse treatment facility (Foley et al., 2005). In individual sessions with 134 American Indians, MI techniques were employed, with a focus on considering risk factors and where changes in attitudes or behaviors could be made. After this, the participants were asked to take a HIV test and to return for the results. Of the group, 78 percent agreed. The authors believe that this was a successful demonstration of the effectiveness of MI because of the general mistrust of American Indians toward governmental agencies. However, the findings are difficult to interpret since there were no control groups and the subjects were paid as an incentive to agree to the testing.

Because MET is a directed, client-centered approach in which motivation and consequences of substance abuse are considered, it has some strengths for potential use with ethnic minorities. Clients' comments and reactions are accepted and respected. Balance sheets regarding positive and negative consequences are formulated. A suggestion for enhancing effectiveness with diverse populations is to bring up cultural and social factors that may be considered as either positive or negative reasons for continuing or reducing alcohol consumption. In building the motivation for change, social and cultural values can also play important roles and the involvement of a significant other can extend to a family or even a community. It may be useful to have significant others attend all sessions when the client's cultural background involves a collectivistic orientation.

Recommended Readings

Miller, W. R., Zweben, A., DiClemente, C., & Rychtarik, R. (1995). *Motivational enhancement therapy manual.* Rockville, MD: National Institute on Alcohol Abuse and Alcoholism.

This manual, which provides a detailed description of the MET intervention for individuals with alcohol abuse and dependence, was evaluated in Project MATCH and is disseminated by the National Institute of Health and the National

Institute of Alcohol Abuse and Alcoholism. This manual, as well as manuals for the two other therapies evaluated in Project Match, Twelve-Step Facilitation Therapy and Cognitive-Behavioral Coping Skills Therapy, are all available from the National Institute of Health free of charge. The steps in the MET approach are clearly explained in the manual.

Miller, W. R., & Rollnick, S. (2002). *Motivational interviewing* (2nd ed.). New York: Guilford Press.

This book provides a comprehensive overview of the conceptual and research background of motivational interviewing. Motivational principles are clearly defined, including strategies for building motivation, responding to resistance, and moving the client toward change. Personal reflections of the authors are also provided, as well as their thoughts regarding implications for clinical training. Varied applications, including techniques for criminal justice populations, medical and public health settings, and for treating dual disorders, are also presented.

Cognitive-Behavioral Theory and Techniques

11

Chapter

My approach to psychotherapy is behavioral, such that I conceptualize the development and maintenance of behaviors according to learning theory (operant conditioning, classical conditioning, etc.). I view the context in which the behavior occurs as critical to accurate conceptualizations and change.... My interventions pull from empirically-supported treatments and principles that are targeted to my behavioral formulations ... *(Wagner, 2005, p. 101)*

Cognitive-behavioral therapy (CBT), now advocated by many in the mental health profession, is rapidly becoming the treatment of choice for many disorders. For example, when 85 psychiatric residents were surveyed regarding therapeutic practices, nearly all rated CBT as "clinically useful," 99 percent anticipated using it in future practice, and all were aware of the research evidence favoring CBT (Cassidy, 2004). For the profession of psychiatry, this shift in favor of cognitive-behavioral approaches is dramatic because psychiatry has traditionally been influenced much more by psychodynamic theories. The increasing emphasis within the mental health profession toward evidence-based practice and the requirement of managed care for short-term treatments with specific goals and interventions has resulted in growing awareness and use of cognitive-behavioral therapies. The clinician quoted above clearly bases her approach on learning theory and interventions that are empirically supported. In fact, the vast majority of empirically supported psychological interventions are some variant of the cognitive-behavioral approach.

Although some differences exist within the different cognitive-behavioral therapies, they are similar in that they extol the virtues of the scientific method and research evidence. Many of the principles and constructs underlying CBT are derived from experimental research. There is emphasis on the importance of observation, the use of objective measures, and the careful evaluation of the process and outcome of therapy. As with the humanistic therapies, CBT focuses primarily on present influences on behavior rather those from past issues. In general, most behavior theorists believe that humans are shaped by environmental variables. In contrast with the humanistic and psychoanalytic approaches, cognitive-behavioral therapies often have clients actively involved in their treatment by practicing skills learned during therapy.

In this chapter, we will present some of the principles associated with the major schools of cognitive-behavioral therapy (classical conditioning, operant conditioning, social learning, and cognitive-behavioral). Although we discuss these branches of CBT separately, it is important to note that there is, in fact, a movement toward combining elements of each within the different perspectives. For example, you will see that the manualized treatments we present in the following two chapters (Beck's cognitive-behavioral therapy for treating depression and Linehan's dialectic behavior therapy for treating individuals with borderline personality) include both cognitive and behavioral strategies. Throughout our discussions, the term *cognitive-behavioral* will be used to encompass all of the different forms of cognitive and behavioral therapies.

Classical Conditioning Theory

At a staff meeting, the case of a 17-year-old young woman seeking therapy for a severe phobia involving birds was brought up for discussion. As the case presentation started, and before further information was given, two psychiatrists expressed the belief that the client's fear symbolized anxiety over sex. From their theoretical perspective, overt behaviors are often manifestations of any underlying conflict. The therapist then reported the client's history. As a child of four, the client had misbehaved while visiting her aunt's farmhouse. As punishment, she was locked in the henhouse for several minutes; her crying upset the hens who flew all around, hit her with their wings, and scratched her arms and face. She was terrified and avoided birds after that incident. (Todd & Bohart, 1999)

Classical conditioning theory is based on the work of Ivan Pavlov (1849–1936; 1927) and John B. Watson and Rosalie Raynor (1920). Pavlov had discovered by accident that dogs would salivate at the sight of his assistant carrying food powder. He hypothesized that food is an *unconditioned stimulus* (UCS), that is, it will automatically produce salivation when placed in the mouth. What he did not understand was why the dogs would salivate when seeing his assistant with the food. He began experiments where he would pair a sound from a bell with food placed in the mouth of dogs. Initially, no salivation would occur with just the bell alone. However, after several repetitions of the bell combined with food powder in the mouth, the dogs would begin to salivate to the bell alone. The bell had become a *conditioned stimulus* (CS); that is, it induced salivation by itself due to its previous pairings with the UCS.

Pavlov also discovered that if he kept presenting the bell (CS) over and over again without following it with the food powder (UCS), *extinction* would occur (i.e., salivation would no longer occur to the bell alone).

J. B. Watson and Raynor (1920) also investigated the role of classical conditioning in the development of fears. By performing experiments with a child, they hoped to determine if there might be a simple method by which emotional responses could spread to other stimuli. Could an 8-month-old infant, Albert, learn to fear objects through classical conditioning? They presented Albert with a number of stimuli, including a white rat. None of the stimuli produced a fear response. They then again showed him the white rat, immediately followed by a loud bang from a hammer striking a steel bar. Albert was initially startled and began crying when the pairing was repeated. After several pairings of the rat and the loud sound, Albert showed a fear response when presented with the rat alone. The rat had acquired fear-producing qualities. In this process, the rat had become a *conditioned stimulus*. Thus, classical conditioning is seen as a model for understanding the etiology of fear responses, including the development of anxiety disorders such as phobias and obsessive-compulsive disorder. However, a question that remains is: Why do fears and other anxiety disorders not go through an extinction process, as seen in the operant conditioning research? It was hypothesized that individuals with fear and anxiety learn to avoid the stimuli or situations that evoke the fear reactions, thus preventing the nontraumatic exposure needed to produce extinction. For example, if an individual has a fear of spiders or snakes, successful avoidance or escape from their presence prevents extinction and maintains the fear.

There is some research evidence that classical conditioning is involved in the development of emotional responses. In one study, women undergoing chemotherapy for cancer were given Kool-Aid in a container with a bright orange lid. After pairing the drink and the chemotherapy repeatedly, the women reported nausea and emotional distress upon seeing the container (Jacobsen et al., 1995). Clinical reports also support the classical conditioning model in the development of fear. Adults with phobias have reported specific conditioning experiences (Öst & Hugdahl, 1981), as have children with a fear of spiders (King, Eleonora, & Ollendick, 1998). In addition, many veterans returning from Iraq report having *Posttraumatic Stress Disorder* (PTSD), symptoms associated with traumatic events they experienced during the war (Hoge et al., 2004). Is there support for the classical conditioning model in terms of treatment? Based on previous research, it would seem that fear reactions could be eliminated through extinction procedures (i.e., exposure to that which is feared). In fact, there is empirical support for the effectiveness of extinction or exposure therapies for phobias, panic, obsessive-compulsive disorder, PTSD, and social anxiety (Chambless & Ollendick, 2001; Taylor et al., 2003).

Therapeutic Strategies Based on Classical Conditioning

There are a number of different therapies based on classical conditioning that involve having clients face their fears either through imagined images or in actual situations. Exposure therapies can employ an extinction process by itself, or can be combined with other interventions such as relaxation or response prevention. The examples we will present include: therapies using exposure only, desensitization, and exposure combined with response prevention.

Therapies Using Exposure Only

Exposure therapy, also known as *extinction therapy,* involve processes by which feared objects or situations are either gradually introduced to minimize overwhelming anxiety (*graduated exposure*) or introduced rapidly in order to produce high levels of anxiety (*flooding*) in the client. For example, an individual who suffers from agoraphobia (a disorder involving severe anxiety in certain situations) may be asked to imagine going outside, or actually go outside for short time periods until anxiety dissipates (graduated exposure), or may be asked to go out to a crowded mall and stay there for an hour or more (flooding). Most therapists prefer to use the graduated approach because of the amount of discomfort that can occur with flooding procedures. However, flooding has been used successfully to treat women recovering from sexual assault. In one study, women were asked to repeatedly imagine and describe the assault "as if it were happening now" and to continually visualize as vividly as possible any sights, sounds, smells, thoughts, and feelings that occurred during the assault; this exposure to the trauma continued until their anxiety was reduced (Foa et al., 1999). Similarly, some therapists use extinction therapy to treat phobias with the assistance of computer-generated images that immerse clients in a realistic setting. One woman who had a spider phobia of 20 years duration viewed three-dimensional images of spiders through a helmet with video monitors. After twelve sessions, she no longer felt compelled to prevent the entry of spiders into her home by sealing her windows with duct tape (Salyer, 1997, p. C2). Extinction techniques have also been used to treat panic disorder and, depending on outcome criteria, the success rate ranges from 52 percent to 78 percent (Lang & Craske, 2000). (See Table 11.1 for an example of the steps involved in an exposure treatment for Panic Disorder.)

Desensitization

Desensitization therapy, developed by Joseph Wolpe (1958), involves having the extinction process occur while the client is in a state of relaxation. The relaxation response, in combination with exposure, is presumed to reduce levels of anxiety. The steps involve (1) teaching the client to relax deeply through progressive relaxation instructions, (2) developing a hierarchy of items related to the feared object or situation that range from high to low

Table 11.1 **Cognitive-Behavioral Treatment for Panic Attacks**

1. **Psychoeducation about anxiety**—Panic is discussed as a "fear of fear." Bodily sensations associated with panic are described, including increase in heart rate, chest pain, sweating, trembling, feelings of distress, dizziness, and a sense that things seem "unreal," and examples of somatic symptoms in individuals undergoing panic attacks are given.

2. **Model for understanding panic symptoms and hyperventilation**—The sequence involved in panic symptoms discussed with the client include: (1) a precipitant, such as stress, exercise, stimulants, fear-provoking thoughts, or fluctuations in physiological states; (2) a perception of a physiological change; (3) a fear response through misappraisal or conditioning; (4) an intensification of the bodily sensations; and (5) a panic attack.

3. **Cognitive restructuring and retraining of the breathing response**—The therapist explains the connection between (1) thoughts and emotional responses and (2) how an event is interpreted and the subsequent emotional reactions to the event. Thoughts that occur just prior to a panic attack are identified, such as, "I will have a panic attack and not be able to breathe." The client is taught how to replace the initial thought with an alternative thought (e.g., "I've had a panic attack before, and have never been unable to breathe").

4. **Symptom induction and interoceptive exposure**—Exposure involves having the client learn the internal cues associated with a feeling of panic. The therapist works with the client using exercises to produce sensations similar to panic. For example, clients might be asked to shake their head from side-to-side for 30 seconds or breathe through a straw for two minutes in order to induce somatic symptoms that occur during a panic attack. Producing these bodily symptoms allows clients to learn that, even if the sensations are present, feared consequences do not occur. Homework exercises might involve running up stairs, watching suspenseful movies, or drinking caffeine to generate similar sensations (without consequences) in a natural setting.

5. **Identification of specific situations that trigger panic and development of alternative or challenging thoughts**—The client lists situations associated with panic and develops a hierarchy from least to most anxiety-arousing for each situation. The client is also taught to challenge the thoughts that maintain the fear in the different situations.

6. **In vivo exposure**—Using the lowest anxiety item in the client's fear hierarchy, the client practices involvement with the fearful situation at least three times a week. The therapist may also encourage the client to perform symptom-induction exercises before exposure to the fearful situation. With each exposure, clients identify and challenge fear-inducing thoughts, use correct breathing exercises, maintain objective focus regarding the situation (e.g., "Okay, I'm in the car and my heart is starting to race"), and rate their level of anxiety. This process increases mastery behavior and reduces escape behavior. The in vivo component is continued for about six to eight sessions.

From Lang & Craske, 2000

anxiety, and (3) having the client imagine these items while in a state of deep muscle relaxation. In the case presented at the beginning of the chapter regarding the 17-year-old woman with the bird phobia, a hierarchy of 12 items regarding birds was developed that ranged from the highest fear ("Touching a large bird") to one that produced only mild anxiety ("Looking out the window and seeing one bird in a tree"). While relaxing, the woman was first asked to imagine the lowest anxiety item. After several repetitions, the item no longer produced anxiety, and the therapist then presented the next item in the hierarchy. This continued until each item no longer produced feelings of anxiety. Desensitization often involves only imagined interactions with the feared objects or situations. However, in this case, the therapists also used *in vivo* (real life) treatment; that is, the client was asked to actually touch feathers and, eventually, a tame parakeet. All tasks were accomplished with the client maintaining relaxation. After five sessions, the client no longer showed anxiety to birds. Desensitization has been an effective treatment for phobias, but has been less successful when used alone to treat another common anxiety disorder, obsessive-compulsive disorder.

Exposure Combined with Response Prevention

Exposure has been found to be effective when combined with *response prevention* (preventing the client from making a particular response when confronted with a stimuli or situation, or from escaping the situation). In the therapeutic approach to obsessive-compulsive disorder, exposure is combined with response prevention. Therapists exposed clients to the object or situation of their fears and prevent them from escaping the situation.

> *Getting dressed in the morning was tough, because I had a routine, and if I didn't follow the routine, I'd get anxious and would have to get dressed again. I always worried that if I didn't do something, my parents were going to die. I'd have these terrible thoughts of harming my parents. That was completely irrational, but the thoughts triggered more anxiety and more senseless behavior. Because of the time I spent on rituals, I was unable to do a lot of things that were important to me.* (National Institute of Mental Health, 2006, p. 5)

The etiology of obsessive-compulsive disorders can be explained by classical conditioning. It is hypothesized that a thought or behavior can become associated with an unpleasant event and that, after several pairings, the thought or behavior can become a conditioned stimulus. Because these actions or thoughts are unpleasant, the individual then develops behaviors or thoughts that help them avoid the initial unpleasant event. These avoidance behaviors are reinforced since they remove the individual from the situation. For example, students may engage in escape activities such as arranging DVDs or CDs over and over again to shield themselves from anxiety over upcoming exams or papers. If this occurs over a long period of time, a compulsive behavior may develop. In treating the problem above, a therapist would have the client bring forth the anxiety-arousing thoughts of harming the parents, and then prevent her from engaging in the ritualistic routines that she believed would negate her thoughts. This process would continue until extinction occurred. Treatments based on exposure and response prevention are empirically supported for obsessive-compulsive disorder.

Operant Conditioning Theory

In a study, researchers gave bananas to two monkeys as a reward for the following behaviors: lifting a paw, holding the paw over the head, and bringing the paw down on the head (i.e., hitting the head with the paw). These behaviors were "shaped" in about 16 minutes. Also, each time a banana was given, the experimenters said "Poor boy! Don't do that! You'll hurt yourself." Because of the association of these comments with a reward, the monkeys began to demonstrate head hitting whenever these words were spoken. (Schaefer, 1970)

As opposed to the involuntary reactions (e.g., sweating, salivating) and emotional responses involved in classical conditioning, *operant conditioning* involves voluntary and consciously controllable behaviors such as walking and talking. Operant conditioning was first formulated by Edward Thorndike (1874–1949; 1911) and further developed by B. F. Skinner (1904–1990; 1953), both of whom developed their behavioral principles based on observations that voluntary behaviors are influenced by events that follow them. *Reinforcers* are anything that increases the frequency or magnitude of a behavior. Notice that the focus is on the *effect* of the stimulus. Teachers have sometimes found that reprimanding a child may actually increase the misbehavior; in such cases, the reprimand is actually functioning as a *positive reinforcer* (something that occurs that *increases* the frequency of the behavior). In the example with the monkeys above, head hitting was produced by the words "Poor boy! Don't do that! You'll hurt yourself" because the monkeys had been given a banana when the words were spoken. A *negative reinforcer* increases the frequency of a behavior by *removing* an aversive event. For example, a student may study for an exam because studying removes the anxiety associated with the upcoming exam. *Extinction* occurs if reinforcement does not follow the behavior; that is, after a period of time, the behavior will no longer occur if the reinforcer is no longer presented. In the case of the monkeys, it is likely that the head hitting disappeared when bananas no longer appeared. *Punishment* reduces the frequency of behavior and involves either the *removal of a positive reinforcer* or the *presentation of an aversive stimulus*. In the case of a misbehaving child, punishment might involve time-out (removal of the child from pleasurable activities) or presentation of a negative consequence, such as requiring the child to do extra chores as a consequence of the misbehavior. Again, it is only a punishment if the frequency of the response decreases. For example, in the situation just mentioned, if a child enjoys helping, asking the child to do extra chores might be a reinforcer rather than a punishment. Interventions based on operant conditioning are used successfully in a variety of counseling situations with children, adolescents, and adults.

Therapeutic Intervention for Depression Based on Lewinsohn's Operant Model

Peter Lewinsohn (1974) developed an operant conditioning model for depression, hypothesizing that the disorder is a result of a reduction in or loss of reinforcements. In Lewinsohn's theory, several variables influence an individual's susceptibility to developing depression. These include:

- The number of reinforcing events in a person's life. When events occur that produce a reduction in the usual level of reinforcement (such as the loss of a loved one or friend, or academic or employment difficulties), the potential for depression increases. The situation may cause an individual to self-label as "depressed," which then leads to more inactivity and even less reinforcement.

- Environmental factors. For example, a change of jobs or move to a new location may produce lower levels of reinforcement than that found in the previous setting, leading to depression.

- The instrumental behaviors of the individual such as their level of social skills or tendency to reach out to others may contribute to depression. Those with deficiencies in interacting with others or in the ability to establish social support systems are more vulnerable to depression.

In line with this perspective, the development of depression generally results from the following pattern: A trigger in the life of an individual, such as a loss or a decrease in reinforcement, results in self-labeling of "depression." The environment is perceived as aversive or no longer as reinforcing as before, so the individual engages in avoidance behaviors such as staying home, not answering the phone, and decreasing social contacts. These avoidance behaviors produce an even larger reduction in positive reinforcements. The individual becomes more depressed, engages in further isolation, and then becomes even more depressed. As the cycle continues, the individual sinks into a deeper and deeper depression. Under this framework, depression can be lifted by teaching or encouraging clients to engage the environment in ways that raise the level of positive reinforcements.

Behavioral activation therapy, a therapy based on principles of operant conditioning and a framework for understanding depression developed by Lewinsohn, utilizes the following steps in therapy. First, the therapist discusses the relationship between depression, activity, and the environment with the client and explains that becoming active again will helps break this pattern. Environmental triggers for the depression are identified. Second, clients describe activities that that might be helpful in lifting their mood. Activities are listed and the client makes a commitment to engage in them. A plan is developed in which the client rates each activity in regards to how pleasurable it was and the degree to which it improved their mood. Third, throughout the therapy, the therapist expresses optimism, understanding, and support regarding the difficulties the client experiences engaging in activities when depressed. The therapist continually stresses the link between *direct activation* (i.e., getting involved in life and activities) and improved mood. This emphasis is very important since individuals with depression often lack the motivation to engage in activities. Fourth, the therapist serves in the role of a coach or consultant who works collaboratively with the client. Behavioral activation therapy has been effective in reducing depression even with severely depressed clients (Dimidjian et al., 2006).

Social Skills Training

> *Philip, an individual with schizophrenia whose psychotic symptoms had been reduced through medication, was actively seeking employment but without success. His therapist asked him about his attire and conversations with prospective employers during job interviews. Philip said he wore the same items that he had on for the session (sweatshirt, exercise pants, head band, and worn sneakers). His description of the job interview demonstrated a lack of conversational skills. (Heinssen & Cuthbert, 2001)*

Social skills training, which involves the teaching of specific skills needed for appropriate social interactions, is an empirically supported therapy for individuals with schizophrenia, attention-deficit-hyperactive disorder (ADHD), and conduct disorder. In their study of individuals with severe mental illness, Heinssen and Cuthbert (2001) found that individuals with schizophrenia displayed "impediments" to obtaining employment or forming social networks because of poor interactional skills, discussion of inappropriate topics, and eccentricities in attire or nonverbal behaviors. They believed that these behaviors could be changed through social skills training and reinforcement for appropriate behavior. The interventions included modeling and use of role-plays to develop interactional skills and discussions regarding choice of attire. For example, Philip, the individual described above, was given feedback about his attire and asked to observe differences in clothing worn by individuals of different occupations. He received training and feedback regarding job interviewing skills and appropriate conversational topics. Following completion of the program, Philip obtained successful employment as a landscape worker, after a successful interview in which he wore a work shirt, blue jeans, and construction boots. Social skills training such as this is widely utilized in a number of different programs that help clients develop appropriate interactions skills.

Assertiveness Training

Assertiveness training is a form of social skills training for individuals who are shy, inhibited in social situations, or who have a hard time making requests or saying no. Assertiveness training usually teaches the difference between *nonassertive behaviors, aggression,* and *assertive responses* (Jakubowski & Lange, 1978) as described below:

- Nonassertiveness—A lack of assertiveness can involve difficulties in (1) expressing one's opinion to others, (2) giving suggestions, (3) correcting others or asking them to change their behavior, (4) accepting compliments, (5) responding to verbal abuse, (6) refusing the requests of others, or (7) standing up for one's rights when feeling intimidated by others. An individual may be nonassertive because they lack the skills to speak up, feel they do not have the right to speak up for themselves, or feel overly concerned about the feelings of others. A lack of assertiveness results in a loss of respect for oneself, lowers self-esteem, and increases the possibility of depression. Friends, family, or colleagues may express frustration when interacting with someone who lacks assertion skills due to the ongoing difficulty understanding what the nonassertive individual wants or how they feel about specific situations.

- Aggression—Some individuals use complaints, sarcasm, and intimidation to get what they want. This sometimes occurs as an overreaction to a situation, as a means of controlling others, or due to the belief that others should always behave according to their wishes. Aggression can substantially inhibit communication since it frequently causes others to feel belittled or attacked.

- Assertiveness—Assertiveness involves the ability to state wishes, feelings, or opinions in a direct and honest fashion and in a manner that also respects the rights of others. Being assertive allows individuals to feel good about themselves and about others. Assertive behavior leads to the development of mutual respect.

When participating in assertiveness training, clients are asked to practice all three types of responses, with the hope that they will come to the realization that being assertive not only benefits them, but also others involved in the interaction. In assertiveness training, role-plays are used to help individuals develop appropriate self-expression and nonverbal skills such as body posture, voice intonations, facial expression, and eye contact. Clients describe difficult, real-life situations and then practice appropriate responses. Clients are taught that there are varying degrees of assertiveness, ranging from very direct forms such as "I need to have this done by 3 p.m." to those that are more interpersonal, such as "I know you are quite busy, but can you prioritize this and get it to me by 3 p.m.?"

Assertion training programs have been helpful for many individuals. As with many social skills training approaches, however, they are based on individualistic Western values and sociocultural aspects are often not considered. Ethnic groups may differ regarding whether a specific behavior would be considered assertive, nonassertive, or aggressive. Additionally, among many ethnic groups, individual rights are perceived as less important than group harmony. In increasing the expressiveness of an individual, the therapist and client should work together to determine if being assertive is, in fact, important for the client and that the client understands the interpersonal consequences of increased assertion. Cultural misunderstanding in communication can occur when therapists impose Western standards on other groups. For example, in one report, an American Indian child was accused of being disrespectful because she did not look directly at her teacher when the teacher spoke to her (Garwick & Auger, 2000). Similarly, shaping was used to increase eye contact in a Navaho girl (Everett, Proctor, & Cortmell, 1989). In both cases, the lack of eye contact was interpreted in a negative fashion, as either a sign of defiance or a deficit in social skills. Among many American Indian tribes and other ethnic minority groups, direct eye contact with authority figures is not considered appropriate. It is essential that the therapist, working in collaboration with the client, determine if the lack of assertion is due to social or cultural values, situational factors, or individual characteristics. In our work with Asian Americans college students (Sue, Ino, & Sue, 1983; Sue, Sue, & Ino, 1990), we found that cultural values do influence assertiveness; students who had the skills to behave assertively in most situations did not do so when interacting with authority figures such as a professor. Thus, this group of students displayed situational nonassertive behavior, most likely influenced by early cultural learning.

We have several suggestions for conducting assertion or social skills training (D. Sue, 1997a). First, it is important to work collaboratively with the client to determine the appropriateness of specific skills training, or the specific behaviors or situations that would be targeted. Are there social and cultural factors that should be considered in terms of nonverbal or verbal expression? Is assertiveness valued within the individual's family, social group, or community? Has the individual considered the consequences on friendships, the family, and the larger community if they were to become more assertive? For example, in our society, assertiveness by women often results in lower social attraction and likeability ratings (Rudman, 1998). We are certainly not saying that women should refrain from being assertive, only that it is important to be aware of possible reactions from others. For clients who come from a hierarchical culture, it would be important to know if assertion to an individual of higher status would be a violation of cultural norms. Second, it is important to explore the roots of the client's lack of assertiveness, considering the possible influence of variables such as family experiences or diversity issues—including sexual orientation, gender, and ethnicity—on assertion. Third, the therapist and client should discuss and role-play different types of assertiveness. In our work with Asian Americans, we found that many understood the importance of being assertive with employers or professors. After realizing that their nonassertive behavior was probably related to cultural values, some made the decision to remain deferential to their parents and within their ethnic community, but also acknowledged the utility of speaking up in class or behaving more assertively when seeking employment. This understanding resulted in more active participation in role-plays during assertiveness training, as well as greater assertion in classroom settings.

Social Learning Theory

In contrast to the strict operant and classical conditioning models, social learning theory focuses on the thought processes involved in learning. In both operant and classical conditioning models, the individual is physically involved in the activity when the learning process occurs. However, social learning theory posits that behaviors can be acquired merely through observation. Bandura and Rosenthal (1966) found that observers who viewed a conditioning experiment in which a subject received a shock that was repeatedly paired with the sound of a buzzer also developed an emotional reaction to the sound. Watching others respond fearfully to a stimulus was enough for them to develop the fear themselves. Thus, it is possible for anxiety and fear reactions to be produced vicariously. Not only that, Bandura (1997) also found that voluntary behaviors can also be learned through observations. In a series of experiments, children exposed to models displaying unique behaviors later demonstrated the very same behavior themselves. These modeling studies led to several conclusions. First, observation of another individual can result in new behavior. Second, watching a model may prompt the observer to engage in the behavior. Third, behaviors that are initially inhibited (perhaps due to social expectations that the behavior not occur) are often performed after a model has been observed engaging in the behavior. Fourth, behaviors may become inhibited if a model is observed being punished for the behaviors. Social learning theory greatly expanded understanding of the ways in which voluntary and involuntary behaviors can be learned. Therapies based on this model have been successful in reducing anxiety and fear reactions and in helping clients learn new behaviors. Bandura (1982) expanded his social learning theory to encompass *self-efficacy,* individuals' belief in their ability to make changes in their environment. No longer were humans seen as merely the subjects of conditioning, but were seen as quite capable of changing their environment. Influence between the individual and the environment became viewed as bidirectional, rather than unidirectional. The focus on such internal processes was further developed by the cognitive theorists.

Cognitive-Behavioral Theory

Cognitive-behavioral therapies in general, and Beckian cognitive therapy in particular, are the fastest growing and most heavily researched orientations on the contemporary scene. The reasons for its current popularity are manifest: cognitive therapy is manualized, relatively brief, extensively evaluated, medication compatible, and problem focused. Let us put it this way: if we were forced to purchase stock in any of the psychotherapy systems, Beck's cognitive therapy would be the blue-chip growth selection for the next five years. (Prochaska & Norcross, 2003, p. 369)

This conclusion by Prochaska and Norcross may be correct. In 2006, Aaron Beck received the $100,000 Lasker Award (often compared to the Nobel Prize) for clinical medical research. Beck was credited for developing the theory and practice of cognitive therapy in the treatment of depression, suicidal behavior, and anxiety disorders, and subjecting the therapy to "unprecedented rigorous tests." Elements of cognitive therapy have been incorporated in nearly all forms of behavior therapy. In addition, while being mainly cognitive in emphasis, most cognitive therapies also contain elements of social skills training, making cognitive-behavioral therapy a more accurate description of the cognitive therapies. A number of therapists have been influential in the development of cognitive therapy, but we will focus on Rational Emotive Behavior Therapy (REBT) as developed by Albert Ellis and Beck's cognitive therapy. Both theorists believe that many disorders of anxiety and mood are the result of specific, maladaptive cognitive patterns. Similarly, they accept the possibility that genetic or early experiences influence susceptibility toward developing distorted thinking.

Rational Emotive Behavior Therapy

Albert Ellis (September 27, 1913–July 24, 2007), the founder of Rational Emotive Behavior Therapy (REBT), conducted therapy and workshops across the country up until his early 90s. He originally practiced psychoanalytic psychotherapy, but found it to be ineffective. He did discover, however, that clients showed more change when he adopted a more active stance. At workshops, Ellis often relates stories of how his own background led to the development of REBT. Ellis described himself as being shy as a young person, to the point that he would delay his entry into the theater until a movie began so he could enter unobserved. As he later noted, "as if I were so important that people would want to look at me." From these experiences of shyness, he began to formulate the idea that it was the thoughts, and not the situations, that were the most important contributors to anxiety.

Assumptions of REBT

According to REBT, emotional distress and psychological disorders are the result of irrational thoughts. Ellis points out that an individual can either have rational or irrational thoughts regarding performance, achievement, or other events. Disturbances occur when one takes a reasonable desire such as "I would very much like to perform well and be approved by others" and then changes it into an "anti-empirically and illogical command" such as "Therefore, I *must* perform well and be approved." This kind of demand or illogical requirement can result in depression, anger, or anxiety. Ellis states, "REBT holds that when people are severely anxious, depressed, enraged, self-downing, or self-pitying, they almost always take their strong preferences for achievements, approval, justice, and comfort and grandiosely elevate them into arrogant, unrealistic commands" (Ellis, 1997, p. 95). Ellis initially described 12 basic irrational beliefs that cause emotional disturbances, but has recently narrowed them into three core beliefs (Ellis, 1999, p. 155).

1. "I must achieve outstandingly well in one or more important respects or I am an inadequate person!"
2. "Other people must treat me fairly and well or they are bad people!"
3. "Conditions must be favorable or else my life is rotten and I can't stand it!"

These core beliefs are irrational. For example, failure to achieve in an area does not mean that an individual is inadequate, but believing it can lead to unhappiness or depression. Ellis believes that we have to change *musts,* or irrational demands, into more rational *preferences.* Failure to achieve a preference (such as performing well or being accepted by others) can lead to feelings of disappointment, frustration, or sadness, but in itself, does not generally develop into an anxiety or mood disorder. So, how do these irrational beliefs develop? Ellis (1993) believes that there is a biological predisposition for some individuals to disturb themselves through irrational thinking and that they learn their musts and irrational beliefs from family members, friends, mass media, religion, and cultural influences.

Ellis's ABC Theory of Human Disturbance

Ellis posits that emotional disturbances are produced by a specific dysfunctional thinking pattern that involves:

A. **Activating Events**—This would include an undesirable event such as not doing well on a test, a breakup in a relationship, or some type of loss.

B. **Beliefs**—Your belief about the event can be either rational (rB) or irrational (iB). Irrational beliefs might involve thoughts such as "How awful that I didn't do well on the exam. My future is ruined," or if a relationship has ended, "This person is the only one for me. I will never be happy with anyone else." A rational belief might be "It's unfortunate I did not do well on the exam; I'll try harder next time," or "Even though breaking up was difficult, there are lots of opportunities for me to meet someone else."

C. **Emotional and Behavioral Consequences**—The consequences of holding on to irrational beliefs are depression and withdrawal. Continuing to believe that your "future is ruined" or that you will "never find happiness with anyone else" produces self-criticism and unhappiness.

In REBT, the therapist identifies and actively disputes or challenges the irrational beliefs. For example, the therapist might ask the client to prove that not doing well on an exam will mean that the individual's future is ruined, or that it is impossible to be happy in another relationship. In therapy, clients learn to dispute the irrational beliefs through logic and by substituting rational thoughts. They are also taught a new and more effective philosophy when encountering problematic situations or events. The following are suggested by Ellis:

> *"When I don't get what I really want (or do get what I greatly dislike), it's a pain in the butt and highly inconvenient. But it's never awful, horrible, or terrible. Just inconvenient!"*

> *"When I fail at important projects, that's bad and disadvantageous. But I am never a bad, rotten person. I make errors and mistakes but I am not what I think, fail, and do. Just a hell of a fallible human!"*

"Other people often will treat me shabbily and unfairly—so they will! They, too, are fallible humans and they have to act badly when they do act badly. I'll never like some of the things they do, but I can bear them and stop whining about them!"

"My life will often be full of hassles and troubles. But I can change what I can change and I can accept—though not like—what I cannot change."

"No matter how bad, uncomfortable, or handicapping my life is, I can practically always find some enjoyments. If I think that way and . . . find them!"

"Absolutic musts won't always kill me and make me thoroughly miserable. But they will help me suffer! I don't have to surrender all my demands on myself, on other people, and on the world. But I'd damned well better!" (Ellis, 1999, p. 97)

Ellis (2000a, b) has been willing to make changes in REBT. In the beginning, he called his therapy rational therapy (RT). Later, acknowledging the importance of emotions on behavior, he changed the name of his therapy to rational emotive therapy (RET), and, finally, to rational emotive behavior therapy (REBT) to acknowledge the importance of behavioral change. His therapy is considered to be at the historical forefront of cognitive therapy and Beck has credited Ellis as having a strong influence on his own theory of emotional disturbances.

Aaron Beck's Cognitive Therapy

Similar to Ellis, Beck had a psychoanalytic background, but became disenchanted with the approach when working with depressed patients. He discovered that it seemed to be clients' cognitions that were important in depression, not repressed anger as predicted by psychoanalytic theory. Beck (1993) gradually came to the view that depression and other emotional disorders were the result of faulty information processing and dysfunctional beliefs. He began to wonder "How does this negative cognitive bias develop?" He concluded that family background and exposure to negative childhood experiences can produce cognitive distortions. For example, one client, Natasha, displayed an arrogant and challenging attitude. In examining childhood contributions, the therapist found out that this behavior developed in childhood as a means of coping with abuse from her mother. Natasha found that when she showed hurt or anger to her mother, she was even more severely punished. Adopting the attitude of not caring helped her maintain self-worth; it was also a means to lessen punishment (Beck, Freeman, & Davis, 2004). In addition to the influence of life experience, Beck believes that certain personality styles and ways of thinking may have evolutionary roots, noting that patterns of behavior shown in childhood often persist to adulthood. Beck acknowledges that mood can also affect cognition, but focuses primarily on changing the client's cognitive processes.

Assumptions of Beck's Cognitive-Behavioral Therapy

Beck and his associates (1979; Robins & Hayes, 1993) believe that each individual responds in a unique way when processing information, and that it is in the interpretation of the incoming data that leads to one's emotional reactions. In his theory, he identifies *schemas, automatic thoughts,* and *cognitive distortions* as the underlying factors in disorders such as anxiety, depression, and personality disorders (Beck, Freeman, & Associates, 1990).

1. **Schemas**—*Schemas* are the cognitive structures that automatically organize and give meaning to information. These are the relatively stable filters through which the individual views the self and the environment. Schemas develop through experience and help facilitate the processing of information by allowing an individual to process incoming stimuli in an efficient manner, as well as deal with issues such as self-evaluation and the perspective of others. Dysfunctional schemas such as "I'm unsuccessful because I'm so inept," "I am helpless," "People are dangerous," or "I'm just an object" result in emotional distress and are revealed in automatic negative thoughts and cognitive distortions. Once activated, schemas act as a lens, and incoming information may be distorted to fit the schema. Schemas are necessary to help an individual process data efficiently. However, dysfunctional schemas can lead to emotional problems. For example, a situation such as giving a speech in front of others may produce an automatic thought such as "I'll look stupid," which comes from an underlying schema of "I'm vulnerable because I'm inept." Sometimes, these negative schemas become quite prominent, producing an even greater systematic bias in interpreting and recalling information or situations; this sequence can result in feelings of anxiety or depression as well as personality disorders.

2. **Automatic thoughts**—These are thoughts that come into a person's mind so automatically that the individual might not even be conscious of their presence or realize that they occur. These thoughts arise when the individual faces situations that fit specific schemas such as "I'll look foolish," or "They will take advantage of me." Individuals may not be aware of the thoughts until the therapist draws their attention to them or when they are asked to reflect on their subjective interpretation of a situation. Whether an individual experiences negative consequences as a result of the automatic thoughts depends on whether the thoughts

are the result of adaptive or maladaptive schemas. Thoughts based on maladaptive schemas can result in psychological symptoms.

3. **Cognitive distortions**—These distortions of thinking can occur when an individual faces an emotionally arousing situation and specific schemas are activated. In such a situation a *cognitive shift* can occur, meaning that a bias in the individual's thought processes, linked to a dysfunctional schema, has been activated. The incoming information is distorted and can result in maladaptive cognitive patterns, which include:

- Dichotomous thoughts—When an individual engages in *dichotomous thinking*, there are no gradations in the way a situation is perceived; only two extreme and diametrically opposed alternatives are considered. Events, choices, or other people are seen as either "good" or "bad," or there is only "success" or "failure."

- Overgeneralization—Sometimes individuals respond to a situation by *overgeneralizing*. They make sweeping exaggerations of situations, responding to a single negative event, such as not doing well on an exam, as an indication that college graduation will be impossible or that they are a total failure.

- Selective abstraction—This occurs when an individual remembers only certain aspects of a situation rather than focusing on all available information or feedback regarding the situation. For example, an individual might focus on minor negative points of a performance review and ignore all positive feedback included in the review.

- Mind-reading—Sometimes individuals assume they know the attitudes of others, even when there is no evidence regarding their assumption. For example, someone might think to themselves, for no logical reason, "I'm sure they thought my ideas were really stupid."

- Personalizing—Some individuals tend to *personalize* problems so that even when events are not under their control, they take responsibility for them. For example, someone who learns that a friend has been taken to the hospital for serious illness might say "If only I had phoned yesterday!"

- Minimizing—*Minimizing* occurs when someone does not take credit for positive experiences or belittles their contribution. For example, someone complimented for their efforts on a large project might think "They would have done just fine, or even better, without me."

Beck's Approach to Cognitive Therapy

The goal of cognitive therapy is to treat cognitive distortions and schemas by having clients become aware of them and to change the negative thoughts and imagery. After this occurs, the focus of therapy is on restructuring the dysfunctional attitudes and beliefs systems that are responsible for the automatic thoughts and the cognitive shifts. For example, individuals who interpret all of their experiences in terms of competence may be processing information based on the schema, "I need to do everything perfectly, otherwise, I'm a failure." If an individual possesses this schema, situations and evaluations of performance are responded to in terms of adequacy, whether or not the situation actually relates to personal competence. The therapist helps clients identify the automatic thoughts, and the cognitive patterns caused by the cognitive shift. They then go through exercises to test the validity of these thoughts and correct the dysfunctional patterns and schemas. Success occurs when the client is able to reevaluate and correct their thinking pattern (Beck et al., 1979). Beck's approach is different from that of Ellis, who directly confronts clients regarding their "irrational" thinking pattern. Beck uses what he terms *collaborative discovery,* working together with clients to help them discover for themselves the distortions in their thinking processes. In the next chapter, we will fully present Beck's method of treating depression.

Research on Cognitive-Behavioral Therapies

Because of the focus on objective measures and outcome, the cognitive-behavioral therapies (which include social learning, operant and classical conditioning, and the cognitive approaches) are highly researched and predominate over other theoretical approaches on the list of empirically supported psychological interventions (Chambless & Ollendick, 2001). The cognitive-behavioral therapies include a number of specific treatments such as relaxation training, modeling, exposure, relapse prevention, stress inoculation, dialectic behavior therapy, and behavioral family therapy, all of which are empirically supported treatments. In a meta-analysis regarding rational emotive behavior therapy (REBT), Lyons and Woods (1992) concluded that REBT is "an effective form of therapy" (p. 20). Although REBT has been highly researched, however, none of the research studies have met the rigorous standards necessary for it to be designated as an empirically supported therapy. For the purposes of this text, we consider REBT to be an evidence-based therapeutic approach because of the large number of research studies supporting its effectiveness. As we mentioned earlier, most cognitive-behavioral therapies include components based on operant and classical conditioning, as well as elements in their treatment. Beck (1979) employs behavioral techniques in his cognitive therapy for depressed clients, such as assertiveness training, role-playing, and requesting that clients engage in homework activities. Beck's cognitive-behavioral therapy is an empirically supported approach for anxiety disorders, panic disorder, posttraumatic stress disorder, and depression. Beck has also recently formulated a treatment for borderline personality disorder (Beck, Freeman, & Davis, 2004).

Although there is research support for the cognitive-behavioral therapies, Mineka and Zinbarg (2006) criticize the behavioral/learning approaches regarding the etiology of anxiety disorders for being simplistic. They point out that not everyone exposed to a frightening or traumatic event develops a phobia or posttraumatic stress disorder. They emphasize that a number of other factors can contribute to or insulate an individual from anxiety disorders including: genetics; nontraumatic experiences with situations or objects (for example, an individual who has had successful contact with dogs may be less likely to develop a phobia when encountering a frightening experience with a dog); experience with others who are nonfearful when facing potentially anxiety-arousing situations; or the type or degree of support received after facing a traumatic or frightening event. Thus, a number of variables should be considered in any etiological theory.

Cognitive-behavioral therapies have also been criticized for focusing more on techniques than on the therapeutic alliance. Although therapist communication skills are seen as important, they are often considered merely a means of obtaining greater client compliance for therapeutic activities (Barlow, 2004). A number of studies do, however, discuss and support the importance of the therapeutic alliance in cognitive-behavioral therapy (Huppert et al., 2001; Ryan & Gizynski, 1990; Svensson & Hansson, 1999) and there is recognition that manualized formats may hamper relationship development (Malik, Beutler, Alimohamed, Gallagher-Thompson, & Thompson, 2003). The therapist-client relationship does appear to have an influence on outcome separate from technique, and has been found to be more influential on therapy outcome than strict adherence to manualized cognitive therapy (Castonguay et al., 1996). Beck (1967), however, has always stressed the importance of a collaborative and empathetic relationship with clients and the need to be aware of transference reactions when working with difficult clients. He describes this relationship as *collaborative empiricism,* whereby the therapist and client work together to establish goals, set the agenda for each therapy session, and jointly design experiments to test out the client's automatic thoughts and beliefs.

As with other forms of therapy, ruptures can occur in the relationship between therapist and client. In cognitive-behavioral therapy, the standard approach to dealing with the issue of ruptures is to increase adherence to cognitive techniques, trying to persuade the client of the validity of the therapeutic approach, and dealing with any negative reactions or concerns that the client is expressing as distorted thoughts that need to be challenged. As you might imagine, such approaches can cause the therapeutic relationship to deteriorate and subsequently interfere with client change. Instead, Castonguay et al. (2004) suggest using procedures developed from the humanistic therapies including:

- Inviting the client to explore the rupture
- Listening carefully and empathetically to the client concerns
- Paraphrasing the client's negative comments or feelings about the therapist or the therapy
- Inquiring in a gentle fashion about the client's negative feelings
- Disarming the criticisms by finding some truth in the client's comments

Cognitive-behavioral therapy is moving beyond the simple application of techniques by acknowledging and incorporating therapist-client alliance research, and by defining client characteristics that may influence successful treatment outcome.

Diversity Issues with Cognitive-Behavioral Therapy

The cognitive-behavioral therapies have been criticized due to their focus on setting goals and making changes without consideration of environmental, social, and cultural factors. Another concern is the emphasis on techniques rather than the importance of therapist attitudes, values, and beliefs, and the way they interact with client values and beliefs. However, within the cognitive-behavioral field, there is an increasing recognition of the influence of person-environment dynamics. For example, Ellis (2000a) acknowledges the necessity of not only working to change an individual's musts and demands, but also the importance of assisting clients in their fight against an "unfair and irrational system." This focus on social conditions that play a role in producing psychological discomfort is a major step forward. It is our strong belief that clinicians who focus on the development of social skills and cognitive strategies should always incorporate information from careful and comprehensive assessment (as outlined in Chapter 4) and include contextual issues regarding familial, cultural, and societal influences. It is essential for therapists to be open to the possibility that automatic and irrational thoughts displayed by a client are, in fact, the result of racism, prejudice, or discrimination. If this is the case, it is important to focus on acknowledging these environmental influences and the need for advocacy for systems change. As we mentioned earlier, cultural considerations, including possible modifications of goals or techniques, are important when employing cognitive-behavioral approaches when working with ethnic minorities.

We thought it would be helpful to describe some of the modifications made by Organista (2000) when using cognitive-behavioral strategies with low-income Latinos suffering from depression:

Engagement Strategies—Because of the value of *personalismo* (personal relationships) within the Latino culture, the first sessions involved relationship building. Time was allotted for *presentaciones* (introductions), during which some personal information was exchanged between the therapist and the client. Clients received information about depression and the CBT model of treatment. They were asked about their experience regarding depression, how it affected their activities, and about some of their thoughts when feeling depressed. Some of the common themes discussed included marital and family conflict, problems with children, acculturation difficulties, culture shock, and discrimination.

Activity Schedules—In the treatment of depression, a common recommendation is for clients to take some time off for themselves, in order to put some focus on their own needs. This idea may run counter to the Latino values of connectedness and putting the needs of the family ahead of oneself. Therefore, instead of solitary activities, clients chose social activities they found enjoyable such as family outings, taking children to the park, or visiting with neighbors. Additionally, recognizing the income status of the clients and the potential impact of financial pressure, activities were encouraged that were affordable or free.

Assertiveness Training—When conducting assertiveness training, therapists recognized the cultural value of being polite and nonconfrontational. Additionally, culturally expected behavior based on status issues (such as the age and gender of the clients and the persons with whom they would be communicating) were taken into consideration. Bicultural clients were able to describe the importance of assertiveness in mainstream American activities. Latino values that are in opposition to assertiveness were discussed, as well as strategies to deal with spouses or higher status individuals. Culturally acceptable ways of expressing assertiveness were developed, such as prefacing statements with *con todo respecto* (with all due respect) and *me permite expresar mis sentimientos*? (Is it okay if I express my feelings?)

Cognitive Restructuring—Rather than labeling thoughts that can reduce or increase depression as rational or irrational, the terms "helpful thoughts" and "unhelpful thoughts" were used. "Helpful thoughts" were developed for different stressful situations and were reinforced. For example, because many of the participants were Catholic, the saying *Ayundate, que Dios te ayudara* (similar to the saying "God helps those who help themselves") was used to assist in behavioral assignments.

Organista believes that this approach was responsible for a reduced dropout rate and better outcome among this group of low-income Latino clients. Similar suggestions on modifying cognitive-behavioral approaches for ethnically different populations have been made by Lin (2002). We believe that such modifications will result in better treatment for ethnically diverse populations.

Cognitive-Behavioral Therapy for Depression

12

Chapter

The 2006 Lasker Award for Clinical Research was given to Aaron Beck "for the development of cognitive therapy, which has transformed the understanding and treatment of many psychiatric conditions, including depression, suicidal behavior, generalized anxiety, panic attacks, and eating disorders."

The National Academy of Sciences (1997) recognized Aaron Beck, stating "You have almost single-handedly restored the relevance of psychotherapy. Your cognitive therapy is the fastest growing form of psychotherapy and has influenced the treatment of psychiatric disorders throughout the world."

Aaron Beck was named in the American Psychologist (1989) as one of the five most influential psychotherapists of all time. (American Psychologist, 1989)

Aaron Beck is a psychiatrist and a Professor Emeritus of Psychiatry at the University of Pennsylvania School of Medicine. He has received numerous awards for his work in cognitive-behavioral therapy. He began his career first as a neurologist and then as a psychoanalyst, conducting research to validate psychodynamic formulations for depression. He was testing the proposition that depression was the result of anger turned inward, manifested in a "need to suffer." However, his research did not support this hypothesis. He found that depressed individuals sought approval and acceptance from others and avoided behaviors that might lead to rejection. The conflict between the clinical hypothesis derived from psychoanalysis and his research findings forced an "agonizing reappraisal" of Beck's belief system. This led Beck to search for an explanation regarding the reasons depressed individuals engage in self-criticism and have such a negative outlook on life (Beck et al., 1979). Through his research and clinical work with depressed clients, Beck came to the conclusion that many mental disorders, including depression, were the result of dysfunctional thinking and cognitive structures, which he later called *schema* or basic beliefs. He discovered that interventions to change thoughts were effective in alleviating depression as well as other emotional disorders. During a joint appearance with Albert Ellis at the American Psychological Association conference in 2000, Beck stated, ". . . the cause of dysfunctional behavior is dysfunctional thinking . . . Thinking processes are shaped by underlying beliefs. Situations are interpreted according to basic beliefs and acted on accordingly. If beliefs do not change," he said, "there is no improvement. If beliefs change, symptoms change. Beliefs function as little operational units" (Fenichel, 2000).

On the basis of his clinical work and research, Beck included several important components with his therapy. First, strategies to identify and change each dysfunctional schema were developed. Second, he introduced the concept of *collaborative empiricism,* through which clients could test out distorted thoughts by engaging in behavioral experiments. These were conducted during homework assignments and were considered to be extended self-therapy. Third, principles and techniques from behavior therapy were incorporated, including behavioral activity assignments. Fourth, although cognitive-behavioral therapy (CBT) is thought to focus only on cognitions and behaviors, Beck's approach emphasizes the importance of therapist qualities and establishing a collaborative relationship with the client. In this chapter, we will give a brief account of Beck's theory regarding depression, describe his approach in therapy, and conclude with an evaluation of CBT and its use with diverse populations. We will focus primarily on the treatment strategies of Beck's approach, since his theory was also discussed in Chapter 11. For this overview, we have relied on material from the following books: *Cognitive Therapy of Depression* (1979) by Beck, Rush, Shaw, and Emery; *Cognitive Therapy of Personality Disorders* by Beck, Freeman, Davis, and associates (2004); and *Essential Components of Cognitive-Behavioral Therapy for Depression* by Persons, Davidson, and Tompkins (2001).

Beck's Theory of Depression

Beck and associates (Beck, Freeman et al., 1990) believe that innate factors render some individuals more vulnerable to depression. These biological influences affect the structures underlying cognitive processing, affect, and motivation. In support of this view, Beck cites the research of Kagan (1989), which shows that emotional behaviors such as shyness, anxiety, fear, or other emotional qualities observed in a child often persist into adulthood. These tendencies or vulnerabilities can become strengthened or weakened during interaction with experiences or environmental conditions (the *diathesis-stress model*). For example, some individuals may be predisposed to respond to common childhood rejection experiences with intense emotion and "catastrophic beliefs" regarding the events. They may develop a negative self-image and believe that they are unlovable. If repeated exposure to rejection during a vulnerable childhood period occurs, the beliefs may be structuralized into a schema, a persistent pattern of thinking or believing. In the following example, childhood experiences are believed to have led to the development of dysfunctional beliefs.

> *A 64-year-old divorced Caucasian woman suffering from depression reported a long history of interpersonal problems. She lacked confidence, had low self-esteem, and felt that others took advantage of her. During her childhood, her parents divorced; she first lived with her mother, who constantly demeaned her and later abandoned her and her sister. The father gained custody and generally ignored the client. Later he remarried and she was abused by her stepmother. The father did nothing during the abuse. She felt unwanted. The client also had conflicts with her older sister, who she described as "promiscuous." Her sister often had sex with boyfriends in the house when the parents were not at home and would brag to her about her sexual prowess. Her sister had an affair with the client's first husband and married him after they divorced. The client remarried and was also abused by her second husband. The client never confronted her parents, sister, or husbands in terms of the pain they had caused her. (Allen et al., 2006)*

In developing a cognitive-behavioral formulation of this case, possible thoughts, core beliefs, and behavioral consequences were hypothesized. Because the client had been referred to a psychiatrist, thoughts such as "I cannot handle my emotions by myself" or "I am weak" might occur. It is also possible that because her sister stole her first husband she might think, "I am not attractive" or "I cannot stand up to my sister." The tendency toward developing these cognitions may have been a result of rejection experiences from her mother, father, or sister, combined with innate vulnerabilities. These beliefs would then lead to conditional beliefs such as "It is better that I do not speak up" and "Good things should not be expected." Behaviors such as not confronting others about their hurtful actions or accepting abusive relationships stem from initial core and conditional beliefs. Thus, the client was unable to confront her parents, sister, or others who had abused her, and her subsequent depression was a consequence of these core beliefs (Allen et al., 2006).

A schema, or core belief, is an underlying cognitive structure that allows individuals to automatically process information about themselves, others, and events. If an individual has a rejection schema, situations such as missing a bus, dealing with an unfriendly salesperson, or differences in opinion with a friend may be interpreted as signs of rejection. Incoming information is often distorted so that it can fit within a particular schema. Schema are not conscious, but can be identified through introspection and are similar to the irrational beliefs in rational emotive therapy (RET). During an APA meeting,

Beck was asked how to identify core beliefs and how could they be dealt with. He said they are evaluated by looking at distortions on the surface level, such as "nobody respects me" or "my family hates me" and then "working your way down" to the underlying core beliefs, such as "I am worthless." To counter the core beliefs, clients need to ask themselves, "What is the evidence?" in regard to each schema they identify (Fenichel, 2000).

Each schema has specific qualities. They are activated by major (e.g., death or loss) or minor (e.g., criticism) external events. They are difficult to alter, since the individual is more likely to notice or remember information consistent with or distorted to fit the schema. A schema can be narrow or broad and can differ in degree of rigidity. When an individual is depressed, a negative schema is more readily triggered; this results in even greater systematic negative bias in interpreting information. The identification of schema can be accomplished through examining the rules clients live by and the statements they make regarding themselves and their life situations. Recognizing surface (conscious) feelings of inadequacy can lead to the identification of core beliefs. Statements by a client regarding deficiencies or inadequacies can also provide information about an underlying schema. Beck indicates that it is important for clinicians to determine the accuracy of negative statements made by a client. If they respond by making a statement such as "I failed completely when I tried to ask Lynn out for a date," the clinician must determine if there is accuracy to the statement, such as an individual lacking in social skills or possessing an abrasive personality. In addition, we believe it is important to determine if there are familial, social, or cultural factors that contribute to the client's beliefs. Generally, schemas become apparent when the client is severely depressed and makes statements such as "I am worthless as a human being" or "I am no good for anyone" (Beck et al., 1979). After a client's core beliefs are identified, the therapist and client proceed with case formulation and the development of interventions.

Components of Cognitive-Behavioral Therapy for Depression

In treating depression, CBT is usually conducted through a course of 15 to 20 sessions. We will begin our discussion with the alliance-building techniques utilized in cognitive-behavioral therapy, followed by behavioral activities and cognitive interventions, with particular emphasis on the approach used by Beck (Beck, 1979; Persons et al., 2001).

Therapist-Client Alliance

According to Beck and colleagues (1979), the therapeutic relationship is necessary, but not sufficient (in most cases) for producing a good outcome in therapy. As with the characteristics considered important with humanistic therapies, Beck believes that the therapist should demonstrate concern, empathy, and acceptance in work with clients, and cautions against being enamored with techniques and forgetting the importance of the therapist-client relationship. The therapist should show warmth and caring for the client and understand the perspective of the client through accurate empathy. Rapport is crucial, since it reassures clients that the therapist is tuned into their feelings. Therapists should be able to mesh their style with that of their clients. These alliance-building behaviors help engage the client in both participating and collaborating in the therapy process. Therapists and clients need to work together to determine client views of the world, evaluate the accuracy of client beliefs, and identify dysfunctional beliefs.

Collaborative Empiricism

As a team, the therapist and client are continually interacting in the process of gathering and analyzing data, determining negative thoughts, and assessing the accuracy of client interpretations. Beck refers to this process as *collaborative empiricism*. After obtaining data about the client's patterns of thinking, the environmental events that activate the beliefs are identified. Behavioral experiments (in the form of homework assignments) are devised jointly in order to test out assumptions underlying the client's beliefs. Hypotheses are generated and evaluated by the client. The therapist and client may analyze the experiments using the following questions: Is the data obtained from the assignment supportive of the client's beliefs (e.g., "nobody likes me")? Would an "objective observer" have evaluated the situation in the same manner as the client?

Guided Discovery

Beck, Freeman, and associates (1990) suggest inducing a sense of adventure into the therapy process as clients work to discover the origins of their dysfunctional beliefs. Turning the search into a puzzle engages the client in a way that makes the task both enjoyable and educational. Guided discovery allows clients to become more independent in seeking explanations for their difficulties. A client may make a statement to the therapist such as, "I feel so depressed today. Why?" Instead of furnishing an answer, the therapist can ask, "When were you first aware of feeling depressed? Was anything happening at that time? What were the thoughts that you had when you started feeling depressed?" Using questions such as these and varying the format in order to avoid redundancy helps clients arrive at their own understanding of the thoughts and beliefs that affect their emotional state.

Impediments to Collaboration

When difficulties in collaboration arise, the blame is often placed on the client, and the problem is labeled "resistance." These problems can be conceptualized in a more productive manner, with a focus on employing strategies that will enhance the working alliance between therapist and client. Beck, Freeman, and associates (1990) suggest that therapists consider the following when there appear to be difficulties in collaboration:

- Some clients may not have the skills needed for collaboration. In these circumstances, the therapist can teach the client the appropriate skills. Lack of skills can also prevent the client from completing homework assignments.

- The therapist may lack the skills for collaboration or in dealing with specific client populations. In these circumstances, the therapist should enhance his or her skills through workshops and should consult with colleagues.

- Environmental conditions may not be conducive to client change, or may reinforce dysfunctional behavior. Family members or friends may give the client direct or indirect messages that discourage change. They may also not be supportive of psychotherapy. If this is the case, it may be necessary to attempt to directly obtain the cooperation of family members or friends or work with the client to decrease their influence.

- Poor understanding of how the CBT model explains and treats depression can also hinder therapy. In this case, the therapist needs to take the time to reeducate the client about how depression is conceptualized in the CBT model and how this relates to treatment strategies and goals. CBT is generally not successful until clients understand the model and how problematic beliefs underlie their depression.

Additional problems that can occur when using cognitive-behavioral therapy are discussed in Table 12.1.

Assessment

Prior to the onset of therapy sessions, intake interviews, assessment, and diagnostic evaluations are conducted. Beck uses measures such as an intake questionnaire, the Beck Depression Inventory, and the Mental Status Exam. These provide information regarding the client's suitability for treatment using cognitive-behavioral therapy. If the client is suicidal, protocols for assessment and intervention such as those discussed in Chapter 15 should be followed.

Table 12.1 **Common Difficulties Encountered by Therapists New to Cognitive-Behavioral Therapy for Depression**

1. Some therapists minimize the importance of the therapeutic alliance. Because CBT is an empirically supported therapy, they may place emphasis on techniques rather than client-therapist interactions. It is important for clinicians to understand that depressed individuals often have difficulty communicating and demonstrate hypersensitivity to rejection. For CBT to be effective, the therapist must focus on the relationship, adopting a style that demonstrates empathy and that meshes with the needs of the client.

2. Some clinicians apply CBT in a rigid manner, model the approach of "expert" therapists too closely, or are too cautious in their use of the therapy. It is important for therapists new to this approach to acknowledge their own style, characteristics, and strengths, and to mesh these with the techniques they are learning. It is important not to be too stiff or too cautious about doing things the wrong way.

3. Therapists may have a simplistic view of CBT, believing that all that is needed for success in therapy is to teach clients to recognize the relationship between thoughts, emotions, and behaviors. It is important for those using the CBT approach to have a thorough grounding in cognitive-behavioral theory and in the use of techniques such as Socratic questioning, behavioral empiricism, and therapeutic collaboration.

4. It is important not to approach clients in an overly didactic manner. Use of questions is important to engage clients in the therapy process, but not to moralize or point out errors in the clients' thinking. Questions should be asked in a way that helps clients increase introspection and begin to independently self-question and test out hypotheses. Therapy is most successful when clients are truly involved in the process of discovery and healthy empiricism. Therapists should adopt a gentle, psychoeducational approach (rather than an "expert" approach) when helping clients identify schema or when introducing homework or other behavioral activities.

5. Therapists and clients may fall into the trap of being overly superficial when identifying thoughts and beliefs. It is important to understand automatic thoughts in terms of the totality of meaning, not just as they relate to one specific situation or experience. Reflection and insight regarding the consequences of the belief in regards to the client's life and future is what makes the process meaningful.

6. It is sometimes difficult for clinicians not to react negatively to depressed clients. Individuals who are depressed often lack energy, feel hopeless, and may be difficult to engage. Instead of characterizing a client as resistant, therapists need to be persistent in working with the client to determine the underlying beliefs and reasons for depression.

7. Sometimes clients indicate intellectual understanding of the thought-feeling-behavior connection, but report that this insight is not helping them change the way they are feeling. In this situation, the client may be saying that the therapist is correct, but are thinking "so what?" They do not yet understand the value of the information in terms of decreasing depression, and so they don't place much value on the information. They may have more confidence in their beliefs about themselves than in what the therapist is saying. Spending additional time explaining the rationale for CBT is essential in a situation such as this.

Source: Beck, Rush, Shaw, & Emery (1979).

Because of the individualistic focus of CBT, we recommend that you also consider using the broader questions recommended in our discussion of assessment in Chapter 4. For all clients, it is important to determine the client's perspective of the problem. This can be done by asking questions suggested by Dowdy (2000):

- What do you think is causing your problem?
- Why is this happening to you?
- What have you done to treat this condition?
- Where else have you sought treatment?
- How has this condition affected your
- How can I help you?

In addition to determining the core beliefs held by the client, the clinician must determine whether these beliefs have an actual basis, perhaps due to the client's behavior or attitude, or because of societal or family messages. For example, gay men and lesbians may receive messages from society that they are defective or abnormal. Exposure to heterosexist or racist attitudes can produce beliefs (e.g., "I am defective" or "If only I weren't . . .") that are continually reinforced in society. In these cases, the therapist must help the client identify the source of his or her beliefs rather than to personalize them. In other situations, the therapist can evaluate the suitability of CBT with diverse clients by determining if this model fits the client's perception of the problem and appropriate interventions. Even mainstream clients may not buy into the cognitive model and, unless this is resolved, therapy will be unsuccessful. The initial interview is very important since the therapist is presenting the model of therapy to the client. Beck describes this process as "socialization for therapy."

Initial Interview and Introduction to CBT

Beck and colleagues (1979) outline the initial interview and the manner in which the CBT model can be explained to clients. The initial session begins by using common therapist responses, such as "What concerns are bringing you in today?" or "What are your feelings about coming in today?" If an emotion such as anxiety or fear is expressed, the therapist may ask the person to further explain his or her thinking with an inquiry such as "What are you thinking of when you feel . . . ?" The manner of presenting these inquiries is varied so that the questioning does not become redundant. The clinician can also ask "I wonder if you are thinking about something when you start to feel . . . ?" Instead of reflecting feeling back to a client, the clinician uses the phrasing "you believe" instead of "you feel." For example, a therapist might say "It sounds like your anxiety starts when you believe people around you are evaluating you" or "So, when you believe people around you don't care about you, you start to feel depressed." Again, this phrasing connects thoughts with feelings. This connection is presented gently rather than in an argumentative manner. It is important to determine the client's receptivity to a focus on cognitions. Ideally, the client will eventually begin to identify the thoughts associated with feelings on their own. This process of helping the client connect thoughts and feeling helps the therapist and client identify automatic thoughts or beliefs and opens the way for collaborative empiricism.

During the first session, the pretreatment therapy address includes an explanation of the cognitive approach to depression and prepares the client for fluctuations in depression levels during treatment. Explanations and examples demonstrating the relationship between thoughts and feelings can be adapted to fit the psychological sophistication, age, and other characteristics of the client. A short statement such as this may be effective:

> *"The approach that I use in work with clients who have problems such as depression is called cognitive-behavioral therapy. Have you heard of it? It's a very useful method that involves identifying the reasons for your problems and then treating them. During this process, we will work together to find out what it is about yourself or situations in your life that is so bothersome to you. From there, we can develop strategies to cope with the stress you're feeling and use the same strategies to prevent or minimize future feelings of depression. Our method will become clearer as we begin the therapy. Do you have any questions?"*

To promote further understanding of cognitive-behavioral therapy, Beck asks clients to read the pamphlet "Coping with Depression" (Beck & Greenberg, 1974), which gives everyday examples of the relationship between feelings and thoughts. We have also had clients read "You Can Change the Way You Feel," a chapter from *The Feeling Good Handbook* (Burns, 1999), another excellent and easily readable resource on cognitive-behavioral strategies. This would constitute the first homework assignment. In addition to doing readings such as these, the homework can be expanded by asking clients to write down questions or to give their reactions to the readings. As with any assignment, it is important to determine the client's reactions to the homework. Having the material available for the client enhances the chances for compliance as does informing clients that a part of the next session will be devoted to discussing their reactions to the readings.

Another component of the first session is discussing the client's expectations regarding treatment. The therapist should indicate that depressive feelings often do not change quickly, but that depression is a treatable condition, especially with cognitive-behavioral therapy. The client is made aware that he or she will likely experience emotional ups and downs during the course of treatment. Drops in mood can be distressing, especially when they follow gains made in previous sessions. It is explained that these can be due to the natural course of depression or caused by external events. The down periods can be portrayed in a positive manner by emphasizing that these downswings allow individuals to obtain information that will help them understand the causes of their depressed mood and changes in their mood. In addition, different strategies to deal with depression can be tested out during this period. This explanation allows clients to understand the uneven course of depression, thus reducing discouragement (Beck et al., 1979).

In CBT, the rationale and specifics of each step of the treatment, each intervention, and each homework assignment are explained in detail to the client. Only by understanding and agreeing with the process can client collaboration be achieved. During the first session, clients help the therapist select the symptoms they would like to address. These might include depressive feelings, behavioral disturbances (e.g., eating, sleeping, social withdrawal), or cognitive difficulties (e.g., reduced concentration). The target symptoms chosen are often those that are the most distressing to the client. Of those symptoms, the ones that are the most amenable to change are addressed first. With the help of the client, behavioral and/or cognitive intervention strategies are then developed.

The goal of the first session is to provide some relief to the client with respect to his or her depressive thoughts and feelings. In doing so, the client develops confidence in the approach and rapport is more easily formed. One way of providing relief is for the therapist to empathetically demonstrate an understanding of the client's distress. For example, in the case discussed at the beginning of this chapter, the therapist might state, "Because of the abuse and rejection you experienced from your mother and father and the actions of your sister, it is understandable why you are feeling depressed. This is something we can work on together." By providing an understanding of the client's problems and possible strategies for treating the problem, hope and confidence is increased.

During the session, the therapist should offer summaries of the information provided by the client and should ask, "Is this an accurate account of what we have covered so far? Do you have anything to add or any reactions?" These summaries should further emphasize the relationship between his or her depressive feelings, thoughts, and behaviors. "So, you find that there are days when you keep thinking 'This all seems so hopeless,' and you find this kind of thinking increases your feelings of depression." The summaries help maintain the collaborative emphasis in therapy and also allow clients to see the perspective of the therapist in regard to the problem. They can also serve as a model to prime clients to be able to analyze their own problems in a similar fashion.

Near the end of the session, the therapist might say, "We have about 15 minutes left in the session and we still need to discuss the homework assignment. Do you have any further questions regarding the session?" The homework assignment is discussed and worked on collaboratively. Assignments selected are specific and concrete, tied into the session work, and are considered both important and doable by the client. The clinician can anticipate possible obstacles by asking, "Is there anything that would prevent you from completing your homework assignment by the next session?" If an obstacle is mentioned, the therapist might ask, "Is there some way that you would still be able to complete the homework?" This inquiry should occur with all homework assignments, so the therapist and client can work together to develop alternative means to complete the assignment if obstacles arise. This allows clients to gain more independence and increase their problem-solving skills. We would also recommend practicing components of the homework in the session and discussing when, where, and how they will perform the homework assignments. It is often helpful to write down the assignment in the session and assign clients to write some brief reflections on the completed assignment.

The Structure and Format of Ongoing CBT Sessions

Cognitive-behavioral sessions are quite structured and generally follow a similar pattern (Persons, Davidson, & Tompkins, 2001). The importance of the format can be explained to the client in the following manner, "In working with depression, we have found that the following components help make therapy more effective. We will first spend a few minutes on finding out how your week went. I would like to know if you had any emotional ups and downs or important situations that we need to discuss further. Then we will look at your homework assignment and the completion of forms. After this, we'll decide together what to focus on today. Do you have any questions or comments? Okay, let's come up with a list of items to work on today."

Check-In

After this explanation, the clinician uses the "check-in" to: (a) find out how the week went, focusing on significant events, current mood, and any positive or negative changes since the previous therapy session, (b) review the outcome of the homework assignments and completed forms, and (c) set the agenda. A maximum of 10 minutes is set aside for the check-in routine. If more time is required, it can be added as an agenda item. The check-in process allows for personal discussion with the client and helps maintain the therapeutic alliance. It is important to keep the check-in separate from the rest of the session.

Problems can occur if the check-in process is allowed to consume too much of the session. If this occurs, it is important to consider if the client is using this period for complaining or venting emotions. It is also possible that the therapist may feel helpless in limiting the duration of the check-in or has poor time management skills. Persons et al. (2001) make several suggestions regarding the effective use of the check-in time. If the problem is arising from the client venting or complaining, the therapist might make a statement such as "What happened was very hurtful for you and it seems you are blaming yourself. That sort of thinking seems to lead you to feeling more sad and withdrawn. It's clear you want to change that pattern so you can change start to feel better." This approach is similar to Dialectical Behavior Therapy, an approach we will discuss in the next chapter, in that the client's feelings are accepted, but the need for change is also communicated. Whenever possible, the clinician identifies and makes use of statements linking cognitions that are associated with the events discussed. Another strategy is to say, "You really seem to need to get your frustrations out today! Why don't we spend about 5 minutes on this and, if necessary, we can add this situation to our agenda items?" It may be beneficial to ask the client if the venting helped. If the client says "yes," the therapist can respond by saying, "It's helpful for some people to vent when emotions build up." If the client says, "no," the therapist can help the client move toward a problem-solving mode by saying, "Venting often brings only brief relief and does not change the reason you are upset." If poor time management appears to be interfering with the efficiency of the check-in period, using a timer or taking turns being the timekeeper may be a helpful strategy to keep to the 10-minute time limit (Persons et al., 2001).

Setting the Agenda

The therapist and client collaboratively develop a list of topics that will be worked on during the session. These items can be arranged in importance and may include suicidal thoughts (which should always be assessed and addressed), current life situations that are causing distress, therapy-interfering behaviors, and behavioral and cognitive intervention strategies to help with current depressive symptoms. The previous week's homework assignment is always one of the first items on the agenda. The therapist helps make sure that the agenda items are not extraneous but are, in fact, related to the client's problem and stated goals. It is important that goals and homework assignments are both doable and concrete. If necessary, goals or skills can be broken down into easier, more achievable steps. The therapist takes note of the topics that will be addressed in the session, making sure that homework and session evaluation are included in the agenda.

Behavioral Activities

Beck uses behavioral activities as an integral part of cognitive-behavioral therapy, and believes that it is especially important with severely depressed clients. Beck and colleagues (1979) use a number of behavioral activities with depressed clients. These include a Weekly Activity Schedule (a log used to document activities), a Mastery and Pleasure Schedule (in which the client rates various activities in which they are engaged), and a Graded Task Assignment (which identifies gradual steps to reach identified goals). See Table 12.2 for a representation of a weekly activity schedule combined with a mastery and pleasure schedule.

This form allows the therapist and client to determine the level of activity that the client engages in during the week and also the degree to which he or she feels a sense of pleasure or mastery after completing the activities. A rating scale from 0 to 5 is used, with zero indicating no mastery or pleasure and 5 indicating a feeling of complete mastery or pleasure. The therapist can give the client a rationale for completing the schedule, such as:

> *"People who are depressed often withdraw, do less, and find less pleasure or feelings of accomplishment with activities. Have you found this to be true? It is important to find out what you are doing during the week and which activities are the most enjoyable for you. Even when depressed, people will find some things that are especially interesting to them or that give them stronger feelings of mastery than others. Here's a copy of the schedule that I'd like you to fill out. Just write down the activity in the correct space and give it a rating from 0 to 5. As an example, it is currently 3:26 PM and you are in therapy. If you write down therapy in the 3 to 4 space for Tuesday, what would be the rating you would give to this activity? I'm very much interested in differences in ratings between different activities, so really try to determine how much of a sense of accomplishment or mastery and pleasure you derive from them. This form also allows us to list activities that might be helpful for you to do during the week and to rate them. Do you have any questions?"*

This schedule is used each session. In addition to gathering data that can be used in therapy and in planning interventions, it allows the therapist to encourage the client to try out different activities. With the help of the client, a list of activities that the client agrees to engage in during the week is developed. It is important to start off with small steps. The Graded Task Assignment sheet breaks larger tasks into discrete events, allowing for a step-by-step ap-

Table 12.2 **Form for Clients to Record Weekly Activities and Mastery or Pleasure Associated with Each Activity**

Weekly Activity and Mastery Pleasure Schedule

Write down activities you engaged in during each time period, each day of the week, and rate each activity on a scale of 0 to 5, with 0 = no pleasure or mastery to 5 = complete mastery or pleasure. Place the rating after each activity. We will sometimes decide on new activities for you to try out that you will also rate.

	Mon	Tues	Wed	Thurs	Fri	Sat	Sun
7–9 A.M.							
9–10 A.M.							
10–11 A.M.							
11–12 A.M.							
12–1 P.M.							
1–2 P.M.							
2–3 P.M.							
3–4 P.M.							
4–5 P.M.							
5–6 P.M.							
6–7 P.M.							
7–8 P.M.							
8–9 P.M.							
9–10 P.M.							
10–11 P.M.							

Source: Beck, Rush, Shaw, and Emery (1979).

proach in which the client can get a sense of accomplishment and success in terms of moving toward an identified goal. For example, an individual with severe depression may have a goal of going to the library, but this may require small steps, which include getting out of bed, getting dressed, eating, cleaning up, putting on a coat, and arranging transportation to get to the library. The graded assignments will depend on the task and the specific characteristics of the client. It may help to mention to the client that research supports the view that engaging in activities reduces depression while inactivity increases it.

Clients often want to wait for their mood to lighten before engaging in activities. The therapist can convey empathy and understanding of how depression has robbed the client's energy, but simultaneously encourage them to try an activity regardless of their feeling (Jacobson, Martell, & Dimidjian, 2001). Beck asks clients to perform a behavioral experiment by seeing if certain activities will improve their mood. Only activities that are positively reinforcing and of interest to the client are selected, since they are the most likely to be performed. In difficult cases, where motivation to try an activity is low, Beck suggests asking the client "What have you got to lose by trying this out?" The therapist can collaborate with the client to determine activities to be performed during the week. It is important to be aware that clients' beliefs regarding the amount of pleasure or feelings of mastery they will experience after completing an activity are often incorrect. An individual who states that taking a walk outside is not pleasurable can be asked to schedule this activity and to rate it in terms of mastery or pleasure. The same can be done with any activity, such as reading, watching television, listening to music, talking to a friend, or going shopping. Often, what happens is that clients are pleasantly surprised to find that activities improve their mood. The therapist should help clients identify activities they previously enjoyed and try to assign tasks that are most likely to be pleasurable according to the client's history and personal preferences (Persons et al., 2001). For some, even talking about past pleasurable activities can improve mood.

Persons and colleagues (2001) suggest the following when using the activity and mastery schedules:

- Use Socratic questioning (questioning that elicits thoughtful responses and contributions) to obtain client collaboration on activities.

- Start at the level where clients are currently rather than where they want to be (e.g., if they are house-bound but would like to go shopping, start with small steps first, such as spending 5 minutes in the garden or outside their house).

- Be specific and concrete about activities such as reading for 15 minutes or watching a particular program on television. Start with shorter time periods to enhance compliance.

- Anticipate obstacles and help clients decide how they will deal with each potential obstacle.

- If a client is unable to come up with any ideas regarding possible activities, the therapist can offer suggestions and modify them with the help of the client.

- If the client is discouraged or unmotivated, the therapist can attempt to identity the thoughts that interfere with willingness to try various activities.

- Therapists can request that clients estimate what their rating of an activity will be, perform the activity, and then rate it, comparing their estimated rating with the actual rating.

Cognitive Interventions

CBT is based on the view that depression is a problem in thinking. Therefore, efforts are directed at identifying, reality-testing, and correcting the dysfunctional belief or schema. In terms of the cognitive aspects of the therapy program, clients are taught to:

1. Monitor their thoughts, especially as they relate to depressive feelings.
2. Understand the connection between their thoughts, emotions, and behaviors.
3. Identify the underlying dysfunctional beliefs.
4. Use scientific thinking by evaluating the evidence regarding connection between their negative thoughts and their mood.
5. Change their thoughts by substituting more realistic thoughts or interpretations. (Beck et al., 1979)

Cognitive Probes

Some clients have difficulty identifying the automatic thoughts (thoughts that unconsciously run though the mind) that are associated with depressive feelings. For these clients, Beck and Freeman (1990) suggest the use of *cognitive probes*. The process of using cognitive probes involves having the client imagine that the upsetting event is currently occurring. They are then asked what they are thinking. This method is generally successful in uncovering the automatic thoughts. The client is instructed to try to "catch" as many as possible of the automatic thoughts that occur after distressing events and then write each one of them down. Through skillful questioning, the therapist can identify core schema—that is, perceptions of the self that are fixed, irreversible, and total. Examples of such thoughts include "I am alone," "I am fearful," or "I will always be unhappy." Once a schema is identified, it can be evaluated.

A number of different strategies are used to help clients see the connection between their thoughts and emotions. The use of a Thought Record can be an important tool for identifying the connection between thoughts, emotions, and behaviors. (See Table 12.3.) The therapist might introduce the use of the Thought Record form in the following manner,

"The way we think about situations can influence how we feel. For example, if a friend or coworker does not show up or cancels an appointment with

Table 12.3 **Form for Clients to Record Situations, Beliefs, and Emotions, with a Focus on Generating Alternative Thoughts**

Thought Record

Throughout the day, consider situations in which you experience strong emotions. For each, write your automatic thought and your emotion. For each situation, also write down an alternative thought and then your emotion with the new thought. For both the original thought and the alternative, rate your belief in the thought on a 0 to 5 scale, with 0 = no belief in the thought to 5 = complete belief in the thought, and place your ratings in the parentheses.

Date: _____

Situation _____

Thought _____ (   )

Emotion _____

Alternative Thought _____ (   )

Emotion _____

Source: Beck, Rush, Shaw, & Emery (1979).

me, I might think that they dislike me. In this case, I may feel down or even depressed. If I'm thinking this way, anything else that happens such as missing a bus or failing to record a program that I had wanted to see would increase my depression. It would reinforce the thought that I am a failure. Has something like this happened to you? We believe that most cases of depression are the result of negative thinking, the kind of automatic thinking that you aren't even consciously aware of. I'd like to find out if this holds true in your situation. The homework assignment that I would like you complete is called the Thought Record. In it, you will note down situations where you feel depressed, indicating both how you felt and the thoughts you had about the situation. Please also rate how strongly you believe in your thoughts on a 0 to 5 scale, 0 meaning you really didn't believe what you were thinking and 5 meaning that you totally believed the thought at the time it went through your head. Ask yourself, 'Did I really believe what I was thinking, and, if so, how strongly did I believe in the thought at the time it was happening?' In the example I gave you, I had the thought that I was a failure because of the following events: a coworker didn't show for the appointment yesterday, I missed the bus, and I was unable to record a television program. I might rate my belief in the thought 'I am a failure' as a 4 when the coworker didn't show up and as a 5 after I missed the bus and missed record-

ing the program I wanted to watch. What would you tell me in regard to my thoughts? How else might I interpret what happened yesterday? You might tell me 'Just because your coworker missed the appointment yesterday doesn't mean the person disliked you. The missed appointment could have had nothing to do with you. Maybe the person forgot or missed the bus, just like you happened to miss the bus. Those kinds of things can happen to anyone. It doesn't mean you're a failure.' In a similar way, I want you to develop an alternative thought regarding your own upsetting situations and rate your belief in the new thought. Do you have any questions about the thought record? Okay, let's practice by charting a recent situation where you felt depressed and go through the steps of completing the thought record."

In a similar fashion, Burns (1999) asked depressed individuals to (1) describe the situation that resulted in depressive feelings, (2) write down their automatic thoughts, (3) rate their belief regarding the thought (0 = no belief in the thought to 100 = complete belief in the thought), (4) identify the distortions associated with each automatic, negative thought recorded, (5) substitute a new thought, and (6) rate their belief in the new thought. He also asks clients to select the type of distortion occurring in their thought process, such as arbitrary inference, selective abstraction, overgeneralization, magnification, minimization, personalization, or absolutistic or dichotomous thinking. Teaching clients about different categories of distortion can be very helpful, since clients can begin to compare their thinking with a list of systematic errors in thinking such as those described by Beck (1979) and Burns (1999).

Schema Change Methods

These methods involve testing the validity of automatic thoughts and core beliefs. Clients are taught to consider evidence for and against each identified schema. Both historical and current experiences are reviewed in terms of supporting or not supporting a particular schema. In one case, an individual's schema was, "I'm fatally flawed" (Persons et al., 2001). The client stated that evidence supporting the view that he was "flawed" involved not being able to play football because of his asthma. He also felt that being sent away by his father to live with his mother also supported the schema. However, the client also acknowledged that there was evidence contrary to the schema, such as his being a member of the swim team and having several jocks as friends. Sometimes therapists need to assist clients in identifying evidence contrary to their automatic schema. After contrary evidence is obtained, a new schema is reinforced, such as "I'm okay" rather than "I'm fatally flawed." Evidence contradicting the negative schema or supporting a replacement schema can be collected contemporaneously as homework. The client can be asked to write down circumstances that reinforce the new and more accurate schema. It is helpful to remind clients that a schema often develops over the course of many years and that schema change is hard work. You can also reinforce clients by giving observations you have of them that are supportive of the new schema.

Persons, Davidson, and Tompkins (2001, p. 136) suggest the following questions as potentially helpful when assisting clients to change a schema:

- Are these thoughts helpful?
- Do these thoughts contain cognitive distortions?
- Are these thoughts consistent with the evidence?
- Are there alternative explanations?
- What would one say to a friend in this situation?
- How did one learn to think this way?

At times, clients may be discouraged and say that nothing positive occurred during the week. If this occurs, the therapist can go through a specific day with the client, carefully looking for positive events. Reframing can sometimes be used to change a potentially negative or neutral situation into a positive one. Focusing on client strengths and ability to survive in difficult circumstances can be helpful. The negative lens through which a client is self-evaluating can be questioned by having the client indicate what could be said to a friend reporting the same circumstance. For example, one woman whose schema was "I am unlovable" discounted the fact that her daughter wanted to spend time with her. The woman was asked what she would say to an individual who stated she was unlovable, but whose daughter sought contact with her (Persons, Davidson, & Tompkins, 2001).

Evaluation of CBT: Scientific Basis, Contextual, and Diversity Issues

At the beginning of this chapter, we cited many of the awards that Beck has received in terms of research and contribution to the field of psychotherapy. Beck's cognitive therapy has strong support as an empirically supported therapy for depression (Chambless & Ollendick, 2001). It has been subjected to the gold standard method of evaluating research in utilizing randomized controlled trials (RCTs). According to Persons, Davidson, and Tompkins (2001), Beck's therapy model is: (1) one of the few psychotherapies found to be effective in RCT studies, (2) more effective in RCT studies with depression than most other forms of psychotherapy, (3) as effective as antidepressant medications and more effective in preventing relapse, and (4) cost effective. Beck has been modifying cognitive therapy for use with other mental health disorders. He has developed an approach to work with personality disorders (Beck et al., 2004) and has found that cognitive strategies can also help patients with schizophrenia challenge their hallucinations. His work with individuals with schizophrenia involves gentle persuasion, and has been found to successfully help patients acknowledge that hallucinations come from within and that they can be challenged and displaced. He believes it is "not the hallucinations causing the distress, but the attached beliefs, such as 'I have to do what the voices say or something terrible will happen to me'" (Fenichel, 2000). Beck teaches his clients to control their beliefs, much like the approach used by Albert Ellis. In addition, Beck identifies underlying fears and how they lead to specific beliefs. In general, there has been strong support for the propositions and hypotheses underlying cognitive-behavioral therapy.

Is the CBT approach effective with diverse populations? We believe that with diverse groups, it is especially important to assess possible social, cultural, and environmental factors that may be contributing to current schema. Because the focus of treatment is on changing one's thoughts and beliefs, some external sources of problems may be overlooked. This is less likely to occur if assessment regarding these factors has been performed early in the therapy process. Research on the effectiveness of cognitive-behavioral therapy on diverse groups is just beginning. There is some support for the view that cognitive errors and hopelessness are related to depression in a similar manner when comparing White American, Hispanic American, and African American youth (Kennard, Stewart, Hughes, Patel, & Emslie, 2006). However, there may be differences in the efficacy of cognitive-behavioral therapy among different ethnic groups. African American children showed less improvement with cognitive-behavioral strategies for depression compared to children from other ethnic groups (Cardemil, Reivich, & Seligman, 2002). Less improvement than expected using CBT was also found among low-income ethnic minority clients as compared to White samples (Organista, Munoz, & Gonzales, 1994). Organista (2000) found that using engagement strategies based on Hispanic cultural norms such as using positive cultural beliefs to "combat irrational thoughts" and using culturally important behavioral activities (e.g., involving family members or focusing on community needs) both increased the effectiveness of cognitive-behavioral therapy and decreased the therapy dropout rate. We believe cognitive-behavioral therapy has great promise as a treatment for depression, but that it may be more effective with diverse groups by considering the following:

1. Is it possible that social or cultural influences are the cause of the dysfunctional beliefs? Would members of the individual's culture consider the thoughts to be irrational?

2. Are there cultural values and norms that need to be taken into consideration? For example, Beck uses the Socratic method (asking a series

of questions rather than giving information directly) in order to impart information or deepen awareness, to engage the client and to stimulate thinking on the part of the client. Members of certain ethnic groups may few awkward with this method and worry that they are not providing the right answer (Chen & Davenport, 2005).

3. Are there cultural or religious beliefs that clients might find helpful in combating irrational thoughts?

4. Are the behavioral activities being considered consistent with the client's cultural values and norms?

5. Are the goals being considered appropriate for the client's cultural group?

Beck's focus on collaboration and empiricism are extremely important with all clients, but even more so when working with clients whose background and worldviews differ from that of the therapist. In true collaboration, clinicians should identify the client's perspective rather than impose their own personal viewpoint on the situation. It is also important to evaluate the effectiveness of the alliance and interventions. When hypotheses and interventions strategies are developed and tested collaboratively, the therapist has a means of determining the effectiveness of the approach with each client and can make modifications, if needed. With this kind of adaptation, we believe that CBT can be a very effective therapy for diverse populations.

Recommended Readings

Beck, A. T., Rush, A. J., Shaw, B. F., & Emery, G. (1979). *Cognitive therapy of depression.* New York: Guilford.

A readable and easily understandable book that presents in-depth coverage of much of the information covered in terms of theory, therapeutic relationship skills, conducting the initial interview, and specific behavioral and cognitive strategies. It also discusses specific techniques with suicidal clients and the use of antidepressant medications. The Beck Depression Inventory, Scale for Suicidal Ideation, and Daily Record of Dysfunctional Thoughts are discussed in the appendix.

Beck, A. T., Freeman, A., Davis, D. D., & Associates (2004). *Cognitive therapy of personality disorders.* New York: Guilford.

The book covers the application of cognitive-behavioral therapy for personality disorder. It contains even greater coverage of the theory than Beck's original book on depression. General issues associated with personality disorders as well as specific approaches for different personality disorders are comprehensively presented.

Persons, J. B., Davidson, J., & Tompkins, M. A. (2004). *Essential components of cognitive-behavior therapy for depression.* Washington, DC: American Psychological Association.

This book provides an excellent overview of the research and theoretical basis for CBT and includes detailed chapters on intake, treatment planning, structure of therapy sessions, behavioral activities, use of the thought record, and other schema change methods. Each of the chapters includes specific examples that illustrate the process of cognitive-behavioral therapy.

Dialectical Behavior Therapy

13

Chapter

*A 35-year-old woman . . . sought outpatient treatment for chronic dyspho-
ria, a pattern of turbulent and unsuccessful interpersonal relationships,
and a state of barely concealed rage that she attributed to the shortcomings
and failure of others . . . About 1 year into treatment, a stormy but long-
term relationship with a man broke up . . . she reported feeling depressed
and suicidal. . . . (Oldham, 2006, p. 20)*

In the case above, the woman seeking treatment received a diagnosis
of borderline personality disorder. Some of the most difficult cases
faced by interns and mental health professionals involve clients with
this diagnosis. The mix of suicidal threats and acts, self-harm behaviors,
extreme emotional displays, and demanding behavior can be both frus-
trating and exhausting. Clinicians frequently present clients with these
characteristics for case supervision. Compounding the problem is that
many individuals with borderline personality disorder also have a mood
disorder, substance abuse disorder, or posttraumatic stress disorder. Because of the chronic instability of individuals with borderline personality disorder, they consume a disproportionate amount of mental health
resources. Females account for about three quarters of those diagnosed
with borderline personality disorder. It is estimated that about 10 percent
of clients seen in outpatient clinics and 20 percent in inpatient settings
have this diagnosis, and that approximately 10 percent will commit suicide (American Psychiatric Association, 2001). Self-injurious behaviors
(e.g., cutting, burning) and suicide attempts are characteristic of this
disorder; both types of behavior may occur in the same client (Oldham,
2006). Some research-based approaches show promise, including Beck,
Freeman, and colleagues (1990) *Cognitive Therapy for Personality Disorders.* In this chapter, we will concentrate on dialectical behavior therapy
(DBT), a comprehensive cognitive-behavioral approach developed by
Marsha Linehan (1993a), which we believe offers a valuable, research-
based contribution to the treatment of this disorder.

A person with borderline personality disorder often has extreme bouts of anger, depression, or anxiety that last for only hours, or, at most, a day. During these episodes, suicide attempts, self-injury, aggression, or substance abuse may occur. These clients may tend to view themselves as bad or unworthy and believe they are misunderstood or mistreated. Their lives are perceived to be empty and isolated, with little social support; this results in frantic efforts to avoid being alone. Although desperately in need of relationships, they develop stormy attachments and show an unstable pattern with friendships. They can shift from idealization of family, friends, or loved ones to displaying intense anger and dislike toward them. Switching from one extreme to another in response to others is common. There is high sensitivity to rejection and frequent impulse behavior such as spending, binge eating, and risky sex (NIMH, 2006).

Theory and Conceptualization

What etiological factors are responsible for these complex symptoms and characteristics? Linehan (1993a, b) developed the Biosocial Theory of Borderline Personality Disorder to account specifically for the emotional dysfunction and dysregulation found in individuals with this disorder. The emotional and behavioral instability is posited to result from both a biological predisposition toward rapid and sustained emotional arousal and invalidating experiences during childhood. Her therapy, dialectical behavior therapy, directly addresses and treats the symptoms and causes of this disorder.

Biological Predisposition

Linehan proposes that individuals with borderline personality have a biological dysfunction within the emotional regulation system that includes: (1) a high emotional vulnerability as exhibited by oversensitivity to emotional stimuli. The individual responds quickly to emotional situations, has a low threshold for emotional reaction, and tends to react with strong emotional intensity, and (2) a dysfunction in the emotional modulation system manifested by difficulty in reducing physiological arousal once emotions are activated. These dysfunctions alone are not sufficient to result in borderline personality. The disorder develops only if the environment is a poor fit or invalidates the individual with these emotional characteristics. Of course, it is also possible that an individual with emotional dysregulation can cause the environment to become invalidating. Linehan hypothesizes that it is the interaction between the biological predisposition for emotional dysregulation and exposure to an invalidating environment that underlies borderline personality disorder. In this theoretical model, as with many other theories, childhood experiences with parents or caretakers play an important role in etiology; parenting style is hypothesized to interact with the predisposition for emotional dysregulation to produce the disorder.

Invalidating Environment

Linehan believes that a specific set of pathogenic, environmentally based, invalidating influences provide the background for borderline personality disorder. This occurs when an individual's subjective reality and experiences are chronically and pervasively dismissed, trivialized, punished, ignored, or responded to erratically throughout childhood. A child who verbalizes "I'm tired" may receive a response such as "No, you're not, you're just lazy," or a parent may make a statement such as "I can see you are angry, but trying to hide it." Personal feelings and subjective experiences are dismissed or reinterpreted, resulting in a lack of confidence regarding the accuracy of perceptions. Most parents do make some invalidating statements to their children; they become problematic only when the dismissal of the child's emotions and perceptions is pervasive. Invalidating environments would also include those that are sexually, physically, or emotionally abusive or intolerant of displays of strong emotions. In the case of sexual abuse, the perpetrator may inform the child that the molestation or abuse is natural or a sign of affection, while warning not to tell anyone about it. The child may feel that the victimization is bad or wrong, and is confused when the abuser contradicts these feelings or beliefs. When a child does report abuse, the revelation may be met with disbelief or blame (Linehan, 1993b). Again, the child's personal experience has been invalidated.

Similarly, cruel acts or neglect by parents may be explained to the child as acts of care or something the child deserves due to misbehavior. Thus, the perceptions of the child are questioned and the child's interpretation of events is challenged. This results in a lack of trust regarding one's own perceptions, emotions, beliefs, or actions, and leads to a dependency on environmental cues regarding how to think, feel, or behave. Intolerance of strong emotional displays without opportunities to learn alternative methods of expressing feelings leads to deficiencies in the ability to modulate emotions. Paradoxically, children living in invalidating environments may need to exhibit strong displays of emotion or extreme behaviors in order to obtain the parent's attention. This pattern leads to some of the behavioral and emotional excesses found in individuals with borderline personality disorder.

The combination of an invalidating environment and biological predisposition toward poor emotional regulation leads to specific characteristics. These are: (1) lack of skill in emotional or behavioral regulation or modulation; (2) development of *dialectic dilemmas* or black and white thinking—where gradations do not exist, and individuals, events, or situations are judged either good or bad; (3) excessive emotional or behavioral patterns that often include suicidal threats and impulsive behaviors; and (4) disturbances in self-identity produced by conflicts between one's own experience and sense of reality and contradictory environmental cues. The lack of trust in one's own ideas and perceptions leads to overdependence on the viewpoint of others. Thus, the biosocial theory postulates that the combination of biologically predisposed emotional dysfunction paired with an invalidating environment leads to symptoms found in borderline personality disorder.

Dialectical Behavior Therapy

Dialectical behavior therapy (DBT) was specifically developed to treat both the biologically and environmentally produced characteristics of borderline personality disorders. In the DBT approach, cognitive and behavioral strategies are used to help the client develop skills in emotional regulation, distress tolerance, and interpersonal effectiveness within the context of a therapeutic environment that strongly emphasizes the interpersonal skills of empathy, reflection, and validation. DBT employs contingency management procedures throughout therapy, reinforcing adaptive behaviors while avoiding the reinforcement of maladaptive behaviors. Clients are educated about reinforcement principles. Components of Eastern philosophy (Zen) are also part of the treatment program—specifically, the use of mindfulness training. Dialectical behavior therapy is different from most traditional cognitive therapies in accepting and validating the client's behavior (such as self-harm or unrealistic demands), strongly emphasizing the therapist-client relationship, focusing on therapy-interfering behaviors that may be displayed by either the therapist or the client, and directing attention to *dialectical* processes. The dialectical process involves having clients come to terms with and to be able to reconcile opposites (e.g., good or bad) through synthesis. This focus is important for individuals with borderline personality because, in many situations, they do not see gradations. For both the therapist and the client, the dialectical process involves accepting the current state of the client and, at the same time, moving toward change.

DBT is a supportive and collaborative therapy. It requires teamwork by the therapist and client to achieve goals. During therapy, the therapeutic alliance is constantly evaluated since problems in the relationship can interfere with progress. In each counseling session, potential conflicts or ruptures are discussed before other issues. The goals of the therapy are to help the client achieve greater interpersonal effectiveness during conflict situations, increase self-regulation of unwanted emotions, and be able to tolerate stress and strong emotions.

In DBT, the therapist is cautioned not to expose clients with borderline personality to an "invalidating environment" during psychotherapy—one in which their motives, behaviors, and perceptions are questioned. Examples of invalidating responses are defining client behaviors as manipulative or not accepting the client's interpretation of a situation; the goal is to avoid duplicating childhood patterns of invalidation. In fact, traditional therapeutic methods that involve requesting behavioral change may precipitate resistance, anger, or abrupt termination of therapy. Requesting changes in the client's behavior does not acknowledge the extreme pain of the client. The primary task of the therapist is to validate clients' experiences and feelings by accepting clients as they are, while simultaneously providing them with the skills needed for change. Validation involves finding a grain of truth or wisdom in the client's responses to the current situation, and communicating to the client that his or her behavior is understandable given their prior life experiences. (This would be similar to the process of dealing with therapeutic ruptures discussed in Chapter 3.)

Linehan (1997) has developed a framework for therapeutic validation that involves six levels of response. The first two levels involve basic empathy responses such as validating the emotional response of the client with statements such as "You seem upset" or "You seem angry." These acknowledge the client's feeling. The next two levels of validation involve empathy with some interpretation. "Given your interpretation of this situation, which is understandable because of the environment you were exposed to growing up, it doesn't surprise me that you responded so explosively" (Sneed et al., 2003, p. 270). This response involves a deeper level of validation in which the therapist demonstrates an empathic understanding of the client's life experience and its influence on the client's interpretation and action in the situation. Notice that it is gently pointed out that the client's interpretation of the situation led to the explosive behavior. The therapist accepts the client's behavior as making sense due to childhood experiences rather than focusing immediately on the need to change.

After hearing the client, change strategies can more effectively be introduced. In the final two levels of validation, the therapist includes an understanding of the problematic behavior or emotion, but also brings up the need for change. For example, a therapist responded in the following manner to a 21-year-old woman who had threatened to jump off the rooftop of the shelter in which she was living: "Given everything you've been through in your life, it makes sense that you sometimes get overwhelmed by your feelings and that one way of coping with this distress is to threaten to kill yourself. However, although this temporarily removes you from the distressing situation, it ultimately sets you back and prevents you from living independently" (Sneed et al., 2003, p. 270). In the response above, the therapist demonstrates understanding of the reasons behind the suicidal threat, but brings in the consequences of the behavior. This approach validates the client's distress and behavior, but also describes the maladaptive nature of her response. In

DBT, the later levels of validation are employed only after a good working relationship has developed.

The therapist understands that clients with borderline personality disorder are truly unable to moderate their behaviors or emotions when they first begin therapy, and that they are trying to deal with their pain, but in a maladaptive manner. Clients are accepted as they currently are, yet there is an honest appraisal about the need to make changes. Some additional assumptions regarding clients with borderline personality disorder and therapy are shown in Table 13.1. Not engaging in an invalidating manner is difficult for many therapists since clients with BPD are sometimes angry and demonstrate behaviors that are threatening or abusive. In addition, traditional therapy approaches used with borderline personality disorder do not employ validating techniques, so this is a new approach for many therapists. In settings where DBT is used extensively, therapists participate in regularly scheduled consultation groups in which they discuss cases, receive training, and actively practice

Table 13.1 **Underlying Assumptions about Clients with Borderline Personality Disorder**

- The current lives of clients with borderline personality disorder are unbearable. Their complaints are valid. We need to accept and validate their behaviors and concerns.

- The dialectic process for the therapist involves accepting clients as they are, yet teaching them to change.

- Clients tend to be mood dependent and must learn to make changes in how they cope when in a highly emotional state.

- Clients are desperately trying to change, although in an inflexible and often pain-producing manner.

- Clients' efforts and motivation may not be up to the task. The therapist and client need to identify factors that inhibit or interfere with the client's efforts and motivation.

- Clients need to change their behaviors and/or alter their environment in order to improve.

- Clients need more than insight, medication, or nurturing.

- Clients do not fail in therapy. In DBT, it is the therapy, the therapist, or a combination of the two that is responsible for failure.

- Therapists working with clients need support. Consultation is especially important because of the frustrations and stress produced by working with individuals with borderline personality disorder.

From Linehan, 1993a

using DBT strategies in the course of their discussions about the challenges of working with their clients.

Goals of Therapy

In DBT, rather than concentrating on helping clients resolve specific problems occurring in their lives, the focus is on teaching clients skills for managing their emotional and behavioral excesses. Through the development of coping skills, clients are able to achieve greater stability in their daily lives. Therapeutic interventions aim to reduce arousal, foster greater affective stability, and improve self-control. The treatment goals for DBT include (Chambliss, 2000): (1) reduction of behavioral excesses, such as dangerous acting out and impulsive behavior; (2) development of plans to prevent suicide and violence toward others; (3) reduction or elimination of substance abuse; (4) development of strategies for containing and controlling emotions; and (5) improvement of skills in areas of self-calming, problem-solving, assertive interpersonal interactions, and structuring leisure time. Linehan's treatment protocol orders the goals or targets for treatment in a hierarchical fashion with the most problematic areas, suicidal or self-injurious acts and therapy-interfering behaviors, receiving first attention.

First Stage Targets: Stability and Control over Current Problematic Behaviors

As treatment begins, the first priority is to decrease suicidal ideation, impulses, and self-injurious acts. These behaviors are treated first and interpreted as maladaptive problem-solving attempts that make sense in terms of the unbearable lives led by individuals whose existence is characterized by crises, social isolation, and encountering one problem after the other. Self-harm is considered to be a genuine, but misguided, attempt by clients to solve their painful existence. Clients need to learn to choose more effective methods of dealing with the distress. Therapists empathize with and validate the emotional upheaval faced by their clients, while simultaneously working to help clients develop more adaptive skills to deal with life's difficulties and to build a more worthwhile life. Traditional assessment and intervention protocols for suicide are employed. (These interventions are addressed in greater detail in Chapters 4 and 15.)

Decreasing therapy-interfering behaviors on the part of both the client and therapist is also a first-stage target. A strong therapeutic alliance is essential because of the collaborative nature of DBT and the need for the client to actively participate in therapy and carry out homework assignments. Behaviors of the client that may be impeding the therapy process (such as inattention, poor attendance, arguing, and pushing limits) are directly addressed when they occur. These kinds of behaviors are framed as misguided attempts by the client to seek assistance. Part of the skills training that occurs in DBT involves teaching clients to ask for help or to state what they want in an appropriate manner. Therapists may also be guilty of displaying therapy-interfering behaviors through responses such as blaming the client, becoming frustrated when client progress seems slow, or failing to balance nurturance with the expectation of change. Therapy-interfering behaviors from either the therapist or the client are important to address because they prevent the formation of a strong therapeutic alliance.

Decreasing behaviors that interfere with quality of life are another important focus during this stage of therapy. An assumption made in DBT is that clients with borderline personality disorder have reasons for being unhappy and suicidal. They have not learned to trust themselves and do not have the skills to modulate their emotions. Not only do they have internalized problems such as poor self-identify, they are also saddled with external problems such as substance abuse, dysfunctional interpersonal relationships, and lack of employment or financial difficulties. To deal with these problem areas and to have a better life, there is a need to make changes in current ways of thinking and behaving.

As behaviors that interfere with the quality of life are decreased, the therapist also assists the client to increase the behavioral and cognitive skills that are needed for an improved quality of life. These are essential skills that individuals with borderline personality disorder need in order to make successful changes. Linehan has four specific areas for skill development. These are: (1) core mindfulness skills, (2) interpersonal effectiveness skills, (3) emotional regulation skills, and (4) distress tolerance skills. We will discuss each of these in detail in the cognitive and behavioral intervention strategy section.

Second Stage Targets: Emotional Processing of Past Events
After resolving first stage targets, attention is directed to the impact of past emotional traumas. This begins with the therapist acknowledging that an invalidating environment can have harmful effects on self-identity and trust in one's own emotions and behaviors. In contrast to many other therapeutic approaches, this *reprocessing* (reviewing past events) occurs only after contemporary emotional and behavioral issues are targeted and improved. During this stage, specific aspects of childhood experiences are linked to the problematic behaviors of the client. Self-blame, difficulties with emotions, and impulsive behaviors are seen to be a product of parental messages. Thus, the individual begins to see him or herself in a more objective and less punitive manner.

Third Stage Targets: The Development of Connection and Serenity
During this stage, clients focus on developing rewarding relationships with others and a sense of peacefulness with themselves. They learn to develop self-respect and synthesize the skills learned from earlier stages. Not all clients are able to reach these latter two stages.

Cognitive and Behavioral Intervention Strategies

As mentioned earlier, individuals with borderline personality disorder show dysfunction in behavior (e.g., impulsivity, self-harm), emotion (e.g., anger and emotional extremes), cognition (e.g., black and white thinking and cognitive distortions), and self-identity (e.g., feelings of emptiness and inadequacy). As therapy begins, behaviors that the client wants to decrease, such as emotional volatility, impulsivity, and interpersonal conflict, are listed. Behaviors to increase might include interpersonal effectiveness, emotional modulation, ability to tolerate stress, and cognitive strategies such as stopping to reflect on what is occurring. Behavioral and cognitive strategies taught in the DBT process are clearly described in the *Skills Training Manual for Treating Borderline Personality Disorder* (Linehan, 1993b). In the following sections, we summarize many of the skills clients learn in order to increase emotional stability and behavioral control.

Core Mindfulness Skills

Linehan considers two cognitive components (*recognizing one's state of mind* and *mindfulness*) to be core skills. These skills, essential for clients who are learning to regulate their emotions, are the taught to clients at the beginning of therapy and are used throughout the treatment process. In the skill of recognizing one's state of mind, three states of mind are described: (1) *reasonable mind*, which involves rational or logical thinking; (2) *emotional mind*, in which responses are dictated by emotional reactions that interfere with reasoning ability. In this state, events and situations are interpreted through an emotional lens and behavioral acts are impulsive and occur based on emotion rather than reason. And the final state of mind is (3) *wise mind*, in which the *reasonable mind* and *emotional mind* are integrated and the skill of *intuitive knowing* is available to help with decision-making. Clients learn that, when they are feeling emotional, taking the time to stop and identify the state of mind they are in results in reduced impulsivity and minimized reactive responding.

The second cognitive component involves mindfulness training. This is based on the Zen Buddhist construct of intentional awareness of one's thoughts and behaviors. It allows clients to view thoughts as mental events rather than as accurate reflections of reality or as aspects of the self (Teasdale et al., 2000). The client is taught to observe, experience, and be aware of the events, behaviors, thoughts, or emotions that are presently occurring without reacting or becoming caught up in them. The goal is for the client to simply experience the event, allowing it to flow in and out of the mind. This is done even when the situation is distressing. By putting oneself in the role

Box 13.1 **Mindfulness Exercises**

OBSERVE

Just Notice the Experience. Notice without getting caught in the experience. Experience without reacting to your experience.

Have a *Teflon Mind,* letting experiences, feelings, and thoughts come into your mind and slip right out.

Control your attention, but not what you see. Push away nothing. Cling to nothing.

Step inside yourself and observe. *Watch* your feelings coming and going, like clouds in the sky.

DESCRIBE

Put Experiences into Words. Describe to yourself what is happening. Put a name on your feelings. Call a thought just a thought, a feeling just a feeling. Don't get caught in content.

NONJUDGMENTALLY

See, but *Don't Evaluate.* Take a nonjudgmental stance. Just the facts. Focus on the what, not the good or bad, the terrible or wonderful, the should or should not.

Acknowledge the helpful, the wholesome, but don't judge it. Acknowledge the harmful, the unwholesome, but don't judge it.

EFFECTIVELY

Focus on What Works. Do what needs to be done in each situation. Stay away from fair and unfair, right and wrong, should and should not.

Play by the Rules. Don't cut off your nose to spite your face.

Act as *Skillfully* as you can, meeting the needs of the situation you are in, not the situation you wish you were in; not the one that is more just; not the one that is more comfortable.

PARTICIPATE

Actively *Practice* your skills as you learn them until they become a part of you . . . Practice changing harmful situations, changing your harmful reactions to situations, accepting yourself and situations as they are.

Adapted from Linehan (1993b, pp. 111, 113). Reprinted with permission, Guilford Press.

of nonjudgmental observer, events are not judged as good or bad, but are simply observed and accepted. The goal of mindfulness training is to allow clients to realize that thoughts have no reality and to counter the tendency to respond to thoughts with strong emotion. (See Box 13.1 for some examples of mindfulness exercises.)

Distress Tolerance Skills

To reduce the psychic pain and extreme emotions experienced by individuals with borderline personality disorder, it is important for them to learn to tolerate feelings of emotional distress. Skills that increase the ability to manage feelings of distress include adopting a nonjudgmental attitude toward oneself or toward a current painful situation without demanding that either the self or the situation be different. This does not require approval of the situation; instead, it involves simply accepting the moment. Along with these cognitive skills, clients learn a set of crisis survival strategies that allow them to deal more effectively with distressing situations. These include: distraction (engaging in different activities, doing things that contribute positively, and focusing on a positive emotion); self-soothing (enjoying visual, auditory, olfactory, or gustatory activities); improving the moment (using prayer, imagery, or relaxation); and reducing vulnerability to the emotional mind by taking care of physical needs such as diet, exercise, sleep, and keeping the body free from drugs and alcohol.

Emotional Regulation Skills

Borderline personality disorder is characterized by emotional lability that often results in suicidal or other serious behaviors. This extreme pain and distress is due to the individual's inability to regulate painful emotions. Validating the emotions of clients is important since they may be resistive if told to control their emotions and may feel the therapist does not understand the depth of their distress. Emotion regulation skills include the mindfulness strategies of observing and being nonjudgmental of the emotional state. In addition, clients are taught to identify their current feelings, the recent event or events that led to their current emotions, and the resulting consequences of the emotion and obstacles to changing emotions, such as recognizing that they are receiving external reinforcement for their emotional displays. Clients learn that they can decrease vulnerability to painful emotions by making sure that their physical needs for healthy eating, sleep, and exercise are met, increasing opportunities for positive experiences in their life, and using mindfulness and distress tolerance strategies.

Interpersonal Effectiveness and Self-Management Skills

Clients with borderline personality often have significant deficits in interpersonal skills. To develop these skills, communication activities involving assertiveness or social skills training are employed. Clients are exposed to appropriate ways of making requests, asking for rather than demanding assistance, saying "no," handling conflict, and respecting the rights of others. To maintain or develop interpersonal relationships, clients practice adopting a gentle demeanor, listening to the other person, using humor, and responding respectfully rather than threatening or judging the response of the other person. Self-management training helps clients learn to use effective interpersonal skills, develop respect, and apply interpersonal effectiveness skills outside of therapy. Self-control is increased as clients learn to (1) make observations regarding situations and behavior rather than always reacting impulsively and (2) understand the consequences of their behavior.

Decreasing Behaviors Related to Posttraumatic Stress

Once the primary target goals regarding stability and control are met, the second stage of therapy begins and past issues are addressed. These deal with posttraumatic emotional episodes and the tendency of the individual to engage in self-blame and self-invalidation for the abuse or trauma. Through exposure processes, the anxiety associated with posttraumatic stress disorder is extinguished and the internalized belief that the client was responsible for the invalidating environment is countered and worked through.

Increasing Respect for Self

The third stage target involves assisting clients to increase their self-respect and feelings of serenity. Individuals with borderline personality disorder often have a strong sense of self-hate or self-loathing. At this stage, the focus is on developing a positive feeling of self-worth and for clients to learn to trust in and value their own opinions, emotions, and behaviors. When trust in their own judgment has developed, clients can begin to engage in self-validation independent of the prompting of the therapist.

The DBT Treatment Process

Linehan's DBT process is both intensive and comprehensive. Clients are expected to complete a 1-year program that includes weekly individual and group therapy sessions along with telephone consultation. Each week, the therapist conducts a 2-hour group-based training module with a focus on specific cognitive and behavioral skills. The individual therapy sessions are directed at dealing with crises and current problems encountered by the client, as well as reinforcing the cognitive and behavioral skills presented during group sessions. The skills modules are taught in the group sessions because Linehan believes that it would be too difficult for an individual therapist to deal with the emotional needs of the client and teach behavioral and cognitive skills during the same session. Realizing the difficulty that many mental health clinics or therapists in private practice would have in providing group training for clients with borderline personality disorder, Linehan does contemplate the possibility of adapting her therapy model to individual therapy alone. She suggests splitting the session into two parts, with the first half directed at immediate client concerns and the second half on skills development. Another option is to meet with the client twice each week, dividing the tasks between the sessions.

Another feature of the program is a weekly telephone consultation between the therapist and client. This is important for several reasons. First, clients with borderline personality disorder lack the skills to ask for help in an appropriate manner. They may feel shame or fear and have difficulty making requests, believing that they are not deserving of help. Conversely, they may demand assistance in an abusive or threatening manner. With the telephone contact, clients are encouraged to use effective means of communicating their needs. This process allows the therapist to engage in the coaching and modeling of appropriate interpersonal skills. The telephone contacts are also used to reinforce cognitive and behavioral skills presented during group sessions. The client may be asked to practice the skills presented in assertion and social skills training during their phone contacts. Second, phone calls can help with any current crisis confronting the client, or can be used to work through possible ruptures or misunderstandings that may have occurred during the previous therapy session. Phone calls allow clients to practice their developing skills in dealing with problems without having to wait for the next session. It is important to note that these contacts are not meant to solve problems, but instead focus on encouraging clients to use the interpersonal and cognitive skills they are learning to manage the situation. Therapists who are not involved in the comprehensive DBT program will need to decide about including regular telephone contact with clients as part of their therapy. At a minimum, secretarial or other staff who may have direct contact with clients should be informed about the importance of responding in a validating manner when clients call.

The way DBT is conducted during the initial sessions is similar to other approaches. However, differences do exist. The therapist gives the client specific information about the disorder and treatment approach. This is the first step in accepting and validating client behaviors and experiences and invokes an attitude of collaboration. During the first meetings, clients are given a pretreatment orientation that includes information about borderline personality disorder, an explanation of DBT and its philosophy, expectations regarding the role and responsibility of the client, and formal agreements. These components are discussed with a client in a Socratic manner to elicit client responses. The biosocial theory of borderline personality disorder is shared, with an emphasis on both biological predisposition toward emotional dysregulation and the role of an invalidating environment. Problematic behaviors such as suicide or self-harm are presented as maladaptive attempts to solve feelings of unhappiness and pain. The client's input is sought regarding this perspective and they are asked whether this description fits their experience. The possibility that clients have experienced invalidation from therapists, physicians, friends, and family members is discussed. Clients are encouraged to give examples of situations where they were misunderstood by others or described as manipulative.

Next, DBT is described as a supportive type of therapy that will help clients decrease harmful behaviors and find more satisfaction in life. They learn that this will be accomplished by having them develop their own strengths and positive qualities. DBT is described as a skills-oriented therapy that helps clients learn to analyze their problematic behavior patterns, the circumstances that elicit them, and to develop more adaptive behaviors. The importance of learning to move beyond all-or-none thinking regarding situations, themselves, or others is also discussed. Clients are told that training will be provided to help them deal with emotional dysregulation using mindfulness, distress tolerance, and other skills to help them regulate their emotions. The therapist emphasizes that DBT is a collaborative therapy in which the therapist and client work jointly to achieve goals, and that it is important for both the therapist and client to directly communicate any problems or concerns with the therapeutic alliance.

After the therapeutic approach is described, the therapist outlines the specific treatment plan. The client is informed that the treatment is for one year, during which they are expected to attend individual and group sessions. Circumstances that may result in unilateral termination are presented. If suicidal behaviors play a prominent role, the agreement involves working toward solutions that do not involve self-harm. A therapy-interfering agreement is also reached, confirming the importance of addressing behaviors that negatively impact the therapeutic alliance. The therapist also agrees to conduct the therapy as competently as possible. It is pointed out that therapists cannot solve problems for clients or keep them from engaging in self-harm behavior. It is reinforced that personal safety is the client's responsibility, and that the therapist can only help the individual develop the skills to handle their own problems. The therapist also agrees to attend all therapy sessions, not to engage in dual or sexual relationships, cancel in advance if necessary, and maintain confidentiality with the exception of situations required by the law. The goal of the pretreatment orientation is to fully explain the process involved in DBT so that that client can give informed consent regarding participation. It also allows the therapist to correct any misconceptions the client may have regarding therapy, and to understand the therapist's role and philosophy. Clients who are ambivalent about the process or the time commitment involved may be asked to make a final decision about DBT after two to four sessions. Once the treatment agreement is signed, sessions begin.

The format of each session is based on a hierarchical model. Behaviors that affect stability and control receive first attention. This would include suicidal or self-harm behaviors, therapy-interfering behaviors, quality-of-life interfering behaviors, and skills deficits. During this first stage of treatment, if a crisis has occurred or the client reports self-harm ideation, the therapist:

1. focuses on the emotion;
2. attends to the recent triggering event;
3. assists the client in generating solutions from the skills that have been taught including mindfulness (activating the wise mind), emotional regulation (experiencing and observing the emotion without judgment), distress tolerance strategies (distracting, self-soothing, and improving the moment), and strategies for enhancing interpersonal effectiveness (attending to relationships and balancing priorities);
4. reinforces adaptive responses and helps identify interfering factors;
5. expresses understanding of the client's pain, but also the necessity of tolerating the pain;
6. helps the client develop and commit to a plan of action that the client believes will be successful in reducing the crisis; and
7. reassesses the potential for self-harm behavior. If the risk for self-harm does not appear to be sufficiently reduced, the therapist proceeds with suicide protocols (see Chapter 15).

Each session deals primarily with behaviors or situations that have occurred since the previous session, with the focus on current rather than historical events. A diary card (containing weekly ratings of thoughts about or use of alcohol, over-the-counter medications, street drugs, suicidal ideation, self-harm, and misery) is provided weekly as homework. This allows for a quick assessment of behaviors such as self-harm, suicidal behavior, or drug use along with other problems. If homework is not completed, this is discussed in the session and may be responded to as therapy-threatening behavior. If suicidal or substance abuse behavior has occurred between sessions, the use of adaptive skills when encountering problems is encouraged. Throughout therapy, the therapist reinforces the use of mindfulness and emotional regulation techniques whenever emotional or behavioral problems are discussed.

Therapists use listening, empathy, and validation skills throughout each session, and interpret problematic behaviors as unsuccessful attempts to solve emotionally painful events. If group training is not available, the therapist allots specific time to teach the core skills. A variety of forms and homework assignments are available in the *Skills Training Manual for Treating Borderline Personality Disorder* by Linehan (1993). During each session, the therapist reviews progress made outside of therapy sessions for each targeted behavior, noting improvements or areas in need of further work. The therapist regularly evaluates the client's use of newly learned skills across a variety of situations, eliciting feedback and collaboration from the client as the client's progress is discussed. Therapists are careful not to take on responsibilities for clients, nor to intervene directly even when a client complains about other mental health professionals involved in their care. For example, a psychiatrist, a social worker, and a counselor might all be working with the same client, but in different capacities. Whenever possible, clients are encouraged to deal with their own problems as they occur. Therefore, if a client has a complaint about someone, the therapist is careful not to become involved in a *splitting* dynamic, where one individual is pitted against another, but instead encourages the client to address the concern directly with the other person using skills that have been taught in therapy sessions.

As each session nears its end, the therapist gives notice to the client that the session will be ending soon, allowing sufficient time for closure on emotional issues. If a strong emotional concern is brought up at this time, the therapist asks the client if it is possible to wait until the next session to bring it up, stressing that important issues should be presented at the beginning of a session. Homework assignments are given and any questions regarding the assignments are discussed. A verbal summary occurs at the end of each session, allowing the client to reflect on the major points of the session. Linehan often tape-records the sessions and allows clients to review the tape at home. Each week, clients are reminded how to access emergency services, if required.

Specific Dialectical Treatment Strategies

There are several kinds of strategies used throughout the DBT process. These include dialectical strategies and core strategies. *Dialectical strategies* are pervasive, underlying strategies that comprise an essential component of the treatment dialogue. As mentioned previously, the goal of dialectical strategies is to help clients reconcile and eventually resolve the rigidity seen in all-or-none thinking. The therapist teaches and models dialectical behavior patterns with the goal of helping the client learn and integrate alternative ways of thinking and behaving. Another dialectical strategy used is that of "making lemonade out of lemons"; that is, taking a difficult or challenging situation and looking at how it might be considered an opportunity for new learning, building character, or for practicing important skills. For example, those who have suffered significant rejections or losses might see how this has increased their understanding of friends with similar circumstances in a way that allows them to be helpful and supportive. Another dialectical focus involves helping the client allow for natural change; that is, realizing that exposure to change can be positive and can offer hidden opportunities.

Core strategies, which consist of both problem solving and validation strategies, are the heart of the treatment. From the very beginning of treatment, therapists validate client behavior, taking the perspective that the behavior makes sense and is understandable in the context of the client's life. Identification of irrational thoughts or schemas, as might occur in traditional cognitive therapy, is specifically avoided because such a focus would only serve to recapitulate the invalidating environment. As mentioned previously, validation involves active observing and listening to the client, reflection and accurate empathy (understanding, but not necessarily agreeing with what the client is saying), and direct validation by looking for "accuracy, appropriateness, or reasonableness" in what the client is saying rather than focusing on how dysfunctional the behaviors or reactions may seem. Emotional validation occurs as the therapist allows time for expressing and processing emotions. This emotional release allows for a calmer atmosphere in which effective problem solving can occur. Core skills also include teaching the client to observe and label emotions, with the goal of integrating emotions into their life in a noncrisis fashion. Specifically, clients are taught self-observation skills that involve observing and describing (1) internal or external events that prompt emotional reactions; (2) the thoughts, interpretations, sensory, and physical responses associated with these events; and (2) any desires or wishes associated with the situation. In these discussions, the therapist outlines possible normative responses of others in similar situations.

A focus on behavioral validation strategies is also important because many clients may tend to invalidate or punish their own behavior. Whenever possible, the therapist looks for the validity of maladaptive behaviors and reflects on that aspect of the behavior, while also directly validating adaptive behaviors. It is hoped that when their behavior is observed and described without judgment, clients may be more clearly able to understand its impact. This is a very important step because clients are often unaware of their own behavior and its effects on others. As behavior is observed, the therapist also works with the client to identify and counter spoken and unspoken self-imposed demands, or "shoulds." Clients learn that understanding how or why something happened is important and does not constitute approval of what happened, and that wishing that things were different does not change the way things are.

Cognitive validation strategies help clients learn to trust their own perceptions and judgments. The therapist works with the client to clearly understand what the client is thinking and what assumptions are being made in specific situations so the client can learn to discriminate facts from interpretations. The therapist finds a "kernel of truth" by focusing on the thoughts or assumptions that appear to be the most valid given the context. Through this process, the therapist validates the idea that people can and do have differing values and opinions, which is fine so long as differences are respected. Another key aspect of validation is to acknowledge the clients' desire to improve, to express confidence in the clients' strengths and ability to overcome current challenges, and optimism about the clients' ability to have a positive and meaningful life. Even when progress seems slow, validation also involves acknowledging that clients are doing their best in moving forward. Eventually, the client and therapist begin to deepen the learning with a focus on problem solving strategies.

Evaluation of DBT: Scientific Basis, Contextual and Diversity Issues

Dialectical behavior therapy is a valuable contribution to the treatment of borderline personality disorder, and appears to be a promising treatment for a number of other mental health disorders. It is considered an empirically supported therapy for borderline personality disorder by the American Psychological Association and is recommended as an efficacious treatment by the American Psychiatric Association. In a review of studies of DBT that used randomized control treatment designs (Robins & Chapman, 2004), participants in DBT showed reductions in reckless and parasuicidal behaviors, anger, substance abuse, and binge eating, and improvement in social functioning. Although the efficacy of dialectical behavior therapy is strongly supported by research, the specific contribution of each component (therapist-client relationship, validation, dialectical focus, mindfulness, emotional regulation modules, cognitive strategies, and behavioral techniques) is not clear. This is an important consideration since DBT integrates so many strategies. One component, mindfulness (awareness of thoughts and detaching from them), has been effective in reducing relapse in depression; teaching depressed individuals to disengage from emotional reactions to their thoughts has been found to prevent the recurrence of depression (Ma & Teasdale, 2004; Teasdale et al., 2000).

There are some reports that modified and briefer forms of DBT have been successful in treating individuals with borderline personality and other disorders. Modifications, especially in duration, are important because insurance companies will generally not pay for 1 year of group and individual treatment. Also, many therapists in private practice or mental health clinics are unable to provide group DBT skills training. Turner (2000) found that incorporating skills training in individual therapy sessions without group training was successful in a community mental health center treating suicidal clients with borderline personality disorder. DBT strategies and techniques have also been used for brief treatment of parasuicidal incidents in psychiatric emergency rooms (Sneed et al., 2003) and with suicidal adolescents (Miller, Glinski, Woodberry, Mitchell, & Indik, 2002). In the latter study, the length of treatment was 16 weeks. A 3-month inpatient program of DBT was also effective in reducing self-injurious acts among females with borderline personality disorder (Bohus et al., 2000).

DBT has also been found to be effective as a treatment for other disorders. Safer, Telch, and Agras (2001) reported that a two-session modified DBT treatment focusing primarily on the development of emotional regulations skills was highly effective in reducing binge/purge eating among individuals with bulimia nervosa as compared to a waiting-list condition. A notable finding was that none of the 14 participants dropped out of the program, while in cognitive-behavioral programs for bulimia nervosa, the average drop out rate is about 28 percent. DBT has augmented the effects of antidepressant medications for depressed older adults as manifested by lower self-rated depression scores and greater interviewer rated improvement on independence and adaptive coping skills as compared to medication only treatment (Lynch, Morse, Mendelson, & Robins, 2003). We believe that DBT will continue to provide mental health professionals with meaningful skills such as validation, mindfulness, and emotional regulation to treat a number of mental health disorders.

We are unaware of any reported effectiveness studies of DBT with ethnic minorities, although Linehan's social skills training manual has been translated into Spanish (Robins & Chapman, 2004). Linehan developed her theory based on work with females with borderline personality disorder. It is not clear how well this conceptualization applies to males with this disorder. The core skill of mindfulness derived from Zen Buddhism might be a particularly good fit for those who embrace this philosophy. Validation of the client would likely be comforting to anyone who is not knowledgeable about therapy or what it entails. In assessing for and working with possible diversity issues, it is important to consider that an invalidating environment might involve societal rejection, prejudice, and discrimination. This is a situation where one's perceptions and self-identity involving race, religion, sexual orientation, or other differences may be judged and contradicted by the society. For example, even though homosexuality is no longer considered a mental disorder, society continues to give the message that it is wrong. Similarly, ethnic minorities often have sets of values that are different from those of the dominant society and their behaviors may be interpreted negatively. Mental health professionals should broaden their assessment to determine if an invalidating environment may stem from societal rather than family sources.

An assumption underlying the use of DBT with borderline personality disorder is that factors such as family dysfunction (which sometimes includes sexual or physical abuse) and invalidation of a child's emotional reactions, combined with a genetic predisposition to emotional reactivity, are necessary conditions for the development of the disorder. Although an invalidating environment may be a risk factor, it is not *pathognomonic* in the sense of being directly linked to borderline personality disorder. Many individuals coming from very difficult backgrounds and challenging environments do not develop the disorder. There is still a need to identify specific aspects of the environment that lead to borderline personality disorder (Paris, 2005). It is also not clear if some of the family conditions that Linehan hypothesizes to be invalidating might apply to child rearing patterns found in ethnic minority families, such as families who have high expectations for self-reliance or self-control. Whether or not the described features of an invalidating environment apply to ethnic groups and whether sociocultural factors can also be etiological factors are areas in need of further investigation.

We believe that mental health professionals using DBT with diverse groups should be willing to modify the approach. This may involve: (1) evaluating sociocultural stressors during assessment; (2) obtaining the client's perspective of the problem; (3) presenting the DBT philosophy and technique, but broadening the concept of invalidating environment to encompass societal and cultural factors, if appropriate; (4) taking care not to pathologize normative ethnic family patterns; (5) determining the degree of fit of the DBT approach from the client's perspective; and (6) collaborating with the client to modify mindfulness, interpersonal effectiveness, and emotional regulation skills, as needed, to take into account the client's background and perspectives.

Recommended Readings

Linehan, M. M. (1993). *Cognitive-behavioral treatment of borderline personality disorder.* New York: Guilford.

This book is an excellent introduction to the historical and current perspectives on borderline personality disorder. It presents the biosocial theory of personality disorder and treatment strategies using the dialectical behavioral approach. For anyone who wants to know the rationale and techniques of DBT, this book provides a solid foundation. It is widely used by clinicians, and contains over 500 pages of clinical wisdom for working with a very difficult population.

Linehan, M. M. (1993). *Skills training manual for treating borderline personality disorder.* New York: Guilford.

The skills training manual is intended to accompany Linehan's text on cognitive-behavioral treatment of borderline personality disorder. It contains the skills required to conduct DBT and has client handouts revolving around specific training such as core mindfulness skills, interpersonal effectiveness skills, emotional regulation skills, and distress tolerance skills. These skill modules are clearly explained. While not as comprehensive as Linehan's text, there are short sections on the etiology of DBT. An advantage of this manual is that purchasers are granted permission to reproduce the handouts and forms for use with clients.

Multicultural Counseling Theory

14

Chapter

. . . most clinicians share a worldview about the interrelationship between body, mind, and environment . . . clinicians view symptoms, diagnoses, and treatments in ways that sometimes diverge from their clients' views, especially when the cultural backgrounds of the consumer and provider are dissimilar. This divergence of viewpoints can create barriers to effective care. (U.S. Department of Health and Human Services, 2001, p. 14)

I recently worked in an infectious disease clinic where I met a patient in her late 60s who was infected with the human immunodeficiency virus (HIV). My surprise at seeing an older woman with an infection associated with unprotected sex or injecting drug use made me realize I had preconceptions about aging and the elderly. . . . My attitudes could be construed as ageist in nature. (McCray, 1998, pp. 1035–1036)

Chinese and Vietnamese immigrants reported that they encountered negative reactions from Western clinicians when revealing that they use traditional medications. Believing that the two cultures could learn from one another regarding treatment, they wanted to talk about non-Western practices with their providers. However, the response was generally negative, "I told the doctor, 'I am taking some angelica and ginseng. Do you think it is OK?' The doctor said, 'I don't know Chinese medicine . . . You should be responsible for the results if you take them!' After that I did not dare mention Chinese medicine again. (Ngo-Metzger et al., 2003, p. 48)

Throughout the chapters of this text, we have infused social and cultural considerations into assessment, diagnosis, conceptualization, and treatment. However, we believe it remains necessary to present a full discussion of a multicultural counseling theory and to illustrate how it contrasts with other theories. The multicultural paradigm has been called the "fourth force" in the field of psychotherapy, following the other major schools of psychoanalytic, cognitive-behavioral, and humanistic therapies, and has assumed increased importance as our population has become more diverse. Despite concerns regarding the use of current Eurocentric therapies with ethnic minorities or other diverse populations, there has not been a specific multicultural theory. Instead, there have been attempts to add or incorporate cultural themes into traditional psychotherapeutic approaches. An exception is the theory of multicultural counseling and therapy as set forth by D. W. Sue, Ivey, and Pedersen (1996). In this chapter, we will consider the proposals and assumptions of this theory, discuss its implications for psychotherapy, and evaluate research support for the theory. As the vignettes at the beginning demonstrate, worldviews and experiences affect the way we view issues and problems.

Multicultural Counseling Theory

Multicultural counseling theory (MCT) is considered to be a "theory of theories," or a metatheory of traditional psychotherapeutic approaches. MCT points out that our theories of counseling and psychotherapy are culture bound in that they are based on a particular set of explicit and implicit assumptions developed within a specific cultural context. In the United States, psychotherapy theories espouse European or Western standards, values, and beliefs. They are monocultural in that perspectives from other cultures are not included in the theories. Some of the basic characteristics of Western therapy include: (1) a focus on the individual—problems are seen to reside within a person and therapy is directed toward helping the individual become healthier and more autonomous; (2) clients are expected to be verbally and emotionally expressive and willing to make self-disclosures; (3) the focus is on the nuclear family and relationships among family members are viewed from an egalitarian perspective; and (4) little attention is placed on environmental, social, or cultural factors (D. W. Sue & D. Sue, 2003).

Although most societies in the world are collectivistic in orientation, there is little recognition that current therapies may be ineffective with diverse cultural groups or with ethnic minorities. Ethnic minorities tend to differ from the Western perspective in the following ways: (1) there is a family or community identification rather than individualism, and interdependence among members may be more highly valued than individual independence; (2) hierarchical communication patterns may be the norm with differing roles assigned to men, women, and children; and (3) communication patterns may differ in terms of emotional and verbal expressiveness. In addition, social or environmental factors involving prejudice and discrimination, poor housing, or financial concerns that may play a large role in psychological distress are not given much attention in traditional counseling theories.

Theories of counseling and therapy constitute worldviews that include philosophical assumptions regarding the nature of the world, a cultural framework from which to view phenomenon and experiences, and a perceived relationship to the world. We have already discussed the general worldview of Eurocentric therapies. However, there are also "mini" worldviews within Western therapies themselves. Psychoanalysis focuses on the unconscious and early childhood experiences and their strong impact on behavior. Client-centered approaches stress that individuals have a potential for self-actualization, which is promoted though therapist qualities of empathy, genuineness, and warmth. Cognitive-behavioral approaches emphasize that dysfunctional thoughts or inadequate behaviors are the roots of mental health issues. Worldviews, including theoretical views, influence how we think, behave, and perceive events. However, difficulties occur when we impose a specific worldview on other groups. Consider the following:

> *In a study comparing poor Black children with White children, the former were found to be more likely to take an immediate, smaller reward rather than wait for a larger reward at a later time. (Mischel, 1958)*

The experimenter was testing the hypotheses that "Negroes are impulsive, indulge themselves, settle for next to nothing if they can get it right away, do not work or wait for bigger things in the future but, instead, prefer smaller gains immediately" (Mischel, 1958, p. 57). This conclusion placed the responsibility for the cycle of poverty on personal characteristics of African Americans, such as an inability to delay gratification. Environmental or alternative explanations were not entertained. Certainly, among lower class Black children or anyone living in poverty, taking what you can when available may be a very adaptive response where there are limited resources (Mio & Iwamasa, 1993). Similarly, the high drop-out rate associated with American Indians has been attributed to cultural values or personal attributes. Instead, many youths who left school reported feeling "pushed out" and mistrusted teachers who represented the White community (Deyhle & Swisher, 1999). The inability to understand environmental influences and how they may affect those living in poverty can lead to biased judgments. In 2005, during Hurricane Katrina, residents living in the poorer parts of New Orleans were criticized for a lack of judgment when they did not evacuate their homes and leave the city. As in the Mischel study, there was a belief by some that poor judgment was an attribute of ethnic minorities. While middle and upper class residents were able to pack up their belongings in their cars, trucks, or SUVs and leave, many lower class residents had no way of leaving. Many families did not own a car or have the money on hand for gas or bus tickets. In the words of one individual trying to cash his paycheck at a local store and waiting in line with more than 100 people, all of whom were either African American or Hispanic:

All the banks are closed and I just got off work . . . This is crazy. How are you supposed to evacuate a hurricane if you don't have money? Answer me that? (Hastings, 2005, p. 1)

Differences in worldviews can lead to misunderstandings and be especially problematic when they exist between a therapist and client during therapy. Because therapies are based on the Western perspective, which may conflict with the worldview of other cultural groups, D. W. Sue and colleagues (1996) believed that a meta-theory was needed to "unmask and demystify the values, biases, and assumptions about human behavior made by each theoretical orientation" (p. 11). Their book begins with a discussion of the shortcomings of current theories of counseling and psychotherapy with respect to culturally diverse groups. Next, a theory of theories, which they called multicultural counseling theory, was formulated to make the theoretical assumptions and biases of counseling theories explicit. These assumptions are then discussed in terms of the appropriateness of their use with specific populations. Suggestions are made regarding ways to include social and cultural contexts and the worldview of the client into therapeutic approaches. MCT is presented in the form of six propositions that will be discussed in the following sections.

Proposition 1: Incorporate Socio-Cultural Considerations

MCT is a "theory of theories." It offers a framework by which theories of counseling and psychotherapy can be understood. Each theory is comprised of a specific worldview with its own set of beliefs and values. Theories are neither right nor wrong, but are generally developed within a particular cultural context for a specific population. Problems can occur when one worldview regarding behaviors and attitudes is applied to a culturally different population. Because of this, MCT hypothesizes that theoretical approaches are most effective for clients who hold the same or a similar worldview. Any theory (psychoanalytic, humanistic, cognitive, behavioral) can be accommodated within MCT and viewed as a complementary means of describing behavior. Although differences exist among different psychotherapeutic theories, they are all influenced by a Eurocentric focus on the individual. MCT suggests improving these approaches by adding environmental, social, and cultural considerations. Hays (2001) demonstrated how this could be accomplished by adapting Lazarus's (1971) multimodal assessment (focused on behavior, affect, sensations, imagery, cognition, interpersonal relationships, and drugs) to include cultural perspectives. (See Box 14.1.)

It is recommended that clients be assessed on these dimensions to determine issues what might be relevant in conceptualizing problems and in

Box 14.1 **Multimodal Assessment for Culturally and Socially Diverse Populations**

- **Behavior**: What are the social and cultural influences, norms, and expectations that may affect the client's behavior? What role, if any, do cultural or social influences play in the client's presenting problems?
- **Affect or Expression of Emotion**: Are there social and cultural influences that might affect the client's expression of emotion? Is the client's method of emotional expression consistent with norms for the client's cultural or social group?
- **Sensation (Physical or physiological symptoms)**: With regard to physical or physiological symptoms, are there social or cultural influences that may increase the tendency for emotional distress to be expressed in physical ways?
- **Imagery**: Are there socially and culturally relevant images that have influenced the client? Has the client's self-image been impacted by oppression or disadvantage?
- **Cognition**: What are culturally or socially related beliefs, values, attitudes, and statements about the self that have been encountered by the client? Have these been internalized by the client? In what ways might they be affecting the client's behavior or view of self?
- **Interpersonal Relationships:** Are there social or cultural influences regarding relationships that might be affecting the client? How might these influences affect relationships with partners, friends, family, and other social networks?
- **Drugs and Health Care:** What are the social and culture-specific conceptualizations of illness and health? Are there social or cultural influences that impact the use of health care systems, including mental health services? Are there any specific cultural or social influences on medication use, or the use of drugs, alcohol, or other substances?

From Hays, 2001

providing treatment. Because MCT emphasizes the degree of fit between traditional theoretical models and the worldview of the client, the MCT theoretical model avoids the problem of either neglecting cultural factors (being culture blind) or overemphasizing cultural differences (stereotyping). Thus, MCT broadens therapy to include social and cultural factors. Because of this, a collaborative relationship with the client with respect to defining problems and solutions is vital. Although most therapies do place importance on the therapist-client relationship, this is usually done with the goal of improving the therapeutic alliance, rather than understanding the worldview of the client.

Proposition 2: Identity is Embedded in Multiple Contexts

Identities of therapists and clients occur at multiple levels and across varied contexts. There may be similarities or differences between a therapist and client with respect to group dimensions such as race, culture, or ethnicity, socioeconomic or religious background, marital status, gender, or age. Traditional psychotherapies have focused primarily on the individual and universal dimensions and have ignored group-level dimensions. Because most therapists trained in the theories of counseling and psychotherapy focus primarily at the individual and universal level, MCT emphasizes the need to consider issues at the group level. This is important because therapists generally operate according to their own cultural worldview and see the client from that perspective.

> *Videotapes of interviews of Chinese and Caucasian American patients were rated by Chinese and Caucasian American psychiatrists. Caucasian therapists were more likely to use the terms "affectionate," "adventurous," and" capable" to describe Caucasian clients, whereas Chinese clinicians used terms such as "active," "aggressive," and "rebellious." While Caucasian therapists described Chinese clients as "anxious," "awkward," "confused," "nervous," and "quiet," Chinese psychiatrists were more likely to use terms such as "adaptive," "alert," and "dependable" for the same clients. (Li-Repac, 1980)*

This study by Li-Repac indicates that the ratings of clients were influenced by differences in the therapists' cultural backgrounds and worldviews. Neither group of psychiatrists realized that their responses to the clients reflected cultural views of what constituted normal behaviors. Both Caucasian and Chinese American psychiatrists ignored the effects of group-level analysis. In a situation such as this, the question should be, "What are the behaviors considered to be normative for the client's specific cultural group?" MCT emphasizes that the totality of identities and contexts for both the therapist and client must be taken into consideration. Additionally, the salience of group affiliation and identity varies over time within the same individual. The therapist must determine what is currently important for the client. Rather than make assumptions based on a client's group membership, this determination must be made on an individual basis. This is to prevent stereotyping and responding in a fixed way just because of a client's membership in a particular group. Over- or underemphasizing group differences is less likely to occur when clients are assessed on different aspects of identify and group membership.

Proposition 3: Cultural Identity Influences Attitudes

The cultural identity of both the client and the therapist influences attitudes toward self, toward others from the same and from different groups, and toward others of the dominant group. These attitudes are not affected only by cultural factors, but also in terms of the differences in power status among different cultural groups.

> *Mikki, a 27-year-old social worker, who immigrated to Israel from Ethiopia at the age of 10, worked in a municipal unit for adolescents in distress . . . Recognizing the huge gap between his family's traditional lifestyle and the modernity of the Israeli, he soon began to feel ashamed of his parents . . . he rejected the boys who represented his traditional Ethiopian self and favored those who represented the Israel part of him . . . (Yedidia, 2005, pp. 165–166)*

In this case, Mikki's rejection of members of his own cultural group was the result of an identity conflict. Only through supervision did he become consciously aware of the effect it has on his work. Some female therapists may also have difficulty working with male clients because of their belief that males have unfair power and privilege in society. Feminist therapists believe that exposure to the patriarchal nature of our society and a subordinate status is responsible for many mental health issues faced by women. Understanding one's reaction to these beliefs is the first step in resolving identity and power conflicts. The degree of identity with a particular group can influence the behavior of both clients and therapists. It is important for therapists to be aware that ethnic minority and diverse populations are hypothesized to go through five stages of identity development (Sue & Sue, 2003) as described below.

Stage 1: Conformity

> *Hector was a 16-year-old boy whose mother was European American and whose father immigrated to the U.S. from Mexico. Hector was referred for counseling because he was acting out in school and making frequent racist remarks. He appeared to be White and openly claimed only his White Identity. . . . He frequently joked about "Mexicans." (McDowell, Fang, Brownlee, Young, & Khanna, 2005, p. 408)*

> *Eric Liu, the son of immigrants from Taiwan, graduated from Yale, wrote speeches for President Clinton and doesn't feel like an "Asian American." He believes the identity is contrived and unnecessary. (Chang, 1998)*

In the conformity stage, racial or diversity identities are of low-salience or may involve self-deprecation. In some cases, diversity or ethnic characteristics may be unimportant to the individual, although some may acknowledge that their group suffers disadvantage. For those who have negative reactions regarding their identity, there may be attempts to emulate the characteristics of the majority group in terms of attitudes, dress, and behaviors. There is little identification with the ethnic or diverse group, and some may feel ashamed of their cultural group. Clients at this stage might not be receptive to discussion of group differences. Individuals at the conformity stage may feel more comfortable with a majority culture or White therapist and may be uncomfortable with any discussion regarding their diversity status.

Stage 2: Dissonance and Appreciation

> *In 1988, I became obviously disabled. I walk with crutches and a stiff leg. Since that time, I no longer fulfill our cultural standard of physical attractiveness. But worse, there are times when people who know me don't acknowledge me. When I call their name and say, "Hello," they often reply, "Oh, I didn't see you." I have also been mistaken for people who do not resemble me. For example, I was recently asked, "Are you a leader in the disability movement?" While I hope to be that someday, I asked her, "Who do you believe I am?" She had mistaken me for a taller person with a different hair color, who limps but does not use a walking aid. The only common element was our disability. My disability had become my persona. This person saw it and failed to see me. (Buckman, 1998, p. 19)*

During the dissonance and appreciation stage, individuals come to the realization that their group may be discriminated against by the larger society. At this stage, for example, individuals who are older, have a disability, or are members of an oppressed ethnic group may begin to accept their group identity and question the prejudicial societal standards. They begin to move toward group appreciation because of feelings of shared experiences, but have still not fully broken from the group-deprecating attitude of Stage 1. In therapy, clients at the dissonance and appreciation stage are open to self-exploration regarding their minority status. It helps when therapists are sensitive to the dissonance and conflicts that are typical at this stage.

Stage 3: Resistance and Immersion

> *I am not elderly, I am old and proud of it. I am aged, like a good cheese. I am a walking history book, an elder of the tribe, tested, tempered, wise. . . . I can leave parties early. . . . I enjoy melancholy, even revel in it. (Frankel, 1998, p. 16)*

During the resistance and immersion stage, individuals have fully adopted their group identity and may become advocates for their group. In some cases, there may be hostility to society-at-large over discriminatory practices. A sense of group pride develops along with a sense of connectedness regarding group membership. During this stage, the individual may over-identify with the group. The dominant society may be viewed as an oppressor and clients may blame their difficulties almost entirely on an oppressive society. Therapists may be viewed with suspicion and seen as societal agents who protect the status quo. It is often necessary to acknowledge and explore these issues before the possible contribution of clients to their own problems can be considered. In situations where prejudice or discriminatory practices play a role in the client's difficulties, discussions of change strategies might involve intervention at the individual, group, or systems level.

Stage 4: Introspection

During this stage, individuals begin to question their unequivocal acceptance of their group and their rejection of those from other groups or from society-at-large. They may begin to realize that they have minimized opportunities to understand themselves or their identity outside of the dictates of their group. An interest in and attempt to reach out to people outside of their own group begins to emerge. At this stage, therapists may be involved in helping clients resolve conflicts between absolute identification with and questioning of their group. Clients may feel a sense of disloyalty to the group if they begin to exercise personal autonomy. Self-exploration is helpful in developing appreciation for other groups and society-in-general, while still accepting the positive aspects of one's group.

Stage 5: Integrative Awareness Stage

In the integrative awareness stage, the individual has developed a sense of security regarding their identity. They feel free to question aspects of their own group and can also appreciate certain aspects of the larger society. Positive and unacceptable elements are acknowledged in all cultural or diverse groups. Preferences for therapists are based on shared understanding and attitudinal similarities.

Identity Conflicts in Therapists

Although, we have focused on the client's identity development, therapists may also display characteristics associated with the different stages of identity. It is possible for identity issues of therapists to become activated during the provision of therapy. A female therapist struggling with the influence of power and gender issues on her work with male clients may be somewhere between Stage 3 (resistance and immersion) and Stage 4 (introspection) with respect to gender identity. She identifies with her group, but realizes that she may be biased against male clients by placing them into the oppressor category. In this next example, the therapist appears to be struggling between Stages 1 (conformity) and Stage 2 (dissonance and appreciation).

> *Kavita, a clinician of South Asian descent, is unsure of her ethnic identity and has trouble balancing being American with being South Asian. Seeing South*

*Asian clients only makes this conflict more salient to her. Will this affect her at-
titudes toward treating minority clients? (Gurung & Mehta, 2001, p. 139)*

Stages of identity may affect the responses of both therapists and clients.
As therapists, we must learn to identify and acknowledge cultural and diversity aspects within ourselves and determine if these may be hindering our ability to provide effective therapy to clients who are culturally different or similar
to us. Do White therapists also go through stages of racial identity? Is there
reason to explore the question "What does it mean to be White?" (Sue & Sue,
2003, p. 241). Although controversial, stages of White identity development
have been formulated (see Table 14.1) and can be helpful in assisting White
therapists to self-assess with respect to their own identity development.

Proposition 4: Cultural Strategies Enhance Therapy

The effectiveness of therapy is enhanced when the modalities and goals of
therapy are consistent with the lifestyle, experiences, and values of the client.
Although this may be most easily achieved when the worldview of the therapist and the client are similar, the effectiveness of therapy can also be increased
by acknowledging perceived differences. Clients may look for commonalities
when they are working with a therapist who appears to be from a different
background. An African American psychology intern working with an older
adult noticed that the client made frequent positive comments regarding African Americans. He repeatedly talked about African Americans with whom
he had served in the army and about their contribution to the unit. The intern
eventually responded by saying "I guess you noticed I'm Black" (Hinrichsen,
2006, p. 31). This led to an open discussion of client concerns over whether or
not the intern could understand the experiences of an older, White male and
the client's fear that he might say something that could be considered racially
offensive. Clients often look for commonalities between themselves and their
therapists, especially if they wonder whether a therapist will understand their
life experiences. A 78-year-old woman asked her therapist if he was Jewish.
The woman explained that she had experienced discrimination and wanted
to know if the therapist would understand her difficulties (Hinrichsen, 2006).
The therapeutic alliance is strengthened when the therapist is perceived to
have values and beliefs similar to those of the client or appears open to the
client's values and beliefs. Collaboration and open communication are important means of accomplishing a sense of mutual understanding.

According to MCT, an avenue for increasing understanding between
therapists and clients is the exploration of indigenous sources of support such
as spirituality and alternative methods of healing. For example, for many African Americans, spirituality and religion play an important role with respect

Table 14.1 **White Identity Development**

Stage	Characteristics
Conformity	This is an ethnocentric stage, with little recognition of the self as a racial being. There is a belief that "everyone has an equal chance to succeed in society." The idea of "White privilege" is not understood or recognized. Either consciously or unconsciously, there is a belief in the superiority of one's own culture and values. Therapists at this stage do not question the assumptions of their therapy.
Dissonance	The individual begins to see inequities in society and injustices to ethnic minorities and other diverse groups. Racism, sexism, ageism, and heterosexism are recognized, but there is still difficulty reconciling these observations. Rather than blaming diverse populations for their plight, the individual begins to recognize that society may also play a role.
Resistance and Immersion	There is understanding that racism and discriminatory practices are prevalent in society. Feelings of guilt over being White, having a privileged status, or anger about repression in society may occur. The individual may display a "White liberal" behavior, including a paternalistic attitude toward or over-identification with minority groups.
Introspective	There is acceptance of being White and less defensiveness about White privilege. The individual develops healthier relationships with minority group members, and is willing to openly explore identity issues and to evaluate intergroup relationships.
Integrative Awareness	A stable awareness of identity allows for the understanding and acceptance of humans as racial and cultural beings. There is an understanding of racism and other -isms. The individual appreciates diversity and places value on efforts to eliminate prejudicial and discriminatory practices.

From Sue & Sue, 2008

to opportunities for self-expression and community involvement. In one case, these aspects were used in treatment:

> *A 42-year-old recently divorced African American woman presented symptoms of depression that included feelings of loneliness, lack of energy, loss of appetite and crying spells. She was raising two children with little support from her ex-husband. (Queener & Martin, 2001)*

During assessment, the woman indicated that religion and spirituality were sources of support for her. The therapist collaborated with the woman to develop a treatment program that included traditional psychological interventions such as cognitive restructuring, changing behaviors, and expression of feelings, but also encouraged her to participate in two church-related programs. This involved her joining the women's ministry of her church, with the goal of decreasing her emotional and social isolation, and participation in a "The Mother to Son Program" that provides assistance to single mothers parenting African American boys (Queener & Martin, 2001). For this client, the use of community support augmented cognitive-behavioral therapy.

Among many ethnic groups, the mind and body are considered inseparable. Emotional distress may be expressed through somatic complaints. Among traditionally oriented Chinese Americans, depression is described with terms such as discomfort, pain, dizziness, or other physical symptoms rather than as feelings of sadness. Many feel that a diagnosis of depression is "morally unacceptable" or "experientially meaningless" (Kleinman, 2004).

Western therapists take a psychosomatic approach to mental disorders, believing that psychological factors can be manifested as physical symptoms. However, other cultural groups believe that emotional problems such as depression are the result of physical symptoms such as headaches, fatigue, restlessness, and disturbances in sleep and appetite (Yeung, Chang, Gresham, Neirenberg, & Fava, 2004). In these groups, physical complaints are a common and culturally accepted means of expressing psychological and emotional stress. Individuals tend to seek treatment for their physical complaints rather than for psychological symptoms. To acknowledge this, therapists can listen to the physical concerns. Psychological issues can be investigated indirectly by asking questions such as "Having headaches and fatigue can be quite troublesome. How are they affecting your mood or your relationship with family or with friends?" In this way, somatic complaints are legitimized, but the question allows a discussion regarding the individual's emotional state and relationships.

Clients can be asked about the use of indigenous healing practices. As the vignette involving Chinese and Vietnamese immigrants at the beginning of the chapter demonstrates, cultural groups often have their own beliefs regarding the etiology and appropriate treatment for problems. *DSM-IV-TR* contains a list of *culture-bound syndromes* (constellations of symptoms or behaviors that are present in specific cultural groups); it is important for therapists to listen to and be open to the explanations of symptoms given by their clients.

Vang Xiong was a former Hmong soldier who settled in Chicago. As with many refugees, he left Southeast Asia under traumatic circumstances. He had witnessed killings, and had had to leave his brothers and sisters behind. In the United States, he lived in an unfamiliar society and was exposed to vast cultural differences. During his first night of sleep in the United States, he dreamed of a cat sitting on his chest and awoke with problems breathing. His second night of sleep was even worse, with dreams of a large black dog sitting on his chest. He could not push the dog off his chest and he became dangerously short of breath. During the third night, he dreamed of a white skinned evil spirit that came into the bedroom and lay on top of him. He was unable to breathe and tried to call out. After about 15 minutes, the spirit left him and he awoke with a scream. (Tobin & Friedman, 1983)

Vang sought help from Mrs. Thor, a shaman in the Hmong community. In investigating the cause of his problem, she began a chant to communicate with spirits. After 1 hour, she announced that his problem was the result of the activities of unhappy spirits who were the former tenants of the apartment. To release the spirits, she had Vang participate in a ritualistic activity in which he briefly wore a cloak, which was burned as soon as he removed it. He was asked to crawl though a hoop and between two knives to prevent the spirits from following him. After this treatment, Vang no longer had breathing problems during sleep.

It is important for therapists to be open to exploring indigenous treatments, especially as they relate to a client's belief system. This does not mean the therapist needs to subscribe to the client's belief; however, the therapist should not invalidate cultural belief, directly or indirectly. The key is for the therapist to listen to the client and sincerely try to understand the client's perspective. Because Vang believed so strongly in the cause of his disorder, methods based on Western approaches may have been ineffective. When appropriate, therapists can attempt to coordinate treatment with indigenous healers. Although you may personally consider indigenous treatments as placebos, it is important to remember that placebos often produce results similar to active treatments. When working with different cultural groups, the goal of therapy is to have clients develop functional ways of thinking, feeling, and behaving within their cultural framework and in interacting with the worldview of others.

Proposition 5: Therapists Can Advocate on Many Levels

MCT emphasizes the importance of therapists taking on multiple roles and the need to intervene at the family, community, and system levels. Some roles for mental health professionals might include (Atkinson, Thompson, & Grant, 1993):

(1) Advisor—In the advisory role, the therapist can provide information regarding community resources that are available to clients. These may include information about housing, financial resources, or academic and occupational opportunities. Knowing how bureaucracies operate, the therapist can advise the client in optimizing the chances for success in working with

agencies. If discriminatory practices occur, the therapist can direct the client to the U.S. Commission on Civil Rights, which investigates discriminatory practices against individuals due to race, religion, gender, age (over 40), and disability in the areas of voting, renting, buying a home, use of a public facility, obtaining a job, or education. Immigrant populations often have fears of deportation, even if they are legal permanent residents. They may need to be informed of services that are available to them and rights such as having an interpreter available during health care. There are also free community clinics that will treat individuals regardless of immigration status. Special services are also available for individuals with disabilities. For instance, the National Library Service produces talking books and magazines on cassettes for individuals with vision limitations.

(2) Advocate—As an advocate, the therapist may promote a client's rights, work to change agency policies, or promote societal changes. At the client level, the therapist may personally intervene to help a client to receive better treatment. At the agency level, the therapist may advocate for changes in clinic policy regarding how to improve and facilitate access to services by multicultural or diverse populations. Important changes at the societal level, such as changes in governmental or organizational policies, have often been the result of the efforts of advocacy groups. In the case below, mental health organizations had only limited success:

> Pentagon guidelines that classify homosexuality as a mental disorder were changed because of concerns expressed by mental health professionals who pointed out that variances in sexual orientation are not considered a mental disorder. Because of the protests, the Pentagon officials finally removed homosexuality from the mental disorder category and placed it with conditions such as bed-wetting, stammering or stuttering, sleep-walking, and insect venom allergies. (Baldor, 2006)

(3) Consultant—As with advocacy, mental health professionals can work as consultants, providing input or specialized knowledge to help facilitate interventions on behalf of a client. Such consultation, which occurs with the permission of the client, might involve parents, teachers, other therapists, administrators, or agencies. MCT stresses the importance of mental health professionals performing activities other than just individual or group counseling, thus broadening their roles and connecting with community agencies and resources.

> Darlene, a 15-year-old, from a low-income family, was considering dropping out of an inner city school because she was not doing well academically and because her mother, who received public assistance, wanted her to get a job to assist the financial well-being of the family, which included five children. (Bienvenu & Ramsey, 2006)

The school counselor utilized a number of different roles to help Darlene. During individual counseling, she focused on Darlene's strengths and worked to make her feel more empowered. She became an advisor by presenting information regarding the advantages of having a high school diploma, such as being able to earn higher wages. When Darlene asked about higher education, the counselor provided information on college admissions and funding resources. In the advocacy role, the counselor arranged for a tutor to provide assistance with current classes, a community mentor to provide social and emotional support, and investigated opportunities for paid internships through the school-to-work program. The counselor even obtained information on job training for Darlene's mother. The roles taken on by this school counselor are roles that any mental health professional can use to assist their clients. This is especially important for clients who have limited skills in navigating systems or accessing community resources.

Proposition 6: Understands Societal Realities

One of the goals of MCT is the "liberation of consciousness." It has been defined as "learning to perceive social, political, and economic contradictions, and to take action against the oppressive elements of reality" (Freire, 1970, p. 19). Many therapists and their clients are unaware of societal, political, and economic influences and the role they play in mental health issues. The following are some examples of societal realities or environmental stressors faced by ethnic minorities and members of diverse populations:

- Republican congressman Virgil Goode of Virginia wrote a letter to his constituents stating, "I feel that in the next century we will have many more Muslims in the United States if we do not adopt the strict immigration policies that I believe are necessary to preserve the values and beliefs traditional to the United States of America . . ." (Frommer, 2006)

- African Americans exposed to videotaped or imaginal depictions of racism showed increases in heart rate and digital blood flow (Jones, Harrell, Morris-Prather, Thomas, & Omowale, 1996). Systolic blood pressure also appears to be influenced by response to discrimination. African Americans who responded by accepting discrimination showed higher blood pressure than did those who challenged the situation. (Krieger & Sidney, 1996)

- A study in the Journal of the American Medical Association reports that girls in their teens are almost as likely as adult women to experience abuse in relationships. One in five girls reported physical or sexual abuse in a relationship. These girls were also more likely to report eating disorders, drug use, suicidal thoughts, and risky sexual behavior. (Palmer, 2001, p. A17)

■ Exposure to societal discrimination may be responsible for the recent findings that lesbian and gay youth report elevated rates of major depression, generalized anxiety disorder, and substance abuse. (Rienzo, Button, Sheu, & Li, 2006)

■ The U.S. Government judged that Indians were incapable of managing their own land, so they placed the property in a trust in 1887, promising that the Indians would receive the income from their land. This financial reimbursement never occurred. In December, 1999, a Federal judge ruled that the government had breached its sacred trust duties. (Maas, 2001)

These are just a few examples of the impact of political and societal prejudice on groups such as women, gay men and women, and ethnic and religious minorities. Feminist therapists have pointed out the sexist nature of our society, emphasizing that sexist perspectives are embedded in both theoretical and therapeutic approaches to psychopathology. They point out that our theories of psychotherapy are male-oriented. In past research, qualities such as submissiveness and being more emotional and relationship-oriented were seen as positive qualities in women (Atkinson & Hackett, 1998). In other cases, behaviors have been pathologized. For example, codependency is defined as being overly involved with another person's problem. D. H. Granello and Beamish (1998) believe codependency in women may stem from a gender role that emphasizes connectedness, nurturance, placing the needs of the family over themselves, and devoting energy to relationships. Although unhealthy attachments do exist, therapists must be careful not to pathologize gender normative behaviors. It is essential that therapists collaborate with their clients to investigate possible societal or cultural dimensions underlying their present concerns. Therapists should take care to be sensitive to and not allow clients to personalize issues that are societal in nature.

Evaluation of MCT

The six propositions in MCT have not been directly investigated because each is very broad in scope and difficult to evaluate. In addition, terms such as culture-bound, ethnocentrism, and racism have not been operationally defined. According to MCT, the very means to test hypotheses from the propositions are culture-bound; that is, they are generated from a specific worldview. As D. W. Sue and colleagues (1996) point out, research on ethnic and other diverse groups has: (1) used Eurocentric standards when evaluating these groups, (2) focused on pathology and deficiencies, rather than strengths, and (3) used research findings to formulate discriminatory practices. Some research has been directed to certain aspects of the propositions. However, the findings are difficult to interpret since they depend on analogue studies regarding therapist preference, involve small samples, may not be representative of larger population groups, and utilize different outcome measures. Given these limitations, we will focus on research findings specific to Proposition 4 from MCT, which suggests that similarities in the worldview of the therapist and client are conducive to a better outcome, taking research on the effects of therapist-client matching in terms of ethnicity, gender, and stage of identity into consideration.

In a meta-analysis of the impact of therapist and client racial-ethnic matching for African American and Caucasian American clients on the variables of overall functioning, drop-out rate, and total number of sessions attended, no significant differences were found between ethnically matched and nonethnically matched dyads (Shin et al., 2005). In a large-scale study that involved 4,483 college students and 376 therapists from 42 university counseling centers, there was little evidence supporting the effectiveness of therapist-client matching on ethnicity with respect to either working alliance or outcome. However, a problem with this study was that the percentage of ethnic minority participants was relatively small (African American, 3.0 percent; Asian American, 4.2 percent; Hispanic American, 7.7 percent; and Alaskan/Native American, 0.3 percent) (Erdur et al., 2000). These findings are in contrast to analogue research that indicates African American clients prefer an African American therapist (Karlsson, 2005). In a review of research on therapist-client match that includes both analogue and actual sessions, Flaherty and Adams (1998) reached the following conclusions:

- Both male and female clients prefer women therapists.
- White clients show no preference in terms of White and non-White therapists while African Americans prefer therapists from their ethnic group.
- Ethnic matching may be important for Asian Americans and is related to decreased dropout.

Linguistic skills of the therapist may be an important factor for immigrant groups. Among Mexican Americans for whom English was not their primary language, ethnic match was found to be a positive predictor of outcome (Sue et al., 1991). There are also some preliminary findings suggesting positive effects of ethnic matching when the therapist is an ethnic minority (Erdur, Rude, Baron, Draper, & Shankar, 2000). Ethnic-matching may also depend on characteristics of the client such as the degree of adherence to cultural values. Asian American clients with traditional Asian values rated Asian American therapists as more empathetic and credible than those who were Westernized (Kim & Atkinson, 2002). Thus, the impact of ethnic matching is influenced by variables such as gender, linguistic ability, and the identity development of the client. We believe that all therapists can enhance similarities by working collaboratively with clients, assessing and respecting their worldview, and jointly deciding on appropriate goals and interventions. This is consistent with the research on therapeutic alliance that stresses the importance of therapist-client agreement on goals and interventions, as well as the relationship skills of empathy and warmth.

What are the practical implications of MCT? It allows therapists to become aware of explicit assumptions regarding their psychotherapeutic worldview and stresses the importance of understanding the worldview of the client. Therapeutic approaches and the theories upon which they are based need to be evaluated for their appropriateness with, or adapted for use with, ethnic minorities and diverse populations. It would be beneficial for all mental health professionals to be open to learning about indigenous healing processes and the use of community resources in treatment. Social, environmental, and cultural issues likely play a much greater role than is commonly recognized in the etiology of psychological distress in diverse populations. It is important for mental health professionals to have the skills to work not only in the traditional therapy role, but also to be advocates, advisors, and consultants for clients, agencies, and government organizations.

Although therapists should consider cultural factors, it is important not to apply cultural knowledge in a stereotypic fashion to clients. It is best for therapists to determine the importance of cultural or ethnic identity and degree of cultural adherence for each individual client. Matching clients with therapists on some characteristics may be important, but even more so, it is the demonstration of warmth and respectful acceptance to the client that is the key to an effective therapeutic alliance with all clients.

Multicultural and Diversity Issues in Counseling and Psychotherapy

Imagine that you are working with a client of a different race from your own. How do you decide whether and, if so, when and how to address the topic of race in the therapy? If you do address race, how does the conversation affect the therapy; if you do not address race, what is the effect of this decision? (Knox, Burkard, Johnson, Suzuki, & Ponterotto, 2003, p. 466)

You are a male social worker who comes from an upper middle class background working in an agency that serves very low-income clients. You find yourself becoming increasingly frustrated with female clients who miss appointments, often with excuses that their car broke down, they couldn't find a ride, they got called in to work at the last minute, or they can't find anyone to baby-sit their children.

You have moved to a new community due to your partner's job transfer. It was a difficult decision to move from a large city to a suburban community in a different part of the country. You are of African-American descent, which was an advantage in your previous counseling job where you had an ethnic and cultural connection with the majority of your clients. However, in your new community, there is little diversity and you feel uncomfortable interacting with your new clients.

15 Chapter

Through the vignettes above, you can begin to get a feel for potential background differences that can affect the client-therapist relationship. Sometimes these differences may be relatively minor, in the sense that they are not salient to the issues discussed or to the therapeutic alliance. In other situations, differences might be quite important to the client or to the therapist. In the multicultural counseling field, attention is often given to "client differences." However, as emphasized throughout our book, it is equally important to consider therapist background characteristics and reactions. In Chapter 4, we discussed the importance of therapists knowing themselves, their values, their reactions, and their prejudices. As we examine the important topic of diversity considerations in counseling, we hope you will take the time to reflect on these topics as they pertain to you individually. If you think of your classmates or colleagues in the fields of counseling, psychology or social work, you will get a feel for the diversity in backgrounds, values, and beliefs of those in the mental health profession.

When individual therapist characteristics are combined with client differences, the potential diversity is immense. Because there is no multicultural therapy, we have decided to use this chapter to present practical issues faced by therapists when working with clients who differ from the therapist in terms of values, or social, cultural, or ethnic background. In the following sections, we will not attempt to provide how-to information, but instead will raise issues that might be important to consider when there are specific differences between therapist and client. We will also discuss issues involved in working with specific diverse populations and conclude with suggestions on how we can improve cultural competence through case presentation and supervision. We will begin by sharing some considerations regarding the perceived effectiveness of therapists regarding cross-racial dyads and the circumstances under which differences should be acknowledged.

Acknowledging Differences: Respect and Understanding Are the Key

Multicultural theory would seem to indicate that to be culturally competent, we need to show respect for clients' ethnicity and background. Should differences between the therapist and client be acknowledged and, if so, when and how? Does recognizing differences increase therapist credibility and strengthen the therapeutic alliance? What kinds of differences should be acknowledged? Should therapists who are ethnically or culturally different from their clients routinely ask questions such as, "How do you feel working with a White (or minority) therapist?" In some cases, it is obvious that differences need to be addressed, such as the case where the woman asked the therapist if he was Jewish. Students, interns, or therapists may also face questions such as "Are you married?" or "Do you have children?" One of our interns was bluntly asked by a 77-year-old widower, "How can you help me? You can't have any idea of how it feels to lose your wife after fifty years of marriage, let alone how it feels to be getting old and seeing friends and family getting sick or dying." In these examples, where characteristics such as race, age, or marital status are brought up, the therapist needs to respond directly.

Hidden or unconscious reactions to the therapist can also occur and are probably more common. Some clients may also have reservations regarding the therapist that they do not voice. These unspoken feelings may affect the therapeutic relationship. In one study, male Hispanic counselors with a Spanish accent were rated lower in expertise by Euro-American students than were Hispanic counselors without an accent (Fuertes & Gelso, 2000). We have worked with a number of interns and mental health professionals who are not native English speakers and who speak with an accent. What advice would you give them when working with clients who speak only English? Before responding, we are going to present some relevant research regarding how therapists have handled cross-racial dyads.

Fifty-three counselors (33 European American, 17 African American, and 3 Native American) were asked regarding their work in cross-racial therapy, "How successful do you think you are in working with majority clients? How successful do you think you are in working with minority clients?" (Davis & Gelsomino, 1994, p.118). Both White and minority counselors considered themselves to be equally effective in working with White clients. However, White therapists considered themselves less successful in counseling minority clients than did minority therapists. Minority counselors reported experiencing racism from some of their clients, while White therapists reported the belief that some minority clients perceived them as having insufficient understanding of their racial experience. From the perspective of the therapists, ethnicity did play a role in cross-racial dyads.

In another study (Fuertes, Mueller, Chauhan, Walker, & Ladany, 2002), interviews were conducted with nine White therapists (six women and three men) regarding their work with African American clients. Most discussed differences in race between themselves and their clients during the first two sessions; some indicated that race was like an "elephant in the room" (p. 774). The therapists varied in both the manner and the directness with which this topic was presented. Here are some examples, ". . . Is it okay with you that I'm your counselor and a person of noncolor?" and "Are there any other issues or sensitivities you have not mentioned, for example, who you would like to work with or who you would find difficult to work with?" (p. 775). Therapists also checked for possible misunderstandings with African American clients with statements such as, "Anytime that you feel I've missed the boat, I want you to tell me I didn't understand, and that your experience or reality is very different" (p. 776). The therapists modified therapy in their work with African American clients to include culture-specific strategies (considering the client's racial identity development and worldview) and attending to reports of racism by the client. The therapists reported that they were careful not to engage in tunnel vision, that is, focusing primarily on race to the exclusion of other factors. Therapists believed the discussion of race contributed to a positive relationship.

Other researchers (Knox et al., 2003) investigated the experience of five African American and seven White therapists regarding the discussion of race in cross-racial therapy. African American therapists routinely brought up the issue of race with clients. This was especially true when race seemed to be part of the presenting problem or if they observed signs of discomfort in their White clients. They also addressed race with clients of color and would directly ask non-African American clients, "How does it feel to talk to an African American therapist?" White therapists were more tentative and uncomfortable in discussing race and some would not normally raise racial issues in therapy. Both groups of therapists avoided discussion of race if the client seemed to be uncomfortable about race. However, both White and African Americans therapists believed that addressing race seemed to strengthen the therapeutic relationship.

Although the research involved cross-race therapy dyads, the findings may also be appropriate to other types of differences between therapist and client. At the beginning of this section, we asked if differences should be addressed, and under what conditions. It is obvious that, as therapists, we need to identify cultural issues, values, beliefs, and experiences that may interfere with the provision of therapy to clients. It is important to acknowledge the distinct possibility that our ethnicity, outward appearance, nonverbal behaviors, or other characteristics may raise questions about our credibility with our clients. We offer the following suggestions based on research and our own experience but caution that clinicians must make their best judgment based on the individual client:

1. Cross-race therapy dyads—In general, both minority and White therapists involved in the above research studies seem to believe it is beneficial to address race during the first sessions. The therapist can do this in a direct manner, inquiring about the possible impact of a cross-race dyad on therapy, or indirectly by talking about differences in life experiences. Minority therapists appear to be the most comfortable addressing racial differences. In the Knox and colleagues' (2003) study, therapists avoided the race issue when it appeared that the client was uncomfortable regarding the topic. Certainly, if race does not appear to be an important issue, it does not seem beneficial to bring it to the client's attention. In our opinion, however, if the discomfort shown by the client is in response to racial differences between the therapist and client, it should be discussed. In general, we believe it is helpful to bring up these differences, either directly or indirectly, in much the same way you would discuss your therapeutic approach.

2. Differences between therapist and client other than race—Aspects or characteristics of the therapist may be salient to some clients. It makes sense to anticipate the possibility that clients will respond to some characteristic that you have and develop different ways of responding. You might preempt possible concerns of the client. One of our students started sessions by saying, "In case you're interested in where my accent comes from, I'm from Bosnia. Do you have any questions regarding me or my background?" Another student mentioned that he was

from Singapore and conversant in English, but requested clients to ask for clarification if they did not understand something that was communicated.

Validation of client concerns can also be helpful. For example, the limited life experience of young professionals is often a concern to clients who are married, have children, or are older. They may ask specifically about the therapist's qualifications in terms of life experiences. In one case, an older adult stated when meeting the therapist for the first time, "You're so young. How can you understand my life or what I am going through?" The intern said, "Maybe I can't, but I'd like to try to understand what is going on in your life." The therapist validated the concern of the client, expressing his wish to work with and understand the client's life. Acknowledging clients' concerns by validating their feelings and stating your wish to understand their view is a useful way of dealing with differences.

It is helpful if you are alert for and prepared to respond to nonverbal signs that appear to question your experience or seem to be in response to some characteristic that you may have. Tentative statements to check out your perception can include questions such as, "I'm wondering if you have some doubts about whether I can understand or be helpful with your problem?" Inquiries should be tentative to allow you to determine the accuracy of your observation. Regardless of whether or not the issue is directly acknowledged or discussed, it is important to remain aware that the therapist's outward appearance, communication style, use of language, accent, or apparent ethnic, cultural, or religious identification may influence the client's perception of the therapist.

What are the conclusions that can be reached regarding differences between therapist and clients? Several options exist. Therapists can: (1) bring up the issue directly, (2) adopt a wait-and-see stance, (3) increase credibility by demonstrating an understanding of social or cultural influences, or (4) attempt to build a strong therapeutic alliance through relationship skills, and thus reduce the impact of differences.

Issues Related to Specific Populations

At your clinic, you are asked to provide services to non-English proficient clients. How would you work effectively with an interpreter? How could you make this partnership work in a productive manner?

"I am assessing to see if that person [counselor] is willing to go that extra mile and speak my language and talk about my Blackness. . . ." (Ward, 2005, p. 475)

As compared to White Americans, fewer American Indians and Alaskan Natives finish high school. Although the blame for high drop out rates has been placed on "cultural factors," youths who left school reported feeling "pushed out." They mistrusted teachers who represented the White community that exerted control over their economic, social and religious lives. (Deyhle & Swisher, 1999)

It was sometimes hard to adjust. When I went outside, I was in America, but inside my house, it was Mexico. My father was the leader of the house. It wasn't that way for some of my American friends. (Middleton, Arrendondo, & D'Andrea, 2000, p. 24)

A study in the Journal of the American Medical Association reports that girls in their teens are almost as likely as adult women to experience abuse in relationships. One in five girls reported physical or sexual abuse in a relationship. These girls were also more likely to report eating disorders, drug use, suicidal thoughts and risky sexual behavior. (Palmer, 2001, p. A17)

Your clinic is providing services to an increasing number of older adults with mental health issues. How would you make the environment user friendly? Are there additional assessments or modifications in therapy that you would employ?

Throughout the chapters of this book, we have attempted to incorporate diversity issues and emphasize the importance of social, cultural, and environmental influences on behavior. We cannot hope to cover all possible groups in this chapter. Instead, we will focus briefly on key issues related to diverse populations and direct therapists to books such as: *Counseling the Culturally Diverse* (5th ed.) by D. W. Sue and D. Sue (2008), *Addressing Cultural Complexities in Practice: A Framework for Clinicians and Counselors* by Hays (2001), and *Multicultural Issues in Counseling* (3rd ed.) by Lee (2006). Often, when working with the culturally diverse, we do not have information regarding their views of or reactions to mental health providers. Because this is an important topic, we will begin our discussion with a study of immigrants and their experiences in the health care system. Such information gives us a rare glimpse into subjective reactions to interactions with professionals.

There are over 33 million immigrants living in the United States, or about 12 percent of the population (U.S. Census Bureau, 2004). Ngo-Metzger and colleagues (2003) wanted to understand the subjective experience of immigrants with respect to their interactions with health care providers. The findings may be unique to the cultural groups in this study, but likely generalize to other immigrants who require interpreters. The study used 12 focus groups, each comprised of 6 to 12 Chinese or Vietnamese immigrants who discussed their experiences in the health care system. The topics for the focus groups involved: (1) positive and negative experiences with health care, (2) communication between themselves and the provider, (3) the use of interpreters, (4) the role of the family in their care, and (5) the use of traditional healing or medicines. In the focus groups, similar themes emerged:

- The clients wanted to talk about indigenous treatments with their providers but felt the physicians disapproved of traditional practices. Many, therefore, discontinued trying to communicate about cultural healing and remedies. As therapists, we should inquire about and be open to client beliefs regarding mental disorders and the use of indigenous treatments. If possible, the clinician should determine how they can be integrated with psychological therapy.

- The immigrants who needed translation services preferred professional interpreters and not family members. The clients believed that the use of their children as interpreters changed family dynamics. As one Vietnamese man indicated, "When your children go with you as your translators, this changes . . . [the relationship] in your family" (p.48). Some expressed dissatisfaction with the behavior of translators who did not demonstrate respect or who responded to them in a cursory fashion. They also wondered if communication was being appropriately translated. Some observed that the doctor often talked quite a bit, but that the translator said only a few words to them. This underscores the importance of providing training for interpreters and assessing the quality of their human relationship skills, especially those working in a therapeutic setting. Clients should be informed about the interpreting process and receive an explanation when long exchanges between the interpreter and the clinician occur. For sensitive matters, the immigrants preferred same-sex translators. Additional factors to consider when using translators are presented in Table 15.1.

- The immigrants expressed appreciation when assistance was given in setting up appointments or completing forms, and when they were given literature in their own language or presented with a clear explanation of diagnosis and treatment. This is particularly important because many immigrants are unfamiliar with the health care system and clinic practices. Therapists, or other staff, should be prepared to assist immigrants in meeting clinic requirements and in negotiating the social service system.

- Receiving respect and dignity was important. When the immigrants were asked what made them or would make them feel supported, they expressed a desire to be treated with courtesy and greeted in a warm and welcoming manner. Due to their lack of English proficiency, they were especially attuned to nonverbal expressions. Signs of emotional

Table 15.1   **Suggestions for Working with Interpreters**

1. When scheduling interpreters, make certain that the interpreter speaks the same dialect as the client. If the interpreter and the client appear to have significant cultural or social differences, monitor to ensure this does not interfere with therapy.

2. It is important for interpreters to understand your counseling style, how you assess and counsel clients; you can orient them before they begin their work with you. Whenever possible, use the same interpreter, especially for the same client.

3. Understanding confidentiality is essential for both clients and interpreters. When explaining confidentiality, therapists often explain the interpreter's code of confidentiality separately from therapist confidentiality. This reinforces the concept of interpreter confidentiality. Undocumented immigrants may be particularly concerned about the confidentiality of information shared during counseling sessions.

4. Extra time is needed during intake and counseling sessions when interpreters are involved or if a client chooses to work without an interpreter, but has limited English proficiency. During intake or the beginning of therapy, clients may not be ready to share their backgrounds, immigration stories, and reactions to their new lives. Such discussion, which can be extremely beneficial to the therapeutic alliance and case conceptualization, can be encouraged once trust develops.

5. Both the interpreter and the client need to understand the role of the interpreter (to relay information) and how the translation process will proceed. Some experienced translators are able to provide simultaneous translation. More common is interpretation that involves the therapist or client stopping after short intervals of speech to allow the message to be translated. Clear, simple, and concise use of language by the therapist facilitates translation.

6. If you believe that an interpreter is not translating all comments fully, interjecting their own opinion, or intervening directly with a client, it is important to have an open discussion of your observations when the client is not present.

7. If a situation occurs where the therapist and interpreter need to speak to each other to clarify something for translation during the session, it is helpful to apologize to the client regarding the interruption and briefly inform the client about the nature of the discussion.

8. Having an interpreter present can change the interpersonal dynamics of counseling sessions; it becomes a three-person rather than a two-person alliance. Therapists need to be aware that the client may initially develop stronger connections with the interpreter due to their ability to communicate directly.

9. Interpreters can be incredible resources in terms of understanding specific cultural issues, and can help provide insight related to case conceptualization and diagnosis by educating the therapist about normative cultural behavior.

10. To help facilitate accurate translation, explain strategies that might be unfamiliar to the interpreter, such as relaxation or reframing techniques.

11. Be aware that interpreters may experience strong feelings when they are exposed to intense emotion or discussion of traumatic experiences in counseling sessions, especially when these issues hit close to home for the interpreter. Therapists can validate these feelings, work with interpreters to understand the issue of vicarious trauma, and support them by allowing time for periodic debriefing after sessions or providing them with suggestions for self-care related to this experience.

From D. W. Sue & D. Sue, 2008

support such as smiling and nodding were welcome. They appreciated having their individuality and needs recognized and respect shown to family members.

Specific Considerations for Diverse Populations

In this section, we provide a brief summary of key information that may be useful when working with specific ethnic groups and diverse populations. Much of the information comes from *Counseling the Culturally Diverse* (5th ed.; D. W. Sue & D. Sue, 2008). The information is not extensive, and is intended to give the reader a brief overview of some key issues regarding worldview, stressors, and values that may pertain to clients who are members of specific groups. (Summary information regarding ethnic and diverse groups can be found in Appendix B.) When working with diverse clients, therapists should gain as much knowledge as possible regarding the client's life experiences, particularly when these experiences differ from those of the therapist. Cultural differences, such as the degree of assimilation, educational level, socioeconomic background, and family experiences impact each individual in a distinct manner. In general, when working with individuals from different groups:

- Be aware that many have experienced individual, group, or institutionalized racism or discrimination, oftentimes resulting in a mistrust of the majority culture. This mistrust may affect how a client relates to you as a therapist, particularly if you are from the majority culture.

- It is important to assess for and acknowledge the possibility that discrimination and racism are causing or magnifying the client's mental health concerns. If so, these issues should be taken into consideration in diagnosis and treatment planning. Sometimes it will be necessary to take on an advocacy role for clients, especially in the case of institutional racism.

- Obtain the worldview and ethnic identity of the client, being careful not to assume just because they are part of a particular group, that they strongly identify with or share the values of that group. For example, acculturated American Indians chose cognitive behavior therapy as their treatment of choice, while those who are more traditionally oriented prefer traditional Native American therapy (Fiferman, 1989).

- Assess not just from an individual perspective but include the effects of family, community, and societal influences on the presenting problem. Have clients summarize their concerns in their own words. Be sure to inquire about religious or spiritual beliefs as they pertain to wellness or healing.

- Strategies and interventions used with clients may vary according to the degree of cultural identification. Individuals who are traditionally oriented may need to develop the skills and resources for dealing with the mainstream society. Clients who are more acculturated may need to examine identity conflicts and values.

- Clients may be unaware of how therapy works. It is important to carefully explain the treatment to be used, why it was selected, and how it will help achieve the goals.

- Clearly discuss confidentiality, explain the client and therapist roles in the therapy process, and describe how you will work together to understand concerns and develop a treatment plan.

- Focus on positive assets of the client and the client's culture, identifying strengths, skills, problem-solving abilities, and social supports available to the client and the family. Determine how they (or friends or other family members) have succeeded with similar problems.

- Determine the structure of the family through questions and observation. Connections to extended family or a nontraditional family may be very important in the life of the client. It is helpful to determine who is living in the home and who is considered a member of the family. With traditional families, try addressing males first.

- Some families with strong connections within the family or beyond the nuclear family may appear to be enmeshed. It is important not to place your own worldview on other cultural groups. It is important to work to strengthen the original family structure and try to make it more functional rather than try to change it.

- Acculturation conflicts between children and their parents are common, especially among first generation immigrants and their children. The children often attribute psychological distress to not quite fitting in with American values and being considered as too Americanized by their parents. One strategy that can be used during family sessions when there is cultural conflict is to frame the cultural differences as the identified problem.

- Many groups are open to holistic approaches that incorporate family members and the religious or social community. Be willing to explore the spiritual or cultural beliefs of clients, such as use of traditional medicines, prayer, or fasting to reduce distress.

- Maintain awareness of the impact of poverty, linguistic difficulties, and limited educational opportunities and assess for external conditions such as poverty, inadequate food or housing, unemployment, neighborhood safety concerns, or stressful interactions with agencies. Some clients may need assistance in understanding and accessing resources.

Failures in Cultural Competence and What We Need to Do

How culturally sensitive are your psychotherapy interventions compared to those of your peers? Are you overlooking interventions that could make your psycho-therapy more culturally responsive? How do your beliefs regarding multicultural competencies compare with those of other clinicians? Do professional psychologists practice what they preach in terms of culturally responsive professional behavior? (Hansen et al., 2006, p. 66)

Guidelines for working with diverse populations, similar to those discussed earlier, are available through university coursework, books, and workshops. Have they been successful in changing the way therapy is provided? Although cultural competence is being promoted by the mental health professions, it has been slow to filter down to clinical practice. There remains a lack of consideration of social, cultural, and environmental influences. Even therapists who consider themselves to be "very" or "extremely" multiculturally competent "do not practice what they preach" (N. D. Hansen et al., 2006, p. 66). For example, only 22 percent of those who self-assessed as multiculturally competent used the cultural formulation in *DSM-IV-TR* with ethnic clients, and only about 33 percent have used multiculturally sensitive data-gathering techniques in work with ethnic clients. As the researchers of the study concluded, "Even though respondents reported that 36 percent of their lifetime caseloads included clients who differed racially/ethnically from themselves, they still reported large and consistent discrepancies between what they knew to be important to competent multicultural practice and what they actually did when working with such clients" (p. 71).

Recognition and awareness of multicultural competences is not sufficient to impact practice. We believe that there are numerous reasons why culturally competent practices are not utilized by therapists. First, many still rely on individualistic theories to conceptualize disorders. Second, many intake forms and interviews do not assess for social or cultural factors. Third, clinical discussions regarding cases rarely address cultural or diversity issues in a systematic manner. Fourth, during supervision, cultural influences are often not considered. To promote culturally competent practice, cultural and diversity issues should be an integral part of diagnosis, case conceptualization, and supervision. The following are suggestions on how multicultural competence can be integrated into clinical practice.

Case Conceptualization

It makes sense for university educators and mental health supervisors to require the consideration of cultural and social influence as part of conceptualization during case presentations and supervision. Practitioners or students should be expected to regularly use information that takes family, social, cultural, and environmental factors into consideration. Additionally, when working with ethnic minorities, data from Axis IV of *DSM-IV-TR* and the cultural formulation in Appendix A could be required. This kind of comprehensive assessment could be done on a regular basis with diverse populations. We demonstrate how this can be achieved in the two cases below:

> *Marcos is a 42-year-old, married father of one child, of Mexican descent, recently promoted to a management position, who came to the first therapy session reporting frequent feelings of unhappiness, stress, and sadness. He reported having frequent insomnia, fatigue, poor appetite, and occasional memory and concentration difficulties. Moreover, during the last month he had started having panic attacks. Marcos denied psychotic and manic symptoms, depressive episodes, or alcohol use. He reported having been unhappy for over two years. He was particularly concerned that these problems could diminish his job performance and decrease his chances of furthering his career. (La Roche, 2005, p. 179)*

> *A 13-year-old boy says he wants to "come out" to his parents and his peers regarding his sexual orientation. How would you respond? What are the factors that you would have to take into consideration? He has come into treatment because of stress, anxiety, and depression.*

If the individuals above came in for treatment of anxiety and depression, how might you conduct a cultural case formulation? We will do so using the Outline for Cultural Formulation in Appendix I of *DSM-IV-TR:*

1. **Cultural (diversity) elements of the relationship between the individual and the clinician.** We might ask ourselves, "Are there differences in values and norms between the client and therapist that might impact diagnosis and treatment?" In doing so, we might consider our personal reactions to these characteristics and ask ourselves, "How might my beliefs, values, and theoretical orientation influence the way I would work with a Latino or with a gay male?" "Will these differences influence my diagnostic and treatment decisions?" "Might my belief in egalitarian and independent functioning interfere with the provision of services to individuals who have a more collectivistic orientation?" "How do I feel about working with an adolescent who self-identifies as gay?" "Do I have the knowledge and skills to deal with these specific diversity issues?" Clinicians can consider differences in values and norms between themselves and individuals from other groups and this can become a part of any case presentation. This would provide the opportunity to bring up issues such as if and when to bring up differences

with a client and to consider possible "blind spots" a therapist may have in working with diverse populations.

2. **Cultural factors related to psychosocial environment and levels of functioning.** Both of the individuals described above potentially face societal standards that may be different from or hostile to their culture or identity. The therapist working with Marcos (vignette above) initially diagnosed his condition as dysthymia and panic disorder and began treatment using desensitization and visualization techniques. Later, the therapist realized that he had only explored the problem from an individualistic perspective and began to develop a cultural formulation. In doing so, he discovered that much of Marcos's stress resulted from internalization of derogatory portrayals of Mexican Americans as being lazy and sloppy. His need to move up the corporate ladder was an attempt to negate this description. When Marcos understood and questioned these social messages, his panic attacks diminished (La Roche, 2005). In the same manner, societal expectations and standards have also affected those with a different sexual orientation. The gay adolescent is living in a heterosexist society in which he has had to hide his orientation, leading to an isolated and inauthentic life. He fears rejection from society, his family, and peers. He wants to "come out," but is uncertain about the reception from others and apprehensive about what will happen if he is honest with others about his true identity. In this case, environmental factors have to be considered when devising intervention strategies. Under this category, consideration of societal issues such as racism, ageism, sexism, and other diversities can be acknowledged and discussed.

3. **Cultural identity of the individual.** The cultural identity of members of ethnic groups can vary from very traditional to very Westernized, or from "not salient to the individual" to "an important aspect of identity." Determining the cultural identity is important since it will influence the way the client views the problem and has implications for diagnosis and treatment. Marcos identified strongly with his Mexican American heritage. He valued family over job promotions and became happier by turning his attention to parenthood. Cultural identity is not just important for ethnic minorities, but can also involve gender, age, religion, or other diversity. For the adolescent who has accepted a gay rather than heterosexual identity, there are profound implications regarding his view of himself and his relationships with others. Sources of support within the family, peer group, and community will need to be established or reestablished.

4. **Cultural explanations of the individual's illness.** Are there ways that the individual perceives his or her difficulties from a cultural perspective? In both of the cases we are discussing, the client may attribute

their problem (e.g., anger, anxiety, depression, confusion) to internal flaws. Certainly, anxiety and depression can come from personal characteristics. However, societal expectations and norms may also play a large role. The therapist and client must collaborate to understand the presenting problem and the relative contributions of both internal and external influences. In our discussion of immigrants and other ethnic groups, we have emphasized the importance of understanding their explanation regarding the symptoms they are experiencing. Only by working in a collaborative manner can we develop interventions that feel genuine to the client and that allow the client to trust in the therapy process.

5. **Overall cultural assessment for diagnosis and care.** As part of a case presentation, presenters can consider the information obtained regarding environmental or cultural influences on the therapist and the client and make a recommendation regarding diagnosis and treatment. If cultural, societal, or environmental issues are involved, strategies should be determined accordingly. We believe that cultural formulation can be appropriate not only for ethnic groups, but also for all diverse populations.

Supervision

What would you do as an Anglo supervisor if a Hispanic American supervisee came to you with the following situation? How might your response differ if you were a member of a non-Hispanic ethnic minority rather than Anglo American?

> I want to work with my (Hispanic American) client and help him deal with his pain. I believe that I have to look at his cultural values and expectations, as well as mine, to really be able to help him. This, however, is difficult for me, because I feel pressured to think like an Anglo, like you think, and treat him like an Anglo man. I feel even more challenged since I want to learn from you and your ways of thinking and behaving as a clinician. However, your reality is Anglo and mine is both Hispanic American and Anglo American. (Jordan, 1998, p. 183)

Supervisors may neglect to consider cultural aspects in cases or fail to recognize differences that may exist between them and their supervisees. During supervision, supervisors may display unintentional racism, sexism, or other forms of biased thinking by not acknowledging the possible influence of social or cultural factors in work with supervisees. Supervisors may assume that their method of supervision and mode of conceptualization can be applied to all clients and all groups of supervisees. To promote openness and to reinforce best practices, ethnic background, age, sexual orientation, and other diversity aspects pertinent to the supervisor and supervisee should be discussed as it relates to supervision and work with clients. Within supervision sessions, both supervisor and supervisee can participate in self-identity discussions that promote personal growth and professional development. During supervision, cultural factors and interventions should be evaluated for relevance regarding a particular client. The possibility of being overly culturally sensitive by inadvertently applying stereotypes should also be entertained. Supervisors should regularly question their supervisees regarding the age, ethnicity, background experience, and worldview of their clients. A supervisor's ability to focus a supervisee's attention on the multicultural issues of clients has been found to significantly improve their skills in case conceptualization (Ladany, Inman, Constantine, & Hofheinz, 1997). In cross-race supervisor-supervisee dyads, Inman (2006) found a positive relationship between supervisor multicultural competence and the ratings of the supervisory relationship.

In this part of the chapter, we have considered reasons why multicultural competence has not been translated into practice and suggested the need to make Axis IV of the *DSM-IV-TR* and the cultural formulation an integral part of case presentations and supervision. Only by infusing these in our clinical practice will they assume importance. By doing so, we will truly allow multicultural competencies to enhance assessment and treatment for diverse clients. Consideration of ways in which to make an office or clinic culturally or environmentally friendly can also promote the importance of diversity issues. Some suggestions include: (1) have materials about the clinic, policies, and mental disorders in the language of groups who frequent the clinic. Lists of interpreters or translators for non-English proficient clients should be available; (2) evaluate your office or clinic in terms of structural barriers that may hamper individuals with disabilities; (3) promote the use of value-free terms with diverse populations, such as "older adult" instead of "elderly," and terms such as "partner" instead of "husband or wife" or "boyfriend or girlfriend" when inquiring about client relationships; and (4) assure that your intake forms, interview procedures, and language are free of ageist or heterosexist bias, or demeaning terms. We believe that multicultural sensitivity can greatly enhance practice when it is a regular part of assessment, diagnosis, and therapy and included during case presentations and supervision.

Assessment and Intervention in Emergency Situations

16
Chapter

You are covering the walk-in desk at a community mental health center. A 45-year-old man is accompanied to the desk by several friends, one of whom is his girlfriend. The girlfriend explains that they are separating and that he has made a suicidal threat. The client has an odor of alcohol and seems somewhat hostile. You begin to interview him, but he ignores your questions and paces around the room. In an agitated way, he states that there is noting wrong with him and he wants to leave. How do you decide whether it is safe to let him go or whether he should be held against his will? What do you do if he walks out? (Kleespies, Deleppo, Gallagher, & Niles, 1999, p. 454)

My professional journey began as a graduate student in clinical psychology . . . H. B. was a 45-year-old Caucasian male who was diagnosed as schizophrenic and who had a history of parental neglect, as well as combat related stress experiences. He was one of my first clinical patients and I had worked with him for several months. While under my care, he killed himself. Over the course of the next 35 years of clinical work, I have been involved with three other psychiatric patients who have died by suicide. Another suicidal patient was being seen by a clinical graduate student whom I was supervising. He was her first patient and he killed himself over the Christmas holidays. (Meichenbaum, 2006, p. 64)

In the scope of their duties, all mental health professionals encounter emergency situations at one time or another. A psychiatric emergency occurs when "an individual reaches a state of mind in which there is an imminent risk that he or she will do something (or fail to do something) that will result in serious harm or death to self or others unless there is some immediate intervention" (Kleespies et al., 1999, p. 454). It is essential for practitioners to be prepared in the event that an emergency situation emerges. You may encounter situations involving threats of self-harm, extreme anger, threats of violence toward others, delusional thinking resulting in safety concerns, or other major psychiatric emergencies. What is your plan if a client discloses suicidal thinking in the course of a counseling session? How do you respond if a client becomes angry and agitated and begins to behave in an unpredictable manner? What strategies do you use if the family member of a client becomes angry or threatening? Not only should you have plans for such situations, it is essential that you and your colleagues review the plans regularly so that, in the event of an emergency, you are readily able to respond. As always, it is very important for you to take into consideration client variables such as gender, religion, race, ethnicity, or socioeconomic status in terms of both assessment and intervention, taking care to understand issues from the client's perspective and background experiences rather than solely from your own perspective.

The therapeutic alliance, always a critical element of therapeutic progress, is even more essential in times of psychiatric emergency. This chapter will review possible emergency situations that you might face, as well as strategies for dealing with such situations. In addition, we address the very difficult topic of suicide and suicidal ideation. Donald Meichenbaum, a well-known clinical psychologist and professor at the University of Waterloo, wrote the above vignette. In sharing his story, he sensitizes readers to the reality of suicidal ideation, behavior, and action in the lives of mental health professionals. In his article, he goes on to say "moreover, with clinical experience the incidence of patient suicide does not greatly diminish. A practicing clinical psychologist will average five suicidal patients per month" (Meichenbaum, 2006, p. 64). This clearly speaks to the importance of the topic, whether suicidal issues come to you in the form of a crisis or, in listening carefully to a client during a regular therapy session, you become alert to the possibility of suicidal thoughts or plans.

Understanding Your Own Response to Crisis

As we consider emergency situations, it is important to reflect on critical incidents you have experienced in your own personal or professional life. Mental health professionals are human and, therefore, subject to a wide range of emotions. Although it may appear obvious that maintaining a calm demeanor and clear thinking is essential in a crisis, it is important to consider the fact that feelings of fear, anxiety, discomfort, or negativity can affect one's ability to respond rapidly and efficiently. You may have colleagues who find that remaining calm when confronted with a suicidal or aggressive client is not difficult. Some may find they respond effectively in some situations, but struggle under certain circumstances. Others may not yet feel confident in their ability to remain calm, collected, and clear in their thinking in emergencies, and recognize that anxiety and fear will likely interfere with an optimal response. In general, mental preparation for and practice in emergency responding will allow you to more confidently deal with such situations. It is important to be aware, however, that specific situations can trigger emotions based on our own personal experiences, such as a therapist who has previously experienced a death due to suicide dealing with a suicidal client, or a therapist who has personally experienced violent behavior dealing with an agitated or potentially violent client. Additionally, it is important to reflect upon your attitudes and values regarding topics such as death, dying, and suicide prior to a psychiatric emergency or to clinical situations in which you may need to address these issues with a client. Ideally, this reflection will occur not only in the process of your graduate coursework and internships, but also during post-graduate supervision (Neimeyer, 2000). It is important to understand the concept of *vicarious trauma,* that is, the thoughts and feelings that occur as a result of close involvement with the traumatic circumstances of another individual. One should not only recognize and deal with such feelings, but also remain aware that such events may affect responses to similar situations in the future.

If you have worked with suicidal clients, you are probably aware of the multiple dilemmas inherent in situations where clients come to you for help and share their profound sense of hopelessness as well as their plan for suicide. This sometimes results in a situation where you are concerned for their safety and contemplate the need to break confidentiality. When this occurs, the boundaries of the relationship, which have been based on confidentiality, may change dramatically, particularly if there is a need for, and the client is not in agreement with, additional help from crisis response personnel. The dynamics may be particularly intense during a situation in which involuntary hospitalization is recommended. What has previously been a strong alliance between the therapist and client may change dramatically (Jobes, 2000). Although you can make reference to the informed consent and exceptions to confidentiality discussed at the onset of therapy, this situation is never easy, and can provoke strong feelings of anxiety and discomfort on the part of both the therapist and the client.

In recent years, there has been a change regarding intervention with significant suicidal concerns. In the past, short-term hospitalization for a period of assessment and observation was likely to occur; currently, however, such intervention occurs with less frequency, resulting in the need for increased training for those working in community mental health settings (Oordt et al., 2005). Practitioners need to be very familiar with protocol for determining which diagnostic constellations can be managed with briefer interventions and which will need longer-term therapeutic intervention. It becomes important for clinicians to understand the dynamics of suicidal thinking and behavior, such as understanding what it is about being suicidal that "works" for the client and then focusing on helping the client increase their tolerance for stress or distress, increase problem solving skills, and substitute more adaptive coping strategies and means of enhancing emotional support. As always, the therapeutic alliance and a true effort on the part of the therapist to understand clients' thinking and the depths of their despair is essential (Jobes, 2000).

As mentioned previously, self-assessment on the part of the therapist is critical, such as asking:

> *"If I am uncomfortable with the topic of suicide, do I respond by avoiding this topic? Am I able to address this issue with clients directly, openly assess for suicidal ideation, and be available to provide needed support when a client does, in fact, share suicidal thinking or planning? Even if it is difficult for me to work with a client who is suicidal, what can I do to understand what is going on for the client? Can I empathize with the life situations that have made suicide seem like a compelling option for my client? How can we work together to make the situation more bearable? Knowing the importance of the therapeutic alliance, can I stay objective, connected, and supportive even when it is difficult for me to understand that someone might see suicide as a viable option?"*

Understanding the Emergency Plan for Your Work Setting

In every work setting, it is essential to have well-designed plans for dealing with emergency situations. In larger organizations, administrative teams or organizational crisis teams may develop these plans, while in private practice or small clinics, you may have the responsibility to develop such plans. In general, it is important to consider what kinds of emergencies could potentially occur. What role would you play in responding to the situation? What role would your colleagues and other staff members play? How do you alert others if there is a need for support during crises? Who in the organization has experience and training in dealing with emergencies? Who tends to have a calm demeanor and good problem-solving skills when confronted with challenging circumstances? What is your plan if an agitated client, who has expressed suicidal or homicidal ideation, attempts to leave? Prearranged assessment, intervention, and consultation strategies may significantly reduce stress and help in maintaining an atmosphere of calm and control in an emergency. As plans and strategies are developed, it is essential that they are consistent with local, state, and federal expectations regarding reporting of the situation to the appropriate authorities, as well as consistent with the specific ethical standards for your profession.

The Importance of Assessing the Prior Histories of All Clients

As was discussed extensively in Chapter 4, knowledge regarding a client's background and life experiences is invaluable, as is taking the time to update assessment and case conceptualization as your understanding of the client deepens during the course of therapy. It may initially be quite clear, based upon intake interviews, that there are concerns about suicidal ideation or potential for violent behavior. However, it is also possible that these issues will emerge at a later time in a client with few initial risk factors. It is, therefore, critical to be aware of the research related to risk factors for self-harm or violent behavior and to have a good working knowledge of clients' stressors, frustration or distress tolerance, and coping strategies. Important knowledge about each client includes: (1) current or prior suicidal ideation or behavior; (2) current or prior impulsive, aggressive, violent, or explosive behavior; (3) history of mental illness and substance abuse, including psychiatric hospitalization or inpatient treatment; (4) grief and loss issues, including any impending losses or anniversaries of loss; (5) family history of suicide or violent behavior; (6) social support systems; and (7) prior responses to depressive symptoms, acute stress, or trauma.

This information can influence therapeutic goals and intervention, and is essential in times of crisis, when there is less time available for information gathering. When conducting an intake assessment or ongoing assessment of a client, it is important to remember that the accuracy of client reporting is sometimes affected by memory, attentional difficulties related to anxiety or depression, trust issues, or a tendency to deny or minimize the severity of symptoms (American Psychiatric Association, 2000b). Trust or denial issues are common when there is substance abuse or alcohol dependence on the part of the client or family members. However, it is critical to assess for these issues, both early in therapy and on an ongoing basis, and to remain aware of the strong link between substance abuse and both suicidal and violent behavior (Canapary, Bongar, & Cleary, 2002). Similarly, it is important to interview both men and women regarding childhood trauma, including sexual and physical abuse (Read, Agar, Barker-Collo, Davies, & Moskowitz, 2001; Young et al., 2001).

You should be aware of the literature supporting a link between such trauma and suicide attempts and suicidal ideation, even in the absence of symptoms of depression. Issues of domestic violence, occurring currently or having occurred in the past, are important to assess in all individuals, including older adults (Wolkenstein & Sterman, 1998) and individuals in same-sex partnerships (Peterman & Dixon, 2003). In considering possible relationship violence, be alert for factors such as fantasies or threats of violence, jealousy, possessiveness, or feelings of ownership toward a domestic partner. During initial interviews as well as during counseling sessions, it is important to ask directly about suicidal ideation, even when this topic is not the presenting problem.

Assessing and Responding to an Emergency Situation

When a mental heath practitioner is confronted with a potentially serious situation involving a client, it is critical that the therapist remain calm and create an environment of safety and security in which the issues can be further explored. In the case of a client experiencing an acute episode of mental illness involving symptoms such as delusions, high levels of agitation, or issues with impaired sobriety due to drug or alcohol abuse, it may be necessary to seek immediate supportive intervention, such as contacting law enforcement or crisis personnel. However, in many situations, collaborative discussion with the client and the gathering of needed information in a supportive atmosphere is possible. The clinician can then work with the client to develop a safety plan, with a focus on specific problem-solving and coping skills, and concrete interventions, such as delineating who to call and what to do if strong thoughts or impulses occur that would compromise the client's safety or the safety of others.

The interview style used by the clinician may vary depending on the presentation of symptoms. For example, a calm, direct, structured interview may work with many individuals; however, when dealing with someone who is quite agitated, particularly if there is paranoid thinking involved, it may be beneficial to be more casual and less direct. If efforts at empathetic containment of the emotional crisis are not sufficient, it may be helpful to involve a colleague or supervisor in the interview process (Kleepies et al., 1999). The presence of a "second set of eyes" may be reassuring for both the client and clinician. The second therapist can assist with emotional containment, serve as a resource in assessing the need for outside emergency crisis services, and help supervise the client if private calls for outside resource support need to be made.

If a client is experiencing an acute psychotic episode, it is essential to interview for suicidal ideation and to assess for *command hallucinations* (i.e., voices telling the client to perform certain actions), or any other characteristics that would suggest harm to the individual or to others. If you are interacting with a client experiencing delusions or hallucinations, it is important to remain calm and reassuring, letting the client know that you care about them and that you will do what you can to help. It is helpful to listen to what the client is saying, checking for understanding as the conversation progresses. If it is possible to do so without increasing agitation, it is helpful to try to keep a delusional client grounded in reality. For example if a client is concerned that the room is bugged, you might ask, "Why do you think someone would want to bug the room?" or "How do you think they would go about bugging the room?" If the client is reporting hallucinations, you might tell the client that although you do not see or hear what is being reported, you believe that the client is, in fact, seeing or hearing things. You can also empathize with the distress the client is feeling. If possible, you can try to decrease agitation by redirecting the client's focus to another topic. It is important to be aware of the potential seriousness of command hallucinations; not only is it important for you to talk to the client about not acting on the command, it may be necessary to seek emergency psychiatric intervention to help keep the client safe if there are command hallucinations suggesting harm to self or others (American Psychiatric Association, 2004).

If a client is too agitated or disoriented to participate in the interview, you might consider interviewing friends or family to rule out suicidal or homicidal delusions. Follow-up may require involvement by medical professionals, including medication to reduce agitation, especially during the acute stages of a psychotic episode, with the goal of suppressing symptoms and reducing the risk of harm to self or others (Herz et al., 1997). Once the crisis phase is resolved, it is important to determine the least restrictive setting for the immediate treatment of the individual. At times, this may involve return to the family home or to a structured community setting, such as a group home or halfway house. On other occasions, the most appropriate alternative may be a psychiatric hospital setting. A determining factor will be the safety of the individual and others, and the ability of the individual to follow the recommended treatment plan.

In many situations, a client in crisis may be taking medications related to mental health or other issues. As we discuss in more detail in Chapter 17, it is important to collaborate with health care providers during a psychiatric crisis to ascertain that there are neither medication side effects nor other physiological factors contributing to the anxious, depressed, or agitated mood. Similarly, it is important to rule out the contribution of alcohol or other substances to the current distress. In the course of intervention in a high-risk situation, other professionals may consider medication or inpatient treatment as an intervention. If this occurs, you may, with the consent of your client, be in a position to assist with assessment and intervention by providing background and response-to-treatment information. If medication is prescribed, you can also support the client with symptom monitoring (to see if the medication is helping or hindering progress) and help the client be alert for medication side effects.

Determining Level of Risk

Managed care admission protocols may contain imminence criteria for patients at risk of suicide before approving insurance benefits, yet no clear-cut suicide risk factors exist for the short-term prediction of suicide. (Simon, 2006)

In the course of assessment or treatment, it is sometimes necessary to determine the level of risk for suicidal or violent behavior. This often includes developing a plan for intervention and making decisions regarding the need to involve others in the intervention. Should a supervisor be involved? Is it necessary to contact the regional mental health crisis line to request further assessment? Is it necessary to involve law enforcement officials? These decisions are never easy. There are not only potential legal and ethical implications (Litwack, 2001), but there is also the need to consider the impact of such decisions on your relationship with the client. The situation is further complicated by the reality that every risk assessment is unique and involves a judgment call based upon the specifics of the situation. Additionally, there is never a guarantee that even the most careful assessment, even when done in conjunction with supervisors or colleagues, will be accurate.

Any determination of risk is subjective. Risk assessment relies on the information obtained and the accuracy of the information provided, combined with the clinician's interpretation of the information and the situation. As you might imagine, even with a skilled clinician, the information obtained may be incomplete or inaccurate. Clinicians are frequently confronted with situations where it is necessary to make an initial judgment regarding risk. Does it appear that there is "little to no" risk of harm to self or others? This determination might be made if the individual has (1) few prior risk factors, (2) does not have a pattern of impulsive behavior, (3) does not have a specific plan or means to carry out a plan, and (4) in the case of suicidal ideation, is willing to sign a no-harm contract. Does there appear to be moderate risk? This evaluation might be made if (1) there are multiple risk factors, particularly when combined with past or current behaviors suggesting risk; (2) a low to moderate degree of intent; (3) limited likelihood of carrying out a stated plan due to lack of access to methods to cause harm, and (4) minimal indication of significant cognitive or emotional impairment, in combination with protective factors (e.g., the presence of a positive support system, a willingness to work with the therapist to develop a safety plan and, in the case of suicide, signing a no-harm agreement). Does it appear that there is a high level of risk? This would include individuals with a current, specific plan involving available or lethal means.

Other factors suggesting high risk include (1) multiple background risk factors, (2) tendencies toward impulsive behavior, (3) low tolerance for distress or frustration, (4) significant current mental health concerns, (5) difficulty or unwillingness to form a therapeutic alliance, (6) limited external support or (7) in the case of suicidal ideation, an unwillingness to sign (or limited expectations for compliance with) a no-harm agreement. Prior suicide attempts, particularly more recent attempts, more serious attempts, or attempts that were made with the belief that they would die from the attempt, significantly increase the risk in a suicidal emergency. Risk is also higher when the individual is not well known to the evaluator or is unwilling or unable to provide information needed for a thorough assessment. Any assessment of risk should also include a close look at protective factors such as supportive personal or community relationships, spiritual beliefs, a resilient temperament, and a positive social orientation (Hillbrand, 2001).

In a situation that appears to present low risk of harm to self or others, the therapist works with the client to enhance coping skills and to develop a plan (including a safety plan) to address the problems confronting the individual. In a situation involving moderate risk, the clinician will likely confer with colleagues, a supervisor, or the regional mental health crisis response system for additional consultation and planning. Simultaneously, the therapist works with the client to develop a safety plan, enhance coping strategies, and focus on alternative solutions to the presenting problems. In the case of a high-risk situation, it will be necessary to involve supervisors and possibly contact law enforcement or regional mental health crisis support personnel. It will also be important to ensure that the client has appropriate supervision for the purpose of safety (i.e., is not left alone or in a situation where self-harm is likely to occur) as you await the arrival of the support agencies.

In mental health inpatient or outpatient settings, clinicians will follow predetermined emergency procedures developed by the agency. Similarly, in the case of a child or adolescent in the school setting, there are likely to be procedures available to guide intervention given different levels of risk. For example, protocol generally involves notifying parents when there is a concern about suicidal thinking, regardless of the determined level of risk, with the hope that they will be involved in supportive follow-up planning. Of course, school counselors and school psychologists seek outside consultation and resources when their initial screening suggests a higher level of risk, or when there is insufficient information to make a determination about risk. It is important for therapists in private practice to also have a set of guidelines to follow in the event of a situation involving potential harm to self or others. It is always best to develop such procedures during a noncrisis time and to review them regularly so that, in the event of an urgent situation, you are prepared to deal with the situation calmly and in accordance with legal and ethical expectations.

Assessing and Responding to a Suicidal Crisis

> *In the United States, there is one suicide every 17 minutes or 83 suicides per day. It is the third leading cause of death among young people between the ages of 15–24. Females make three times more suicide attempts than males, but males complete suicide at a rate four times higher than females. More than 90 percent of completed suicides are done by individuals with one or more mental disorders. (American Association of Suicidology, 2004)*

Most mental health practitioners gain experience dealing with suicidal thoughts or feelings in clients early in their training or professional experience. Many work in settings where they confront these issues frequently. When confronted with a suicidal emergency, prior experience or contact with the client might range from a therapist conducting an intake interview with an unfamiliar client at a mental health clinic to a therapist who has worked with a client over a period of years. Knowledge of background information will vary from situation to situation. A practitioner faced with the circumstance of someone contemplating suicide will need to gather information, perform a comprehensive risk assessment within the context of a supportive and caring environment, and then work with the client to develop a plan to maintain safety and well-being. This process may vary, to some degree, depending on the setting, how well the professional knows the client, and whether it is the client who brought up the suicidal concerns or if these concerns have been brought to the therapist by a third party. In their summary of recommendations for managing suicidal emergencies, Kleepies and colleagues (1999) reinforce the importance of approaching all situations involving suicidal thinking as a possible emergency until you are convinced otherwise. Regardless of the circumstances, the goal of the counselor is to assess the situation while developing or maintaining a strong therapeutic alliance with the client.

There has been a great deal written about understanding both group and individual risk factors for suicide (Laux, 2002). The American Psychiatric Association (2003) has compiled an extensive review of research related to suicide risk and considerations pertaining to suicide assessment, including a list of questions (discussed in Chapter 4) that are beneficial to refer to in the course of the clinical interview. It is valuable for therapists to be aware of this literature during assessment and therapeutic intervention with any client, but it is particularly critical during times of crisis. Specifically, it is important to be aware of: (1) the symptoms of severe depression in adults, adolescents, and children; (2) warning signs of suicide; (3) background factors that may increase suicide risk; and (4) the potential impact of critical events that may push a client who has not been previously suicidal to the brink of suicide. (Refer to Box 16.1 for a summary of statistics and risk factors). It is extremely important to directly address the issue of suicide when (1) risk factors are present, (2) the client has mentioned suicide directly or alluded to it indirectly, or (3) you have reason to believe that the client has been contemplating suicide. As you are gathering information and assessing the situation, it is essential to listen intently, and to ask directly about recurrent thoughts of death and any suicidal ideation, plans, or attempts. While initially exploring the extent of suicidal thinking, it is essential not to minimize the client's feelings, nor to confront the apparent illogic of the feelings.

Risk assessment involves the gathering of information on the frequency, intensity and lethality of suicidal thoughts and plans, with the goal of prediction and prevention. When an individual is reporting infrequent or transient suicidal thinking combined with no specific suicidal planning, it is generally concluded that there is a lower risk of suicide. Individuals who (1) have frequent, pervasive thoughts of suicide, (2) have developed a specific plan,

Box 16.1   Are You Informed about Suicide Risk Factors?

Statistics on Suicide

- Adolescents and adults older than age 65 have significantly higher rates of suicide.
- For every completed suicide, there are 8 to 25 suicide attempts, with the ratio even higher among women and youth.
- Up to 15% of those with severe major depressive disorder die from suicide.
- Individuals who have a major depressive disorder and are age 55 or older have a four times greater probability of death by suicide.
- Native Americans have a suicide rate about 1.5 times the national rate, with young male Native Americans at greatest risk.
- Asian American women have the highest suicide rate among women age 65 or older.
- The suicide rate is highest for young White men, but is increasing rapidly among young African-American men (aged 15 to 19).
- Although statistics do not consistently support the frequently quoted assertion of a much higher suicide risk for gay and lesbian youth, there is a growing concern about suicide risk for this group, particularly for young men who are homosexual or bisexual.
- Among high school students, Hispanic students, particularly females, are the most likely to have made a suicide attempt.

Background Factors That May Be Associated with Suicide

- Previous suicide attempts or self-mutilating behavior, particularly more lethal attempts or more recent attempts
- History of domestic violence, rape, child abuse, or physical assault
- History of incest, sexual abuse, or physical abuse
- Drug or alcohol abuse
- Social isolation or disconnection from family, friends, and other social supports
- Self-destructive or impulsive behavior
- Direct experience with suicide by family or friends
- Major Depressive Disorder, Anxiety Disorder, Schizophrenia, Personality Disorder, particularly Borderline Personality
- Chronic severe stress
- Physical illness or chronic pain

Possible Warning Signs of Suicidal Risk

- Acknowledgment of thoughts or plans about suicide
- Prior suicide attempts
- Recurrent thoughts of death or suicidal ideations, plans, or attempts
- Suicidal threats or talk of death
- A sense of hopelessness, guilt, or shame
- Significant changes in behavior or personality
- Interest or preoccupation with public figures who have committed suicide
- Increasingly withdrawn or isolated behaviors

(continued)

Box 16.1   Continued

- Decline of performance on the job or in school
- Lack of purpose or sense of belonging
- Irrational beliefs
- Inability to generate alternative solutions to problems
- Strong desire to end the painful emotions associated with a life circumstance
- Feelings that current problems are insurmountable
- History of inability to cope with strong negative feelings
- Giving away favorite possessions
- Sudden appearance of energy after a depressive period

Possible Triggers for Suicidal Behavior

- Suicide of a friend, family member, acquaintance, or public figure
- Loss of employment
- Lack of success in school
- Breakup of an important relationship
- Severe conflict with family members
- Unplanned pregnancy
- Public humiliation
- Perceived failure to meet culturally defined norms

From American Psychiatric Association, 2000b; American Psychiatric Association, 2003; Surgeon General's Call to Action to Prevent Suicide, 1999; Westefeld et al., 2000

and (3) have access to means by which to commit suicide are at higher risk. However, the research suggests that is just not possible to predict accurately whether or when a particular individual will attempt suicide (American Psychiatric Association, 2000b). *There are no guarantees that even the most careful or detailed assessment can accurately predict risk.* A great deal has been written about understanding suicidal behavior from various theoretical perspectives, and more recently, about empirically identifying correlates of suicidal behavior and using this information in the assessment and treatment planning process (Westefeld et al., 2000). For example, factors that have been associated with higher suicide risk include hopelessness, negative feelings toward self, confusion, reduced problem-solving skills, and increased rigidity in thinking, such as "all or nothing" thinking patterns (Neimeyer, 2000). In considering risk factors, it is important to be aware that the absence of prior suicide attempts does not eliminate risk since almost three-fourths of suicide completers commit suicide on the first known attempt. Similarly, a denial of suicidal ideation or denial of a plan does not necessarily mean there is limited risk (Kleespies et al., 1999). Oordt and colleagues (2005) emphasize that individuals who have attempted suicide on multiple occasions are at chronic risk for suicide and require a higher level of care. The belief that an individual who demonstrates an increase in energy during a depressive episode might be at heightened risk for suicide has not received research support; however, a recent investigation of this issue (Joiner, Pettit, & Rudd, 2004) has led to the conclusion that incomplete remission of depression (i.e., improved energy, but continuing affective symptoms) may be the critical factor, emphasizing the importance of augmenting psychopharmacological or therapeutic treatment for these clients.

It is important for clinicians to be aware of groups that have a statistically higher prevalence of suicide, including individuals with schizophrenia and elderly Chinese Americans, particularly women (Dai et al., 1999). Elderly men have among the highest rates of suicide (Luoma, Martin, & Pearson, 2002). In a study comparing outpatients with mood disorders who committed suicide with a group of matched controls, the individuals who ultimately committed suicide had attended fewer sessions of therapy, showed higher levels of hopelessness at their last therapy session, and were more frequently judged to still need therapy at the time that they terminated treatment. In addition, this group had greater incidence of unemployment, prior suicide attempts, prior hospitalizations, prior use of psychiatric medication, and family history of suicide (Dahlsgaard, Beck, & Brown, 1998). Awareness of the increased risk of completed suicide among individuals with certain psychiatric diagnoses (depression, substance abuse, schizophrenia, posttraumatic stress, borderline personality, and antisocial personality) may be helpful in estimating risk (Kleespies et al., 1999). Ongoing assessment of suicidal ideation when working with individuals with schizophrenia is essential, not only because of the statistical risk of suicide in this group, but because of the limited coping strategies, stronger intent toward self-harm, and seriousness of the attempts employed (American Psychiatric Association, 2004; Schwartz, 2000).

Awareness of cultural differences in perceptions toward suicide and specific stressors for men and women of specific cultural groups is an important component of suicide risk assessment. The expression of suicide both within and across cultures varies significantly, as do preferred methods of self-harm (Mishara, 2006). For example, elements of the African American culture, such as close family and community ties and religious and personal values that are contrary to suicide, appear to decrease suicide risk. Similarly, the social connectedness and strong church allegiance seen in Latino communities may serve as a protective buffer. Different factors may account for the lower suicide rates in most Asian American subgroups, particularly the perception that suicide may bring shame to the family. It is important to be aware, however, that there is an increased risk of suicide with increasing age in Asian Americans (Westefeld et al., 2000). Potential environmental stressors or stressors related to acculturation that may contribute to increased feelings of isolation, helplessness, or hopelessness in certain cultural groups should be addressed. For example, there is higher suicide risk in Native American populations, particularly for individuals with less of a sense of cultural cohesion. Similarly, in gay and lesbian individuals it is important to consider factors associated with increased suicide risk such as family dysfunction, the stress of coming out, substance abuse as a method of coping with stress, and identity confusion variables (Westefeld et al., 2000). Additionally, the risk of suicide attempts related to issues of sexual orientation was found to be greater for youth who had greater identifiability of and early openness about same-gender sexual orientation, as well those considered to have gender atypical behavior by parents, and whose parents tried to discourage the behavior; this was particularly true for males (D'Augelli et al., 2005) The authors of this study stress the importance of assessing for the risk factors of past parental psychological abuse, parent reactions to the adolescent, and history of psychological abuse from others related to identifiability as gay or lesbian. When evaluating the "subculture" of adolescents, Hacker, Suglia, Fried, Rappaport, and Cabral (2006) found that early use of drugs as well as experiences of abuse increased the risk of suicide attempts in 9th graders, whereas for 11th graders interpersonal violence at school and substance abuse heightened suicide risk Statistical information is important, but when considering correlates of suicide, either in terms of individual or group factors, it is very important to consider each client as an individual. It is essential not to base conclusions about risk primarily on specific background factors or membership in a particular ethnic or social group.

Best Practices in Managing Situations Involving Suicidal Ideation

The idea of managing a client who is actively considering suicide may feel daunting, especially for students or clinicians new to the field. In this kind of a situation, you will play a critical role at many different levels. You will need to gather specific information related to suicidal thoughts or plans, while at the same time providing an opportunity for your client to share thoughts and feelings and explain the sense of hopelessness that has led to the suicidal thinking. You will need to simultaneously listen and assess, and consider options for addressing the emotional and safety needs of your client. Try to maintain a balance between gathering information needed for risk assessment, and truly listening and attempting to understand your client's distress. Even while you are asking direct questions and gathering information, you are providing emotional support, showing empathy and understanding, and helping your client to realize his or her worth and importance to others. It is essential to understand that the client has entrusted you to help in a time of emotional crisis. As you listen, you may hear a very gloomy and negative perspective of circumstances and a strong sense of hopelessness. Do not allow yourself to be drawn into this negative frame of thinking. You should remain objective and, if possible, attempt to elicit some positives to focus on, including family or friends who are part of the client's support system. When there is social isolation and limited support systems, you and the client might work together to develop plans to decrease isolation and enhance social supports, which may include contact with support groups, involvement in activities of interest, or strengthening religious support. Above all, it is important for your client to know that you and others care, and that there is hope for a positive future once the current, overwhelming concerns are resolved.

Even if it is personally difficult for you to enter into a discussion of thoughts about dying or suicidal plans, stay engaged with the conversation and continue to listen and probe. If your discomfort is apparent or if you appear frightened, shocked, or overwhelmed by the discussion, your client may curtail conversation and you may lack essential information. Similarly, if you begin to argue with your client or minimize expressed feelings, further communication may be jeopardized. Often, by listening carefully, you can help clients who are overwhelmed put their problems into perspective. By asking open-ended questions, you open the door to further communication and an opportunity to gain an understanding of the depth of the pain. As you listen, you can help the client clarify the situation and perhaps specifically identify the problems that need to be addressed. Problem identification allows for a focus on problem-solving and developing strategies for relieving stress. In most situations, clients have reached out for help by sharing their intense despair. Validate their feelings and acknowledge that you are there to help them problem-solve and develop a plan for feeling better. As you listen to and interact with the client and you hear about positive factors in their lives, reasons for living, or methods they have used to cope productively in previous situations, you can emphasize these protective factors and use them in your collaborative planning.

Once you have had an opportunity to understand the most significant factors affecting your client, and how these relate to their feelings of hopelessness, you can begin to develop a plan. Initially, you will work collaboratively to identify, clarify, and prioritize the problems overwhelming the client. Next, you will work collaboratively to consider alternatives for addressing the most critical problems. If time is limited, you may want to have the client prioritize their needs so you can address the problem perceived to be the most significant first. In addition to a focus on possible solutions to the problems, it will be important to take time to identify supportive resources, including friends, family, colleagues, or acquaintances in religious or social organizations. You and your client can also work to develop a list of relaxing, enjoyable, or stress-reducing activities and include these in the plan. Remember, your goal is to calmly and empathetically help your client clarify current stressors, and then to instill hope by working to mobilize resources and develop strategies to deal with the problems. As discussed in previous chapters, it is important to take into account the whole picture, including your client's cultural background and life history as you assess the situation and work to develop a safety plan.

Jobes (2000) emphasizes the importance of collaborative assessment of suicidality, as opposed to the more traditional "expert" approach focused on psychiatric diagnosis. He encourages ongoing screening for the presence of suicidal thinking. If such thinking is acknowledged, the client and the therapist can collaborate to assess the situation. Given the emotional distress of a client contemplating suicide, the therapist may need to help the client define problems and express their thoughts, feelings, and perceptions, including the thoughts, impulses, and plans related to suicide. In this approach, the central focus of the assessment becomes the suicidality expressed by the client, including the depths and origins of the current psychological pain and feelings of hopelessness, and the reasons for living as well as reasons for wanting to die. Once the dynamics of the suicidal thinking are better understood by both the therapist and client, they can then work together to develop a plan to ensure client safety and well-being. A copy of this written plan, which includes concrete goals (with specific timeliness), coping strategies (specifically outlined), and specific steps to address some of the most difficult problem areas confronting the client, is kept by both the client and the therapist. Such plans also include resources for support if an emotional crisis occurs between therapy sessions. The goal is for the client to feel understood and empowered. This will motivate their work with the therapist since they are focusing on improving the circumstances that led to the distress and developing strategies for coping with stressful events or circumstances. This approach attempts to serve the same function that hospitalization has served in the past—creating a temporary safe haven—with the critical difference being that this safe haven is based upon a therapeutic alliance in an outpatient setting. Although the goal of this approach is to do everything possible to keep the client out of the hospital, it is important to be aware that there may be circumstances when hospitalization is the only safe alternative for a client.

As mentioned previously, an important component of treatment for a suicidal individual is that the therapist and client have a shared understanding of the issues of suicidality. It is important to ask questions such as, "Why do you think you are feeling so bad that you want to kill yourself?" It is important to assess the thoughts and attributions of those who suffered childhood abuse, particularly the aspect of self-blame that is often seen in these individuals. Such assessment can help significantly in the formulation of a treatment plan and can serve to instill hope that the issues will be addressed and resolved (Read et al., 2001).

A common approach used in assessment and intervention with a suicidal client is a no-harm agreement, sometimes referred to as a no-suicide contract or suicide-prevention contract. Typically, this is a written agreement developed between the client and therapist (or with a regional mental health professional who is assisting with a risk assessment). Generally, the agreement involves a commitment on the part of the client to not engage in self-harm for a designated period of time, together with a plan to assist the client to keep safe in the event that thoughts or impulses of self-harm emerge between treatment sessions. Agreements such as these are frequently used, despite a lack of research supporting their effectiveness as an intervention (Weiss, 2001). When attempting to negotiate a no-harm agreement with a client, useful information is obtained by the therapist. Some individuals may give serious consideration to signing the agreement, but then decline to do so because they do not have confidence that they can keep the agreement. Similarly, a refusal to agree can be a strong indicator of risk. In these circumstances, the therapist may try to negotiate a no-harm agreement for a more limited period of time, scheduling phone appointments or a therapy session sooner than usual; it is also important to seek consultation from a supervisor or regional mental health professional. If the client perceives that the therapist's primary concern is legalistic in nature (focused on avoiding liability), rather than a true effort to keep the client safe, an attempt to negotiate an agreement may, in fact, reduce the strength of the therapeutic alliance and add to the client's negative cognitions (Egan, Rivera, Robillard, & Hanson, 1997). Therapists need to be aware that no-harm agreements, even when willingly signed by the client, are by no means a guarantee against suicidal behavior, nor malpractice claims (Weiss, 2001; Westefeld et al., 2000). It is not unusual for clients to sign a contract if they believe that doing so will give them the freedom to escape closer scrutiny regarding suicidal ideation, involvement with a crisis mental health worker, or, in some cases, involuntary hospitalization. It is critical that you do not allow a signed no-harm agreement to give you a false sense of security about suicide risk. The fact that suicide completers frequently have no-harm contracts (Knoll, 2000; Miller, Jacobs, & Gutheil, 1998) speaks for itself and serves as a reminder that we cannot reduce our vigilance about suicide risk. However, when a no-harm agreement is used in conjunction with a continued focus on maintaining a strong therapeutic alliance, comprehensive risk assessment, and a risk-benefit analysis of the decisions made in the course of intervention, the overall intervention could be viewed as consistent with the expected standard of care (Simon, 1999).

Monitoring the safety of an individual who comes to your office in the midst of a suicidal crisis is essential. It is important that you not leave the person alone until it has been clearly established that there is not a risk of self-harm. Additionally, it is important to assess for the availability of means by which a client could hurt themselves (e.g., knives, medications, firearms). Some form of consultation and support is often necessary during a suicidal crisis. This may involve a supervisor who works on-site, consultation with a colleague, or consultation with the regional mental health crisis professional. This consultation, which you should document in a detailed fashion, may involve reviewing the situation and plans you are considering or have developed, or requesting advice or assistance. As mentioned earlier, it is important for us to be aware of our own responses to crisis situations; if you are emotionally shaken by a situation it is especially important to seek consultation.

Long-Term Intervention with Suicidal Clients

Although short-term crisis intervention is a critical component for individuals with suicidal ideation, it is also essential that counselors be aware of empirically validated approaches to ongoing therapy (Westefeld et al., 2000). After a suicidal crisis has passed, the therapist and individuals involved in the support system of the client should keep in touch and continue to express caring and provide emotional support. It is often helpful to target suicidal behavior directly in the treatment plan and, whenever possible, to collaborate with the client's health care provider (Ordt et al., 2005). Research aimed at decreasing suicide risk in a managed care setting has reinforced the benefits of ongoing use of client self-report measures (regarding symptoms, substance use, daily functioning, and direct questioning about suicidal ideation) in improving therapist awareness of client needs and risk for suicide (Brown, Jones, Betts, & Wu, 2003). And increase in level of monitoring (through avenues such as more frequent appointments, phone calls, e-mails, or letters) is also beneficial when there are suicidal concerns (Oordt et al., 2005).

One therapeutic alternative that has been validated as effective as a long-term intervention for suicide is *dialectical behavior therapy*. This therapy, the focus of Chapter 13, is a long-term intervention that combines humanistic, cognitive-behavioral, and psychoeducational therapies. Clients are taught very specific skills, using both group and individual therapy, with a focus on interpersonal effectiveness, emotional regulation, distress tolerance, and mindfulness (Linehan, 1987). Another form of therapy that has received a great deal of empirical support with both depression and suicidal ideation is cognitive therapy. As we have seen, individuals with suicidal ideation and depression frequently experience rigid or exaggerated thinking, with a tendency to overgeneralize situations, magnify events, engage in "black and white" thinking, and personalize events, thereby reaching faulty conclusions about situations or events. Cognitive therapeutic interventions such as those discussed in Chapters 11 and 12 address strategies for helping the client recognize these distortions and look at the situation from a different perspective. Participation in group therapy with a focus on interpersonal skill development, problem-solving, and adaptive coping, combined with a focus on enhancing positive emotions, has also been a successful intervention (Joiner, Voelz, &

Rudd, 2001). These authors also have used a very direct crisis planning approach. In a counseling session, the therapist and client develop a plan that includes specific suggestions if there is a reemergence of suicidal thinking:

If thinking of suicide I'll . . .

- use what I have learned in therapy to identify what is upsetting me
- write down and review some reasonable, nonsuicidal responses
- try to do some things that, in the past, have helped me feel better
- call or go to the emergency room, if the thoughts continue or get specific

We refer you also to an article recently written by Donald Meichenbaum entitled "35 Years Working with Suicidal Patients: Lessons Learned" in which he compiled a multitude of questions that therapists can ask themselves or supervisors can ask supervisees regarding their response to suicidal ideation or behavior in a client. His suggestions align with the idea of therapist self-assessment and the focus on best practices discussed throughout the text. In the article, he suggests questions under each of the following major categories (Meichenbaum, 2006, pp. 69–72):

- What are you doing to establish a therapeutic relationship with the suicidal client?
- What assessment strategies are you using to determine ongoing risk of suicide?
- What background factors have been assessed?
- How have you assessed for comorbidity and determined level of suicidal risk?
- What have you done explicitly to reduce the presence of risk factors?
- Have you involved family members and significant others?
- How have you gone about determining the role of medication?
- What specific psychotherapeutic interventions are you providing or have you provided?

Suicidal Clients' Input Regarding Therapist Responses

In an attempt to evaluate the effectiveness of therapy for suicidal individuals, Paulson and Worth (2002) interviewed a group of previously suicidal clients, a process that resulted in some very valuable suggestions for therapists. Specifically, these clients identified factors that were *not* helpful (i.e., errors in treatment) including:

1. Failure to really understand the client and what was going on with the client emotionally (i.e., the counselor was perceived as nonaccepting or disbelieving of the extent of the feelings)
2. Therapist anxiety and difficulty coping with the client's strong, negative feelings
3. Difficulty dealing with the client's expression of anger and hostility
4. Succumbing to the client's attitude of despair and hopelessness
5. Allowing dependency on the therapist
6. Failure to explore avenues of emotional support for the client
7. Failure to openly discuss and confront the suicidal thoughts and behaviors

Factors that were seen to be helpful included: (1) a positive, supportive working relationship with the therapist (i.e., a strong therapeutic alliance); (2) acknowledging and validating the client's feelings of despair, yet working with the client to help overcome these feelings and develop strategies to cope with these intense emotions; and (3) confrontation of the choice of self-destructive behavior combined with a focus on empowering the individual to make better choices. In summary, this study strongly validated the importance of the therapist moving beyond the role of solely assessing risk factors and managing the suicidal crisis, to calmly listening to, acknowledging, and working with the intense and overwhelming feelings and thinking that led the client to the point of considering suicide as a means of problem resolution.

The authors emphasize that if clients do not receive validation for their powerful feelings, it is very difficult to move beyond the feelings. Activating and working through these emotions within the therapeutic alliance paves the way for behavior change by confronting negative thoughts and patterns, and overcoming them by establishing more positive coping patterns. Rosenberg (1999) also emphasizes that, in addition to action-based steps to handle the immediate suicidal crisis, it is important to focus on the client's emotional pain, with an effort to reframe the situation, suggesting that the client's willingness to share despair and thoughts of suicide reflects a desire for help and a desire to live. Discussion can focus on the idea that clients may be feeling that the pain will go on forever, but that by seeking help they are indicating that they want to work to help stop the pain. Similarly, suicidal thoughts can be reframed as a way of communicating the depth of the feelings being experienced rather than as intent to take action, particularly taking into account the finality of death. Such discussions can lead to a focus on strategies to express emotional pain in more healthy ways, as well as ways to decrease stress and manage the specific problems confronting the client. (Refer to Box 16.2 for a summary of intervention suggestions.)

Box 16.2   **Intervention Ideas for Suicidal Ideation**

Affective Interventions

- Listen carefully to the concerns expressed, taking care not to minimize feelings.
- Acknowledge the client's interest in seeking help by sharing thoughts of suicide.
- Discuss how a desire for help is positive and suggests ambivalence about death.
- Discuss feelings of hopelessness, anger, or desire for revenge.
- Discuss the desire to get away from the intense feelings.
- Frame thoughts of suicide as a means of communicating the depth of current feelings.
- Discuss how overwhelming emotion can lead to feelings of hopelessness.
- Discuss how thoughts of suicide sometimes result from feelings of anger directed inward.
- Discuss the finality of death and the potential impact on loved ones.
- Frame intensely painful feelings as temporary, and reinforce the value of discussing concerns as a way of making problems seem more manageable.
- Gently assist client to recognize rigid or inflexible thinking.
- Assist client to list and rank (i.e., on a 1–10 scale) the most overwhelming feelings; develop concrete ideas for addressing the most distressing feelings (Joiner et al., 2001).
- Assist in prioritizing concerns and begin to problem-solve the most overwhelming concerns.
- Discuss times when the client has been able to overcome negative emotions or when the client has felt positive and happy.
- Guide the client through positive visualization activities.

Action-Based Interventions

- Develop a no-harm agreement.
- Discuss availability of means for self-harm and develop a safety plan.
- Schedule more frequent counseling sessions.
- Share crisis and emergency numbers with the client and/or family.
- Initiate a short-term phone check-in schedule.
- Notify others of the client's need for support.
- Assist the client to decide if staying with friends/family would be beneficial.
- Develop a crisis card with a specific plan to follow if suicidal thinking emerges (Joiner et al., 2001).
- Encourage the client to engage in positive, relaxing activities (exercise, spending time with friends, listening to music, reading, playing with pets, writing).
- Consult with colleagues or supervisor or initiate an assessment by a regional mental health crisis professional, if necessary.

From Rosenberg, 1999

The Impact of Suicide on Therapists

In a study of 34 therapists who had experienced the death of a client by suicide, over one-third were severely distressed. Factors associated with this distress included: (1) believing that they were responsible for not hospitalizing an imminently suicide client, (2) making an incorrect treatment decision such as allowing a client to leave a secure setting by authorizing a visit outside the facility, (3) receiving negative reactions from administrators about the client death, and (4) being fearful of a lawsuit by the client's relatives. In one case, the hospital director looked at the therapist and said "The patient appears to have died the way she was treated, with a lot of people around her, but no one effectively helping her." (Hendin, Haas, Malsberger, Szanto, & Rabinowicz, 2004, p. 1442)

A completed suicide can be extremely traumatic for all involved, including grief over the death itself combined with grief over the circumstances of the death. Feelings of guilt and self-blame are common among those left behind. Friends and family members may try to second guess the situation, with thoughts of "if only I had . . ." Therapists are not immune from feelings of shock and grief, and may experience the impact very intensely. All involved should have an opportunity to engage in the grieving process. This means taking the time to reflect on the meaning of the client's suicide and its impact on future functioning as a therapist, including the possible emergence of feelings of anxiety or helplessness when confronted with future clients presenting with suicidal ideation (Kleespies, 1993). There may also be an intense focus on recordkeeping and legal liabilities, a tendency to over-refer clients for hospitalization, a loss of self-esteem, or intrusive thoughts and feelings of anger or guilt (McAdams & Foster, 2000). If one of your friends or colleagues in the mental health field is in the extremely difficult situation of confronting a client's suicide, it is very important to encourage that person not to become isolated and to talk about their feelings. Of course, if malpractice or legal implications arise from the suicide, which is not uncommon, the therapist should follow the advice of their attorney regarding any discussion of the case. Often it is difficult to know what to say to people who have experienced a suicide in their personal or professional lives. For those who have to deal with a client's suicide, we should remember that clients make their own choices, and that suicide sometimes occurs despite the best efforts of all involved. Circumstances of the death may range from a suicide that comes very suddenly and apparently without warning, to a suicide that occurs after multiple attempts, warnings, and despite intensive therapeutic interventions. In both situations, the deceased individual has made a choice that will forever impact those closely involved. It is important to encourage those experiencing such impact to reflect on the person's whole life and not just on the person's death, and to anticipate and plan for the fact that strong emotions may reemerge on dates such as the anniversary of the suicide.

Assessing and Managing an Angry or Potentially Violent Client

It is sometimes necessary to distinguish between the presentation of innocuous aggressive thoughts or feelings and the potential for *targeted violence* (i.e., a circumstance in which there is a specific threat of intentional harm to an individual or group). If, in the course of an intake appointment or a session with a client, you become concerned about the potential for violence, it is important for you to calmly keep the communication open, ask open-ended questions, and attempt to assess the intensity of thoughts and feelings as well as the lethality of any methods discussed. A threat may be very vague or implausible with little likelihood of true risk, or it may be very specific in terms of setting, means, and motive, clearly suggesting a serious potential for harm. You may also be confronted with an ambiguous situation, with the client making a clear threat that would be possible to carry out, but with no suggestion that the first steps (such as obtaining a weapon) have occurred. When assessing risk for violence, it is important to ask about access to and past use of weapons. Most critically, just as in the case of suicidal ideation, it is incumbent upon the therapist to thoroughly assess the situation with the client.

Violent behavior, like any other behavior, is a function of the characteristics of the individual combined with what is going on in the individual's environment. It is, therefore, important to pay close attention to situational variables that may increase the risk of violence. When a client is discussing possible violence, it is important to keep in mind: (1) the individual's prior history (is there a history of violent or impulsive behavior?); (2) the individual's current mental and emotional state (Is there an impairment in functioning and decision-making? Is the client depressed? Is there a risk of a homicidal/suicidal event?); and (3) previous patterns of conversations with the client or those close to the client (Does the client tend to "talk big," but not follow through on threats? Is there evidence from the client or expressed by family or friends suggesting the potential for violence?). It is important to remember that the single greatest risk factor for future violence is a history of violent behavior. A substance abuse diagnosis is also a contributor to risk as well as the presence of delusions, manic behavior, or command hallucinations (Otto, 2000).

Certain characteristics increase the risk of violent behavior, including being male, in the late teens or early twenties, belonging to a racial minority, having a lower level of education, lacking stability in residential and employment history, and having a history of alcohol or drug abuse. The closer an individual comes to this profile, the higher the statistical risk of violent behavior. Often, the strongest predictor of violent behavior is a history of such behavior, especially when the behavior has occurred recently, has occurred frequently, or has involved more severe forms of violence. Situational factors to consider include access to weapons or other means of violence, levels of stress, and the use of alcohol or other substances that may decrease inhibitions (Truscott, Evans, & Mansell, 1995). In addition to concerns about the violence risk for clients seen in an outpatient mental health setting, there is the need for school counselors, school psychologists, and school social workers to be aware of best practices with threat assessment (Reddy et al., 2001) particularly given events such as the shootings at Columbine High School and Virginia Tech in recent years.

When dealing with an agitated client, it is important to keep safety in mind. To reduce the risk of increasing agitation, speak calmly (perhaps reminding the client that you are there to help), avoid moving rapidly or approaching the client from behind, keep an adequate distance from the client, and remain close to the door. It is also important to assess the environment for furniture or other items that could be dangerous if agitation increases. If possible, calmly and professionally alert a nearby colleague so they can unobtrusively monitor the situation. Establishing or maintaining rapport through active listening, using nonthreatening body language, and maintaining a calm demeanor is extremely important. If agitation increases, it may be necessary to verbally set limits with the client. If the client makes a verbal threat, it may be helpful to: (1) acknowledge that what the client has said is perceived as a threat ("What you just said sounds like a threat"); (2) offer an interpretation ("Using words like that pushes people away"); (3) express your own feelings ("Your words are causing me to worry"); and (4) make an advisement ("If threats are made, I need to contact the police") (Tishler, Gordon, & Landry-Meyer, 2000).

Agitation and assaultive behavior may occur for a variety of reasons. It is possible that the client's cognitive or emotional responses are impaired due to drug or alcohol intoxication or due to an acute psychiatric situation, such as a psychotic episode. The agitation may also be an impulsive behavioral response in an individual with low frustration tolerance who is fearful, frustrated, or angry, or who is using aggressive talk and behavior as a means of intimidation. Understanding the aggressive behavior and its origin can be helpful in determining the level of intervention needed. A client with whom you have a strong therapeutic alliance and who seems to be reacting out of anger or fear may be someone you can coax to sit down and safely problem-solve the situation. In the case of someone who is demonstrating potentially dangerous behavior and who appears to be severely psychotic or under the influence of intoxicants, it may be necessary to immediately request assistance from law enforcement.

The ability to rapidly and efficiently assess and manage a situation where there is client agitation or the potential for violence is a critical skill. If a therapist, dealing with an agitated client, becomes aware that the client has a weapon, it is important to attempt to intervene calmly by acknowledging the situation: "I see you have a knife." Again, while letting the client know you are there to help, you can ask the client to place the weapon, and any other weapons, on the floor. If this occurs, the next step would be to ask the client to go with you to another room (where you can indirectly notify colleagues and request assistance in dealing with the situation). It is critical to remain calm, since a therapist's fear, discomfort, or negativity may increase client agitation and make communication and intervention more difficult (Tishler et al., 2000). You should keep up-to-date with the professional literature on risk assessment, such as research-based structured assessment interviews (Webster, Douglas, Eaves, & Hart, 1997) combined with detailed review of the individual's history of violent or aggressive behavior, including history of making threats of violence. Refer to Otto (2000) for additional information on assessing and managing violence risk in outpatient settings, and Borum (2000) on assessing violence risk among youth.

When you have a strong therapeutic alliance with a client and you perceive that there is a risk of violence, collaborate with the client to create a plan for safety. This may include a plan to reduce environmental triggers for anger, remove access to weapons, or work with medical professionals to adjust medication levels. It may also be decided by the therapist and client that therapy should occur more frequently. Treatment goals will vary depending on the case formulation, but may include stress management, strategies for anger control, and identifying and avoiding trigger situations such as a focus on decreasing substance use. Of course, in circumstances where there appears to be a high risk of violence and there is an identifiable victim, legalities involving a "duty to protect" or "duty to warn" will come into play.

Be aware that homicidal ideation can coexist with suicidal ideation, and that best practices dictate screening clients for both suicidal and aggressive tendencies. Investigations of homicides followed by a suicide suggest that the pattern and risk factors parallel those associated with suicide. In homicide-suicide situations, there is less likely to be a history of violent or impulsively reckless behavior, and the individuals involved are more likely to have risk factors such as depression, psychosis, substance abuse, and triggers such as paranoia, jealousy, feelings of helplessness or despair, absence of social support, and connections with a specific religious or political ideology (Hillbrand, 2001).

As mentioned in Chapter 3, it is also important to assess for the presence of violence in relationships with others (Wolkenstein & Sterman, 1998). A therapist may become aware that a client is in a relationship where there has been a history of domestic violence or is with someone who appears to be at heightened risk for violence, or the client may enter into such a relationship during the course of therapy. In such situations it is important for the therapist to understand the severity, frequency, and context of the violence (Lawson, 2003), and to work with the client to assess issues of safety and to determine if the safest course of action is to leave (perhaps in conjunction with obtaining a protection order) or to remain in the situation. If the client chooses to stay in the relationship, safety planning may involve: maintaining access to a cell phone for emergency calls, developing an awareness of items in the home that could be used against the client as a weapon, recognizing situations that trigger the partner's violent behavior, and considering a plan in the event the client needs to leave the situation (Peterman & Dixon, 2003). Additionally, during the course of therapy, it will be important to address the personal, economic, and cultural issues that impact the dynamics of the relationship, coping strategies, and decisions to stay in the relationship (Yoshihama, 2002). Similarly, if there are children in the home, discuss the impact of conflict on the "silent witnesses" of abuse (Burrows-Horton, Cruise, Graybill, & Corrett, 1999) and be cognizant of the co-occurrence of spousal violence and child abuse, and the increased risk of socioemotional and behavioral problems in children exposed to domestic violence (Shipman, Rossman, & West, 1999).

Best Practices in Crisis Management

Each region has a unique system for responding to mental health emergencies. Practitioners should be aware of the resources in their own community, as well as the specifics of the implementation system. Many areas have a mental health professional designated by the state or county as the official resource for responding to a mental health crisis. This individual can be accessed at a designated number by the police, by staff at hospital emergency rooms, by mental health crisis lines, or by mental health professionals working in the community. When you are confronted with a suicidal situation or a situation with the potential for violence, you must decide the most appropriate level of intervention:

1. Do I need to contact 9-1-1 for immediate support in the situation? This may be the case if a client is extremely agitated or intoxicated or acutely suicidal and is presenting imminent risk to self or others.

2. Is it appropriate to make a plan to have the client taken by a friend or family member to a local hospital for mental health assessment? This may be the case if there is a reliable friend or family member who agrees to accompany the client to the hospital and the client expresses willingness for the intervention and has a history of reliable follow through.

3. Is it appropriate to contact the designated mental health professional to request an on-site assessment of mental health needs? This may be the

case when there is a high risk of self-destructive or violent behavior, it is unlikely that the client would be able to arrange to go to the emergency room, and the situation does not appear to require involvement by law enforcement officials.

It is important to know the response process and procedures when you contact your local mental health crisis professional. Is there a triage system where you first speak to a mental health worker who assesses the next steps in response? Will you wait on the line until you are connected to the individual, or will a message be forwarded to someone who will then contact you within a designated period of time? As much as possible and appropriate, it is important to make these decisions for back-up support jointly with the client. However, this may not always be possible, particularly in a high-risk suicidal situation where the client does not want additional intervention or an acute situation requiring law enforcement support.

Assessment of risk for the potential to inflict harm on self or others is a continuing process, rather than an event that occurs only during intake or during times of crisis (Otto, 2000). All new clients should be screened during intake regarding their violence history (Borum, Swartz, & Swanson, 1996) and history of suicidal ideation or behavior. If a client has a history of violent behavior or psychiatric illness that has resulted in violent episodes, a component of the treatment plan may include working with the client (and possibly individuals close to the client) to monitor for signs of increasing agitation, and to have a plan to intervene if such symptoms are observed. The involvement of significant others in such planning is important because violent behavior generally results from interpersonal interactions. Friends or family members may also be involved in plans to create a safer environment by removing potential weapons from the environment or having telephones strategically located to allow for emergency calls, thereby reducing the risk of serious injury during a violent episode.

Another strategy used is "target hardening," which refers to interventions designed to help keep potential victims safe, such as notifying a potential victim (if ethically and legally appropriate), suggesting the use of alarm systems or availability of a cellular phone to call for help, and strategies for recognizing signs of escalating risk and knowing when and how to intervene. It is important for the clinician and client, as well as significant others, to be aware that the potential for violence occurs along a continuum and is not static. Problematic risk behaviors can gradually emerge, or the escalation from calm to violent behavior can occur very rapidly (Otto, 2000). When working with a suicidal or depressed client on an outpatient basis, you will want to monitor suicidal ideations during therapy sessions, provide the client with a 24-hour emergency access number, and make sure that the negotiated safety plan is not in need of modification. Some counselors also use telephone contacts in between counseling sessions to monitor safety (Kleespies et al., 1999).

When confronting any psychiatric emergency, it is essential to follow best practices related to risk management, including documentation that there has been a comprehensive evaluation of the situation, including a risk-benefit analysis that supports the actions taken (or not taken) by the therapist. Consultation with a supervisor or colleague to review the situation and the plan is also a critical component of risk management (Bongar, Greaney, & Peruzzi, 1998). As we discussed in Chapter 4, a comprehensive assessment of the client's needs and circumstances (including current coping strategies and the multiple variables impacting their situation and life view) taken during the initial stages of therapy can be invaluable when evaluating and formulating plans in a crisis situation. It is also essential to understand the legal and ethical implications of managing a psychiatric emergency or situations that may involve self harm or harm to others.

Understanding Psychopharmacology

Dr. Andrew Mosholder, an FDA medical reviewer, stated that he had been pressured to alter and hide information on documents submitted to congressional investigators concerning the possible link between antidepressant use and suicide in children. (Vedantam, 2004)

$$17$$

Chapter

It is important for mental health professionals to have a working knowledge of the medications prescribed to treat psychological conditions. This is particularly true as more and more people are turning to their physicians for relief from psychological symptoms, combined with the extensive marketing of medications to health care providers and to the public. Many who seek psychotherapy are already taking medication for their symptoms at the time they initiate therapy (Wiggens & Cummings, 1998). It is argued that mental health professionals have the responsibility to be knowledgeable about the biochemical processes involved in the development and treatment of psychological disorders (Rivas-Vazquez & Blais, 1997), and that it is difficult for therapists to provide comprehensive treatment planning, ensure well-being of clients, and minimize professional liability without some background knowledge in psychopharmacology (King & Anderson, 2004). It is well documented that psychotherapeutic intervention can assist clients both in managing adverse effects from medication and understanding the importance of regular adherence to recommended medication schedules (Rivas-Vazquez, Johnson, Blais, & Rey, 1999).

If mental health professionals move into discussions of medication with their clients, it is essential that they take the time to examine their own beliefs regarding the use of medication, in general, and in the treatment of psychological disorders. You might want to ask yourself the following questions: Do you believe that psychological problems can have a physiological basis? Do you consider the use of medication necessary with some psychological disorders, but unnecessary with others? If medication is to be used as part of a comprehensive treatment plan, would you recommend that therapy and medication begin simultaneously? If not, which do you believe should start first? Do you hold the view that the use of medication disguises symptoms and is, therefore, a hindrance to the therapeutic process? Do you believe that psychotropic medication should only be prescribed by a psychiatrist, or are you comfortable when such medications are recommended and prescribed by a family physician? Should medication be used only as a last resort? Do you feel frustrated about the extensive marketing of medications and, if so, do these feelings influence your attitudes toward pharmacological interventions? The use of medication in the treatment of psychological disorders is complex from many perspectives. Certainly, it is crucial for the medical practitioners who prescribe medications for emotional issues to have training in differential diagnosis and psychopharmacology. Additionally, it is important for mental health professionals to be informed about research-based and best practice guidelines for specific disorders, regardless of one's personal or professional opinions. It is essential for mental health professionals to investigate and be knowledgable about ethical and legal aspects of discussing medications with clients. Depending on where you practice and your professional affiliation, there may be ethical or legal restrictions on such discussions, even when the discussion is initiated by the client.

Overview of Psychopharmacology Basics

Biochemical abnormalities in the brain are recognized as playing a significant role in a variety of psychological disorders, including anxiety, depression, bipolar disorder, and schizophrenia. The human brain and central nervous system is comprised of billions of cells, called *neurons,* which have a complex system for communicating sensation, movement, thoughts, and feelings. The *axon* of each neuron (located at the tip of the cell) has a connection to the *dendrites* (the branches) of adjacent cells and allows the transmission of nerve impulses from cell to cell. Dendrites bring information to the body of the cell and axons carry information away from the cell. The *synapse* is the tiny space between cells and between the axon of one cell and the dendrites of another cell. Chemicals, called *neurotransmitters,* help relay biochemical messages between neurons. Signals move from neuron to neuron, with neurotransmitters playing a critical role in the transmission of the nerve impulses. When a signal reaches the end of a neuron that specializes in sending messages (the *presynaptic neuron*), the cell secretes a chemical message into the synapse; the neurotransmitter then floats through the synapse and binds to the correct receptor neuron on the other side (the *postsynaptic neuron*), like a key fitting into a lock. Depending upon the specific neurotransmitter and other complex factors, the binding either excites the postsynaptic cell, (meaning it continues to transmit the signal) or inhibits it (meaning that it stops further transmission of the signal). Once the neurotransmitter has performed its function, it is either broken down by enzymes in the synapse or is reabsorbed into the presynaptic neuron. When these neurotransmitters are not functioning appropriately, messages can be blocked or sent incorrectly, resulting in the symptoms seen in some psychological disorders.

Many *psychotropic medications* (i.e., medications used to treat psychological disorders) work to correct biochemical imbalances, often by increasing or decreasing the amount of neurotransmitter available, thus impacting the process of binding, reabsorption, or breakdown by enzymes. Some medications work by enhancing the transmission process, while others block the communication of messages. Different disorders are caused by different biochemical abnormalities, and psychotropic medications should be selected based upon careful differential diagnosis and analysis of symptoms. It is critical, especially for those prescribing medication, to carefully assess each client, not only to ensure a correct diagnosis, but also to rule out other factors (e.g., physical illness, excessive caffeine consumption, lack of sleep, substance abuse, reaction to herbal remedies or other medications) that may be contributing to (or even causing) the presenting symptoms. Medication needs to be used with particular care in children and adolescents, those who are elderly, pregnant or considering pregnancy, or individuals who have other physical risk factors (e.g., seizures, compromised liver or kidney functioning, eating disorders, cardiovascular concerns). *Psychopharmacology* refers to the use of medications in the management of psychological disorders. The term *titration of dose* used in the pharmacological literature refers to the gradual increase or decrease in medication that may occur as the medical professional attempts to find the correct *therapeutic dose* (i.e., the lowest dose of the medication needed to produce the desired effects). It is important for clients to be aware that the time needed to reach a therapeutic response differs from medication to medication, with some providing almost immediate relief from symptoms and others requiring many weeks of regular use before a therapeutic level is reached. Readers are referred to Buelow, Herbert, & Buelow (2000), Diamond (2002), Gorman (1998), Julien (2001), Keltner and Folks (2001), and Ruiz (2000) for comprehensive explanations of these complex processes.

It may be helpful to understand the process involved when a pharmaceutical company gains approval by the Food and Drug Administration (FDA) to sell a specific medication. When a new compound that may have potential as a medication for humans is discovered, the company developing the drug seeks a patent. Such patents generally last for many years, during which time the drug is tested on animals and, if the animal studies have been promising, testing begins on humans. The human studies involve three phases, beginning with a trial where safety and effectiveness are evaluated on both healthy volunteers and on individuals with the condition being treated. The next phase involves more controlled studies, comparing drug effects with placebo effects. If this phase yields positive results, the last phase involves testing the drug in more comprehensive trials with larger groups of subjects. If success is achieved at each of these stages, the company submits an application for formal approval by the FDA. Once approved, the drug is manufactured by the company that developed the drug, under a brand name chosen by the company. At this stage, the medication is often quite expensive because the drug manufacturer is recovering the costs of research and development. After the patent expires, any company that meets FDA standards can manufacture and market the drug (with the same active ingredients as the original) in a *generic* form, under a trade name chosen by the company.

It is also important to understand the limitations of FDA testing. Clinical trials, which are generally paid for by the drug manufacturer, tend to have a number of built-in biases, including reliance on clinician ratings and difficulty maintaining the "blind" (i.e., the goal that the participants and their physicians be unaware if they are taking a medication or a placebo) of the study when individuals begin to display side effects consistent with expected physiological responses for the medication being evaluated (Antonuccio, Burns, & Danton, 2002). Additionally, the studies often include a process for determining, prior to the start of a clinical trial, which individuals tend to be strong, immediate responders to placebo medications and then eliminating these individuals from the study. It has been argued that this process works to minimize the measured placebo response of drugs, thereby magnifying the apparent medication effects (Brown, 2002). In addition, even when combining the three phases of testing, most drug trials are brief and involve only two to three thousand people, often excluding certain groups such as the elderly or individuals with complicated medical histories (Holland & Degruy, 1997). Monitoring side effects and the developing literature on new medications is very important due to limited information on long-term side effects, possible drug interactions, and the potential of newly discovered adverse reactions. In fact, it is not uncommon for adverse drug reactions to be reported after a drug has been on the market for a period of time (Lasser et al., 2002). When concerns emerge, suggested precautions may simply be added to the warnings section of the medication package insert. If a more significant *black-box drug warning* (i.e., a warning related to significant safety concerns with a medication that is placed in a black-bordered box in the medication instructional insert) occurs, letters from the drug manufacturer are sent to health care providers alerting them to the heightened level of concern. These alerts may occur when a drug is new to the market, or when concerns emerge after the drug has been available for a long period of time. Unfortunately, unless there happens to be publicity about a black box warning, these admonitions often do not reach consumers. On rare occasions, drugs are removed from the market due to severe concerns. At times, drugs are removed from the market in other countries, but remain available in the United States. As with any change in medication, if individuals become concerned about the safety of a particular medication, it is essential that they discuss their concerns with their health care provider.

Following the literature on psychopharmacology and understanding the use of medication can be confusing because medications are referred to both by their chemical name and by their brand name. Each medication has only one chemical name, but can have multiple brand names. For example, bupropion is marketed under the name Wellbutrin when it is used as an antidepressant, but is sold under the name Zyban when it is used to help someone stop smoking. The popular press and some of the professional literature use the brand name in discussion of the medication; however, professional journals frequently discuss research with specific medications using only the chemical name of the medication. For ease of reference, Appendix C contains a list of psychopharmacological medications listing both chemical and brand names, as well as some common side effects and precautions.

Understanding Side Effects and Adverse Reactions

Although the majority of individuals in one survey reported that antidepressants were helpful, between 10 and 21 percent reported feeling drowsy or disoriented, from 21 to 51 percent indicated decreased sexual interest or performance, and 12 to 21 percent reported weight gain, depending on the specific medication used. (Consumer Reports, 2004)

There are many possible side effects associated with the use of medication, involving both physiological and psychological reactions. Not everyone experiences side effects, and the experience, intensity, and tolerance for the effects can differ from person to person. Understanding and interpreting the side effects that are reported when someone begins a trial of medication is much more complex than might be expected. In order to comprehend and interpret reported side effects, it is important to understand how a *placebo* (an inactive substance that is administered in a form similar to the active substance) is used in drug research to ascertain the true effects of a medication, apart from psychological reactions. In a *double-blind placebo trial,* neither the patient nor the physician knows if the pills the patient is taking contain an actual medication or an inert placebo. With double-blind medication trials, not only do the individuals taking actual medication report side effects, but so do individuals taking only a placebo. Adverse side effects reported when someone is administered a placebo are referred to as a *nocebo effect* (Barsky, Sainfort, Rogers, & Borus, 2002). Understanding this phenomenon involves recognizing that most healthy adults experience a variety of somatic symptoms (e.g., fatigue, difficulty concentrating, drowsiness, headaches) on a regular basis, so when a new substance is taken, be it medication or a placebo, there is a good chance that these symptoms might be misattributed to the pill they have taken. The experiencing of side effects may occur, in part, due to an *expectancy* effect—the individual is aware of possible side effects, attends to an uncomfortable sensation, and then attributes the sensation to the medication. Given the numerous studies showing placebo effects in at least 25 percent of the individuals taking a placebo, we can assume that some of the side effects we see with any medication can be attributed to the placebo effect. In fact, we also know that the number of side effects reported in response to a placebo increases when there is active questioning about possible side effects. It is important not to immediately assume that all side effects reported are due to the medication being taken. This is particularly true for clients who are anxious or depressed, already demonstrate a variety of somatic symptoms, are concerned about possible side effects, or have a history of being sensitive to a variety of different medications (Barsky et al., 2002). For clients who may be anxious about starting a medication, the health care provider may decide to wait until the individual is certain about trying medication or may start with a very low dose of the medication, allowing time for the individual to get used to the idea of medication and to allow the individual's body to slowly adjust.

Recent evidence suggests that antidepressant placebos not only produce psychological effects, but also produce chemical changes in the brain. Review of positron emission tomography (PET) imaging in a six-week double-blind trial comparing a placebo to the antidepressant Prozac, revealed that not only did the medication produce changes in brain functioning, there were also clear metabolic changes in certain parts of the brain for those taking the inactive placebo (Mayberg, Silva, Brannan, & Tekell, 2002). Similarly, in another drug trial comparing a placebo with Prozac with all participants involved in counseling sessions, Lecter, Cook, and Witte (2002) found that both groups showed improvement in symptoms and brain changes, although the exact nature of the changes differed between the groups.

When health care providers prescribe medications, they research possible *drug-drug interactions* (i.e., when the effect of one medication is changed, enhanced, or diminished when taken with another drug). For example, certain antianxiety medications need to be prescribed at lower doses when used with certain antidepressants. *Drug incompatibility* (i.e., potential harmful or uncomfortable effects that occur when two drugs are combined) is also a necessary consideration when prescribing medications. For example, an extremely serious reaction can occur when certain antidepressants are combined; this can also occur when a change in medication has been made and there has not been enough time for the first drug to be cleared from the body before the second drug is started. Similarly, combining certain medications with tobacco, alcohol, or marijuana, or with certain foods (such as processed meats or grapefruit juice) can produce undesired effects (Rivas-Vazquez, 2001d). Food, or even specific nutrients, can affect how a medication is absorbed, so health care providers and pharmacists generally provide information on whether a medication should be taken with food or on an empty stomach, or if there are certain foods, or other substances, that should be avoided. Not only are predictable side effects possible, there is always the remote possibility that someone may experience an idiosyncratic adverse reaction to a medication. The chances of such a reaction are increased when a drug is new to the market and has not yet been used by a wide range of individuals or those using multiple medications (Holland & Degruy, 1997).

With side effects that are not life-threatening, the health care provider may recommend waiting a while before considering a change in dose or a change in medication because side effects sometimes resolve as the body adjusts to a medication. This "wait and see" approach may be distressing to the client. The experiencing of harmless side effects can be framed positively, as a sign that the medication is taking effect (Rivas-Vazquez & Blais, 1997). Efforts to educate about ways to minimize discomfort (e.g., increasing fluid intake, sucking on sugarless candy, chewing gum to counteract dryness in the mouth) may increase willingness to continue with a medication trial. This kind of support is particularly important for chronic disorders such as schizophrenia or bipolar disorder that require maintenance medications to prevent relapse. It is also important to be aware, however, that some distressing side effects, such as the sexual dysfunction reported by the users of some antidepressants, do not always improve with time (Rivas-Vazquez & Blais, 1997). Sexual dysfunction is a side effect that a client may be uncomfortable discussing with their health care provider. In some cases, medication may be discontinued with only a vague explanation such as, "I don't like the way it makes me feel." It is important for health care providers prescribing medications to openly ask about side effects, including sexual side effects, because a change of medication might be an option. There is always a delicate balance between making sure that distressing side effects are not ignored, and avoiding a self-fulfilling prophecy by focusing too much attention on the issue of side effects.

The Role of Therapists in Medication Management

From 50 to 75 percent of individuals with schizophrenia will relapse within one year if they discontinue antipsychotic medications as compared to only 25 percent of those who continue their medications. Factors such as the therapist-client relationship, the complexity of the medication regimen, and family support play an important role in compliance with treatment. (Valenstein et al., 2001)

Accurate diagnosis of a disorder is critical, particularly if medication is selected as an intervention. As discussed in the assessment chapter, a comprehensive physical exam to rule out contributing physiological factors is an important component of the diagnostic process and important before medications are prescribed. Once medical conditions are ruled out, collaboration with the therapist is important for a clear understanding of the mental health diagnosis. This is particularly true when, as is often the case, the prescribing medical practitioner is not a psychiatrist. As part of the diagnostic process, any factors that could be causing or contributing to symptoms should be thoroughly assessed. This would include: sleep deprivation, lack of exercise or proper nutrition, caffeine intake, alcohol intake, the intake of any other recreational drugs, and the use of both prescription and nonprescription medications (including laxatives, herbal remedies, and health food products). Any of these can have an impact on symptoms and may, in fact, be the primary cause of symptoms. For example, caffeine, a commonly used substance (found in many products including coffee, tea, chocolate, soft drinks, and aspirin), can produce symptoms of anxiety, insomnia, or irritability. Of course, it is always critical to ask about medical conditions (e.g., hypothyroidism, sleep apnea, heart arrhythmias) that may be causing the presenting symptoms. Interviewing the client regarding their response, both physical and psychological, to any previously prescribed medications is also imperative.

The relationship between the physician and client can also play an important role in effective pharmacological management. In the health care field, *compliance* (i.e., adherence to recommendations in accordance with the expectations of the health care provider) is an important issue. In general, patients take only about half of the medication prescribed for them; this results in less effective treatment, invalid assessment of therapeutic effects, and the mistaken belief that higher doses or stronger medications are needed (Williams, Rodin, Ryan, Grolnick, & Deci, 1998). Medical professionals make recommendations (e.g., prescribing a medication, requesting blood tests, suggesting abstinence from alcohol while taking a medication) based upon medical knowledge, whereas individuals may make decisions based upon personal priorities. It has been found that compliance with recommendations is enhanced when there is a strong therapeutic alliance—when the health care professional communicates their opinion of the problem and develops a treatment plan jointly with the patient, taking into account the patient's values, goals, and expectations. Important variables in this interaction are trust in the health care provider and the degree to which the individual feels listened to, understood, and independent in making choices (Langer, 1999). Williams and colleagues (1998) emphasize the relationship between personal autonomy and increased compliance, suggesting that compliance is enhanced when feelings are acknowledged, pressure to comply is minimized, recommendations are carefully explained, and choices are offered.

Discussion of concerns about medication can have a positive impact on compliance and ultimately improve the effectiveness of a medication (Krupnik et al., 1996). This is not surprising given concerns that might exist about the use of medication, including fears or negative beliefs about medication on the part of the client or members of the client's support system, concerns about side effects, or even frustration about the time it takes to reach therapeutic doses with some medications. Mental health professionals can encourage clients to become educated, not only about their specific disorder, but also about expected medication side effects, particularly any serious side effects to which they should be alert. The therapist can help clients develop a system to ensure that they are taking their medication regularly and can discuss information the client has been provided, such as whether to take the medication with food or on an empty stomach, or any potential interactions with food, alcohol, or other medications. Assisting a client in becoming an informed consumer and self-advocate in the area of health care can be a very important life-long skill, and an appropriate therapeutic goal. Friends, family members, and caregivers can support the client's autonomy in medication management. This may be particularly important if the client is feeling pressured to take medication, and responding with noncompliance.

It is important for mental health professionals to understand that there are many barriers that can affect adherence to a medication regime recommended by the health care provider. Studies investigating the acceptability of treatment options for psychological disorders have shown that medication is generally perceived to be a less acceptable and less effective treatment than counseling (Hall & Robertson, 1998). If a client is having a difficult time adhering to a medication recommendation, it is extremely important to find out why and then to encourage discussion of the issues with the health care provider. Seeking input regarding the perceptions of close friends and family regarding the medication is critical, since their beliefs and reactions can have a strong impact on client reactions. Some of the potential barriers to successful use of medication include:

1. *The client, or family, may not truly understand the nature of the disorder and the role of medication in treating the disorder.*

    It can be very helpful to talk with the client, and close friends or family members, about the biochemical basis of a disorder, explaining how the medication works to help control symptoms and the importance of taking medications on schedule (i.e., maintaining the correct therapeutic level of medication). Clients dealing with more chronic disorders such as schizophrenia or bipolar illness will need to understand the importance of maintenance medication. It is important for the client to understand that medications do not cure psychological disorders, but that they can relieve symptoms of a disorder. They should understand that some medications require weeks before much effect is noticed, and that sometimes the health care provider will need to try different medications before results are seen.

2. *The client may encounter negative beliefs of family and others.*

    A client may be open to the concept of a medication trial, particularly when they are experiencing distressing symptoms or are tired of battling a psychological disorder without success, but may find that family members or close friends have negative feelings toward the use of medication. The client may feel pressure to avoid medication or to try alternate therapies. This can be a very challenging and frustrating situation for therapists and health care providers, particularly when dealing with a disorder such as schizophrenia or bipolar illness, in which pharmacology plays a critical role. It may be necessary to intervene and attempt to educate family members about the role of medication in treating the disorder. This is particularly important given the common view that drugs prescribed for psychological conditions are addictive.

3. *The client, or family, may believe that there is no need to continue taking medication once they start feeling better.*

Many individuals may not understand the biochemical basis of a disorder, or the importance of taking a medication as prescribed. Clients may believe they no longer need to continue a medication once they are feeling better or have experienced a reduction in acute symptoms. They may believe that the medication can be used on an "as needed" basis, such as aspirin or cold remedies might be used. Reeducation about the biochemical basis of the disorder and how the medication works to help symptoms may be necessary; this discussion may be particularly important for medications requiring the maintenance of therapeutic blood levels for ongoing effectiveness. Clients need to understand that it is essential to consult with their health care provider if they are considering discontinuation or reduction of a medication. The health care provider can further explain the effects of abruptly stopping—or periodically starting and stopping—medications.

4. *The client, or family, may feel that taking medication is a sign of weakness or inability to deal with problems on their own; the medication may be perceived as a constant reminder of the individual's psychological difficulties.*

Again, education about the biochemical basis of the illness may be helpful. Most people are familiar with diabetes and the need for the regular use of insulin in order to stay healthy. The client can also be given the analogy that, for some psychological conditions, medication is necessary to help the person stay healthy. Therapists sometimes explore issues of resistance to or ambivalence about medication use, perhaps focusing on the client's commitment to become and remain healthy, and to explore various methods for meeting that goal. Clients can also be reassured that it is common for the dosage to decrease (or the medication to be discontinued) following successful therapy (Wiggins & Cummings, 1998).

5. *The client, or family, may be concerned about side effects of the medication.*

Clients can be encouraged to become more knowledgeable about the specific medications they are taking or that their health care provider is considering. They can be encouraged to ask the health care provider direct questions about risks and benefits of the medication.

Box 17.1 Questions Clients Can Ask Their Health Care Providers

- How long do you expect it will take for the medication to help my symptoms?
- How does this medication work?
- What kind of improvements should I expect to see?
- Are there other remedies that I could try instead of medication?
- Why does it seem that this medication is the best choice for me?
- What is the lowest dose I can take to gain a benefit from the medication?
- How do you plan to monitor to see if the medication is helping?
- How do you usually monitor to see if I am experiencing side effects?
- How often will you need to see me while I am taking this medication?
- Are there any special lab tests that will be required before I start or while I am on the medication?
- What are typical side effects of the medication?
- Are there any serious risks or side effects that I need to be aware of?
- Have the risks been adequately studied?
- Are there side effects that need to be reported to you immediately?
- Are there any side effects that will require me to seek immediate medical attention?
- Are there any addiction or drug dependence concerns with this medication?
- Do I take the medication after eating, or on an empty stomach?
- Is it best to take the medication in the morning or the evening?
- Are there foods, beverages, medications, vitamins, or herbal remedies that should not be combined with this medication?
- Is it possible to have once-a-day dosing of this medication?
- What should I do if I miss a dose of the medication?
- Is it acceptable to crush or to chew the pills?
- If I decide to discontinue this medication, do I need to stop it gradually?
- Do you have a list of the medications I am taking? Can I have a copy?
- Is one of my health care providers keeping track of all of the medications I am taking?
- Are there any concerns with this combination of medication?

(Refer to Box 17.1 for a list of possible questions.) They can learn about the statistical probability of serious side effects, and the more common, less serious side effects. They may feel reassured if they have been reassured that the side effects of most medications are not serious, do not require medical attention, and often disappear as the body adjusts to the medication. Those taking medication should be educated about any potentially serious side effects, the symptoms to be reported immediately, and the remote possibility of an idiosyncratic adverse reaction. An understanding of the difference between dangerous side effects (which are rare) and more common side effects (that may be disturbing, but are not dangerous) may relieve anxiety and may allow the client to feel comfortable tolerating innocuous side effects.

Acknowledge any side effects that the client reports and be supportive and encouraging when discussing common, benign side effects that are disturbing, but not dangerous. Clients can also be educated about the placebo effect, explaining how the symptoms that they experience in daily life are sometimes blamed on medication, or how worrying about the side effects of medication can create a "self-fulfilling prophecy." If a client has been started on a low dose of the medication, reassurance can be given that their body will have a chance to slowly adjust to the medication.

Continuing open discussion about the client's anxieties or fears about side effects, trying to understand their exact reservations, and recognizing that the side effects may be truly distressing and frightening to clients can act to reassure them. Further examination of the client's (or the family's) feelings about the diagnosis, the convenience of obtaining the medications or getting recommended blood tests, or the ease of taking the medication according to the recommended schedule can yield helpful information (Sainfort, 2002). Continued or exaggerated reports of side effects, particularly in individuals or families with ambivalence regarding medication, may be an indirect way of requesting discontinuation of the medication.

6. *The client may not remember to take the medication due to depression or other symptoms such as confusion or impaired thinking.*

If a client does not appear to have the organizational skills, energy, or alertness necessary to adhere to a medication schedule, it may be necessary to help the client develop a plan to ensure that the medication is taken regularly. (See Box 17.2 for some suggestions for remembering to keep appointments or to take medication on time.) The assistance of close friends or family members may be needed in the early phases of treatment, particularly for medications that require a period of weeks before a therapeutic response occurs. However, as the situation improves it is important that clients take on the responsibility, to the greatest extent possible, of managing their own medication. However, for some individuals with schizophrenia who continue to have difficulty taking medication on schedule, it may be necessary to consider antipsychotic medication via an intramuscular injection once or twice per month rather than oral medications.

7. *The cost may be prohibitive.*

Prohibitive costs may affect a client's decision to continue with a prescribed medication, even when there is obvious improvement in symptoms. Some insurance companies, in their efforts to cut costs, may charge higher co-payments for newer, brand name medications. For in-

BOX 17.2   **Assisting Clients to Remember Appointments and Medication**

- Work collaboratively with the client to develop a structure that works for the client.
- Ask the client about why they are missing appointments or forgetting their medication.
- Listen carefully to the client's perspective regarding the difficulties.
- Remember that issues may be much deeper than simply forgetting.
- Inquire about successful methods that were used in the past.
- Ask about ideas the client might have for modifying previous strategies to enhance success.
- Consider structures to help with memory:
  - Outline the schedule for monitoring medication effects (physician visits, lab tests).
  - Keep a written list of all medications taken and medication schedule.
  - Use a calendar or daily planner.
  - Program an alarm in a cell phone.
  - Use a Palm Pilot or computer calendar reminder system.
  - Place the medication in a location where it will be easily visible.
  - Use a daily or weekly pillbox.
  - Use reminder "notes to self" or Post-It notes.
  - Develop a chart.

dividuals with limited insurance or without medical insurance, efforts to make medication supplies last longer may include reducing the frequency or quantity of the dosage (Becker, 2001). Clients may feel guilty about using household funds to purchase medication or may believe that they do not deserve to have the money spent on them. Clinicians can assist clients in applying for medical insurance or lower cost health care, and can encourage clients to ask their health care provider for free samples of medication, a prescription written for a smaller quantity of medication, or for a *generic* (i.e., non-brand name) equivalent of the medication. Generic medications are close to, but necessarily identical to, the original brand name medication. (For this reason, it is often recommended that individuals initially trying a medication not switch from a brand name to a generic during the course of the medication trial because this change may confound the results. However, they may later begin a trial of the generic if the original medication proves to be effective.)

8. *The ability to get to the pharmacy or to appointments may be a barrier; this may be particularly true with medications that require monitoring of blood levels or with medications that require a new written prescription each month.*

    Some psychotropic medications are classified as *Schedule II drugs,* which means they have the potential for abuse. For this reason, Schedule

II drugs (e.g., the stimulant medications used to treat attention-deficit disorder) cannot be refilled (they require a new prescription) and, in some areas, a paper prescription must be carried to the pharmacy each month (rather than using telephone or fax prescription options). These requirements, which may involve the inconvenience of getting to the physician's office and then to the pharmacy, may be a barrier to regular adherence to the medication schedule, particularly in single-parent families, families with limited transportation, or when clients or caretakers work long hours. In this situation, the mental health professional can help consider ways of facilitating these required trips to the physician's office and the pharmacy. Some medications require that blood testing be done periodically, either to check that the medication is at the therapeutic dose, or to check for specific adverse side effects. This testing can also be perceived as inconvenient or distressing, or both. Offering an opportunity to discuss the concerns, combined with discussion of the rationale of periodic blood testing with certain medications, may be beneficial.

9. *The client may have concerns that the medication is not working adequately, that the medication is taking too long to work, or that tolerance to the medication might develop.*

   Some clients may become impatient when they start taking a medication and see no immediate results. In this situation, the therapist can explain that for some medications the dosage is increased gradually until a therapeutic level of the medication is reached, and that some medications, especially antidepressants, may take as long as 4 to 6 weeks for the client to begin to feel the effects. Some clients are pleased with reduced symptoms, but may become noncompliant in the regular use of medication because they are worried that the effectiveness of the medication may wear off if they use it too regularly. For most psychotropic medications, the therapist can help reassure the client that a tolerance does not develop. It can be explained that physicians typically start with a low dose of a medication and increase the dose until a therapeutic level is reached, with the goal of finding the lowest possible dose needed for symptom relief. The therapist can educate clients about why health care providers do not recommend stopping medications suddenly, but instead will gradually reduce the dosage, thus eliminating the unpleasant, or even dangerous, side effects than can occur when some medications are stopped suddenly. Clients who are considering the discontinuation of medication need to understand that it is essential to do so in consultation with their health care provider.

10. *The client may have concerns that there is just too much medication being used these days and that medications are being overprescribed or used without sufficient information on their effectiveness.*

It is true that there has been a significant increase in the advertising of medications and a 50 percent increase in outpatient drug prescriptions since 1992 (Ukens, 1999). In fact, in 2001, pharmaceutical companies spent 1.5 billion dollars to market antidepressants to doctors, and 200 million dollars on television and magazine advertisements targeted at consumers (Goode, 2002). Medications are being used to treat a wider range of psychological conditions and are being prescribed with increased frequency by primary care physicians (Rivas-Vazquez & Blais, 1997). At times, medications are prescribed not only for the original condition, but also to combat drug side effects. Given these realities, it is important for clients to receive a thorough assessment, accurate diagnosis, and to be informed about treatment alternatives, including nonpharmacological treatment. Clients can be encouraged to express any concerns about medication directly to their health care provider, who may agree that, given the reluctance to try medication, it is best to try therapy as a first step. This may not be an option with conditions such as schizophrenia or bipolar illness. Best practice guidelines support medication use in the treatment of acute symptoms of these disorders, as well as maintenance medication to prevent relapse.

Clients may appreciate information on the FDA process of medication testing and data on the medication's effectiveness with respect to their specific symptoms. Clients can also be reassured that they can talk to their health care provider if it seems a medication is not effective (i.e., does not provide symptom relief within the expected time period). Similarly, if distressing side effects continue even after their body has adjusted to medication, they can openly discuss these concerns with their health care provider. Some individuals may feel uncomfortable or intimidated asking questions or discussing side effects with their physician. If this is the case, therapists can offer to help engage in role-play activities with the client to practice these skills.

Special Considerations with Medication

Certain Asian groups believe that western medications are "hot" and too potent for Asian physiology; therefore, they sometimes dilute or discontinue medication, preferring to rely on herbal medications. (Chen and Hawks, 1995)

Beliefs in Traditional Folk Healing and Alternative Medicine

Cultural beliefs regarding the nature of illness and appropriate treatment can also affect compliance. Folk beliefs serve an important role in the lives of many ethnic minority clients, especially new immigrants. Asking about clients' understanding of their condition can help the therapist determine potential challenges related to medication use. For example, Asian and Latino clients who believe that herbs are important for healing and that the mind, body, and spirit are interconnected may still show a willingness to try prescription medications. However, a preference for herbal remedies, concerns about the side effects of prescribed medicines, or reluctance to continue a medication once relief from the presenting symptoms is noted may result in premature termination of medication. This is particularly true if there is a perception that the health care provider does not approve of herbal remedies. Clients may choose to be dishonest about whether they are taking the prescribed medication rather than risk disapproval for not complying (S. Lee, 1993). This reinforces the importance of educating the client, and possibly the family, about the long-term need for some medications, such as with psychotic and bipolar disorders, and the importance of some Western medications in balancing the biochemistry of the body (Kung, 2001). It is always important to understand and respect the client's conceptualization of a problem. For example, if a client believes that psychological problems are related to problems with internal organs, the therapist can focus on the goal of getting the mind and body in balance (Kung, 2001). Folk beliefs can also affect reactions to medication side effects. Some Asians believe that individuals have a hot or a cold body constitution. Bipolar symptoms may be viewed as the individual having excessive heat in the body. If lithium is prescribed and they experience typical side effects such as dry mouth or constipation, it may be problematic because these symptoms are also attributed to a hot constitution (Lee, 1993). This conflict may result in an unwillingness to use lithium, or other medications that have similar side effects. Again, when there is noncompliance, open discussion about a client's concerns or about concerns expressed by family members is essential.

Alternative medicine is used with increasing frequency in the United States. In fact, in 1993, consumers spent over 21 billion dollars on various forms of alternative medicine, and there were 243 million more visits to alternative practitioners than to conventional primary care physicians (Eisenberg et al., 1998). Those who subscribe to these alternative philosophies may view psychological and physical illness very differently from those subscribing to a conventional Western biomedical model. The worldview of the client may include a focus on the interconnectedness of the mind, body, and spirit, and belief in the concept of a life energy that is responsible for the development of the body throughout life, beginning at conception (White, 2000). Psychological as well as physical healing may be seen as interconnected with an individual's life force; healing occurs through recognizing and rebalancing patterns of disharmony. Herbal remedies, dietary interventions, or lifestyle changes may be initiated in an attempt to rid the body of toxins, or the individual may use remedies such as acupuncture, acupressure, meditation, or massage. Readers are referred to White (2000) for a comprehensive overview of alternative healing philosophies including Chinese medicine, Ayurvedic medicine (a philosophy originated in India), homeopathy (with origins in Germany), and naturopathy. Such information can help us understand the worldviews of clients with respect to health and healing. Some beliefs may come from the professional health sector, while others come from the popular sector or from folk lore. For this reason, it is essential for mental health professionals to have a firm understanding of what the client (or the client's family) believes caused the symptoms, what the client fears most about the symptoms or condition, and what the client is hoping will be achieved by treatment (Ailinger & Dear, 1997).

Medication with Different Racial and Ethnic Groups

Medicine in the United States was originally one-sided, with doctors sharing only a limited amount of information and patients deferring to the doctor's wishes regarding their care. This approach has changed due to newer ethical and legal codes that emphasize *informed consent* (i.e., providing patients with all information, including the benefits and risks of treatment options, and allowing the individual to make an informed decision about the course of treatment). The individualistic focus of our system of health care may differ significantly from the collectivistic or paternalistic decision-making systems seen in the native countries of many immigrant groups (e.g., the health care provider dictates the course of treatment or decisions are made as a family group, with the decision focusing on the needs of the entire family unit rather than on the needs of the individual). It is important to be aware that decision-making regarding the medication use of a family member may be influenced by cultural values (McLaughin & Braun, 1998). Conflicts may arise due to issues of family privacy, lack of familiarity with and possible distrust toward mental health professionals, lack of understanding of Western medical practices, or feeling overwhelmed by a complex health care system (Choi & Wynne, 2000). The immediate and extended family is often very central to the lives of members of some ethnic groups, and they can be valuable allies in attempts to gain adherence to prescribed medication regimes. For example, Lin, Miller, Poland, Nuccio, and Yamaguchi (1989; 1991) found that family members of Asian Americans with schizophrenia were more likely to accompany them to outpatient visits and that family involvement resulted in improved compliance with outpatient visits and compliance with prescribed medication.

The educational background and cultural beliefs of clients may greatly influence their understanding not only of psychological disorders, but also of physical illness. This is particularly true of immigrants whose understanding of disease and prevention may come primarily from their country of origin. Immigrants who come from nonindustrialized, agrarian societies frequently practice alternative medicine. Some immigrants may have very limited familiarity with health care of any kind, and their primary understanding of illness may primarily result from exposure to cultural beliefs and local healers (Coppens, Silka, Khakeo, & Benfey, 2000). In addition, due to a lack of understanding of English, immigrants may not have access to health information from the popular media. For example, a group of Latina women were studied regarding their knowledge of risk for cancer; many of the women, particularly those who were immigrants, believed that cancer is the result of physical stress and trauma to the body, including rough sex and abortion (Chavez, McMullen, Mishra, & Hubbell, 2001). In the Filipino culture, where stoicism is highly valued, religious beliefs may serve to further reinforce the idea that suffering is an opportunity to demonstrate virtue; additionally, physicians in the Philippines tend to prescribe less due to the scarcity of medication (Galanti, 2000). It is essential for professionals to be alert to and to inquire sufficiently to gain a clear understanding of the sociocultural experience from which their client's view of health and illness emerges (Ailinger & Dear, 1997). When mental health issues are identified, ethnic minority clients may be less likely to follow through with recommendations for medication use or counseling (Miranda & Cooper, 2004).

Many individuals for whom English is a second language navigate through day-to-day life with some difficulty. Medical or psychiatric vocabulary, particularly when medication options are discussed, may be overwhelming, even for native English speakers. If an interpreter is used, it is important to remember that, even when terms are translated, the client may have no familiarity with the word or concepts, even in their native language. Conditions such as depression and anxiety are viewed differently in different cultures. In the United States, the stigma associated with these conditions has been decreasing as the public has learned more about the biological basis for various disorders. It is not unusual for friends and family to talk openly about feeling anxious or feeling depressed. However, in some groups, psychological conditions are associated with personal weakness, so symptoms may be more comfortably expressed through somatic complaints (Ballenger, Davidson, Lecrubier, & Nutt, 2001).

Clinicians should remain aware of concerns about the reliability of mental health diagnosis in certain ethnic populations. For example, there is concern that African Americans may be inaccurately diagnosed as schizophrenic, and therefore given inappropriate medications. Additionally, African Americans are more likely to receive higher doses of antipsychotic medication, despite medical evidence suggesting that due to genetic and ethnic differences in metabolism, they may actually require lower levels of medication to achieve a therapeutic response (Lawson, 1996). In a study of adolescents with bipolar disorder, the African American adolescents were twice as likely to receive antipsychotic medication compared to the White adolescents (DelBello, Soutullo, & Strakowski, 2000). Additionally, African Americans are less likely than Whites to receive antidepressant medication following a diagnosis of depression (Melfi, Croghan, Hanna, & Robinson, 2000; Blazer, Hybels, Simonsick, & Hanlon, 2000). African Americans may be more cautious about treatment, fearful of hospitalization, and skeptical about the health care system; a factor in this distrust may be the infamous Tuskegee syphilis study (curative antibiotics were withheld from a group of African American men in order to study the long-term effects of syphilis), which came to public attention in 1972 (W. B. Lawson, 1996). Certain ethnic groups are less likely to have medical insurance and are more likely to delay treatment until symptoms are more severe. It is estimated that one-third of Latinos and one-fourth of African Americans do not have health coverage (Becker, 2001).

Racial and ethnic differences in response to medications have been reported, particularly with antianxiety and antidepressant medications; it is unclear if differences result from ethnic dietary effects or from innate metabolic differences (Hines, 2000). In addition, there have been ethnic differences found in response to neuroleptic medications (Ruiz, Varner, Small, & Johnson, 1999). K. M. Lin (2001) emphasizes the need for lower initial doses and slow dose increases in ethnic populations, as well as close monitoring for possible side effects and careful evaluation for a positive response to the medication even at low doses. Unfortunately, many clinical trials of medications do not include representative samples of ethnic minorities; this may, in part, be due to suspicion about medical research or a lack of familiarity or comfort with the concept of medication research on humans. It is equally important, however, to remember that there is often as much variability within a group as is seen between groups. Therefore, it is important to remember that most individuals within the ethnic group require standard doses (Lee, 1993). It is essential to always focus on the individual and the individual response to the medication (Ballenger et al., 2001).

Gender Differences in Reactions to Medications

Although gender differences in response to psychotropic medication have been acknowledged (Matthews, 1995; Yonkers, Kando, Cole, & Blumenthal, 1993), it is surprising that there has not been more focus on gender specific information about medication. Research is beginning to address the effects of women's monthly hormonal changes, as well as normal variations that occur during or following pregnancy or during or prior to menopause (Kornstein et al., 2000), as well as basic variables such as muscle-to-fat ratios in the body (Martin, 2001). Knowledge of differential effects of medication is particularly important given the higher incidence of depression, anxiety disorders, and eating disorders in the female population. Mental health professionals working with women can assist in evaluating the relationship of symptoms experienced and hormonal changes. Additionally, special consideration must be given to women who are taking medication and considering pregnancy.

Medication with the Elderly

In addition to the range of psychosocial disorders seen in the general population, depression, dementia, and sleep difficulties are seen with increasing frequency in the elderly, as are stressors such as changes in physical health, financial difficulties, loss of independence, and grief related to the death of a spouse or close friends. The impact of social isolation on both physical and mental well-being is a significant concern with this group. A reluctance to use medication as an intervention for psychological illness is particularly true for the elderly (Burgio et al., 1995).

The rate of medication absorption may be much slower in the elderly. In general, older individuals require a reduced dose of most medications and more careful monitoring when they are taking medications—even nonprescription medications. The elderly take a longer time to respond to treatment with antidepressant medications, with an average response time of 6 to 10 weeks. Wellbutrin is a medication sometimes used to treat depression in the elderly due to its potential effectiveness in combating symptoms, combined with the reduced risk of cardiac side effects (Rivas-Vazquez & Blais, 1997). In the elderly, many medications, including common nonprescription medications, can cause sleepiness, confusion, anxiety, or agitation. For this reason, it is important to carefully ask about current medication use in the process of differential diagnosis. Physical illness, including something as simple as a urinary tract infection, can produce significant symptoms of mental confusion. Other organic causes of confusion in the elderly include dehydration, pneumonia, congestive heart failure, poor nutrition, poorly managed diabetes, hearing or vision difficulties, reactions to newly prescribed medications, or inadvertent drug overdose resulting from failure to recall whether a medication (either prescription or nonprescription) has been taken. It is also critical to be alert for signs or symptoms of heart failure or stroke, and to be sensitive to the fact that older individuals may be fearful of becoming ill and being sent to a hospital or nursing home and, therefore, may minimize or try to hide symptoms of physical illness or psychological stress.

The elderly, especially the frail elderly, are more likely to experience adverse side effects from medications. This may be due to a slower metabolism (resulting in higher levels of medication in the system), drug interactions due to increased frequency of multiple medications, difficulty keeping to a medication schedule, or inadvertent overdose. These side effects may result in poor adherence to medication schedules or to a decision to prematurely terminate a medication. Lack of transportation to the pharmacy or medical facilities or the costs of medication are additional barriers to medication compliance that should be considered with the elderly.

Medication with Children

Although psychotropic medications are being used increasingly with children, most psychotropic medications have not been well researched with youth. In fact, many of the medications being used with increased frequency do not have FDA approval for use with children. Other than the research involving stimulant medications for attention-deficit/hyperactivity disorder (ADHD), there is a paucity of well-controlled, double-blind studies or studies with outcome measures apart from clinician ratings. The use of double-bind trials is especially critical because youth have been shown to be strong placebo responders (Sommers-Flanagan & Sommers-Flanagan, 1996) and have differential absorption of medication due to a lower fat-to-muscle ratio and a faster metabolism (Hall & Gushee, 2002). In addition to the increasing use of antidepressants with children and adolescents, prescriptions for lithium and anticonvulsants for the treatment of bipolar disorder symptoms are increasing. Atypical antipsychotics are also being used with children. As with adults using these medications, children taking atypical antipsychotics demonstrate weight gain and the associated medical risks (McClure, Kubiszyn, & Kaslow, 2002). Given the difficulty that children may have articulating emotions or accurately reporting behavior changes or side effects, it is critical that information from other sources including parents, teachers, or mental health professionals who work in the schools be gathered. A recent review of pediatric pharmacology continued to conclude that "the clinical use of most psychotropic medications far exceeds their safety and efficacy" (Brown & Sammons, 2002, p.135). Similarly, concerns continue regarding the growing use of medication with children and adolescents in the absence of scientific support for these practices, as do calls for mental health practitioners to use an evidence-based focus when working with parents to educate about treatment options for childhood disorders (Ingersoll, Bauer, & Burns, 2004) and to develop systems and standards to assess medication safety (Vitiello et al., 2003).

In this chapter, we have focused on the increasing need of the mental health professionals to increase their knowledge about psychotropic medications. Although we know that medications new to the market have gone through rigorous drug trials, questions remain regarding tests that are subsidized by pharmaceutical companies, how participants are included or excluded in the studies, and other methodological issues. Because many clients are receiving or will receive medication for psychological symptoms, it is essential that in providing complete treatment, the psychotherapist understands the effects of specific medications, how they work, side effects associated with the medications, and barriers to compliance with recommendations made by health care providers.

Medications Used with Psychological Disorders

In treating depression, the combination of antidepressants and psychotherapy produced the best outcome, although psychotherapy alone for 13 or more sessions was nearly as effective as medication. Medication produces more rapid improvement during earlier sessions, but plateaus without the addition of psychotherapy. (Consumer Reports, 2004)

18
Chapter

The use of medication in conjunction with therapy is considered the standard of care for some mental health disorders. As noted in the previous chapter, it has become increasingly important for mental health professionals to have an understanding of basic pharmacology and an awareness of new developments in the field. In this chapter, we present current information and research related to the use of medications with some of the major mental health disorders. For ease of reference, Appendix C contains a listing of information on common psychotropic medications, organized by the disorders treated by each medication. Box 18.1 contains a glossary of pharmacological terms used in this and the previous chapter. The information provided is only a brief introduction, not an exhaustive review of the literature. It is important to remember that the psychopharmacological literature is evolving, and, in some cases, rapidly changing. Therefore, it is incumbent upon practitioners to remain updated through monitoring of reports related to medications, as well as professional reading and other professional development activities.

Medications Used to Treat Depression

On October 15, 2004, the FDA, after an extensive review of the effectiveness of SSRIs for children and adolescents, decided to require that all antidepressants carry a black box warning on the package inserts indicating possible increases in suicidal thoughts and behavior when these medications are used by children and adolescents.

Box 18.1   **Glossary of Psychopharmacological Terms**

Anticholinergic side effects—side effects of dry mouth, constipation, difficulty urinating, or blurry vision caused by antipsychotic medication and some antidepressant medication.

Discontinuation syndrome—a biochemically based constellation of symptoms resulting from biochemical changes that occur as the body adjusts to a decrease in levels of some antidepressant medications.

Depot antipsychotic—injectable antipsychotic medication that is released into the body slowly over an extended period of time.

Drug-drug interactions—when the effect of a medication is changed, enhanced, or diminished when taken with another drug, including herbal substances.

Drug incompatibility—potential harmful or uncomfortable effects that occur when two drugs are combined.

Extrapyramidal side effects—side effects of neuroleptic medication that involve the extrapyramidal system, which controls motor activities involved in posture, movement, and overall support of the body. They include odd facial expressions or odd movements caused by muscular tension, difficulty with speech or swallowing, drooling, involuntary rhythmic movements of the arms or legs, and slow or shuffling gait.

Generic—the lower-cost copy of a drug that can be manufactured once a drug patent expires.

Neuroleptic malignant syndrome—potentially fatal condition that can occur in those taking neuroleptics. Onset can be rapid or gradual, involving changes in mental status, heart rate, and/or body temperature.

Neuroleptics—conventional antipsychotic medications, also referred to as major tranquilizers.

Neurotransmitters—chemicals in the brain that allow communication from one brain cell to another.

Psychopharmacology—the use of medications in the management of psychological disorders.

Psychotropic medications—medications used to treat psychological disorders.

Schedule II medications—the medications in this federally defined category (also referred to as class 2, CII, or controlled substances) have great potential for abuse and have specific prescription requirements; some of the most well-known medications in this category are stimulant medications such as Ritalin and pain relievers such as Percocet and Oxycontin.

Seratonin syndrome—an extremely serious, even deadly, reaction involving confusion, agitation, twitching, changes in vital signs, and eventual coma that can occur when SSRI antidepressants are inadvertently combined with monoamine oxidase (MAO) inhibitors.

Tardive dyskinesia—a side effect of neuroleptic medication that involves abnormal involuntary movements, often of the face, mouth, tongue, trunk, arms, and legs. This condition sometimes continues even after medication is stopped or can spontaneously appear even after the medication has been discontinued.

Therapeutic dose—the lowest dose of the medication needed to produce the desired effects.

Titration of dosage—a gradual increase or decrease in medication that may occur as the medical professional attempts to find the correct dose.

In general, antidepressant medications are believed to be effective through their impact on specific neurotransmitters (e.g., dopamine, epinephrine, norepinephrine, serotonin). The availability and use of serotonin has received particular attention, not only pertaining to depression, but also in relationship to anxiety disorders. Newer research has focused on processes occurring within the neuron rather than solely within the synapse, and on the possibility of different subtypes of depression involving various biochemical abnormalities (Rivas-Vazquez, 2001a). Antidepressant medications are thought to work by correcting chemical imbalances in the brain. They are not addictive, but they do have a variety of potential side effects (American Psychiatric Association, 2000b) including sexual dysfunction, weight gain, dry mouth, dizziness, and constipation. It is important to monitor blood pressure–related side effects such as dizziness or weakness, especially in individuals already taking medication for high blood pressure, since drug interactions sometimes cause a significant drop in blood pressure. Any of the antidepressants can produce a manic or hypomanic response in certain individuals, which may result in the need to discontinue the medication. It is important for clients taking antidepressant medications to be aware of the potential effects of combining the medication with alcohol or products containing alcohol, including some cold medications. Consumption of alcohol is an issue because alcohol may increase the risk of side effects and intoxication may occur more rapidly when someone is taking antidepressant medication. Monitoring caffeine intake is also important given the tendency to self-medicate with caffeine to counteract symptoms of depression (Larson & Carey, 1998).

There has been a notable increase in media reports about psychotropic medications. After much public debate, the FDA recently required manufacturers of antidepressants to provide black box warnings regarding the possibility of increased risk for suicidal thinking and behavior in children and adolescents taking them. Physicians are now encouraged to inform patients and caregivers about risks and benefits of the medication and to offer a Medication Guide, developed by the FDA, which summarizes risks and possible side effects. The FDA warning emphasizes the importance of monitoring individuals in this age group for symptoms of agitation and anxiety as well as for worsening depression. In December 2006, an FDA panel proposed that the black box warning be extended to include individuals ages 18 to 24. The FDA has also recommended that individuals of all ages be monitored for suicidal thoughts and behavior, "clinical worsening," or unusual behavior, particularly when they first begin taking an antidepressant or during increases or decreases in dosage. The warning states that families and caregivers should be advised about the need for close observation. The FDA suggests close observation by the prescribing physician, including weekly face-to-face contact, at the minimum, with the child, parent, or caregiver for the first 4 weeks of treatment, then contact twice during the next 4 weeks, then once within the next month, and every 3 months thereafter. Given the relationship between depression and suicide, it makes sense for therapists to closely monitor suicide risk in all depressed clients, not just those taking antidepressants.

Mental health professionals should be aware of the concept of *discontinuation syndrome*, a biochemically based constellation of symptoms resulting from biochemical changes that occur as the body adjusts to a decrease in antidepressant levels in the body (i.e., from a dose reduction in the process of supervised discontinuation of the medication, a skipped or forgotten dose, an abrupt, unsupervised discontinuation of the medication). The symptoms of this syndrome can include shakiness, dizziness, stomach upset, headaches or muscle aches, fatigue or intense sleepiness, insomnia, or increased emotionality, including frustration, anger, sadness, or suicidal thinking. There may be a temporary reoccurrence of depressive symptoms during this phase, but this does not mean that there has been a relapse. Some degree of discontinuation effects occur in approximately one-third of those who use antidepressants. The effects typically appear within 1 to 3 days, usually last no longer than 2 weeks, and can occur when the client has been closely adhering to a medication regime or when the medication has not been used consistently (Rivas-Vazquez et al., 1999). These effects can be seen when an individual has missed only one daily dose of medication, when a physician begins to slowly decrease the dosage, or in the final step of tapering when the medication is completely discontinued. If these effects are the result of failure to take the medication as prescribed, the client can be educated about the importance of adhering to a regular medication schedule. Collaboration between the client and the health care provider to prevent, recognize, and manage discontinuation effects is an important task. The presence of discontinuation effects does not mean that there was an addiction to the medication. This is particularly important to understand in the event that the client, or someone they know, needs antidepressant medication in the future.

The decision of the health care provider regarding which specific antidepressant medication to choose depends on the presenting symptoms, the client's health history, other medications the client might be taking, and the side effects of the medications being considered. For example, if an individual is overweight, the health care provider may choose to avoid a medication with the side effect of weight gain or increased appetite. Openness with the health care provider regarding any previous medication use and side effect concerns is essential. The gender of the client may also influence decision making; for example, premenopausal women have been found to respond much better to Zoloft than Tofranil (Baca, Garcia-Garcia, & Porras-Chavarino, 2004; Kornstein et al., 2000). It is important for individuals who are depressed to know that approximately 30 to 50 percent of depressed individuals do not respond to the first antidepressant medication chosen, even after the initial 6 to 13 weeks (Rivas-Vazquez & Blais, 1997). It is not known how much of this lack of response is due to failure to take the medication as prescribed, or failure on the part of the physician to monitor progress and side effects and make needed adjustments. If there is not an effective result with a specific medication, the health care provider generally chooses another medication within the same class of antidepressants for an additional medication trial, or may choose to add an additional medication, if this can be done safely. When a decision is made to change classes of antidepressant, the dose of the original medication is slowly decreased and the new medication is not started until the original medication has cleared from the patient's system. Antidepressant medication trials often begin with either SSRIs or the atypical antidepressants; MAOIs are typically used only if other medication trials have not been successful (Rivas-Vazquez & Blais, 1997).

Treatment of depression with medication generally involves medication use not only for the relief of acute or chronic symptoms, but often involves the use of the antidepressant for 6 to 12 months beyond the initial resolution of symptoms, with the goal of keeping the individual free from depressive symptoms and preventing a relapse. Generally, slow discontinuation of the medication is attempted after this period of time. Longer term, maintenance use of antidepressants is sometimes considered for individuals who have had a history of extremely chronic depressive symptoms or multiple acute episodes of major depression (Rivas-Vazquez & Blais, 1997). The use of antidepressant medication is not without controversy. Recently, in an attempt to examine placebo effects with antidepressants, Kirsch, Moore, Scoboria, and Nichols (2002) conducted a comprehensive meta-analysis of the FDA database of medication trials used to gain FDA approval for the six most commonly pre-scribed antidepressants. They found that the medication effects had only a small statistical advantage over the placebo, but that the differences seen were not clinically significant, suggesting that much of the effect seen with antidepressants is attributable to a placebo effect.

In a large nationwide multistep study of antidepressant medication, the STAR*-D (Sequenced Treatment Alternatives to Relieve Depression) study, funded by the National Institute of Mental Health, researchers aimed to sys-tematically monitor treatment for major depressive disorder in a real-world setting through the use of specific treatment protocols and systematic rating of depressive symptoms and reported side effects, in order to judge patients' responses to antidepressant medication and to guide health care providers in adjusting dosage. The study concluded that using systematic ratings of symptoms and side effects to inform treatment decisions was both possible and effective, and that complete remission of symptoms associated with major depressive disorder often required a trial of more than one medication (either a change of medication or the use of a second medication to supplement the first), particularly when the depression was more chronic and more severe (National Institute of Mental Health, 2006a, b).

Tricyclic Antidepressants (TCAs)

Tricyclic antidepressants (TCAs) work by increasing the activity of the neuro-transmitters serotonin and noradrenalin and by blocking the re-absorption of both of these chemicals into the body, allowing them to remain in the synapse and produce neural-communication effects for a longer period of time. Medications included in this class are doxepin (Adapin; Sinequan), nortriptyline (Aventyl; Pamel), amitriptyline (Elavil; Endep), desipramine (Norpraime; Pertofane), imipramine (Tofranil), and clomipramine (Anafranil).

Typical side effects for the tricyclics include dry mouth, constipation, blurred vision, sexual dysfunction, and weight gain. Alcohol combined with tricyclic antidepressants can result in extreme drowsiness and impaired coordination. Discontinuation syndrome effects for tricyclic antidepressants may include flulike symptoms, sleep disturbance, movement disorders, cardiac arrhythmias, or even possible precipitation of a manic state (Rivas-Vazquez et al., 1999). Given the increased risk of suicide with depression, it is important to be aware that tricyclic antidepressants, particularly desipramine, can be highly toxic in overdose.

Selective Serotonin Reuptake Inhibitors (SSRIs)

Selective serotonin reuptake inhibitors (SSRIs) work by increasing the activity of serotonin with *serotonogeric* (serotonin-enhancing) effects similar to the tricyclic antidepressants. The SSRIs work by blocking the re-absorption of serotonin into the cells that originally release this chemical, allowing serotonin to remain in the synapse and retain effectiveness longer. Medications included in this class are fluvoxamine (Luvox), sertraline (Zoloft), fluoxetine (Prozac), paroxetine (Paxil), citalopram (Celexa), and escitalopram (Lexapro). The primary difference between the SSRIs and the tricyclic antidepressants is that the SSRIs specifically target the neurotransmitter serotonin whereas the TCAs target multiple neurotransmitters, resulting in a greater range of side effects. TCAs, however, may be superior in the management of severe depression with melancholic features (Rivas-Vazquez & Blais, 1997). SSRIs tend to be as effective as TCAs with less severe depression, and seem to be superior in regard to atypical depressive symptoms such as mood reactivity, increased need for sleep, and sensitivity to rejection (Rivas-Vazquez & Blais, 1997). In addition to being used as antidepressants, some of the SSRIs are used for bulimia and for anxiety disorders, including panic disorder and obsessive-compulsive disorder. SSRIs are often chosen because they have fewer side effects and less toxicity in overdose than previous antidepressants, an important factor when there are suicide concerns (Rivas-Vazquez & Rey, 2002). Recently, there has been considerable controversy regarding the use of SSRIs with children and adolescents (Jureidini et al., 2004; Whittingdon et al., 2004). Specifically, there are questions about the effectiveness of the medications with this population and more serious concerns about increased suicide risk with this age group. Prozac is the only antidepressant that has FDA approval for use with childhood depression.

Common side effects with the SSRIs include physical restlessness, difficulty falling asleep, tremor, headaches, stomach upset, and sexual dysfunction (which may be a major issue for patients but not necessarily something that is discussed with the health care provider; Clayton, Pradko, & Croft, 2002). Caffeine intake should be monitored, since the SSRIs tend to decrease the body's ability to metabolize caffeine, resulting in a build-up of caffeine effects (Larson & Carey, 1998). Discontinuation syndrome effects are similar to those seen in tricyclic antidepressants and may include flulike symptoms, sleep disturbance, movement disorders, cardiac arrhythmias, or even possible precipitation of a manic state. Additionally, there may be tingling in the extremities, dizziness, or a spaced-out feeling. These effects are more likely when an SSRI has been used for at least 2 months, and tend to be most common with Paxil and seen least often with Prozac. There may be a delay in noticing discontinuation effects with Prozac since it is more slowly metabolized and can linger in the body for over a month. When originally introduced, there were media reports that Prozac seemed to increase suicidal or aggressive potential in adults taking the medication, although this has not been substantiated in subsequent research (Rivas-Vazquez & Blais, 1997); however, these concerns remain under discussion and investigation for many of the antidepressants. It is important to be aware that concerns based on media reports may affect an individual's willingness to try antidepressants.

Monoamine Oxidase Inhibitors (MAOIs)

Monoamine oxidase inhibitors (MAOIs) reduce the activity of monoamine oxidase, an enzyme that works to prolong the effects of norepinephrine in the brain. This class of antidepressants includes phenelzine (Nardil), isocarboxazid (Marplan), and tranyleypromine (Parnate). Selegiline (Emsam), an MAOI introduced in 2006, is administered via a skin patch, and is marketed in three dose sizes. The lowest-dose patch is said to be safe from the potential dangerous food interactions seen with the other MAOIs (discussed below). Due to some of the concerns specific to these medications, they are often not the first medication of choice in the treatment of depression, but are sometimes used when other medications have not been effective (Rivas-Vazquez & Blais, 1997).

Typical side effects for the MAOIs include dizziness, weight gain, and sexual dysfunction. Discontinuation syndrome effects for MAOIs include delirium, catatonia, agitation, confusion, and aggression, particularly when discontinued abruptly (Rivas-Vazquez et al., 1999). It is essential for individuals using MAOIs to be aware of possible dangerous reactions, including sudden and severe increases in blood pressure that can lead to stroke and death, when MAOIs are combined with foods containing tyramine. Tyramine is a substance that occurs naturally in foods, especially in foods that are ripened, aged, or fermented, such as raisins, soy sauce, fava beans, avocados, overripe bananas, certain aged cheese, deli meats, yogurt, wine, and beer. Symptoms indicative of a hypertensive crisis and the need for emergency medical treatment may include severe headache, nausea, increased heart rate, sweating, and confusion. Antihistamine and decongestant use is also a concern when using MAOIs. Additionally, caffeine should be consumed only sparingly due to possible side effects such as increased nervousness, arrhythmias, or high blood pressure (Larson & Carey, 1998).

It is also very important to know that *serotonin syndrome,* an extremely serious, even deadly, toxic reaction resulting from excessive serotonin activity can occur when SSRIs, TCAs, or atypical antidepressants are inadvertently combined with MAOIs (Rivas-Vazquez, 2001d). Symptoms can have a very rapid onset and include confusion, agitation, twitching, changes in vital signs, coma, or even death. These reactions can also occur when an MAOI is given after another class of antidepressant has been discontinued but has not sufficiently cleared the body. Particular caution needs to be used with Prozac, which can take as long as 5 weeks to completely leave the body.

Atypical Antidepressants

This group of antidepressants includes medications with biochemical properties that are distinct from the other three classes of antidepressants; medications in this group are also distinct from each other. In general, these antidepressants are equally effective as the SSRIs and TCAs. Similarly, they should not be combined with MAOIs (Rivas-Vazquez & Blais, 1997).

Bupropion (Wellbutrin) is an antidepressant that has been used with increasing frequency since it first became available in 1989; it is a unicyclic amnioketone, and has properties similar to psychostimulant medications combined with biochemical changes in dopamine and norepinephrine. This medication has few effects on sexual functioning, and few cardiac side effects. However, typical side effects include agitation, appetite suppression, dry mouth, insomnia, headache, and tremor. Bupropion is not recommended for use by individuals who have a history of seizures, anorexia, or bulimia (Rivas-Vazquez & Blais, 1997). This medication is sold under different brand names; it is called Wellbutrin when used for depression, but is marketed as Zyban when used to assist in the discontinuation of smoking. This dual labeling is very important to know, because high doses of any medication can have hazardous effects. It is recommended that alcohol be completely avoided when using bupropion.

Nefazadone (Serzone), was first available in 1995. After 7 years on the market, Serzone received a black box warning due to multiple cases of life-threatening liver failure. Its use was discontinued in many countries and was eventually pulled from the United States' market in 2004. Venlafaxine (Effexor), which has been available since 1993, is classified as a selective serotonin and norepinephrine reuptake inhibitor (SSNRI) due to the effects on both serotonin and norepinephrine. Side effects include headache, dizziness, insomnia, weight loss, increased heart rate, and increased blood pressure.

Reboxetine (Edronex), which has been available in the United States since 2000, works by inhibiting neuronal serotonin and norepinephrine reuptake, and has some effects on dopamine availability. This medication, a nontricyclic selective norepinephrine reuptake inhibitor (NRI), is similar in function to the TCAs, but has fewer side effects. Reboxetine produces a more rapid response than other antidepressants (symptom relief generally appears within 2 weeks), appears to be more effective than the SSRIs with severe depression, and has a positive impact on social functioning (Burns, 2000; Rivas-Vazquez, 2001b; Rivas-Vazquez & Blais, 1997). This medication is generally well tolerated, with typical side effects including nausea, dry mouth, insomnia, and dizziness; additionally, there is a reduced need to closely monitor blood pressure with this medication.

Mirtazapine (Remeron), which has been available since 1996, has a tetracyclic chemical structure and affects levels of serotonin and norepinephrine by stimulating their release and blocking their reuptake. This medication tends to have sedating, anti-anxiety properties. The most common side effects include sedation, dry mouth, blurred vision, insomnia, increased appetite, and weight gain. This medication should not be combined with alcohol or Benzodiazepines; liver function and white blood cell count should be monitored. Additionally, caution should be exercised when using this medication with the elderly (Rivas-Vazquez & Blais, 1997). The newest atypical antidepressant on the market is duloxetine hydrochloride (Cymbalta), available since 2003. Cymbalta is a serotonin norepinephrine reuptake inhibitor that is used to treat chronic nerve pain related to diabetes as well as depression. Alcohol should be avoided when taking this medication.

Medications Used with Anxiety Disorders

Benzodiazepine use in the elderly is associated with a 24% increase in hip fracture. Risk is somewhat greater during the first two weeks of use, although this only accounted for a small percentage of cases of hip fracture. (Wagner et al., 2004)

Anxiety disorders, which are among the most prevalent psychological disorders, generally involve the experiencing of significant anxiety or attempts to avoid anxiety, such as seen with obsessive-compulsive disorder. As with all psychological conditions, it is important to consider medical factors that might be causing anxiety symptoms (e.g., hyperthyroidism, hyperglycemia, asthma, anemia, cardiac arrhythmia, sleep apnea, mitral valve prolapse). Medical evaluation is particularly important when there is a sudden onset of panic episodes or anxiety symptoms in adulthood without a precipitating event or precipitating environmental factors.

There has been a recent shift in the medical treatment of anxiety disorders, with SSRIs and atypical antidepressants becoming a first-line treatment (Rivas-Vazquez, 2001a). Historically, barbiturates were used to treat anxiety disorders until the benzodiazepines (i.e., minor tranquilizers) came on the scene. There have always been serious concerns regarding the addictive potential and withdrawal symptoms produced by barbiturates; unfortunately, there are similar concerns with the benzodiazepines. The SSRIs and some of the atypical antidepressants have been viewed as a positive alternative because they do not have the addictive potential of the benzodiazepines. In addition, buspitone (BuSpar) is a medication used specifically for anxiety symptoms.

Benzodiazepines work by increasing the activity of an inhibitory neurotransmitter, gamma-amniobutric (GABA), reducing the transmission of nerve impulses, which then results in the reduction of symptoms of anxiety. Short-acting benzodiazepines, such as lorazapam (Ativan), oxazezepam (Serax), and alprazolam (Xanax) may be taken several times per day if needed, and are used for acute panic attacks or in situations that are anticipated to be of a relatively short duration, such as anticipated acute anxiety (e.g., someone with aviophobia taking a plane trip). Long-acting benzodiazepines, such as chlordiazepoxide (Librium), clonazepam (Klonopin), halazepam (Paxipam), clorazepate (Traxene), and diazepam (Valium) are administered only once per day and are used for more generalized anxiety and for longer-term treatment needs. In view of the controversy about the potential for abuse and physiological dependence, and the need to examine the risk–benefit ratio of the use of benzodiazepines, Oswald, Roache, and Rhoades (1999) conducted a study in which volunteers with generalized anxiety disorder or panic disorder were given Xanax or a placebo, to be used as needed. Xanax was found to be clearly preferred over the placebo. However, there was considerable variability between subjects in the frequency of use of the Xanax; those who self-medicated more frequently were more introverted and had an external locus of control and greater avoidance behavior.

Common side effects of the benzodiazepines include drowsiness, dizziness, weakness, poor coordination, and blurred vision; the side effects generally resolve with time. It is important to understand the side effects of the medications because the symptoms of anxiety (restlessness, agitation, heart palpitations) can be mistaken for medication side effects. It is also important that clients be educated to avoid caffeine, especially self-medication with caffeine in response to drowsiness, because caffeine can both produce anxiety symptoms and counteract the effects of the benzodiazepines (Larson & Carey, 1998). Although the benzodiazepines can produce effective and rapid relief from anxiety, there is a potential for physiological tolerance and dependence; when discontinued, withdrawal symptoms can include insomnia, nervousness, headache, drowsiness, lack of energy, and loss of appetite, particularly with the use of higher doses for an extended period of time. For this reason, medical professionals typically discontinue these medications or reduce the dose as soon as the acute symptoms of anxiety have subsided. In addition, care is taken to decrease the medication gradually in order to minimize withdrawal effects.

Selective serotonin reuptake inhibitors (SSRIs) are also used for anxiety disorders, including obsessive-compulsive disorder and panic disorder (American Psychiatric Association, 1998). They work by increasing the activity of the neurotransmitter serotonin, which appears to have an impact on the chronic overarousal and apprehension seen in anxiety disorders, including obsessive or compulsive symptoms. To date, different antidepressants have received approval for specific anxiety disorders, including Paxil and Zoloft for panic disorder, Paxil for social phobia, Zoloft for posttraumatic stress disorder, and Effexor for generalized anxiety disorder (Rivas-Vazquez, 2001a). The medications that have been found to be more effective than placebo in treating obsessive-compulsive disorder are Prozac, Luvox, Zoloft, and Paxil, as well as clomipramine (Anafranil), which is related to the tricyclic antidepressants (Franklin, Abramowitz, Bux, Zoller, & Feeny, 2002). Side effects of these medications include stomach upset, insomnia, headaches, sedation, and sexual dysfunction. Side effects may be a particular concern because antidepressant medications generally require higher doses for effectiveness with anxiety disorders (Rivas-Vazquez, 2001a).

Abramowitz (1997) confirmed the effectiveness of the use of serotonergenic antidepressants (Anafranil, Luvox, Paxil, and Prozac) in the treatment of obsessive-compulsive disorder when compared with placebo or non-SSRI antidepressants. It is important to note, however, that both behavior therapy techniques (involving exposure and response prevention) and cognitive-behavioral techniques were equally effective compared to pharmacological interventions. Franklin, Biever, Moore, Clemens, and Scamardo (2002) also studied cognitive-behavior therapy alone, compared with cognitive-behavior therapy combined with the use of SSRIs, and found that the cognitive-behavior therapy was effective both with and without the pharmacotherapy. These authors suggest, however, that if OCD is accompanied by severe depression, the therapist may want to delay cognitive-behavioral intervention until after a therapeutic benefit has been achieved with an antidepressant medication, since success with cognitive-behavioral techniques requires a level of motivation and optimism that may not be seen when an individual is severely depressed.

Medications Used with Psychotic Disorders

> *Peter was a twenty-nine-year-old man with chronic paranoid schizophrenia . . . When off medication, he had constant hallucinations and his behavior became unpredictable . . . Peter complained that he was feeling quite restless, and did not want to take the medication. (Liberman, Kopelowicz, & Young, 1994, p. 94)*

Conventional antipsychotic medications (also referred to as neuroleptics or major tranquilizers) have served an important role in the treatment of acute psychotic episodes and in the prevention of future schizophrenic symptoms. These medications tend to work primarily on what are considered the *positive symptoms* of the psychotic disorders, such as hallucinations, delusions, paranoid thinking, agitation, and confused thinking, with minimal impact on the *negative symptoms,* such as apathy, withdrawal, blunted affect, or slow thinking processes. It is thought that individuals with schizophrenia may have an excessive amount of the neurotransmitter dopamine; neuroleptics work by blocking the movement of dopamine from one cell to another, stopping the nerve activity that relies on dopamine, and thereby controlling the psychotic symptoms. In addition to the conventional antipsychotics, newer medications have emerged; these are referred to as "atypical antipsychotics" because they work on different neurotransmitters. At times, antidepressant medications, mood stabilizers, or benzodiazepines are used in combination with antipsychotic medications to help with symptoms of withdrawal, anxiety, or agitation. The American Psychiatric Association (2004) presents a comprehensive overview of medication use with acute psychotic episodes, as well as the role of maintenance medication in reducing the risk of relapse.

In acute episodes of schizophrenia, it is essential to interview for suicidal ideation or to assess for "command" hallucinations or any other characteristics that would suggest harm to the individual or to others. Medication is very important in this phase of treatment, since the goals are to suppress the acute symptoms and reduce the risk of harm to self or others. The required dose of antipsychotic medication is affected by gender and by body weight. The goal for the health care provider is to find a dose of medication that is high enough to be effective in suppressing the acute symptoms and low enough to avoid or minimize side effects. It is also important to determine if the individual has been abusing alcohol or has been taking benzodiazepines, because withdrawal from either of these substances while taking antipsychotic medications can result in seizures (Herz et al., 1997). The use of caffeine can increase the metabolism of antipsychotic medications. This is particularly important to monitor given the relatively high rate of caffeine consumption in psychiatric populations (Larson & Carey, 1998). A recent, carefully controlled study (Straus et al., 2004) revealed a three-fold increase in sudden cardiac deaths in individuals taking antipsychotic medication, even at low doses, with the risk being greatest for those taking the medication for less than 3 months, those taking higher daily doses, those taking butyrophenone antipsychotics (pipamperone and haloperidol), and those taking the medication for reasons other than schizophrenia (i.e., dementia, stress, anxiety, bipolar disorder).

Sedation is a typical side effect of neuroleptic medications. It is often only a temporary side effect, but health care providers sometimes recommend reducing the dose or taking the medication at bedtime. Individuals taking neuroleptics should completely avoid the use of alcohol, since alcohol can significantly increase sedation effects. Compliance with a specified medication regime can be problematic for individuals with schizophrenia; it is estimated that less than half of those taking antipsychotic medications do so as prescribed (Ziguras, Klimidis, Lambert, & Jackson, 2001). For this reason, health care providers often check blood levels of the medications to ensure therapeutic doses; at times, it is necessary to change to a liquid form of the medication (which can be taken under supervision) or use periodic intramuscular injections, referred to as *depot antipsychotics.* Valenstein and colleagues (2001) found that depot antipsychotics significantly increase compliance and decrease relapse. However, depot antipsychotics appear to be both an underused option and, when used, patients appear to be receiving unnecessarily high doses.

Conventional Antipsychotics

Conventional antipsychotic medications (neuroleptics) include mid- and higher-potency medications such as haloperidol (Haldol), thiothixene (Navene), and trifluoperazine (Stelazine), and lower-potency antipsychotics including thioridazine (Mellaril), prochorperazine (Compazine), chlorpromazine (Thorazine), and loxapine (Loxitane). In general, with the lower-potency medications, a higher dose of medication is needed to treat symptoms. Neuroleptics typically produce *anticholinergic* side effects, which include dry mouth, constipation, difficulty urinating, and/or blurry vision. Low-potency neuroleptics tend to lower blood pressure, produce sedation, and have more of the anticholinergic side effects (Gorman, 1998). Another cluster of side effects produced, particularly by higher-potency neuroleptics, is referred to as "drug-induced Parkinsonism" or extrapyramidal side effects. *Extrapyramidal side effects* involve the extrapyramidal system, which controls motor activities involved in posture, movement, and overall support of the body, both at rest or in motion. These side effects include odd facial expressions or movements caused by muscular tension, difficulty with speech or with swallowing, drooling, involuntary rhythmic movements of the arms or legs, or symptoms seen in Parkinson's disease (slow movement, a shuffling gait, tremors, muscular rigidity, and a masklike expression). Sometimes these symptoms appear within days or weeks of the initiation of neuroleptic medication, and sometimes they are not seen for years.

These side effects can occur suddenly and can be very frightening to the client, family members, or other caregivers; it is important to reassure all involved that most of these symptoms are not dangerous. However, spasms in the larynx can be life-threatening; emergency medical services should be immediately alerted if this symptom occurs. Sometimes the symptoms resolve spontaneously; on other occasions, they can be minimized through the use of anti-Parkinsonism medications. These medications, however, have their own potential set of side effects, including drowsiness, dry mouth, constipation, and blurred vision; they also may cause the original psychotic symptoms to re-emerge. Another serious side effect of antipsychotic medications is *tardive dyskinesia*, the development of abnormal involuntary movements, usually beginning in the area of the face, mouth, and tongue, and later involving the trunk and extremities. This condition is of particular concern because, although it gradually resolves for some individuals even when still taking low or moderate neuroleptic doses, the symptoms sometimes appear spontaneously after the patient has stopped taking the medication. The risk of tardive dyskinesia tends to be greater in schizophrenics who display negative symptoms and increases with increasing age, higher doses, and longer duration of use of anticholinergic medications (Caroff, Mann, & Campbell, 2001; Wszola, Newell, & Sprague, 2001).

Atypical Antipsychotics

> *A 35-year-old schizophrenic man has developed tardive dykenisia on 200 mg of clozapine. He had undergone two courses of Botox injections on a 5-monthly basis with only partial relief. He is also on lithium 800 mg (nocturnal), low-dose clonazepam, and propranolol. High-dose (1,000mg) vitamin E has also been tried for more than 6 months to no avail. What other options exist? (Medscape Neurology and Neurosurgery, 2004, p. 1)*

The group of newer medications for schizophrenia, referred to as the *atypical antipsychotics*, include clozapine (Clozaril), risperidone (Risperidal), quetiapine (Seroquel), ziprasidone (Geodon), and olanzapine (Zyprexa). In general, these medications are less likely to produce extrapyramidal side effects, although blood sugar levels need to be monitored and there is an increased tendency to gain weight (Geddes, Freemantle, Harrison, & Bebbington, 2000). These medications also do not have the extremely narrow margin between efficiency and adverse side effects, and they have the advantage of demonstrating some effect on "negative symptoms," producing improved cognitive functioning in some patients (Rivas-Vazquez, 2001e).

One of the more recent atypical antipsychotics, Geodon, is well tolerated, results in only minimal weight gain, and is less likely than other similar medications to induce manic symptoms. The biggest concern with this medication is the potential for fatal alterations in cardiac function. With all of the atypical antipsychotics, it is important that the health care provider monitor weight, triglycerides, cholesterol, blood glucose levels, and cardiac functioning (Rivas-Vazquez & Rey, 2002). One of the newer antipsychotic medications, Clozaril, has been found to be effective in schizophrenics who do not respond to other antipsychotic medications. Whereas Clozaril does not have the typical side effects of the other neuroleptic medications, it has its own set of side effects, including weight gain, metabolic disturbance, cardiac effects, and a rare, but serious, blood disorder (requiring close monitoring of leukocyte levels). It is recommended that Clozaril be considered only when a combination of up to two antipsychotics (from two different classes) has not been effective in controlling psychotic symptoms, and is to be avoided for patients with preexisting arrhythmia, blood disorders, or for clients who will not come in regularly for blood testing (Herz et al., 1997). A new antipsychotic, asenapine, entered Phase III FDA testing in 2004 for use with both schizophrenia and bipolar disorder.

Medications Used with Bipolar Disorder

Medications used with bipolar disorder work to correct multiple chemical imbalances in the brain. Bipolar disorder, a complex and serious illness involving multiple neurotransmitters (norepinephrine, serotonin, GABA, glutamate), as well as secondary chemical messengers and calcium ions, tends to be a difficult disorder to manage (Rivas-Vazquez, Johnson, Rey, & Blais, 2002). Medication decisions vary depending on the presenting needs and symptoms (e.g., acute mania, acute depression, rapid cycling, stable symptoms, but a desire to prevent relapse) and whether there are psychotic symptoms. The medications used with bipolar illness all have some side effects, especially when first used. Side effects can include drowsiness or dizziness, stomach upset, dry mouth or increased thirst, weight changes, or mild weakness or unsteadiness. Blood levels of individuals taking many of these medications are checked periodically to ensure that the dose is both safe and effective. There is general agreement that the use of medication is an essential component in the treatment of bipolar disorder, not only in managing the acute symptoms, but also in the prevention of relapse (American Psychiatric Association, 2002).

There is controversy regarding the use of antidepressants in bipolar illness, including concern that use of an antidepressant might induce mania or may initiate a pattern of rapid cycling. Among the antidepressants, Paxil and Wellbutrin are the least likely to initiate negative effects and are considered when significant depression is a concern. If antidepressants are used, increasing the dose very gradually may reduce the risk of triggering a manic episode (Rivas-Vazquez et al., 2002). Antipsychotic medications are sometimes used in bipolar illness with psychotic features. Symbyax, the only medication with FDA approval for bipolar depression, was introduced to the market in 2004; it is unique in its combination of the antipsychotic olanzapine (Zyprexa) and the antidepressant fluoxetine (Prozac). In 2006, the FDA posted a warning about possible serotonin syndrome when this medication is combined with any of the tripan medications used to treat migraine headaches. Additionally, the antipsychotic, Seroquel (quetiapine fumarate), has recently received FDA approval for the short-term treatment of acute mania. The benzodiazepines are also sometimes used for behavior control and to allow an individual to sleep during periods of acute mania. It is often challenging to treat a depressive episode without triggering mania (Rivas-Vazquez et al., 2002). Although the manic phase of the disorder is overtly problematic, the very high risk of suicide with bipolar illness suggests that not only is medication management essential to combat depression, but ongoing therapeutic and psychosocial intervention to address life stressors that may trigger a relapse are also essential. In bipolar illness, there is a temptation for clients to discontinue medication because of concerns about the side effects. They may miss the excitement and creativity associated with the "highs" and may not feel a need for medication during manic phases (Lee, 1993). In the course of therapy, mental health professionals can serve an important role in terms of monitoring medication compliance and providing ongoing education about the importance of continuing medication to prevent relapse.

Lithium

Lithium affects multiple neurotransmitters and calcium ions at the intracellular level, and is often the first medication chosen for use during an acute manic phase and for the ongoing management of bipolar illness; however, approximately one-third of all individuals treated fail to respond to lithium, resulting in the need to use alternate or adjunctive medication. It takes approximately 2 weeks to achieve a therapeutic level of lithium. Typical side effects for lithium include weight gain, tremor, and stomach upset. Also, about half of the individuals using lithium for maintenance develop a resistance to it after 3 years (Rivas-Vazquez et al., 2002). It is very important for anyone taking lithium (even when there are no adverse side effects observed) to have his or her blood levels checked regularly to ensure the dose is at therapeutic, not toxic, levels. It is also important to monitor the thyroid and renal functioning of individuals taking lithium. Those taking lithium need to drink fluids regularly, avoid becoming dehydrated, and not allow their intake of salt to vary greatly from day to day. Alcohol consumption should be avoided due to increased chance of stomach upset and effects on the blood concentrations of lithium. Care should be taken with caffeine consumption, since caffeine results in increased urine output, which can result in reductions in lithium levels (Larson & Carey, 1998). Caution is particularly important when the client also struggles with bulimia because lithium levels can be impacted by binging and purging; the increased weight gain associated with lithium may also be an issue for those with an eating disorder (American Psychiatric Association, 2000).

Anticonvulsant Medications

There are three anticonvulsant medications that are used fairly regularly in the treatment of bipolar disorder. It is generally found that there is better compliance with the use of these medications compared to lithium. Divalproex sodium/valproic acid (Depakote), a medication generally used in the treatment of seizure disorders, works in the treatment of bipolar disorder by enhancing levels of the neurotransmitter GABA. It was first approved by the FDA in 1995 for use with mania. It tends to be the preferred medication for individuals who demonstrate rapid cycling. A therapeutic response is generally seen within 3 days of beginning the medication. It is generally well tolerated, with the most common side effects being drowsiness and tremors. However, caution is urged in the use of this medication with young women due to concerns about increases in testosterone (NIMH, 2002). Carbamazepine (Tegretol), another medication commonly used with seizures, also has positive effects on bipolar symptoms by enhancing levels of the neurotransmitter GABA and decreasing levels of glutamate. It takes several weeks to achieve a therapeutic level of Tegretol. Common side effects include sedation, ataxia, severe rash, and stomach upset. It is essential for individuals taking Tegretol to be closely monitored due to the more serious side effects of developing a blood disorder or liver toxicity. Other anticonvulsant medications, including gabapentin (Neurontin) and lamotrigine (Lamictal), as well as calcium channel blockers, are also being used experimentally in the treatment of bipolar illness (American Psychiatric Association, 2002; Rivas-Vazquez et al., 2002).

Medications Used with Attention-Deficit/Hyperactivity Disorder

In February 2006, an FDA panel recommended that a black box warning be placed on stimulant medication to warn about possible cardiac effects, including sudden death, particularly in adults. Several months later another panel stopped short of recommending a black box warning about psychotic symptoms, includ-

ing hallucinations, which occur in 2–5% of the children taking stimulants; however, they did agree that a lower level warning should be included in packaging of these medications. An additional concern discussed by the panel was that physicians might be prescribing additional medication to treat the hallucinations when they are, in fact, a side effect of the stimulant medication. (Harris, 2006)

Attention-deficit/hyperactivity disorder (ADHD) is a complex disorder involving cognitive, behavioral, psychological, and social factors. The role of the brain and genetic factors have been increasingly recognized and researched. Specifically, researchers have focused on the role of the frontal and prefrontal areas of the brain and an apparent failure of systems designed to inhibit emotional and behavioral responses. Some individuals with the disorder exhibit symptoms of high activity and impulsivity, combined with a short attention span, whereas others display a primarily inattentive type of the disorder (ADD). ADD individuals tend to be more inattentive, may appear to be socially withdrawn or frequently "daydream," and are more likely to be depressed or anxious (Erk, 2000).

Psychostimulant medications (i.e., central nervous system stimulants) are the most commonly used and most comprehensively studied for use by individuals with ADD/ADHD. Stimulants are Schedule II medications (controlled substances) because they have the potential for illicit use and abuse and psychological or physiological dependence. This means that no refills are allowed on the prescription, and no more than a 30-day supply is given at a time. Unlike many of the medications previously discussed that require days or weeks to reach a therapeutic level, these medications have a rapid onset and short duration of effect. Side effects typically include poor appetite, stomachache, headache, and irritability. It is recommended that growth, both in weight and height, be closely monitored when children are taking stimulant medications. Many health care providers believe that stimulants should be used cautiously, if at all, in individuals with a tic disorder or familial history of tic disorder due to the possibility of tics occurring as a side effect (Brown, 2000). It is important that those living with or working with children using stimulant medications be familiar with the concept of *behavioral rebound* (i.e., as the medication wears off, there may be temporary deterioration of behavior to a level that is of even greater concern than baseline behavior). This effect can sometimes be managed by adjusting the dosing schedule or by providing increased structure in the environment as the medication effects wear off. Concerns about stimulants include reports of increasing recreational use of the medication as a street drug, risk of drug dependence, and the potential that abuse can lead to serious physiological side effects. Additionally, there is concern about psychosis or severe depression with abusive levels of the drug.

Methylphenidate (marketed as Ritalin, Concerta, Metadate, and Methylin) is the most recognized and most frequently used medication for ADHD. Stimulant medications are generally administered two to three times per day, with the doses timed to minimize interference with sleep or appetite, or to control rebound effects. Sustained release versions are available for some of the psychostimulants, with their effects lasting up to 12 hours. These have the advantage of requiring only one dose per day. A new methylphenidate transdermal system (marketed as Daytrana) involves wearing a patch on the hip for up to 9 hours each day; medication effects continue up to 3 hours after removal of the patch. An FDA panel recommended that Daytrana be used only as an alternative treatment (i.e., when pills cannot be used successfully). Dextroamphetamine (Dexedrine) lasts somewhat longer in the system than methylphenidate, but is reported to have a more pronounced effect on growth than the other psychostimulants. Adderal, derived from mixed amphetamines salts, has the properties of dextroamphetamine; it has been available since 1995 and lasts for 4 to 10 hours, depending on the individual's response to the medication. Magnesium permoline (Cylert) is given only once per day. Cylert has less potential for abuse than the other stimulants and is listed only as a Schedule IV substance. The use of Cylert has decreased since warnings about possibly fatal liver toxicity have been published (Hall & Gushee, 2002).

A newer medication, atomoxetine (Strattera), is a nonstimulant alternative that works on the neurotransmitters norepinephrine and dopamine, and is the only medication with FDA approval for treatment of ADHD in adults. Strattera, similar to the SSRI antidepressants, can take weeks for maximal effectiveness; dosing can occur either once or twice daily, depending on the individual's tolerance for a larger single dose. Strattera has an advantage in not being listed as a Schedule II medication (controlled substance) since it does not have the same potential for illicit abuse (Rivas-Vazquez, 2003). In December, 2004 the manufacturer of Strattera added a warning that the drug should be discontinued in individuals who show signs of jaundice (e.g., yellowing of the skin or the whites of the eyes) or if blood tests show signs of liver damage.

Approximately, 10 to 30 percent of children believed to have ADHD do not respond to psychostimulant medication (Julien, 1998) or respond to one of the medications, but not others. This reinforces the importance of individualizing both the medication chosen and the dose (R. T. Brown & La Rosa, 2002). Antidepressants are not approved for the treatment of ADHD, but the SSRIs and the atypical antidepressant Wellbutrin are sometimes used instead of stimulants, especially when symptoms include depressed mood, anxiety, or over-focusing. It is very important to be aware that there have been reports of sudden death in children using tricyclic antidepressants, specifically imipramine (Tofranil) and desipramine (Norpramine), resulting in a reluctance by many physicians to use tricyclics with children. Unexpected deaths have also been reported in children using clonidine (Catapres), an antihypertensive medication, which is sometimes used for the treatment of hyperactive behavior, despite side effects of sedation and a need to monitor salt intake and blood pressure, combined with limited evidence of its effectiveness (Hall & Gushee, 2002). Antipsychotic medications are also being prescribed for ADHD and other nonpsychotic conditions (Tanner, 2006). The increase in this controversial practice, which began in the mid-1990s with the introduction of the atypical antipsychotics, is of particular concern, because the safety and effectiveness of these medications for children has not been established.

There has been significant controversy over the years regarding the overprescription of Ritalin and other stimulant medications. Some stress the importance of careful analysis of the medication dose and avoidance of overmedication (Smith, 2002). A major concern is that pills are sometimes "pushed" by schools or used without appropriate diagnostic and management procedures. The American Academy of Pediatrics recently released guidelines regarding best practices in treating ADHD, emphasizing the importance of educating parents about the chronic nature of the condition and the importance of setting specific goals for treatment focused on the problems of daily life. Success in treatment is greatest when goals are developed by the health care provider in conjunction with parents, school staff, and mental health professionals. It is essential to have a plan for monitoring progress toward these goals that takes into account the developmental changes that occur from childhood to adolescence to adulthood. It is recommended that the diagnosis and plan be reevaluated if treatment goals are not met.

Best practices in the treatment of ADHD involve a comprehensive approach including education about how attention, memory, and learning work, and strategies for self-monitoring and self-control, including the control of attention (Brown, 2000). It is hoped that if individuals develop strategies for controlling and compensating for the symptoms of ADHD, their personal and social development will be enhanced with a positive impact on lifetime functioning. The American Psychological Association's Working Group (2006) report on the use of psychoactive medication for children and adolescents presents a very comprehensive overview of psychotropic medication use with children. The report contains background and up-to-date information on medication, psychosocial interventions, and combined interventions, diversity issues, risk-benefit analyses, and future directions for a variety of childhood disorders. However, it is estimated that between one-third and one-half of children with ADHD continue to display symptoms in adulthood such as inattention, increased activity, and impulsivity that are disruptive to their lives. Some individuals may continue to require medication to control their symptoms, in addition to continued interventions, such as education about the disorder, strategies to compensate for ADHD symptoms, attention management training, and anger management or self-control skills training (Jackson & Farrugia, 1997).

Herbal Remedies

The use of herbal remedies is quite common for a variety of conditions, including symptoms of stress, depression, or anxiety. The use of these remedies is also common in certain cultural groups (particularly Asian and indigenous groups), both for healing and to facilitate mystical experiences (Ingersoll, 2005). There is a perception by consumers that herbal remedies are safe because they are natural. However, not only are there concerns about the safety and quality of herbal remedies, there is often minimal documentation as to whether or not herbal substances work for the purpose they are being used. It is difficult to gather clear information about the use of herbal remedies because the products tend to be unregulated (lacking specific standards for production and systems for quality control) and there is very limited data regarding their safety and effectiveness (Grueb & McNamara, 2000). It is important for those using herbal remedies to understand that such remedies, although derived from plants, do possess strong pharmacological properties. Examples of other plant-derived substances that are well understood to have chemical properties are marijuana, cocaine, and opium.

Of additional concern is the possibility that herbal remedies might interact negatively with other medications. For example, warfarin (Coumadin), a blood thinner frequently prescribed for the prevention of strokes, is known to interact with over 25 herbal compounds (Pancrazio, 2001). If a client initiates discussion of herbal remedies, therapists should remember general ethical and legal issues relevant to the discussion of any medication. As with prescription medications, it is important that mental health practitioners not suggest or endorse the use of any particular herbal remedy (Rivas-Vazquez, 2001c). Given the frequent use of herbal remedies, however, it is helpful for therapists to have some knowledge of the more commonly used substances.

An herbal remedy commonly used for depression is St. John's wort, which is derived from the buds and flowers of the plant *hypericum perforatum*. In the case of St. John's wort, initial research suggests that it works better than placebo in treating mild to moderate depression, although it is not clear if it is as effective as conventional antidepressants. It is thought to have chemical properties most similar to tricyclic antidepressants. It has been associated with side effects including upset stomach, constipation, fatigue, sedation, confusion, and rash. As with other antidepressant medication, there have been reports of St. John's wort precipitating manic episodes or psychotic relapse (Rivas-Vazquez, 2001c).

The rhizomes of the kava shrub (*piper methysticum*), native to the South Pacific Islands, have been used both socially and medicinally for many generations in native cultures. Kava kava, sold as an herbal remedy, is promoted for its relaxing and stress-reducing properties and is used to treat symptoms of anxiety. There has been some research supporting an anxiolytic effect with Kava (Ingersoll, 2005). Kava has been proposed as a useful adjunct to cognitive-behavior therapy in the treatment of anxiety disorders, as it appears to reduce anxiety and has fewer common side effects compared to benzodiazepines and antidepressant medications (Dattilio, 2002). However, there has also been concern expressed about side effects (Ernst, 2005), which could include liver toxicity (Brauer, Stangl, Siewart, Pfab, & Becker, 2003) and tolerance/dependence issues (Mischoulon, 2002).

Considerations and Best Practices Regarding the Use of Medication

We assume that the majority of readers of this text are most interested in learning about psychotherapeutic skills, techniques, and therapies. However, it is likely that the clients who approach you for therapy may already be taking medication or are considering medication. Therefore, it is crucial to remain aware of the pharmacological basics of medications used to treat disorders commonly seen in your field of practice, as well as the risks and benefits associated with each medication and, as discussed in the previous chapter, possible barriers to adherence. You can help your client self-advocate by encouraging him or her to ask the medical professional about the benefits and risks of medications used or considered. Any time a medication is being considered or prescribed, a close working relationship with the health care provider increases the chances of a positive outcome for your client.

In this chapter, we have covered medications typically used with mood disorders, anxiety disorders, psychotic disorders, and attention-deficit/hyperactivity disorder. It is important to keep in mind that this represents only a brief review of these medications and that the information is subject to change based on future research. It is important to note that this chapter and Appendix C are intended as a brief summary of this large, changing body of literature. Despite attention to detail when compiling the information, it is important for readers to understand that we cannot guarantee the accuracy or the currency of all the information. We hope that this review has sensitized readers to the complexities of medication use, medication marketing, and the need for those prescribing medications to clearly weigh the risks and benefits of any medication prescribed. Our goal has been to do our best to provide you with an up-to-date assessment of the constantly changing psychopharmacological literature. In this way, you will be prepared for discussions with your clients about physiological symptoms they are experiencing when their physician is initiating, reducing, or discontinuing psychotropic medications. At the very least, you can educate clients about the benefits of becoming fully informed about medications.

Many questions remain unanswered as one reviews the psychopharmacological literature. It is clear that the majority of the research comes from physicians and those whose worldview strongly supports the medical model and the use of medication. Therapists who review the literature may be astonished by what appears to be a lack of critical thinking and a focus on medication without consideration of the uniqueness of the individual, particularly in terms of the etiology of symptoms. There is little discussion of best practices in terms of when to consider medication in the course of comprehensive treatment. Under what circumstances, if any, should medication be used prior to psychotherapy? If a course of medication and therapy are both instituted, is this best done simultaneously or in a staggered fashion? Should the approach differ based on the nature of the disorder and the severity of the symptoms? How can collaboration with the health care provider best be initiated when a client begins therapy already taking multiple psychotropic medications? Does the literature address the issue of diversity in terms of both physiological response to medication as well as attitudes toward the use of medication and adherence to physician recommendations? Is there sufficient research related to the long-term effects of medication use? Is the evidence clear and compelling in terms of short-term efficacy for symptom relief? How might mental health professionals, health care providers, and clients most effectively collaborate? These questions become even more critical as the sale and marketing of psychotropic medications continue to grow exponentially. Off-label use and the combining of psychotropic medications is also occurring with increased frequency. In addition, more and more pediatricians and general practitioners are prescribing psychotropic medication. Medication is frequently prescribed in the absence of a clear plan for (1) systematically monitoring the effects of the medication on targeted symptoms and (2) for gathering data on any side effects the individual is experiencing. The previously mentioned STAR*-D study (NIMH, 2006) provides excellent guidelines for systematic data gathering regarding both symptoms and side effects; most importantly, protocols are sufficiently succinct for consistent use. In the mental health field, there is focus on evidence-based practice and contextual perspectives. It is clear that ultimately the decision to use or not use any medication lies with the client. However, are clients being provided with the information they need to make informed decisions? Does the information provided include up-to-date information on risks and benefits, including both long- and short-term safety? Is there a clear plan for how long the medication will be used? Mental health professionals can encourage their clients to ask some of these critically important questions.

Intake Assessment Form

Appendix

INTAKE ASSESSMENT

Client Name:	ID:	Assessment Date:

A.

Diagnosis

Axis I _____

Change in Diagnosis

Date	Diagnosis	Initials

Axis II _____

Axis III _____

Axis IV _____

Axis V _____ GAF (Adult) _____ CGAS (Childrens Global Assessment Scale)

GAF/CGAS Justification:

Demographic Summary *(include demographic information, presenting need/referral):*

DSM IV TR Diagnostic Criteria *(Diagnostic justification, including <u>exclusion</u> criteria for diagnoses ruled out)*

Page 1

B. Treatment Package

☐ Meets funding criteria *(specify)* _____   ☐ Client does not meet eligibility criteria

☐ Meets "A" diagnostic criteria

☐ Meets "B" diagnostic criteria with added Risk factor: _____

☐ High Risk Behavior Last 90 days   ☐ Child at Risk due to Abuse or Neglect
☐ Two or more MH hospital admissions during the last 2 years.   ☐ Child < age of 6 Atypical Behavioral patterns
☐ Outpatient MH Treatment last 90 days   ☐ Child < age of 6 Atypical Behavioral patterns
☐ MH hospitalizations or residential for 6 months during last year, D/C MH hospital.

Service Level: _____ Initial hours authorized: _____ Initial Tx. Recommendation: ☐ Groups ☐ CM
                                                                          ☐ Therapy *(primary Clinician)* _____

Special Population Status: ☐ Child   ☐ OA   ☐ Deaf   ☐ DD

                             ☐ Ethnic: _____   ☐ Other: _____

_____
MHP Assessor Signature, Degree/Specialty/ID   *Printed Name*

_____
MHP Supervisor Signature, Degree/Specialty/ID (if needed)   *Printed Name*

Client Name: ID:

C. Presenting Issues

- Current needs, status, chronology:

- Client/family strengths:

- Transition planning and desired outcomes *(document using measurable outcomes of what will the client be able to do that they can't do now, or what won't be happening in their life that is happening now and from whom will they receive support and/or services?):*

D. Treatment History

- Dates and places of previous outpatient and inpatient treatment, medications used past and present, consumer's perceptions of what worked/didn't work:

E. Psychosocial History *(consider strengths, as well as cultural and spiritual issues):*

- Family *(family of origin current status, include knnown family history of mental health issues/Treatment):*

- Natural supports *(community and family supports):*

- Cultural *(expand beyond ethnicity and include socioeconomic, religion, and geographic, etc):*

- Major life events *(e.g., notable trauma, criminal history, deaths, CPS involvement, military):*

- Employment/Education *(historical, current and plans):*

Client Name: ID:

F. Substance Abuse Screening *(Review Health & Medical Substance Use/Abuse):*

	No	Yes
1. Does the identified client use prescription/street drugs or alcohol to cope with life?	☐	☐
2. Do others think the identified client has a substance use problem?	☐	☐
3. Do family members have a history of substance use/aduse?	☐	☐
4. Has substance use ever lead to family, legal or work problems?	☐	☐
5. Has the identified client ever received outpatient/inpatient drug/alcohol treatment?	☐	☐

Comments *(required for ALL yes answers)*

G. Risk Management:

- Danger to self

Current			History		
	Yes	**Denied**		**Yes**	**Denied**
Ideation:	☐	☐	Ideation:	☐	☐
Plan:	☐	☐	Plan:	☐	☐
Attempts:	☐	☐	Attempts:	☐	☐

- Danger to Others

Current			History		
	Yes	**Denied**		**Yes**	**Denied**
Ideation:	☐	☐	Ideation:	☐	☐
Plan:	☐	☐	Plan:	☐	☐
Attempts:	☐	☐	Attempts:	☐	☐

- Other risk factors *(gravely disabled, victimization, etc):*

- Comments/protective factors/clinically relevant information *(required for ALL yes answers above):*

Client Name: ID:

Page 4

H. FUNCTIONING IN LIFE DOMAINS *(Describe strengths and needs in each area)*

Sleep ☐ Adequate (strengths) ☐ Decreased ☐ Increased ☐ Other

Describe:_____

Food/appetite ☐ No current issues (strengths) ☐ Needs ☐ Impaired by MH Issues ☐ N/A for Client

Describe:_____

Employment/School ☐ No current issues (strengths) ☐ Needs ☐ Impaired by MH Issues ☐ N/A for Client
Pre-school/daycare
Describe:_____

Finances/Income ☐ No current issues (strengths) ☐ Needs ☐ Impaired by MH Issues ☐ N/A for Client

Describe:_____

Legal Issues DOC ☐ No current issues (strengths) ☐ Needs ☐ Impaired by MH Issues ☐ N/A for Client

Describe:_____

Housing ☐ No current issues (strengths) ☐ Needs ☐ Impaired by MH Issues ☐ N/A for Client

Describe:_____

Other Daily Activities ☐ No current issues (strengths) ☐ Needs ☐ Impaired by MH Issues ☐ N/A for Client

Describe:_____

Cultural/Spiritual ☐ No current issues (strengths) ☐ Needs ☐ Impaired by MH Issues ☐ N/A for Client

Describe:_____

Personal Safety ☐ No current issues (strengths) ☐ Needs ☐ Impaired by MH Issues ☐ N/A for Client

Describe:_____

Transportation ☐ No current issues (strengths) ☐ Needs ☐ Impaired by MH Issues ☐ N/A for Client

Describe:_____

Social Life/Family ☐ No current issues (strengths) ☐ Needs ☐ Impaired by MH Issues ☐ N/A for Client

Describe:_____

Self Care ☐ No current issues (strengths) ☐ Needs ☐ Impaired by MH Issues ☐ N/A for Client

Describe:_____

Medical Needs ☐ No current issues (strengths) ☐ Needs ☐ Impaired by MH Issues ☐ N/A for Client
Medications ☐ No current issues (strengths) ☐ Needs ☐ Impaired by MH Issues ☐ N/A for Client
Dental ☐ No current issues (strengths) ☐ Needs ☐ Impaired by MH Issues ☐ N/A for Client

Describe: *(Note severity/urgency and address both Medical and Dental)*_____

Client Name: ID:

H. Mental Status Examination *(at time of interview — consider cultural norms in completing this section)*

Appearance	Thought Processes	Orientation
☐ Age/culture appropriate ☐ Meticulous ☐ Unkempt ☐ Inappropriate ☐ Eccentric ☐ Poor Hygiene Children Only: ☐ Age/size congruent ☐ Slumped ☐ Relaxed ☐ Rigid/tense ☐ Other: Comments: _____	☐ Age/culture appropriate ☐ Circulstantial ☐ Concrete ☐ Tangential ☐ Aggressive ☐ Obsessive ☐ Phobias ☐ Blocking ☐ Paranoid Ideation (specify) _____ ☐ Delusions (specify) _____ ☐ Other: _____	☐ Age/culture appropriate ☐ Disorientated to: 　☐ Person 　☐ Place 　☐ Date 　☐ Situation
Mood/Affect	**Cognitive Functioning**	**Motor Activity**
☐ Age/culture appropriate ☐ Flat/blunted ☐ Labile ☐ Incongruent ☐ Depressed ☐ Expansive ☐ Anxious/fearful ☐ Angry ☐ Other: _____	Remote Memory ☐ Present ☐ Limited Recent Memory ☐ Present ☐ Limited Ability to Abstract ☐ Present ☐ Limited	☐ Age/culture appropriate ☐ Agitated ☐ Hyperactive ☐ Lack of movement ☐ Tremors ☐ Tics ☐ Mannerisms ☐ Facial grimacing ☐ Other: _____
Perceptual Processes	**Behavior**	**Speech**
☐ Age/culture appropriate ☐ Imagination (child only) ☐ Depersonalization Hallucinations (specify): 　☐ Auditory 　☐ Visual 　☐ Tactile 　☐ Olfactory 　☐ Somatic 　☐ Other: _____ **Insight/Judgment** ☐ Age/culture appropriate ☐ Understands consequences ☐ Denial/resistance ☐ Blames other ☐ Aware of problem ☐ Poor impulse control ☐ Discern right/wrong	☐ Age/culture appropriate ☐ Poor eye contact ☐ Attends to task ☐ Distractible ☐ Cooperative ☐ Friendly ☐ Withdrawn/passive ☐ Suspicious ☐ Guarded ☐ Ingratiating ☐ Hostile ☐ Bizarre Verbally: ☐ Interacts ☐ Initiates ☐ Interrupts ☐ Redirects Children Only: ☐ Separation reactions 　(specify): ☐ Other: _____	☐ Age/culture appropriate ☐ Slow ☐ Rapid ☐ Soft ☐ Loud ☐ Mute ☐ Profuse ☐ Pressured ☐ Age Intelligible ☐ Unintelliginle ☐ Impaired/medical condition: _____ ☐ Slurred ☐ Mumbled ☐ Clear ☐ Whiny ☐ Blocked ☐ Preservations ☐ Stuttering ☐ Other: _____
Sleep ☐ Adequate ☐ Decreased ☐ Increased ☐ Other: _____	**Appetite** ☐ Adequate ☐ Decreased ☐ Increased ☐ Weight Change	

Client Name: _____   ID: _____

I. ASSESSMENT CLINICAN'S RECOMMENDATIONS/INTERIM TREATMENT PLAN (Provide treatment "orders" for the next 30 days, or until an ongoing Treatment Plan is completeed by the clinician and client. Be sure to order all medically necessary services that may fall within that peroid).

Modality	Frequency
☐ Individual Psychotherapy	
☐ Case Management	
☐ Psychiatric or Medication evaluation	
☐ Group Psychotherapy	
☐ Crisis Plan Development, if client consents	
☐ Client to meet with CM within 14 days	
☐ Continuing CM assessment of client need	
☐ Development of ongoing treatment plan	
☐ Other (specify)	
☐ Other (specify)	

Additional Recommendations:

Issues Related to Specific Populations

Remember that the observations we are sharing in the next section are very general, and that there is significant variability in life experiences between members of the same ethnic, social, or cultural group. It is important to determine if the information applies to the specific individuals or families that you are working with. The material is adapted from D. W. Sue & D. Sue (2008). We recommend reading the resources suggested earlier in Chapter 15 or books on specific groups for more comprehensive information.

an American Populations

1. There is significant variability in family structure. The family structure of African Americans tends to be both flexible and hierarchical. African American families are often headed by a female, with relatives, older children, and close friends frequently helping with childrearing and emotional support. Grandmothers play an important role in childrearing.

2. There are high expectations for children's behavior. Strict discipline and physical punishment are common.

3. Communication patterns between family members may be more direct and appear to be more critical than that found in White, middle-class families. In many cases, family members respond well to this communication style because it demonstrates care and concern. Therapists must evaluate family communication, not by their own background experience, but by determining the effect on the client.

4. Many African American parents strongly encourage their children to achieve and have high aspirations for the future despite social or economic obstacles.

5. Many school systems do not appear to be meeting the needs of

African American youth; many drop out of school or experience failure in school, especially African American males.

6. One of the greatest barriers for less educated African Americans is poverty, crime, substance abuse, and high rates of unemployment.

7. Strengths in the African American family structure include flexible family roles, strong family connections, a strong work ethic, and strong spiritual and religious ties. There is a strong commitment to caring for family members who are ill or elderly.

8. Mistrust may be observed during therapy sessions, especially when there is a cross-race dyad. Directly discussing cross-race issues may strengthen the therapeutic alliance.

Native American Populations

1. There is great variability in the acculturation rates of various Native American groups; the majority of Native Americans live in suburban or urban areas rather than on reservations.

2. Based upon a variety of historical events, Native Americans may be very familiar with the history of oppression from the majority culture and therefore suspicious of non-Indians. Similarly, many do not expect to be treated fairly by non-Indian agencies.

3. Even for those living in urban or suburban areas, the tribe and tribal structure remain very important. Collectivism is a strong value for tribes. The tribe and family are generally seen as more important than the individual. Many Native Americans see themselves as an extension of their tribe, which provides a sense of belonging and security. It is important for therapists to understand the importance of the tribe for the individual and to gain an understanding of the tradition of tribal involvement in individual or family treatment or decision-making.

4. There is a unique relationship between tribal members and local, state, and federal laws. This affects law enforcement and child welfare issues, particularly concerning events that occur on tribal land.

5. There is great variability in family structure depending on the tribe and region. In some areas, a clear matriarchal or patriarchal structure is evident. In general, families tend to have a strong role for women, high fertility, and a high rate of out-of-wedlock births. It is common for children to spend time living with different members of the extended family, such as grandparents, aunts, uncles, or older siblings.

6. It is important to avoid therapeutic goals or techniques that will lead to discord within the family or tribe. For some clients, it may be best to involve family, friends, elders, or tribal leaders in the development of interventions.

7. Nonverbal communication is valued, as is the philosophy that learning occurs by listening rather than talking. Direct eye contact and direct questioning should be avoided, especially with elders or authority figures.

8. A client-centered listening style may work best initially. Therapists can gradually determine if and when to use more structure and direct questioning. It is important not to hurry clients and to allow adequate time for them to finish statements and thoughts.

9. Traditional healing approaches, such as the vision quest or sweat lodge ceremonies, focus on restoration of harmony between the mind, body, and spirit.

10. There are common values held by many Native American individuals, tribes, and families. These include the sharing and giving of time and material possessions. This sometimes means that a client will prioritize spending time and energy with family and friends or in ceremonial activities over other activities, such as work or school. Working may be seen as a temporary means of meeting daily living needs in order to be able to enjoy time with others. Cooperation, which includes sensitivity to the opinions and attitudes of others, is also considered very important. This may mean active avoidance of argument or disagreement.

11. The incidence of domestic violence, along with physical and sexual assault, is quite high in many native communities; Native American women suffer violence at a rate that is almost four times higher than the national average. This may be an underestimate because of a lack of trust in law enforcement agencies (Bhungalia, 2001).

12. Substance abuse is a significant concern, as are high mortality rates from alcoholism, motor vehicle accidents, drowning, homicide, and suicide. Community focused substance abuse treatment programs have shown some success.

Asian American Populations

1. There are large between-group differences within the Asian American population; this population is composed of at least 40 distinct subgroups that differ in language, religion, and values (Sandhu, 1997). This includes Chinese, Filipinos, Koreans, East Asian Indians, Japanese, refugees and immigrants from Southeast Asia (Vietnamese, Laotians, Cambodians, and Hmongs), and Pacific Islanders (Hawaiians, Guamanians, and Samoans). There is significant variability in culture, acculturation, English language skills, and educational and occupational level both within and between the different subgroups.

2. Although sometimes referred to as a "model minority," Asian Americans continue to face both direct and indirect anti-Asian sentiments, including stereotyping and discrimination.

3. Among traditionally oriented Asian Americans, psychological and emotional stress and depression are often described with physical complaints such as fatigue, headaches, and difficulty eating or sleeping. There is a belief that physical disturbances cause emotional problems and that treatment of the physical illness will cure the emotional symptoms. It is important for therapists to closely attend to physical complaints as well as emotional issues.

4. Asian Americans tend to underutilize mental health services. This may be due to cultural factors such as feelings of shame or disgrace associated with acknowledging emotional difficulties, a desire to keep issues private and handle them within the family, or a focus on the somatic aspects of distress rather than emotional symptoms.

5. Traditional Asian American families are often authoritarian and hierarchical in structure; males and older individuals occupy a higher status. Communication occurs from parent to child, with the expectation of allegiance, respect, and obedience. When expectations are not met, the result may be verbal or physical punishment. Shame and guilt are often used to control the behavior of children, even after they have reached adulthood. There are strong expectations for males to carry on the family name and tradition, and for males to demonstrate primary allegiance to the parents, even after they have married.

6. Asian Americans tend to have a family and group focus rather than an individualistic orientation. They make decisions based on benefit to the family rather than individual family members. There is an emphasis on family harmony, which often means considering the wishes of the parents rather than those of the children. For some Asian Americans, a therapeutic focus on individual needs and wishes may run counter to

the value of collectivism. Interventions may need to be developed or modified to take parent wishes and family values into consideration.

7. Asian children and adolescents are expected to focus on family goals and demonstrate "correct" behavior so they do not bring dishonor to the family. Conflicts with parents, feelings of guilt or stress over academic performance, cultural confusion, identity issues, negative self-image, and personal struggle between interdependence and independence are common.

8. Academic achievement and having a successful career are emphasized by parents since such success reflects well on the family. Often, parents have specific ideas of careers they would like their children to pursue, so career choices may reflect parental expectations rather then personal interest or aptitude. Despite high expectations, there may be little praise for accomplishments.

9. Strong emotional displays, especially in public, are discouraged for both adults and children. In many Asian families, care and concern are demonstrated by attending to the physical needs of family members rather than verbalization or open display of emotions. In counseling, a direct focus on emotion may be uncomfortable; a more indirect acknowledgment of emotions such as "some people might feel very sad to leave their homeland" may be most effective.

10. In general, Asian Americans prefer a problem-focused approach rather than one that involves contemplation. The therapist should take an active role, but allow the client to give feedback regarding the therapeutic approach and suggested interventions.

Latino Populations

1. A large percentage of Latinos are from Mexico or of Mexican descent. Other areas of origin include Central America, South America, and the Caribbean Islands (primarily Puerto Rico and Cuba). Although many Latinos are immigrants or children of immigrants, there are many whose families have lived in the United States for generations. There is variability in background and culture both within and between Latino subgroups.

2. Traditional Latino families are hierarchical, with the greatest voice given to the parents, older family members, and males. The father is generally the primary authority figure.

3. Interpersonal relationships with an extended network of family and friends are very important. The extended family generally includes close friends (*madrina, padrino, comadre, copadre*) who serve supportive roles within the family. When emotional concerns for a family member are present, extended family and close friends may be relied upon rather than outside help. Physical discipline is used in some Latino families, and there may be fear that their childrearing practices are being judged.

4. Traditionally, men are expected to be dominant, strong, and in charge (*machismo*), whereas women are expected to be pure, self-sacrificing, nurturing, and submissive (*marianismo*). Given these traditional gender role expectations, it can be stressful for males when linguistic, social, or economic barriers make it difficult to fulfill the traditional role. Feelings of insecurity, isolation, frustration, anxiety, or anger and an even more rigid desire to adhere to gender roles may result. Women may experience stress in response to their partner's behavior or feelings of not living up to expectations. They may not have avenues for expressing feeling of sadness, anger, and isolation. This may be particularly true for families who have immigrated and who do not have access to the close interpersonal ties they experienced in their country of origin.

5. A warm and respectful first meeting is important. Although the client may be somewhat formal, after trust (*confianza*) is developed, close emotional bonds are easily formed. Therapists may find that they are treated as a family member or close friend. This is an indication of trust, deep affection, and respect, not dependency or a deliberate violation of boundaries.

6. Discussions of confidentiality are very important. Even Latinos born in the United States or immigrants with legal status may be concerned

about confidentiality, particularly with respect to immigration authorities.

7. Family unity, cooperation, and loyalty are very important for Latinos. Family allegiance is strong and sometimes takes precedence over other responsibilities, such as work or school. Older children sometimes are absent from school to take care of younger siblings, to translate for parents who have appointments, or to visit relatives.

8. Parents expect their children to be well-behaved and to cooperate with parental decisions, including restrictions on activities for adolescent females. Adolescents often leave school at an early age so they can work and contribute financially. Teenage pregnancy and early marriage are also common.

9. Despite strong family support for education and a belief that education will allow children opportunities the parents never had, standardized test scores for Latino children are often low and the drop-out rate for Latino adolescents remains high.

10. Cultural or ethnic identity concerns and problems with acculturation can result in low self-esteem and a lack of social or personal responsibility. Pressure for gang involvement may be a concern in some areas. This is particularly true when children, adolescents, and young adults are no longer connected to the positive, protective aspects of the Latino culture.

11. Religiosity (often Catholicism) and spiritual beliefs play an important role in the lives of many Latinos. Fatalistic thinking (i.e., a belief that events are predetermined and inevitable) is common. The therapist may validate this belief, but also suggest change strategies by asking, "Even though this was meant to happen, how can you deal with it now?"

12. Within the Latino population, there are some families who speak only indigenous dialects (e.g., Mixtec, Trique, Zapotec, Quechua) and whose Spanish skills are limited or nonexistent. Even Spanish speaking counselors require interpreters when working with these individuals.

Immigrant Populations

1. The U.S. Census Bureau (2004) estimates that about half of the 33 million immigrants living in the United States have been here less than 20 years. Although many immigrants are either naturalized citizens or legally documented and admitted as permanent residents, more than one-fourth are undocumented (i.e., they entered the United States without documents or have overstayed their visas).

2. The September 11, 2001 terrorist attacks significantly affected attitudes toward immigrants and individuals appearing to be foreign. In addition, increases in discrimination have occurred as a result of the debate over immigration policy.

3. Because of the recent political struggle over illegal immigration and the sometimes negative reception from both the government and the public, even those who have legal status may be hesitant to seek services or to reveal personal information. Immigrants may worry that therapists are somehow connected to the government, or that therapy might affect their immigration status or that of parents, siblings, or other close family members.

4. It is important to have immigrants share their backgrounds, immigration stories, and changes in their lives since immigrating. Immigrants typically encounter multiple stressors as they adjust to a new country, including the struggles with a new language, combined with new and challenging social, economic, and educational systems.

5. Immigrants may be hesitant to reveal family issues or matters of personal concern because of the cultural importance of privacy. Women who are abused by their husbands or victims of sexual assault may not talk about these issues because of shame or cultural norms regarding family privacy.

6. Disruptions in family structure are common in immigrant families, with changes in roles occurring when the children acculturate more rapidly than the parents. For various reasons, immigrants may not be able to return to their previous level of occupational and social functioning. This loss of status can result in a sense of failure, lowered self-esteem, and economic stress.

7. Immigrants face a variety of additional barriers when it comes to seeking mental health services, including a lack of understanding about mental health care or how the health care delivery system works, limited English proficiency, or fear of judgment of themselves or their families. Because of the lack of bilingual counselors, problems in explaining services

or in diagnosis can occur with clients who are not conversant in English, even when translators are used.

8. Anyone who is born in the United States is a citizen and eligible for health and mental health services, if needed, regardless of the immigration status of the parents. Hospitals must offer emergency care regardless of immigration status. There are many local clinics, available to anyone with a low income, including undocumented immigrants. These clinics offer free or inexpensive health care, including mental health and dental services.

9. *Refugees,* individuals who leave their countries to escape racial, religious, or political persecution, may be under even greater distress due to trauma experienced in their country of origin, the sudden exit from their homeland, and loss of friends and family who have been left behind. Posttraumatic stress syndrome and symptoms such as anxiety, fear, or sleep disturbance are common.

Gay Men, Lesbians, Bisexuals, and Transsexuals

1. Take care not to make assumptions about anyone's sexual orientation and to refrain from using heterosexist language; for example, asking if the client has a "partner" rather than "spouse," "boyfriend," "girlfriend," "husband," or "wife," conveys openness and allows for later discussion of sexual orientation. Assuring that intake forms and interview procedures are also free from heterosexist language and offer an opportunity for indicating sexual orientation can also open communication.

2. Many GLBT (gay, lesbian, bisexual, or transsexual) clients have been targets of hate crimes, which may lead to depression or posttraumatic stress. Even if not directly affected by direct harassment or violence, societal discrimination can be an ongoing stressor.

3. It is important not to assume that the presenting problems with GLBT clients are necessarily the result of sexual orientation. However, remain alert to the reality that a client's mental health issues may be the affected by prejudice and discrimination or a lack of peer, family, school, and community support.

4. Not only do GLBT individuals face relationship issues typical of those faced by heterosexual couples and families, they also have additional stress due to prejudice and discrimination from society and decisions related to the extent to which they decide to hide their sexual orientation or come out to family, friends, neighbors, and acquaintances. Be careful not to use a heterosexual framework when working with lesbian and gay male relationship issues, such as offering a book on heterosexual relationships.

5. Be aware of common mental health issues including distress due to harassment, assault, prejudice, or discrimination; internalized homophobia; stress or indecision related to the coming out process; a lack of family, peer, school, or community support; suicidal ideation or attempts; and substance abuse.

6. The decision to come out can be extremely difficult, with potential social and economic implications. Counseling can focus on helping the client carefully evaluate the consequences of coming out (e.g., anger or rejection) or continuing to hide sexual orientation (e.g., isolation or lowered self-esteem). These issues are particularly complex for adolescents or young adults, who are often emotionally or financially dependent on their families. GLBT youth are at higher risk for suicidal thoughts or attempts, substance use and abuse, personal safety issues (e.g., molestation or assault), and high-risk sexual behaviors.

7. Examine your own attitudes and behaviors with respect to GLBT indi-

viduals. There continue to be reports of biased or inappropriate practice among clinicians including: (1) assuming that all clients are heterosexual, which reduces client comfort in bringing up the topic of sexual orientation; (2) failure to understand or acknowledge the impact of societal response to homosexuality on identity development and on psychological symptoms such as anxiety or depression; (3) belief that homosexuality is a mental illness, sometimes even demeaning homosexuality or encouraging clients to try to change their sexual orientation; (4) viewing homosexuality primarily in terms of sexual activity and underestimating the importance of permanent, intimate relationships; and (5) failure to understand the social and psychological consequences of both "keeping the secret" and coming out (Garnets, Hancock, Cochran, Goodchilds, & Peplau, 1998).

Considerations with Gender

1. Most counseling theories are male-centered and do not consider the impact of societal messages on the self-esteem and mental health of women. It is critical to be aware of all forms of societal oppression and understand how they interact with sexism. Therapists of both genders need to self-examine for possible biases when working with female clients, including biases in diagnosis (e.g., some of the personality disorders focus on gender characteristics).

2. All counselors should be careful not to make sexist assumptions or promote traditional gender roles. It is crucial to understand that sexism impacts expectations for girls and women and that the devaluation of women is a common occurrence at the societal level. Many parents and educators continue to unconsciously give messages that reinforce gender restrictive roles and behavior for females.

3. It is essential for therapists working with women and female adolescents to have accurate, up-to-date information on psychological and physiological issues impacting women, including overall health and wellness, menstruation, birth control, pregnancy (including unplanned pregnancy), miscarriage, infertility, childbirth, lactation, childcare, balancing multiple roles, pressure to be thin and other stereotyped standards of beauty perpetrated by the mass media, discrimination in the workplace, and discrimination based on age and gender.

4. Violence and sexual harassment towards adolescent girls and young women is common and is associated with increased use of drugs, binge drinking, suicidal ideation and attempts, eating disorders, and early sexual activity.

5. Females continue to earn less than males; this trend is particularly evident comparing salaries of White men and women, with women earning less than three-fourths of that earned by men. The impact of low earnings is especially evident for single mothers, who head less than 20 percent of all families, but account for nearly half of the families living in poverty (U.S Census Bureau, 2002).

6. Career fields that tend to be dominated by men are often not easily open to women. Many women remain in traditionally feminine careers. Common obstacles include difficulty finding a job; discrimination, harassment, or feelings of isolation in the workplace; and less mentoring and camaraderie (i.e., not being invited into the "good old boys" network), which can all be barriers to career advancement. This is often true even for college graduates, particularly women of color.

7. Women experience depression at approximately twice the rate found

in men (Schwartzman & Glaus, 2000). There are many factors thought to contribute to the increased incidence of depression. These include socioeconomic stress, societal gender standards and pressure, posttraumatic stress, poor body image and eating disorders, focus on relationships at the cost of personal needs and wishes, and equating relationship failure with personal failures.

8. Interventions that may be particularly appropriate for the needs of women and adolescent females include career counseling, connecting young women with female mentors, assertiveness training, gender role analysis, and same gender support groups.

Considerations with Older Adults

1. The number of individuals over 65 is increasing and is expected to double and reach 70 million by the year 2030 (U.S. Census Bureau, 2006). The 85 years and older age group is increasing at a rapid rate, and this growth is expected to continue for decades.

2. *Ageism,* negative attitudes toward aging or toward older individuals, is prevalent in our society. Negative stereotypes and discrimination are common; this bias occurs at an even earlier age for women. It is important for clinicians to evaluate their own attitudes, stereotypes, and prejudices related to aging.

3. Presume competence in older adult clients unless the contrary is obvious. Ask about medical conditions and the use of prescription and over-the-counter medications because mental conditions can be the result of health problems, drug interactions, or drug side effects. It is beneficial to assess using multiple tools and including varied sources of information (client, family members, significant other, and health care providers).

4. Physical impairments or health issues such as cardiovascular diseases, insomnia, or vision or hearing impairment is more common in older adults. However, many older individuals are active, healthy, and living independently.

5. Most older adults do not have cognitive problems. If cognitive slowing is evident, information can be presented at a slower pace or can be visually augmented through writing on notepads or a white board. For those who do have cognitive difficulties, show respect and allow as much autonomy as possible.

6. Abuse of alcohol or prescription drugs occurs in almost 20 percent of older adults. Alcohol abuse sometimes begins in later years when individuals are coping with depression, grief and loss, health concerns, financial stress, caregiving responsibilities, family conflict, or other life changes. Misuse of prescription drugs may occur when there are multiple medications, memory issues, or misunderstanding of dosing instructions.

7. The incidence of depression increases with increasing age in men, with the opposite occurring with women once they reach midlife. Suicide rates are high among older adults. Suicides in the 65 and older age group accounted for 19 percent of all suicides in 1997, with the suicide rate for White males aged 85 and older reaching almost six times the national rate (Miller, 2005). Older men are seven times more likely to commit suicide than older women (Roose, 2001). Increased suicide risk occurs with individuals who are: living alone, separated or divorced,

depressed or anxious, or experiencing declining health, financial stress, family conflict, or loss of a significant relationship.

8. Physical abuse or neglect is a concern for older individuals, especially in families where there is a pattern of marital stress or domestic violence, high levels of emotional or financial stress, or crowded living conditions (U.S. Department of Health and Human Services, 1998).

9. If family members are involved in caregiving, it may be helpful to offer to include them in therapy sessions or to provide them with information on reducing burnout.

10. Older couples may need to focus how to spend their time, balancing time spent alone and together (especially after retirement).

11. For adults close to the end of their lives, a sense of control may be gained by focusing on decisions such as deciding how heirlooms, keepsakes, and photo albums will be distributed and cared for. A *life review* can be helpful, focusing on the positive aspects of their experiences, such as having done their best with their life, meeting and surviving challenges, and making plans for priorities for the future.

13. There is a clear need for clinicians with interest and background knowledge related to the social, psychological, and physiological aspects of aging. Awareness of issues that are prevalent in these populations, such as hearing or vision loss, insomnia, or specific health conditions, is important.

Considerations with Disability Issues

1. Of the almost 50 million individuals with disabilities, most do not have visible disabilities (e.g., blindness or difficulties with mobility). Most have disabilities related to health issues (e.g., cardiovascular problems or epilepsy), learning or developmental disabilities, limited vision or hearing, or significant mental illness.

2. As a therapist, you can strive to understand the impact of prejudice, discrimination, inconvenience, and barriers on individuals with disabilities and help advocate for changes in societal attitudes. Negative attitudes and stereotypes can be both distressing and discouraging.

3. Be sure that you interact with individuals who have a disability in accordance with their skills, personality, and other personal attributes rather than their disability. Avoid targeting your interactions to someone who is accompanying the client rather than communicating directly with the client.

4. If a client appears to require assistance, ask before helping; if your offer is accepted, ask for instructions on how you can help. Devices used by individuals such as wheelchairs, walkers, or canes are considered personal and should not be moved without permission.

5. Determine if the disability is related to the presenting problem or if it needs to be considered in the development of intervention strategies. Family members and other social supports may be important in intervention planning. They can be included as part of assessment, goal formulation, and selection of therapeutic techniques.

6. Clients with disabilities (and their families) will be varied in terms of how they view the disability and how the disability impacts social, emotional, and occupational functioning.

7. Be aware that lack of employment, underemployment, and discrimination in the workplace are significant issues for individuals with disabilities. Many want to work, but are unable to find appropriate jobs.

8. Take care not to underestimate the quality of life for individuals with disabilities or to view depression or suicidal ideation as expected because of a low quality of life. Many individuals with disabilities have happy, productive, and fulfilling lives. In addition to treatment focused on ameliorating depressive thinking, encouraging depressed clients to take charge of their lives to the greatest extent possible can increase self-esteem and self-efficacy.

9. Consider how your office can be made accessible for all clients. This may include looking at environmental or procedural modifications

such as physical accessibility, accommodations for service animals, or communicative support such as sign-language interpreters, Braille or large-print materials, videotapes and audiotapes, and computers.

10. When meeting someone with vision loss, identify yourself and anyone else they will be interacting with. Offer the use of your arm and guide the client, giving verbal cues. When offering a seat, place the client's hand on the back of the chair to orient the client. If a service dog is present, less assistance will be needed. Let the client know if you move within the room and give a verbal cue when the conversation is close to ending. Ask the client about the best way of presenting written information (e.g., in large text format, in Braille, with audiotapes).

11. For clients who are deaf or hard of hearing, ask about their preferred communication. If someone is accompanying them, be sure to address the client. Make direct eye contact, keep your face and mouth visible, and speak clearly.

12. For clients with speech impediments, it is important to listen carefully and not rush conversation. Checking for understanding can enhance communication.

13. Promote the development of self-advocacy skills for all clients; family members and friends can also be strong advocates.

14. Mental health professionals should become familiar with the Americans with Disabilities Act (ADA), which is civil rights legislation signed into law in 1990 that contains information on legal rights and protections for individuals with various disabilities.

Psychotropic Medications

C
Appendix

Medications Commonly Used in the Treatment of Depression

Brand Name	Generic Name	Common Side Effects	Serious Effects/ Other Information
Trycyclic Antidepressants			
Anafranil	clomipramine	Dizziness, drowsiness, dry mouth, constipation, sexual dysfunction, blurred vision, weight gain	Alcohol use should be avoided. Dangerous if combined with MAOIs. Overdose can be fatal.
Elavil	amitriptyline		
Norpramin	desipramine		
Pamelor	nortriptyline		
Sinequan; Adapin	doxepin		
Tofranil	imipramine		
SSRIs[1]			
Celexa	citalopram	Upset stomach, anxiety/ restlessness, insomnia, tremor, headaches, fatigue, difficulty concentrating, weight gain, sexual dysfunction, SSRI discontinuation syndrome	Also used for body dysmorphic disorder and anxiety (including OCD). Approved for pediatric OCD.
Luvox	fluvoxamine		
Paxil	paroxetine		Less weight gain than with other SSRI antidepressants. Approved for Panic Disorder and Social Phobia

(continued)

Note: Shading indicates effects apply to all of the medications in the category or subcategory.

[1]Seratonin Syndrome, an extremely serious toxic reaction, is possible with all SSRIs. SSRIs should not be combined with MAOIs or certain cough medications. SSRIs may initiate manic behavior. SSRIs should not be discontinued abruptly.

Brand Name	Generic Name	Common Side Effects	Serious Effects/ Other Information
Prozac; Sarafem	fluoxetine	Upset stomach, anxiety/ restlessness, insomnia, tremor, headaches, fatigue, difficulty concentrating, weight gain, sexual dysfunction, SSRI discontinuation syndrome	Approved for pediatric use in major depression and OCD and adult panic disorder. Sold as Sarafem for premenstrual mood disorder.
Lexapro; Cipralex	escitalopram		Used for generalized anxiety disorder.
Zoloft	sertraline		Also approved for panic disorder, PTSD in adults, and for pediatric OCD.
Symbyax	fluoxetine and olanzapine	Drowsiness, weakness, swelling, tremor, sore throat, difficulty concentrating, weight gain	A combination antidepressant and antipsychotic.
MAOIs			
Marplan	isocarboxazid phenelzine tranylcypromine	Edema, weight gain, low blood pressure when standing, sexual dysfunction, headaches, insomnia, sedation, dizziness	Food with tyramine (e.g., aged cheese, fermented products, yeast, overripe or spoiled food) can cause an hypertensive crisis. Avoid decongestants and cold medications. Never combine MAOIs with other antidepressants or stimulants, or start an MAOI before they have had time to clear the body; a toxic reaction, Serotonin Syndrome, can occur.
Nardil			
Parnate			
Emsam	selegiline		Transdermal patch; the lowest dose patch is reported to be free of the serious side effects seen in MAOIs.
Atypical Antidepressants			
Desyrel	trazodone	Nausea, vomiting, restlessness, dizziness, drowsiness, low blood pressure	Also used with chronic nerve pain, must be taken shortly after eating.
Cymbalta	duloxetine hydrochloride	Nausea, vomiting, sexual dysfunction, restlessness, dizziness, drowsiness	Do not combine with alcohol. Also used with chronic nerve pain.

Note: Shading indicates effects apply to all of the medications in the category or subcategory.

Brand Name	Generic Name	Common Side Effects	Serious Effects/ Other Information
Edronax	reboxetine	Dry mouth, constipation, sweating, vertigo, insomnia, impotence, nausea	Monitor blood pressure.
Effexor	venlafaxine	Nausea, headaches, drowsiness, insomnia, sexual dysfunction, dizziness, weight loss	Used with anxiety disorders, including OCD. Monitor blood pressure.
Remeron	mirtazapine	Sleepiness, weight gain, dry mouth, blurred vision	Should not be combined with alcohol or Benzodiazepines. Liver function and white blood cell count should be monitored. Monitor cholesterol.
Serzone	nefazodone	Upset stomach, drowsiness, insomnia, dry mouth	Can cause liver failure. No longer sold in the United States as of May 2004.
Wellbutrin (Zyban)	bupropion	Agitation, headaches, tremors, seizures, insomnia, stomach upset, suppressed appetite	Do not use with individuals with history of anorexia or bulimia. Avoid alcohol use. Zyban is prescribed for smoking cessation.

Note: The FDA requires manufacturers of all antidepressants to include a black box warning about increased risk of suicidal thinking and behavior in children and adolescents taking antidepressants.

Medications Commonly Used as Mood Stabilizers in Bipolar Disorder

Brand Name	Generic Name	Common Side Effects	Serious Effects/Other Information
Anticonvulsant Medications			
Depakene; Depakote	valproic acid/ divalproex sodium	Sedation, stomach upset, tremor, weight gain	Used with rapid cycling bipolar disorder. Can affect blood platelets and capacity to clot.
Lamictal	lamotrigine	Drowsiness, upset stomach, headache, insomnia	Do not combine with alcohol. Risk of fatal rash.
Neurontin	gabapentin	Fatigue, edema, dizziness, shaky movements	Used with chronic, neurogenic pain. Keep well-hydrated, monitor kidney function.
Tegretol	carbamazepine	Sedation, stomach upset, vertigo, skin sensitivity to sunlight	Do not combine with alcohol. Used with chronic, neurogenic pain. Can cause a serious blood disorder.
Topamax	topimarate	Dizziness, drowsiness, fatigue, loss of appetite	Keep well-hydrated, monitor kidney functioning.
Trileptal	oxcarbazepine	Fatigue, stomach upset, dizziness, blurred vision	May require monitoring of sodium levels in the blood.
Other Medications Used with Bipolar Disorder			
Cibalith	lithium citrate	Weight gain, thirst, frequent urination, mental confusion, hand tremor, sedation, stomach upset	Monitor caffeine intake. Monitor cardiac, thyroid, and kidney function and for dose toxicity.
Eskalith; Lithobid; Lithonate; Lithotabs; Lithane; Lithium	lithium carbonate		
Seroquel	quetiapine	Sedation, agitation, weight gain, headache, upset stomach, low blood pressure	Antipsychotic also used for acute mania. Liver functioning may be monitored. Do not combine with alcohol or Benzodiazepines.

Note: Shading indicates effects apply to all of the medications in the category or subcategory.

Medications Commonly Used in the Treatment of Anxiety Disorders

Brand Name	Generic Name	Common Side Effects	Serious Effects/Other Information
Benzodiazepines			
Ativan*	lorazepam	Sedation, fatigue, slurred speech, weakness, clumsiness, memory impairment, dizziness, blurred vision	These are Schedule IV substances due to potential for abuse. Tolerance or physiological dependence may develop. Do not combine with caffeine. Dose is tapered for discontinuation—monitor for withdrawal symptoms and return of symptoms after medication is stopped.
Klonipin	clonazepam		
Librium	chlordiazepozide		
Paxipam	halazepam		
Serax*	oxazezepam		
Traxene	clorazepate		
Valium	diazepam		
Xanax*	alprazolam		
Other			
BuSpar	buspirone	Drowsiness, stomach upset, headache	Also used with premenstrual symptoms.

Note: Shading indicates effects apply to all of the medications in the category or subcategory.

*Short-acting

Medications Commonly Used in the Treatment of ADD/ADHD

Brand Name	Generic Name	Common Side Effects	Serious Effects/ Other Information
Stimulants			
Adderall	amphetamine/ dextroamphetamine	Stomach upset, loss of appetite, insomnia, nervousness, dizziness, headaches	These are Schedule II controlled substances because they have a high potential for abuse and drug dependence. Do not combine with MAOIs. Monitor for rash, racing heartbeat, tics, decreased rate of growth (in children). Should not be taken if there are heart conditions, including structural abnormalities. Symptoms that should be reported to the physician immediately include: Chest pain or fainting; high blood pressure; suicidal thoughts or behavior, abnormal thoughts or hallucinations, hostility or aggression, and blurred vision.
Dexedrine	dextroamphetamine		
Focalin	dexmethiphenidate		
Ritalin; Concerta; Methadate; Methylin	methylphenidate		
Cylert	pemoline		Cylert is a Schedule IV substance (less potential for abuse). Monitor for liver irritation or toxicity.
Daytrana	methylphenidate transdermal system		Patch is worn on the hip for up to 9 hours; medication effects continue up to 3 hours after removal. Should be used only as an alternative treatment for children ages 6–12.
Other Medications Used for ADHD			
Catapres	clonidine	Sedation, dizziness, constipation, drowsiness, dry mouth	Blood pressure medication. Need to monitor blood pressure and salt levels. Do not discontinue suddenly.
Strattera	atomozetine	Drowsiness, upset stomach, dry mouth, insomnia, sexual dysfunction	Nonstimulant alternative; may take 4 weeks for therapeutic effects. Do not combine with MAOIs. Monitor for jaundice or other signs of liver damage.

Note: Shading indicates effects apply to all of the medications in the category or subcategory.

Medications Commonly Used in the Treatment of Psychotic Symptoms

Brand Name	Generic Name	Common Side Effects	Serious Effects/Other Information
Conventional Antipsychotics			
Haldol	haloperidol	Headache, insomnia, stomach upset, rapid heart rate, weight gain, low blood pressure, dizziness, sedation, drowsiness, weakness, dry mouth, sore throat, constipation, diarrhea, agitation, difficulty concentrating, difficulty urinating, blurry vision, atypical motor movement	Avoid coffee, tea, alcohol, or caffeinated beverages. Avoid overheating. Monitor cardiac functioning.
Mellaril	thioridazine		
Moban	molindone		
Navane	thiothixene		
Serentil	mesoridazine		
Thorazine	chlorpromazine		Used also in manic phase of bipolar disorder.
Taractan	chlorprothixene		Antipsychotic also used for acute mania. Structurally related to chlorpromazine, but with lower potency.
Atypical Antipsychotics			
Abilfy	aripiprazole	Headache, insomnia, stomach upset, rapid heart rate, weight gain, dizziness, sedation, drowsiness, weakness, dry mouth, sore throat, dizziness, jerky movements, fatigue, hyperactivity, constipation, diarrhea, sedation, agitation, weight gain, headache, upset stomach, low blood pressure, difficulty concentrating	
Clozaril	clozapine		Risk of blood disorder (agranulocytosis), requires regular blood tests. Monitor for seizures and cardiovascular and respiratory effects.
Geodon	ziprazidone		Antipsychotic also used for acute mania. Can cause potentially fatal heartbeat irregularities, routine ECGs recommended.
Risperdal	risperidone		Antipsychotic also used for acute mania. Liver and kidney function may be monitored.
Seroquel	quetiapine		Antipsychotic also used for acute mania. Liver functioning may be monitored.

(*continued*)

Note: Shading indicates effects apply to all of the medications in the category or subcategory.

Brand Name	Generic Name	Common Side Effects	Serious Effects/ Other Information
Symbyax	fluoxetine and olanzapine	Headache, insomnia, stomach upset, rapid heart rate, weight gain, dizziness, sedation, drowsiness, weakness, dry mouth, sore throat, dizziness, jerky movements, fatigue, hyperactivity, constipation, diarrhea, sedation, agitation, weight gain, headache, upset stomach, low blood pressure, difficulty concentrating	A combination antidepressant and antipsychotic medication.
Zypreza	olanzapine		Antipsychotic also used for acute mania. Risk of very low blood pressure.

Note: Many medications should not be combined with alcohol. It is important to review any such restrictions with the pharmacist or health care provider.

Note: Combining two or more medications that increase serotonin levels such as some antidepressants, amphetamines, or the Tripan medications used to treat migraine headaches can cause a life-threatening reaction (Serotonin Syndrome) with symptoms that may include mental status changes, instability of the autonomic, gastrointestinal, and neuromuscular systems.

Note: It is recommended that those taking antipsychotics be routinely monitored for weight gain, hyperglycemia, diabetes, signs of tardive dyskinesia, and extrapyramidal side effects (American Psychiatric Association, 2004); it may require 2–4 weeks for an initial medication response and up to 6 months for a full response. Cholesterol monitoring is also recommended with some antipsychotics. Neuroleptic Malignant Syndrome—a rare, life-threatening side effect affecting the central nervous system—sometimes occurs with antipsychotic medications. Spasms of the larnyx also require immediate medical attention. Antipsychotics are not approved for use in elderly patients with dementia and have been linked to higher rates of mortality when used in this group.

Sources: www.nimh.nih.gov/publicat/medicate.cfm; www.rxlist.com/cgi/generic; www.webmd.com; http://www.fda.gov/cder/drug/InfoSheets; www.nlm.nih.gov/medlineplus/print/druginfo/medmaster.html; American Psychiatric Association, 1998; 2000; 2004.

REFERENCES

Ablon, J. S., & Jones, E. E. (1999). Psychotherapy process in the National Institute of Mental Health Treatment of Depression Collaborative Research Program. *Journal of Consulting and Clinical Psychology, 67,* 64–75.

Abramowitz, J. S. (1997). Effectiveness of psychological and pharmacological treatments for obsessive-compulsive disorder. *Journal of Clinical and Consulting Psychology, 65,* 44–52.

Ackerman, S. J., Benjamin, L. S., Beutler, L. E., Gelso, C. J., Goldfried, M. R., Hill, C., et al. (2001). Empirically supported therapy relationships: Conclusions and recommendations of the division 29 task force. *Psychotherapy, 38,* 495–497.

Addis, M., & Krasnow, A. (2000). A national survey of practicing psychologists' attitudes toward psychotherapy treatment manuals. *Journal of Consulting and Clinical Psychology, 68,* 331–339.

Adler, A. (1964). *Social interest: A challenge to mankind.* New York: Capricorn Books. (Original work published in 1929).

Ahn, H., & Wampold, B. E. (2001). Where oh where are the specific ingredients? A meta-analysis of component studies in counseling and psychotherapy. *Journal of Counseling Psychology, 48,* 251–257.

Ailinger, R. L., & Dear, M. R. (1997). Latino immigrants' explanatory models of tuberculosis infection. *Qualitative Health Research, 7,* 521–529.

Allen, D. M., Wahid, Z., Khan, H., Bienenfeld, D., Gillig, P. M., Kramer, S. I., et al. (2006). Clinical exchange: Integrating psychotherapy and psychopharmacology—The case of the certified nursing assistant. *Journal of Psychotherapy Integration, 16,* 263–312.

American Association of Suicidology. (2004). U.S.A. Suicide: 2004 Official final data. Retrieved 10/14/2006 from http://www.suicidology.org/displaycommon.cfm?an=1&subarticlenb.

American Counseling Association. (1997). *ACA Code of Ethics.* Alexandria, VA: Author.

American Counseling Association. (2005). *ACA Code of Ethics.* Alexandria, VA: Author.

American Psychiatric Association. (1998). Practice guidelines for the treatment of patients with panic disorder. *American Journal of Psychiatry, 155,* 1–34.

American Psychiatric Association. (2000a). *Diagnostic and statistical manual of mental disorders* (4th ed., text rev.). Washington, DC: Author.

American Psychiatric Association. (2000b). Practice guidelines for the treatment of patients with eating disorders. *American Journal of Psychiatry, 157,* 1–39.

American Psychiatric Association. (2000c). Practice guidelines for the treatment of patients with major depressive disorder (revision). *American Journal of Psychiatry, 157,* 1–45.

American Psychiatric Association. (2001). Practice guidelines for the treatment of patients with borderline personality disorder. *American Journal of Psychiatry, 158,* 2–53.

American Psychiatric Association. (2002). Practice guidelines for the treatment of patients with bipolar disorder. *American Journal of Psychiatry, 159,* 1–47.

American Psychiatric Association. (2003a). Assessment of patients with suicidal behavior. *American Journal of Psychiatry, 160,* 7–27.

American Psychiatric Association (2003b). Practice guidelines for the assessment and treatment of patients with suicidal behaviors. *American Journal of Psychiatry, 160,* 1–50.

American Psychiatric Association. (2004). Treatment recommendations for patients with schizophrenia. *American Journal of Psychiatry, 161,* 3–54.

American Psychological Association. (1993). Guidelines for providers of psychological services to ethnic, linguistic, and culturally diverse populations. *American Psychologist, 48,* 45–48.

American Psychological Association (APA) Committee on Legal Issues. (1996). Strategies for private practitioners coping with subpoenas or compelled testimony for client records or test data. *Professional Psychology: Research and Practice, 27*, 245–251.

American Psychological Association. (2002). Ethical principles of psychologists and code of ethics. Retrieved 12/14/2005 from http://www.apa.org/ethics/code2002.html#principle_e.

American Psychological Association. (2003a). *Code of Ethics*. Washington, DC: Author.

American Psychological Association. (2003b). Guidelines on multicultural education, training, research, practice, and organizational change for psychologists. *American Psychologist, 58*, 377–402.

American Psychological Association. (2003c). *Guidelines on psychological practice with older adults*. Washington, DC: Author.

American Psychological Association (APA) Committee on Professional Practice and Standards. (2003d). Legal issues in the professional practice of psychology. *Professional Psychology: Research and Practice, 34*, 595–600.

American Psychologist. (1989). Aaron T. Beck, Recipient of the APA Scientific Contributions Awards. *American Psychologist, 44*, 630.

Anderson, C. E. (2000). Dealing constructively with managed care: Suggestions from an insider. *Journal of Mental Health Counseling, 22*, 343–353.

Anderson, C. M. (2003). Cassandra notes on the state of the family research and practice union. *Family process, 42*, 323–327.

Antonuccio, D., Burns, D. D., & Danton, W. G. (2002). Antidepressants: A triumph of marketing over science? *Prevention & Treatment, 5*, Article 25. Retrieved 8/21/2004 from http://www.journals.apa.org/prevention/volume5/pre0050025c.html.

APA Division 44/Committee on Lesbian, Gay, and Bisexual Concerns. (2000). Guidelines for psychotherapy with lesbian, gay, and bisexual clients. *American Psychologist, 55*, 1440–1451.

APA Presidential Task Force on Evidence-Based Practice. (2006). Evidence-based practice in psychology. *American Psychologist, 61*, 271–285.

APA Working Group on the Older Adult Brochure. (1998). *What practitioners should know about working with older adults*. Washington, DC: American Psychological Association.

APA Working Group on Psychoactive Medications for Children and Adolescents. (2006). *Report of the working group on psychoactive medications for children and adolescents*. Washington, DC: American Psychological Association.

Archer, R., Forbes, Y., Metcalfe, C., & Winter, D. (2000). *British Journal of Medical Psychology, 73*, 401–406.

Arnold, M. S. (1993). Ethnicity and training marital and family therapists. *Counselor Education and Supervision, 33*, 139–147.

Asay, T. P., & Lambert, M. J. (2002). Therapist relational variables. In D. J. Cain & J. Seeman (Eds.), *Humanistic psychotherapies: Handbook of research and practice* (pp. 531–557). Washington, DC: American Psychological Association.

Associated Press. (1998, August 14). Psychiatrist is sued over multiple bad personalities. *Seattle Post-Intelligencer*, A12.

Atkinson, D. R., & Hackett, G. (1998). *Counseling diverse populations* (2nd ed.). Boston: McGraw-Hill.

Atkinson, D. R., Thompson, C. E., & Grant, S. K. (1993). A three-dimensional model for counseling racial/ethnic minorities. *The Counseling Psychologist, 21*, 257–277.

Babits, M. (2001). Using therapeutic metaphor to provide a holding environment: The inner edge of possibility. *Clinical Social Work Journal, 29*, 21–33.

Baca, E., Garcia-Garcia, M., & Porras-Chavarino, A. (2004). Gender differences in treatment response to sertraline versus imipramine in patients with nonmelancholic depressive disorders. *Progress in Neuropsychological and Biological Psychiatry, 28*, 57–65.

Baer, J. S., & Peterson, P. L. (2002). Motivational interviewing with adolescents and young adults. In William R. Stephen Rollnick (Ed.), *Motivational interviewing* (2nd ed., pp. 320–332). New York: Guilford Press.

Baldor, L. C. (2006, Nov 16). Pentagon alters homosexuality guidelines. Yahoo News, http://news.yahoo.com/s/ap/20061116/apongocasstpe/military_gays.

Ballenger, J. C., Davidson, J. R., Lecrubier, Y., & Nutt, D. J. (2001). Consensus statement on transcultural issues in depression and anxiety from the international consensus group on depression and anxiety. *The Journal of Clinical Psychiatry, 62,* 47–58.

Bandura, A. (1982). Self-efficacy mechanism in human agency. *The American Psychologist, 37,* 122–147.

Bandura, A. (1997). *Self-efficacy: the exercise of self-control.* New York: Freeman.

Bandura, A., & Rosenthal, T. L. (1966). Vicarious classical conditioning as a function of arousal level. *Journal of Personality and Social Psychology, 3,* 54–62.

Barber, J., Muenz, P., & Larry, R. (1996). The role of avoidance and obsessiveness in matching patients for cognitive and interpersonal psychotherapy: Empirical findings from the Treatment for Depression Collaborative Research Program. *Journal of Consulting and Clinical Psychology, 64,* 951–958.

Barber, J. P., Crits-Christoph, P., & Luborsky, L. (1997). A guide to the CCRT standard categories and their classification. In L. Luborsky & P. Crits-Christoph (Eds.), *Understanding transference: The core conflictual relationship theme method* (2nd ed., pp. 43–54). Washington, DC: American Psychological Association.

Barkham, M., & Hardy, G. E. (2001). Counselling and interpersonal therapies for depression: Toward securing an evidence-base. *British Medical Bulletin, 57,* 115–132.

Barlow, D. H. (2004). Psychological treatments. *American Psychologist, 59,* 869–878.

Barrett, M. S., & Berman, J. S. (2001). Is psychotherapy more effective when therapists disclose information about themselves? *Journal of Consulting and Clinical Psychology, 69,* 597–603.

Barsky, A. J., Saintfort, R., Rogers, M. P., & Borus, J. F. (2002). Nonspecific medication side effects and the nocebo phenomenon. *Journal of the American Medical Association, 287,* 622–627.

Bartels, S. J. (2003). Evidence-based geriatric psychiatry for the general psychiatrist. *Psychiatric Times, 20,* Retrieved 2/13/2007 from http://www.psychiatrictimes.com/p031159.html

Baruth, L. G., & Manning, M. L. (2003). *Multicultural counseling and psychotherapy: A lifespan perspective.* Columbus, Ohio: Merrill Prentice Hall.

Bassman, R. (2000). Agents, not objects: Our fights to be. *Psychotherapy in Practice, 56,* 1395–1411.

Baucom, D. H., Shoham, V., Mueser, K. T., Daiuto, A. D., & Stickle, T. R. (1998). Empirically supported couple and family interventions for marital distress and adult mental health problems. *Journal of Consulting and Clinical Psychology, 66,* 53–88.

Bean, R. A., Perry, B. J., & Bedell, T. M. (2002). Developing culturally competent marriage and family therapists: Treatment guidelines for non-African-American therapists working with African-American families. *Journal of Marriage and Family Therapy, 28,* 153–165.

Beck, A. T. (1967). *Depression: Clinical, experimental, and theoretical aspects.* New York: Hoeber Medical Division, Harper & Row.

Beck, A. T. (1991). Cognitive therapy as the integrative therapy. *Journal of Psychotherapy Integration, 1,* 191–198.

Beck, A. T. (1993). Cognitive therapy: Past, present, and future. *Journal of Consulting and Clinical Psychology, 61,* 194–198.

Beck, A. T., & Freeman, A., & Associates. (1990). *Cognitive therapy of personality disorders.* New York: Guilford Press.

Beck, A. T., Freeman, A., & Davis, D. D., & Associates (2004). *Cognitive therapy of personality disorders* (2nd ed.). New York: Guilford Press.

Beck, A. T., & Greenberg, R. L. (1974). *Coping with depression.* New York: Institute for Rational Living.

Beck, A. T., Rush, A. J., Shaw, B. F., & Emery, G. (1979). *Cognitive therapy of depression.* New York: Guilford Press.

Becker, G. (2001). Effects of being uninsured on ethnic minorities' management of chronic illness. *Western Journal of Medicine, 175,* 19–23.

Behnke, S. (2004). Informed consent and APA's new ethics code: Enhancing client autonomy, improving client care. *Monitor on Psychology, 35,* 80–81.

Behnke, S. H., & Kinscherff, R. (2002). Must a psychologist report past abuse? *Monitor on Psychology, (May, 2002),* 56–57.

Belar, C. (2003, May). Training for evidence-based practice. *Monitor on Psychology, 57.*

Belar, C. D., Brown, R. A., Hersch, L. E., Hornyak, L. M., Rosensky, R. H., Sheridan, E. P., et. al. (2001). Self assessment in clinical health psychology: A model for ethical expansion of practice. *Professional Psychology: Research and Practice, 32,* 135–141.

Berg, I. K., & De Jong, P. (1996). Solution-building conversations: Co-constructing a sense of competence with clients. *Families in Society, 77,* 376–394.

Berlin, E., & Fowkes, W. (1983). A teaching framework for cross-cultural health care. *Western Journal of Medicine, 139,* 934–948.

Betancourt, J. R. (2003). Cross-cultural medical education: Conceptual approaches and Frameworks for evaluation. *Academic Medicine, 78,* 560–569.

Beutler, L. E. (2000a). Empirically based decision making in clinical practice. *Prevention & Treatment, Volume 3,* Article 27. Available on the World Wide Web: http:// journals.apa.org/ prevention/volume3/pre0030027a.html.

Beutler, L. E. (2000b). Empirically based decisions: A comment. *Prevention & Treatment, Volume 3,* Article 31. Available on the World Wide Web: http://journals.apa.org/prevention/volume3/pre0030031r.html.

Beutler, L. E. (2004). The empirically supported treatments movement: A scientist-practitioner's response. *Clinical Psychology: Science and Practice, 11,* 225–231.

Beutler, L. E., Kim, E. J., Davison, E., Karno, M., & Fisher, D. (1996). Research contributions to improving managed care health care outcomes. *Psychotherapy, 33,* 197–206.

Bhungalia, L. (2001). Native American women and violence. *National NOW Times, 33,* pp. 5, 13.

Bieling, P. J., & Kuyken, W. (2003). Is cognitive case formulation science or science fiction. *Clinical Psychology: Science and Practice, 10,* 52–69.

Bienvenu, C., & Ramsey, C. J. (2006). The culture of socioeconomic disadvantage: Practical approaches to counseling. In C. C. Lee (Ed.), *Multicultural issues in counseling* (3d ed., pp. 345–353). Alexandria, VA.: American Counseling Association.

Blazer, D. G., Hybels, C. F., Simonsick, E. M., & Hanlon, J. T. (2000). Marked differences in antidepressant use by race in an elderly community: 1986–1996. *American Journal of Psychiatry, 157,* 1089–1094.

Bledsoe, S. E., Weissman, M. M., Mullen, E. J., Ponniah, K., Gameroff, M. J., Verdell, H., Mufson, L., et al. Empirically supported psychotherapy in social work training programs: Does the definition of evidence matter? *Research on Social Work Practice, 17,* 449–455.

Bohart, A. C., O'Hara, M., & Leitner, L. M. (1998). Empirically violated treatments: Disenfranchisement of humanistic and other therapies. *Psychotherapy Research, 8,* 141–157.

Bohus, M., Haaf, B., Stiglmayr, C., Phol, U., Boehme, R., & Linehan, M. (2000). Evaluation of inpatient dialectical behavior therapy for borderline personality disorder: A prospective study. *Behavior Research and Therapy, 38,* 878–887.

Bombardier, C. H., & Rimmele, C. T. (1999). Motivational interviewing to prevent alcohol abuse after traumatic brain injury: A case series. *Rehabilitation Psychology, 44,* 52–67.

Bongar, B., Greaney, S., & Peruzzi, N. (1998). Risk management with the suicidal patient. In P. Kleepies (Ed.), *Emergencies in mental health practice: Evaluation and management* (pp. 199–216). New York: Guilford Press.

Book, H. E. (1998). *How to practice brief psychodynamic psychotherapy.* Washington, DC: American Psychological Association.

Bordin, E. (1979). The generalizability of the psychoanalytic concept of the working alliance. *Psychotherapy, 16,* 252–260.

Borum, R. (2000). Assessing violence risk among youth. *Journal of Clinical Psychology, 56,* 1263–1268.

Borum, R., Swartz, M., & Swanson, J. (1996). Assessing and managing violence risk in clinical practice. *Journal of Practical Psychiatry, and Behavioral Health, 2,* 205–215.

Bourgeois, L., Sabourin, S., & Wright, J. (1990). Predictive validity of therapeutic alliance in group marital therapy. *Journal of Consulting and Clinical Psychology, 58,* 608–613.

Bowlby, J. (1969). *Attachment.* New York: Basic Books.

Bradley, C., & Fiorini, J. (1999). Evaluation of counseling practicum: National study of programs accredited by CACREP. *Counselor Education and Supervision, 39,* 110–119.

Brauer, R. B., Stangl, M., Siewart, J.R., Pfab, R.,

& Becker, K. (2003). Acute liver failure after administration of the herbal tranquilizer Kava-Kava (piper methysticum). *Journal of Clinical Psychiatry, 64*, 216–218.

Brems, C. (2000). *Dealing with challenges in psychotherapy and counseling.* Pacific Grove, CA: Brooks/Cole.

Brodley, B. T. (1991). Instructions for beginning to practice client-centered therapy. http://world.std.com/~mbr2/cct.beginning.practice.html.

Brodley, B. T. (2006). Client-initiated homework in client-centered therapy. *Journal of Psychotherapy Integration, 16*, 140–161.

Brody, A. L., Saxena, S., Stoessel, P., Gillies, L. A., Fairbanks, L. A., Alborzian, S., et al.(2001). Regional brain metabolic changes in patients with major depression treated with either paroxetine or interpersonal therapy: Preliminary findings. *Archives of General Psychiatry, 58*, 631–640.

Brott, P. E. (2001). The storied approach: A postmodern perspective for career counseling. *The Career Development Quarterly, 49*, 304–313.

Brown, D. (1997). Reply to Sue: Looking for common ground and moving forward. *ACES Spectrum, 57*, 9–10.

Brown, G. S., Jones, E. R., Betts, E., & Wu, J. (2003). Improving suicide risk assessment in a managed-care environment. *Crisis: The Journal of Crisis Intervention and suicide prevention, 24*, 49–55.

Brown, L. M., Bongar, B., & Cleary, K. M. (2004). A profile of psychologists' views of critical risk factors for completed suicide in older adults. *Professional Psychology: Research and Practice, 35*, 90–96.

Brown, M. E. (2000). Diagnosis and treatment of children and adolescents with attention-deficit/hyperactivity disorder. *Journal of Counseling and Development, 78*, 195–200.

Brown, P. D., & O'Leary, K. D. (2000). Therapeutic alliance: Predicting continuance and success in group treatment for spouse abuse. *Journal of Consulting and Clinical Psychology, 68*, 340–345.

Brown, R. T., & LaRosa, A. (2002). Recent developments in the pharmacotherapy of attention deficit/hyperactivity disorder. *Professional Psychology: Research and Practice, 33*, 591–595.

Brown, R. T., & Sammons, M. T. (2002). Pediatric psychopharmacology: A review of new developments and research. *Professional Psychology: Research and Practice, 33*, 135–147.

Brown, W. A. (2002). Are antidepressants as ineffective as they look? *Prevention & Treatment, 5*, Article 26. Retrieved 11/12/2004 from the World Wide Web http://www.journals.apa.org/prevention/volume5/pre0050026c.html.

Bryant, R. A., & Harvey, A. G. (2000). *Acute stress disorder: A handbook of theory, assessment, and treatment.* Washington, DC: American Psychological Association.

Bucci, W. (2002). The challenge of diversity in modern psychoanalysis. *Psychoanalytic Psychology, 19*, 216–226.

Buckman, D. F. (1998). The see-through syndrome. *Inside MS, 16*, 19.

Buelow, G., Herbert, S., & Buelow, S. (2000). *Psychotherapists resource on psychiatric medications: Issues of treatment and referral* (2nd. ed.). Belmont, CA.: Brooks/Cole.

Burgio, L. D., Cotter, E. M., Stevens, A. B., Hardin, J. M., Sinott, J., & Hohman, M. J. (1995). Wilder's acceptability ratings of behavioral treatments and pharmacotherapy for the management of geriatric behavioral disturbances. *The Gerontologist, 20*, 91–93.

Burkard, A. W., & Knox, S. (2004). Effect of therapist color-blindness on empathy and attributions in cross-cultural counseling. *Journal of Counseling Psychology, 51*, 387–397.

Burkard, A. W., Knox, S., Groen, M., Perez, M., & Hess, S. A. (2006). European American therapist self-disclosure in cross-cultural counseling. *Journal of Counseling Psychology, 53*, 15–25.

Burns, D. D. (1999). *The feeling good handbook.* New York: Plume.

Burns, D. D., & Auerbach, A. (1996). Therapeutic empathy in cognitive-behavioral therapy: Does it really make a difference? In P. Salkovskis (Ed.) *Frontiers of cognitive therapy* (pp. 135–164). New York: Guilford Press.

Burns, M. J. (2000). The pharmacology and toxicology of reboxetine. *International Journal of Medical Toxicology, 3*, 26–32.

Burrows-Horton, C., Cruise, T. K., Graybill, D., & Corrett, J. Y. (1999). For children's sake: Training students in the treatment of child witnesses of domestic violence. *Professional Psychology: Research and Practice, 30,* 88–91.

Cain, D. J. (2002a). Defining characteristics, history, and evolution of humanistic psychotherapies. In D. J. Cain & J. Seeman (Eds.), *Humanistic psychotherapies: Handbook of research and practice* (pp. 3–54). Washington, DC: American Psychological Association.

Cain, D. J. (2002b). A time for reflection. *Journal of Humanistic Psychology, 42,* 7–15.

Cain, D. J., & Seeman, J. (2002). *Humanistic psychotherapies: Handbook of research and practice.* Washington, DC: American Psychological Association.

Canapary, D., Bongar, B., & Cleary K. M. (2002). Assessing risk for completed suicide in patients with alcohol dependence. *Professional Psychology: Research and Practice, 33,* 464–469.

Cardemil, E. V., Reivich, K. J., & Seligman, M. E. P. (2002). The prevention of depressive symptoms in low-income minority middle school students. *Prevention and Treatment,* Retrieved 1/15/2007 from http://www.journals.apa.org/prevention/volume5/pre0050008a.html.

Carlson, J. M., & Carlson, J. D. (2000). The application of Adlerian psychotherapy with Asian American clients. *Journal of Individual Psychology, 56,* 214–225.

Caroff, S. N., Mann, S. C., & Campbell, E. C. (2001). Neuroleptic malignant syndrome. *Adverse Drug Reaction Bulletin, August 2001, 209,* 799–802.

Cashwell, C. S., Shcherbakova, J., & Cashwell, T. H. (2003). Effect of client and counselor ethnicity on preference for counselor disclosure. *Journal of Counseling and Development, 81,* 196–201.

Cassidy, K-L. (2004). The adult learner rediscovered: Psychiatry residents' push for cognitive-behavioral therapy training and a learner-driven model of educational change. *Academic Psychiatry, 28,* 215–220.

Castonguay, L. G., Goldfried, M. R., Wiser, S., Raue, P. J., & Hayes, A. M. (1996). Predicting the effect of cognitive therapy for depression: A study of unique and common factors. *Journal of Consulting and Clinical Psychology, 64,* 497–504.

Castonguay, L. G., Schut, A. J., Aikins, D. E., Constantino, M. J., Laurenceau, J-P., Bologh, L., et al. (2004). Integrative cognitive therapy for depression: A preliminary investigation. *Journal of Psychotherapy Integration, 14,* 4–20.

Cepeda, L. M., & Davenport, D. S. (2006). Person-centered therapy and solution-focused brief therapy: An integration of present and future awareness. *Psychotherapy: Theory, Research, Practice, Training, 43,* 1–12.

Chambless, D. L., Baker, M. J., Baucom, D. H., Beutler, L. E., Calhoun, K. S., Crits-Christoph, P., et al. (1998). Update on empirically validated therapies, II. *The Clinical Psychologist, 51,* 3–16.

Chambless, D. L., & Ollendick, T. H. (2001). Empirically supported psychological interventions: Controversies and evidence. *Annual Review of Psychology, 52,* 685–716.

Chambliss, C. H. (2000). *Psychotherapy and managed care: Reconciling research and reality.* Boston: Allyn & Bacon.

Chang, Y. (1998, Jun 22). Asian identity crisis. *Newsweek,* p. 68.

Chavez, L. R., McMullen, J. M., Mishra, I. M., & Hubbell, F. A. (2001). Beliefs matter: Cultural beliefs and the use of cervical cancer screening tests. *American Anthropologist, 103,* 1114–1129.

Chen, M. S., Jr., and Hawks, B. L. (1995). A debunking of the myth of healthy Asian Americans and Pacific Islanders. *American Journal of Health Promotion 9:* 261–268.

Chen, M-W., Froehle, T., & Morran, K. (1997). Deconstructing dispositional bias in clinical inference: Two interventions. *Journal of Counseling and Development, 76,* 74–81.

Chen, S. W-H., & Davenport, D. S. (2005). Cognitive-behavioral therapy with Chinese clients: Cautions and modifications. *Psychotherapy: Theory, Research, Practice, Training, 42,* 101–110.

Choi, K., & Wynne, M. A. (2000). Providing services to Asian Americans with developmental disabilities and their families: Mainstream service providers' perspective. *Community Mental Health Journal, 36,* 589–595.

Chung, R. C-Y., & Bernak, F. (2002). The relationship of culture and empathy in cross-cultural counseling. *Journal of Counseling and Development, 80,* 154–159.

Chwalisz, K. (2001). A common factors revolution: Let's not "cut off our discipline's nose to spite its face." *Journal of Counseling Psychology, 48,* 262–267.

Chwalisz, K. (2003). Evidence-based practice: A framework for twenty-first-century scientist-practitioner training. *The Counseling Psychologist, 31,* 497–528.

Clayton, A. H., Pradko, J. F., & Croft, H. A. (2002). Prevalence of sexual dysfunction among newer antidepressant. *Journal of Clinical Psychiatry, 63,* 357–366.

Cobia, D. C., & Boes, S. R. (2000). Professional disclosure statements and formal plans for supervision: Two strategies for minimizing the risk of ethical conflict's in post-mater's supervision. *Journal of Counseling and Development, 78,* 293–296.

Cohen, J. A. (2003). Managed care and the evolving role of the clinical social worker in mental health. *Social Work, 48,* 34–43.

Conners, G. J., Carroll, K. M., DiClemente, C. C., Longabaugh, R., & Donovan, D. M. (1997). The therapeutic alliance and its relationship to alcoholism treatment participation and outcome. *Journal of Consulting and Clinical Psychology, 65,* 588–598.

Constantine, M. G. (2001). Multicultural training, theoretical orientation, empathy, and multicultural case conceptualization ability in counselors. *Journal of Mental Health Counseling, 23,* 357–372.

Consumer Reports. (2004). Drug therapy vs talk therapy. *Consumer Reports,* pp. 22–29.

Coombs, M. M., Coleman, D., & Jones, E. E. (2002). Working with feelings: The importance of emotion in both cognitive-behavioral and interpersonal therapy in the NIMH Treatment of Depression Collaborative Research Program. *Psychotherapy: Theory/Research/Practice/Training, 39,* 233–244.

Cooper, L. A., Roter, D. L., Johnson, R. L., Ford, D. E., Steinwachs, D. M., & Powe, N. R. (2003). Patient-centered communication, ratings of care, and concordance of patient and physician race. *Annals of Internal Medicine, 139,* 907–916.

Coppens, N. M., Silka, L., Khakeo, R., & Benfey, J. (2000). Southeast Asians' understanding of environmental health issues. *Journal of Multicultural Nursing & Health, 6,* 31–38.

Corcoran, J. (1999). Solution-focused interviewing with child protective services. *Child Welfare, 78,* 461–479.

Corcoran, J., & Stephenson, M. (2000). The effectiveness of solution-focused therapy with child behavior problems: A preliminary report. *Families in Society, 81,* 468–474.

Cornelius-White, J. H. D. (2002). The phoenix of empirically supported therapy relationships: The overlooked person-centered basis. *Psychotherapy: Theory, Research, Practice, Training, 39,* 219–222.

Coursey, R. D., Keller, A. B., & Farrell, E. W. (1995). Individual psychotherapy and persons with severe mental illness: The clients' perspective. *Schizophrenia Bulletin, 21,* 283–299.

Crane, D. R., Wampler, K. S., Sprenkle, D. H., Sandberg, J. G., & Hovestadt, A. J. (2002). The scientist-practitioner model in marriage and family therapy doctoral programs: Current status. *Journal of Marital and Family Therapy, 28,* 78–83.

Creed, T. A., & Kendall, P. C. (2005). Therapist alliance-building behavior within a cognitive-behavioral treatment for anxiety in youth. *Journal of Consulting and Clinical Psychology, 73,* 498–505.

Crits-Christoph, P., & Connolly, M. B. (1998). Empirical basis of supportive-expressive psychodynamic psychotherapy. In R. F. Bornstein & J. M. Masling (Eds.), *Empirical studies of the therapeutic hour* (pp. 109–151). Washington, DC: American Psychological Association.

Crits-Christoph, P., Cooper, A., & Luborsky, L. (1988). The accuracy of therapists' interpretations and the outcome of dynamic psychotherapy. *Journal of Consulting and Clinical Psychology, 56,* 490–495.

Crits-Christoph, P., Frank, E., Chambless, D. L., Brody, C., & Karp, J. F. (1995). Training in empirically validated treatments: What are clinical psychology students learning? *Professional Psychology: Research and Practice, 26,* 514–522.

Cummings, N. A., Busman, S. H., & Thomas, J. L.

(1998). Efficient therapy as a viable response to scarce resources and rationing of treatment. *Professional Psychology: Research and Practice, 29,* 460–469.

Curtis, R., Field, C., Knann-Kostman, I., & Mannix, K. (2004). What 75 psychoanalysts found helpful and hurtful in their own analyses. *Psychoanalytic Psychology, 21,* 183–202.

Dahir, V. B., Richardson, J. T., Ginsburg, G. P., Gatowski, S. I., Dobbin, S. A., & Merlino, M. L. (2005). Judicial application of *Daubert* to psychological syndrome and profile evidence: A research note. *Psychology, Public Policy, and Law, 11,* 62–82.

Dahlsgaard, K. K., Beck, A. T., & Brown, G. K. (1998). Inadequate response to therapy as a predictor of suicide. *Suicide and Life-Threatening Behavior, 28,* 197–204.

Dai, Y., Zhang, S., Yamamoto, J., Ao, M., Belin, T. R., Cheung, F., et al. (1999). Cognitive behavioral therapy of minor depressive symptoms in elderly Chinese Americans: A pilot study. *Community Mental Health Journal, 35,* 537–542.

D'Andrea, M. (2000). Postmodernism, contructivism, and multiculturalism: Three forces shaping and expanding our thoughts about counseling. *Journal of Mental Health Counseling, 22,* 1–16.

Dankoski, M. E., & Deacon, S. A. (2000). Using a feminist lens in contextual therapy. *Family Process, 39,* 51–66.

Danzinger, P. R., & Welfel, E. R. (2000). Age, gender and health bias in counselors: An empirical analysis. *Journal of Mental Health Counseling, 22,* 135–149.

Danzinger, P. R., & Welfel, E. R. (2001). The impact of managed care on mental health counselors: A survey of perceptions, practices, and compliance with ethical standards. *Journal of Mental Health Counseling, 23,* 137–150.

Das, A. K. (1995). Rethinking multicultural counseling: Implications for counselor education. *Journal of Counseling and Development, 74,* 45–52.

Dattilio, F. M. (2002). The use of kava and cognitive-behavioral therapy in the treatment of panic disorder. *Cognitive and Behavioral Practice, 9,* 83–88.

Daubert v. Merrell Dow Pharmaceuticals, 509 U.S. 579 (1993).

D'Augelli, A. R., Grossman, A. H., Salter, N. P., Vasey, J. J., Starks, M. T., & Sinclair, K. O. (2005). Predicting the suicide attempts of lesbian, gay, and bisexual youth. *Suicide and Life-Threatening behavior, 35,* 646–660.

Davis, J. T. (2002). Countertransference temptation and the use of self-disclosure by psychotherapists in training: A discussion for beginning psychotherapists and their supervisors. *Psychoanalytic Psychology, 19,* 435–454.

Davis, L. E., & Gelsomino. (1994). As assessment of practitioner cross-racial treatment experiences. *Social Work, 39,* 116–123.

Daw, J. (2002). New Mexico becomes the first state to gain RX privileges. *Monitor on Psychology,* 24–25.

De Jong, P., & Berg, I. K. (2001). Co-constructing cooperation with mandated clients. *Social Work, 46,* 361–374.

De Shazer, S. (1988). *Clues: Investigating solutions in brief therapy.* New York: Norton.

De Shazer, S., Berg, I. K., Lipchick, E., Nunnally, E., Molnar, A., Gingerich, W., & Weiner-Davis, M. (1986). Brief therapy: Focused solution development. *Family Process, 25,* 207–221.

DeAngelis, T. (2005). Shaping evidence-based practice. *Monitor on Psychology, 36,* 26–31.

Deegear, J., & Lawson, D. M. (2003). The utility of empirically supported treatments. *Professional Psychology: Research and Practice, 34,* 271–277.

DelBello, M. O., Soutullo, C. A., & Strakowski, S. M. (2000). Racial differences in the treatment of adolescents with bipolar disorder. *American Journal of Psychiatry, 157,* 837–838.

DeLeon, P. H. (2000). Beyond the 21st century. *APA Monitor, 31,* 5.

Dermer, S. B., Hemesath, C. W., & Russell, C. S. (1998). A feminist critique of solution-focused therapy. *American Journal of Family Therapy, 26,* 239–250.

DeVoe, D. (1998). Feminist and nonsexist counseling: Implications for the male counselor. In D. R. Atkinson & G. Hackett (Eds.), *Counseling diverse populations* (2nd ed., pp. 283–291). Boston: McGraw-Hill.

Deyhle, D., & Swisher, K. (1999). Research in American Indian and Alaska Native education: From assimilation to self-determination. *Review of Research in Education, 22,* 113–194.

Diamond, R. J. (2002). *Instant psychopharmacology: A guide for the non-medical mental health professional* (2nd ed.) New York: Norton.

Dillon, F. R., Worthington, R. L., Savoy, H. B., Rooney, S. C., Becker-Schutte, A., & Guerra, R. M. (2004). On becoming allies: A qualitative study of lesbian-, gay-, and bisexual-affirmative counselor training. *Counselor Education and Supervision, 43,* 162–178.

Dimidjian, S., Hollon, S. D., Dobson, K. S., Schmaling, K. B., Kohlenberg, R. J., Addis, M. E., et al. (2006). Randomized trial of behavioral activation, cognitive therapy, and antidepressant medication in the acute treatment of adults with major depression. *Journal of Consulting and Clinical Psychology, 74,* 658–670.

Dowdy, K. G. (2000). The culturally sensitive medical interview. *JAAPA, 13,* 91–104.

Duncan, B. L., & Miller, S. D. (2000). *The heroic client: Doing client-directed, outcome-informed therapy.* San Francisco: Jossey-Bass.

Dunn, E. C., Neighbors, C., & Larimer, M. E. (2006). Motivational enhancement therapy and self-help treatment for binge eaters. *Psychology of Addictive Behaviors, 20,* 44–52.

Dyche, L., & Zayas, L. H. (2001). Cross-cultural empathy and training the contemporary psychotherapist. *Clinical Social Work Journal, 29,* 245–258.

Edmond, T., Megivern, D., Williams, C., Rochman, E., & Howard, M. (2006). Integrating evidence-based practice and social work field education. *Journal of Social Work Education, 42,* 377–396.

Eells, T. D., Lombart, K. G., Kendjelic, E. M., Turner, L. C., & Lucas, C. P. (2005). The quality of psychotherapy case formulations: A comparison of expert, experienced, and novice cognitive-behavioral and psychodynamic therapists. *Journal of Consulting and Clinical Psychology, 73,* 579–589.

Egan, M. P., Rivera, S. G., Robillard, R. R., & Hanson, A. (1997) The "no suicide contract"; Helpful or harmful? *Journal of Psychosocial Nursing, 35,* 31–33.

Eisenberg, D. M., Davis, R. B., Ettner, S. L., Appel, S., Willey, S. VanRompay, M., et al. (1998). Trends in alternative medicine use in the United States 1990–1997. *New England Journal of Medicine, 328,* 246–252.

Eisendrath, S. J., Lichtmacher, J. E., Haller, E., Fleming, A. M., Fritch, M., Weiss, D. S., et al. (2003). Training psychiatry residents in evidence-based treatments for major depression / reply. *Psychotherapy and Psychosomatics, 72,* 108–183.

Elkin, I. (1994). The NIMH treatment of depression collaborative research program: Where we began and where we are. In A. E. Bergin & S. L. Garfield (Eds). *Handbook of psychotherapy and behavior change* (4th ed.). New York: Wiley.

Elkin, I., Shea, T., Watkins, J. T., Imber, D. D., Sotsky, S. M., & Collins, J. F. (1989). National Institute of Mental Health Treatment of Depression Collaborative Research Program: General effectiveness of treatments. *Archives of General Psychiatry, 46,* 971–982.

Elliott, R. (2002). The effectiveness of humanistic therapies. In D. J. Cain & J. Seeman (Eds.). *Humanistic psychotherapies: Handbook of research and practice* (pp. 57–81). Washington, DC: American Psychological Association.

Elliot, R., & Greenberg, L. S. (2002). Process-experiential psychotherapy. In D. J. Cain & J. Seeman (Eds.), *Humanistic psychotherapies: Handbook of research and practice* (pp. 279–306). Washington, DC: American Psychological Association.

Elliott, R., Shapiro, D. A., Firth-Cozens, J., Stiles, W. B., Hardy, G. E., Llewelyn, S. P., et al. (2001). Comprehensive process analysis of insight events in cognitive-behavioral and psychodynamic-interpersonal psychotherapies. In C. E. Hill (Ed.), *Helping skills: The empirical foundation* (pp. 309–333). Washington, DC: American Psychological Association.

Ellis, A. (1971). *Growth through reason.* Palo Alto, CA.: Science and Behavior Books.

Ellis, A. (1985). Cognition and affect in emotional disturbance. *American Psychologist, 40,* 471–472.

Ellis, A. (1993). Reflections on rational-emotive therapy. *Journal of Consulting and Clinical Psychology, 61,* 199–201.

Ellis, A. (1997). Must musturbation and demandingness lead to emotional disorders? *Psychotherapy: Theory, Research, Practice, Training, 34,* 95–98.

Ellis, A. (1999). Why rational-emotive therapy to rational emotive behavior therapy? *Psychotherapy, 36,* 154–159.

Ellis, A. (2000). A continuation of the dialogue on issues of counseling in the postmodern era. *Journal of Mental Health Counseling, 22,* 97–106.

Ellis, A. (2000). Can rational emotive behavior therapy (REBT) be effectively used with people who have devout beliefs in God and religion? *Professional Psychology: Research and Practice, 31,* 29–33.

Ellis, A., Rogers, C., & Perls, F. (1975). *Three approaches to psychotherapy.* Corona Del Mar, CA: Psychological Films.

Epp, L. R. (1998). The courage to be an existential counselor: An interview with Clemmont E. Vontress. *Journal of Mental Health Counseling, 20,* 1–12.

Erdur, O., Rude, S., Baron, A., Draper, M., & Shankar, L. (2000). Working alliance and treatment outcome in ethnically similar and dissimilar client-therapist pairings. *Research Reports of the Research Consortium of Counseling and Psychological Services in Higher Education, 1,* 1–20.

Eriksen, K., Artico, C., Schmitt, J., Quinn, M., Waters, S., & Wilson, P. (1997). Trends in counseling. *ACES Spectrum, 58,* 7–9.

Erickson, E. (1968). *Identity: Youth and crisis.* New York: Norton.

Erk, R. E. (2000). Five fundamentals for increasing understanding of effective treatment of attention-deficit/hyperactivity disorder predominantly inattentive type. *Journal of Counseling and Development, 78,* 389–399.

Ernst, E. (2002). The risk-benefit profile of commonly used herbal therapies: Ginkgo, St. John's wort, ginseng, echinacea, saw palmetto, and kava. *Annals of Internal Medicine, 136,* 42–53.

Everett, F., Proctor, N., & Cortmell, B. (1989). Providing psychological services to American Indian children and families. In D. R. Atkinson, G. Morten, & D. W. Sue (Eds.), *Counseling American minorities* (3rd ed., pp. 53–71). Dubuque, IA: W. C. Brown.

Falvey, J. E. (2001). Clinical judgment in case conceptualization and treatment planning across mental health disciplines. *Journal of Counseling and Development, 79,* 292–303.

FDA–U.S. Food and Drug Administration (2004).

Retrieved 8/21/2004 from the World Wide Web: http://www.fda.gov/cder/drug/anti depressants/AntidepressantsPHA.htm.

Fenichel, M. (2000). The historic dialogue between Beck and Ellis. Retrieved 12/10/2006 from http://www.fenichel.com/Beck-Ellis.shtml.

Fenton, W., James, R., & Insel, T. (2004). Psychiatric residency training, the physician-scientist, and the future of psychiatry. *Academic Journal of Psychiatry, 28,* 263–266.

Fiferman, L. A. (1989). *Native American and Anglo ratings of acceptability of four treatments for depression.* Unpublished doctoral dissertation, University of South Dakota.

Fisher, P. L., & Durham, R. C. (1999). Recovery rates in generalized anxiety disorder following psychological therapy: An analysis of clinically significant change in the STAI-T across outcome studies since 1990. *Psychological Medicine, 29,* 1425–1434.

Flaherty, J. A., & Adams, S. (1998). Therapist-patient race and sex matching: Predictors of treatment duration. *Psychiatric Times, 15,* 1–4.

Fleming, J. S., & Rickord, B. (1997). Solution-focused brief therapy: One answer to managed mental health care. *Family Journal, 5,* 286–294.

Flores, E., Tschann, J. M., Marin, B. V., & Pantoja, P. (2004). Marital conflict and acculturation among Mexican American husbands and wives. *Cultural Diversity and Ethnic Minority Psychology, 10,* 39–52.

Foa, E. B., Dancu, C. V., Hembree, E. A., Jaycox, L. H., Meadows, E. A., & Street, G. P. (1999). A comparison of exposure therapy, stress inoculation training, and their combination in reducing posttraumatic stress disorder in female assault victims. *Journal of Consulting and Clinical Psychology, 67,* 194–200.

Foley, K., Duran, B., Morris, P., Lucero, J., Jiang, Y., Baxter, B., et al. (2005). Using motivational interviewing to promote HIV testing at an American Indian substance abuse treatment facility. *Journal of Psychoactive Drugs, 37,* 321–329.

Fonagy, P., Roth, A., & Higgitt, A. (2005). Psychodynamic psychotherapies: Evidence-based practice and clinical wisdom. *Bulletin of the Menninger Clinic, 69,* 1–57.

Fortune, D. G., Richards, H. L., Griffiths, C. E. M., &

Main, C. J. (2004). Targeting cognitive-behaviour therapy to patients' implicit model of psoriasis: Results from a patient preference controlled trial. *British Journal of Clinical Psychology, 43,* 65–82.

Foster, V. A., & McAdams, C. R. (1999). The impact of client suicide in counselor training: Implications for counselor education and supervision. *Counselor Education and Supervision, 39,* 22–33.

Foxhall, K. (2000). How to protect your practice from fraud and abuse charges. *Monitor on Psychology (February 2000),* 64–66.

Frank, A. F., & Gunderson, J. G. (1990). The role of the therapeutic alliance in the treatment of schizophrenia: Relationship to course and outcome. *Archives of General Psychiatry, 47,* 228–235.

Frank, E., Kupfer, D. J., Buysse, D. J., Swartz, H. A., Pilkonis, P., Houck, P., et al. (2007). Randomized trial of weekly, twice-monthly, and monthly interpersonal psychotherapy as maintenance treatment for women with recurrent depression. *American Journal of Psychiatry, 164,* 761–767.

Frank, K. A. (2002). The "ins and outs" of enactment: A relational bridge for psychotherapy integration. *Journal of Psychotherapy Integration, 12,* 267–286.

Frankel, M. (1998, May 24). The oldest bias. *New York Times Magazine,* pp. 16–17.

Frankl, V. (1959). *Man's search for meaning.* Boston: Beacon.

Franklin, C., Biever, J., Moore, K., Clemons, D., & Scamardo, M. (2001). The effectiveness of solution-focused therapy with children in a school setting. *Research on Social Work Practice, 11,* 411–434.

Franklin, M. E., Abramowitz, J. S., Bux, D. A., Zoeller, L. A., & Feeny, N. C. (2002). Cognitive-behavioral therapy with and without medication in the treatment of obsessive-compulsive disorders. *Professional Psychology: Research and Practice, 33,* 162–168.

Freire, P. (1970). *Pedagogy of the oppressed.* New York: Continuum.

Freud, S. (1900/1913). *The interpretation of dreams.* New York: Macmillan.

Freud, S. (1909). Notes upon a case of obsessional neurosis. *Collected Papers, 3,* 293–383.

Freud, S. (1910/1957). The origin and development of psychoanalysis. *American Journal of Psychology, 21,* 181–218.

Freud, S. (1955). Lines of advance in psycho-analytic therapy. In J. Strachey (Ed.), *The standard edition of the complete psychological work of Sigmund Freud* (Vol. 17). London: Hogarth Press (Original work published 1918).

Freud, S. (1957). Instincts and their vicissitudes. In J. Strachey (Ed.), *The standard edition of the completed psychological works of Sigmund Freud* (Vol. 14, pp. 117–140). London: Hogarth Press (Original work published 1915).

Freud, S. (1958). Recommendations to physicians practicing psycho-analysis. In J. Strachey (Ed.), *The standard edition of the completed psychological works of Sigmund Freud* (Vol. 12, pp. 109–120). London: Hogarth Press (Original work published 1912).

Freud, S. (1961). The Economic Problem of Masochism. In J. Strachey (Ed.), *The standard edition of the complete psychological works of Sigmund Freud* (Vol. XIX). London: The Hogarth Press (Original work published 1923).

Freud, S. (1962). The aetiology of hysteria. In J. Strachey (Ed.), *The standard edition of the complete psychological works of Sigmund Freud* (Vol. 3). London: Hogarth Press (Original work published 1896).

Fried, D., Crits-Christoph, P., & Luborsky (1997). The parallel of the CCRT for the therapist with the CCRT for other people. In L. Luborsky & P. Crits-Christoph (Eds.), *Understanding transference: The core conflictual relationship theme method* (2nd ed., pp. 165–287). Washington, DC: American Psychological Association.

Frommer, F. J. (2006, Dec 20). Congressman criticized for Muslim letter. Retrieved 12/20/2006 from http://seattlepi.newsource.com/printer2/index.asp?.

Frosch, A. (2002). Transference: Psychic reality and material reality. *Psychoanalytic Psychology, 19,* 603–633.

Frye v. United States, 54 D.C. App. 46, 293 F. 1013 (C.C. Cir. 1923).

Fuertes, J. N., & Gelso, C. J. (2000). Hispanic counselors' race and accent and Euro Americans' universal-diverse orientation: A study of initial perceptions. *Cultural Diversity and Ethnic Minority Psychology, 6,* 211–219.

Fuertes, J. N., Mueller, L. N., Chauhan, R. V., Walker, J. A., & Ladany, N. (2002). An investigation of European American therapists' approach to counseling African American clients. *The Counseling Psychologist, 30,* 763–788.

Gabbard, G. O., Gunderson, J. G., & Fonagy, P. (2002). The place of psychoanalytic treatments within psychiatry. *Archives of General Psychiatry, 59,* 505–512.

Galanti, G. (2000). Filipino attitudes toward pain medication. *Western Journal of Medicine, 173,* 278–280.

Gambrill, E. (2005). *Critical thinking in clinical practice.* Hoboken, NJ: Wiley.

Garber, B. D. (2004). Therapist alienation: Foreseeing and forestalling third-party dynamics: Undermining psychotherapy with children of conflicted caregivers. *Professional Psychology: Research and Practice, 35,* 357–363.

Garfield, S. (1998). Some comments on empirically supported treatments. *Journal of Consulting and Clinical Psychology, 66,* 121–125.

Garnets, L., Hancock, K. A., Cochran, S. D., Goodchilds, J., & Peplau, L. A. (1998). Issues in psychotherapy with lesbians and gay men: A survey of psychologists. In D. R. Atkinson & G. Hackett (Eds.), *Counseling diverse populations* (2nd ed., pp. 297–316). Boston: McGraw-Hill.

Gartner, J., Harmatz, M., Hohmann, A., Larson, D., & Gartner, A. F. (1990). The effects of patient and clinician ideology on clinical judgment: A study of ideological countertransference. *Psychotherapy, 27,* 98–106.

Garwick, A., & Auger, S. (2000). What do providers need to know about American Indian culture? Recommendations from urban Indian family caregivers. *Families, Systems & Health, 18,* 177–190.

Gaston, L. (1990). The concept of the alliance and its role in psychotherapy: Theoretical and empirical considerations. *Psychotherapy, 27,* 143–153.

Gaston, L., Marmar, C. R., Callaghes, D., & Thompson, L. W. (1991). Alliance prediction of outcome beyond in-treatment symptomatic change as psychotherapy process. *Psychotherapy Research, 1,* 104–113.

Geddes, J., Freemantle, N., Harrison, P., & Bebbington, P. (2000). Atypical antipsychotics in the treatment of schizophrenia: Systematic overview and meta-regression analysis. *British Medical Journal, 321,* 1371–1376.

Geller, J., Brown, K. E., Zaitsoff, S. L., Goodrich, S., & Hastings, F. (2003). Collaborative versus directive interventions in the treatment of eating disorders: Implications for care providers. *Professional Psychology: Research and Practice, 34,* 406–413.

Gelso, C. J., & Carter, J. A. (1994). Components of the psychotherapy relationship: Their interaction and unfolding during treatment. *Journal of Counseling Psychology, 41,* 296–306.

Gelso, C. J., & Hayes, J. A. (1998). *The psychotherapy relationship: Theory, research, and practice.* New York: Wiley.

Gelso, C. J., Kivlighan, D. M., Wine, B., Jones, A., & Friedman, S. C. (1997). Transference, insight, and the course of time-limited therapy. *Journal of Counseling Psychology, 44,* 209–217.

George, L. K., Larsons, D. B., Koeing, H. G., & McCullough, M. E. (2000). Spirituality and health: What we know, what we need to know. *Journal of Social and Clinical Psychology, 19,* 102–116.

Gershon, M. J. (2002). Psychosomatics and psychoanalytic theory: The psychology of ulcerative colitis and Crohn's disease. *Psychoanalytic Psychology, 19,* 380–388.

Gibbs, L., & Gambrill, E. (2002). Evidence-based practice: Counterarguments to objections. *Research on Social Work Practice, 12,* 452–476.

Ginsburg, J. I. D., Mann, R. E., Rotgers, F., & Weekes, J. R. (2002). Motivational interviewing with criminal justice populations. In William R. Stephen Rollnick (Ed.). *Motivational interviewing* (2nd ed., pp. 333–346). New York: Guilford Press.

Glass, G., & Kliegl, R. (1983). An apology for research integration in the study of psychotherapy. *Journal of Consulting and Clinical Psychology, 51,* 28–41.

Glauser, A. S., & Bozarth, J. D. (2001). Person-centered counseling: The culture within. *Journal of Counseling and Development, 79,* 142–147.

Glicken, M. D. (2005). *Improving the effectiveness of the helping professions: An evidence-based approach* to practice. Thousand Oaks, CA: Sage Publications.

Glosoff, H. L., Herlihy, B., & Spence, E. B. (2000). Privileged communication in the counselor-client relationship. *Journal of Counseling and Development, 78,* 454–462.

Goldfried, M. R., Castonguay, L. G., Hayes, A. M., Drozd, J. F., & Shapiro, D. A. (1997). A comparative analysis of the therapeutic focus in cognitive-behavioral and psychodynamic-interpersonal session. *Journal of Consulting and Clinical Psychology, 65,* 740–748.

Goldfried, M. R., & Wolfe, B. E. (1996). Psychotherapy practice and research: Repairing a strained alliance. *American Psychologist, 51,* 1007–1016.

Gonzalez, D. M. (2002). Client variables and psychotherapy outcomes. In D. J. Cain & J. Seeman (Eds.), *Humanistic psychotherapies: Handbook of research and practice* (pp. 559–578). Washington, DC: American Psychological Association.

Goode, E. (2002). Researchers scramble for the next Prozac. *The Seattle Times,* June 30, pp. A7. (from the *New York Times*).

Gorman, J. M. (1998). The *essential guide to psychiatric drugs.* New York: St. Martin's Press.

Granello, D. H., & Beamish, P. M. (1998). Reconceptualizing codependency in women: A sense of connectedness, not pathology. *Journal of Mental Health Counseling, 20,* 344–358.

Granello, P. F., & Granello, D. H. (1998). Training counseling students to use outcome research. *Counselor Education and Supervision, 37,* 224–237.

Gratz, K. L., & Orsillo, S. M. (2003). Scientific expert testimony in CSA cases: Legal, ethical, and scientific considerations. *Clinical Psychology, 10,* 358–364.

Greenberg, L. S. (2002). Integrating an emotion-focused approach to treatment into psychotherapy integration. *Journal of Psychotherapy Integration, 12,* 154–189.

Greenberg, S. A., & Shuman, D. W. (1997). Irreconcilable conflict between therapeutic and forensic roles. *Professional Psychology: Research and Practice, 28,* 50–57.

Greene, G. J., Lee, M-Y., Mentzer, R. A., Pinnell, S. R., & Niles, D. (1998). Miracles, dreams, and empowerment. *Families in Society, 79,* 395–399.

Grencavage, L. M., & Norcross, J. C. (1990). Where are the commonalities among the therapeutic common factors? *Professional Psychology: Research and Practice, 21,* 372–378.

Greub, B. L., & McNamara, J. R. (2000). Alternative therapies in psychological treatment: When is consultation with a physician warranted? *Professional Psychology: Research and Practice, 31,* 58–63.

Guidelines for providers of psychological services to ethnic, linguistic, and culturally diverse populations (1993). *American Psychologist, 48,* 45–48.

Guinee, J. P., & Tracey, T. J. G. (1997). Effects of religiosity and problem type on counselor description ratings. *Journal of Counseling and Development, 76,* 65–73.

Gurung, R. A. R., & Mehta, V. (2001). Relating ethnic identity, acculturation, and attitudes toward treating minority clients. *Cultural Diversity and Ethnic Minority Psychology, 7,* 139–151.

Gutheil, T. G., & Hilliard, J. T. (2001). "Don't write me down": Legal, clinical and risk-management aspects of patients' requests that therapists not keep notes or records. *American Journal of Psychotherapy, 55,* 157–165.

Guthrie, E., Moorey, J., Margison, F., Barker, H., et al. (1999). Cost-effectiveness of brief psychodynamic-interpersonal therapy in high utilizers of psychiatric services. *Archives of General Psychiatry, 56,* 519–527.

Haaga, D. A., & Davison, G. C. (1993). An appraisal of rational-emotive therapy. *Journal of Consulting and Clinical Psychology, 61,* 215–220.

Hacker, K. A., Suglia, S., Fried, L. E., Rappaport, N., & Cabral, H. (2006). Developmental differences in risk factors for suicide attempts between ninth and eleventh graders. *Suicide and Life-Threatening Behavior, 36,* 154–166.

Hagen, M. A. (2003). Faith in the model and resistance to research. *Clinical Psychology, 10,* 344–349.

Hall, A. S., & Gushee, A. G. (2002). Medication interventions for ADHD youth: A primer for school and mental health counselors. *Journal of Mental Health Counseling, 24,* 140–153.

Hall, G. C. N. (2001). Psychotherapy research with

ethnic minorities: Empirical, ethical, and conceptual issues. *Journal of Consulting and Clinical Psychology, 69,* 502–510.

Hall, L. H., & Robertson, M. H. (1998). Undergraduate ratings of the acceptability of single and combined treatments for depression: A comparative analysis. *Professional Psychology: Research and Practice, 29,* 269–272.

Halleck, S. L. (1996). A different kind of education for psychiatric residents. *Psychiatric Quarterly, 67,* 95–110.

Hansen, J. T. (2000). Psychoanalysis and humanism: A review and critical examination of integrationist efforts with some proposed resolutions. *Journal of Counseling and Development, 78,* 21–28.

Hansen, N. D., Randazzo, K. V., Schwartz, A., Marshall, M., Kalis, D., Frazier, R., et al. (2006). Do we practice what we preach? An exploratory survey of multicultural psychotherapy competencies. *Professional Psychology: Research and Practice, 37,* 66–74.

Hardy, G. E., Stiles, W. B., Barkham, M., & Startup, M. (1998). Therapist responsiveness to client interpersonal styles during time-limited treatments for depression. *Journal of Consulting and Clinical Psychology, 66,* 304–312.

Harris, G. (2006, Mar 23). Stimulants can give children hallucinations. *Seattle Post-Intelligencer,* A1, 7.

Hartmann, H. (1964). *Essays on ego psychology: Selected problems in psychoanalytic theory.* New York: International Universities Press.

Hastings, D. (2005, August 9). No way out: Many poor stuck in Houston. Retrieved 12/05/2006 from http://www.comcast.net/includes/article/print.jsp.

Hays, P. A. (2001). *Addressing cultural complexities in practice: A framework for clinicians and counselors.* Washington, DC: American Psychological Association.

Heinssen, R. K., & Cuthbert, B. N. (2001). Barriers to relationship formation in schizophrenia: Implications for treatment, social recovery, and translational research. *Psychiatry, 64,* 126–132.

Hendin, H., Haas, A. P., Malsberger, J. T., Szanto, K., & Rabinowicz, H. (2004). Factors contributing to therapists' distress after the suicide of a patient. *American Journal of Psychiatry, 161,* 1442–1446.

Herz, M. I., Liberman, R. P., Lieberman, J. A., Marder, S. R., McGlashan, T. H., Wyatt, R. J., et al. (1997). APA guidelines for treating adults with schizophrenia. *Medscape Mental Health, 2* (5).

Hillbrand, M. (2001). Homicide-suicide and other forms of co-occurring aggression against self and others. *Professional Psychology: Research and Practice, 32,* 626–635.

Hillman, J., & Stricker, G. (2002). A call for psychotherapy integration in work with older adult patients. *Journal of Psychotherapy Integration, 12,* 395–405.

Hilsenroth, M. J., & Cromer, T. D. (2007). Clinician interventions related to alliance during the initial interview and psychological assessment. *Psychotherapy: Theory, Research, Practice, Training, 44,* 205–218.

Hines, S. (2000). Intelligent prescribing in diverse populations. *Patient Care, 34,* 135–149.

Hinrichsen, G. A. (2006). Why multicultural issues matter for practitioners working with older adults. *Professional Psychology: Research and Practice, 37,* 29–35.

Ho, D. Y. F. (1995). Internalized culture, culturocentrism, and transcendence. *The Counseling Psychologist, 23,* 4–24.

Hodge, D. R. (2003). Value differences between social workers and members of the working and middle classes. *Social Work, 48,* 107–119.

Hoffman, I. Z. (1998). *Ritual and spontaneity in the psychoanalytic process: A dialectic-constructivist view.* Hillsdale, NJ: Analytic Press.

Hoffman, M. A., Hill, C. E., & Taffe, R. (1996). The relationship between in-session significant events and session outcome for prepracticum counselor trainees and their volunteering clients. *Counselor Education and Supervision, 36,* 25–36.

Hoge, C. W., Castro, C. A., Messer, S. C., McGurk, D., Cotting, D. I., & Koffman, R. L. (2004). Combat duty in Iraq and Afghanistan: Mental health problems and barriers to care. *New England Journal of Medicine, 351,* 13–22.

Hoglend, P. (2003). Long-term effects of brief dynamic psychotherapy. *Psychotherapy Research, 13,* 271–292.

Holland, E. G., & Degruy, F. V. (1997). Drug-induced disorders. *American Family Physician, 56,* November 1, 1997.

Holtforth, M. G., & Castonguay, L. G. (2005). Relationship and techniques in cognitive-behavioral therapy—A motivational approach. *Psychotherapy: Theory, Research, Practice, Training, 42,* 443–455.

Hubble, M. L., Duncan, B. L., & Miller, S. D. (1999). *The heart & soul of change: What works in therapy.* Washington, DC: American Psychological Association.

Huey, S. J., Jr., & Pan, D. (2006). Culture-responsive one-session treatment in phobic Asian Americans: A pilot study. *Psychotherapy: Theory, Research, Practice, Training, 43,* 549–554.

Huffman, J. C., Stern, T. A., Harley, R. M., & Lundy, N. A. (2003). The use of DBT skills in the treatment of difficult patients in the general hospital. *Psychosomatics, 44,* 421–447.

Hunsley, J. (2007). Addressing key challenges in evidence-based practice in psychology. *Professional Psychology: Research and Practice, 38,* 113–121.

Huppert, J. D., Barlow, D. H., Gorman, J. M., Shear, M. K., & Woods, S. W. (2006). The interaction of motivation and therapist adherence predict outcome in cognitive behavioral therapy for panic disorder: Preliminary findings. *Cognitive and Behavioral Practice, 13,* 198–204.

Huppert, J. D., Bufka, L. F., Barlow, J. M., Gorman, J. M., Shear, M. K., & Woods, S. W. (2001). Therapists, therapist variables, and cognitive-behavioral therapy outcome in a multicenter trial for panic disorder. *Journal of Consulting and Clinical Psychology, 69,* 747–755.

Hyer, L., Kramer, D., & Sohnle, S. (2004). CBT with older people: Alterations and the value of the therapeutic alliance. *Psychotherapy: Theory, Research, Practice, Training, 41,* 276–291.

Ibrahim, F. A. (1991). Contribution of cultural world view to generic counseling and development. *Journal of Counseling and Development, 70,* 13–19.

Ingersoll, R. E. (2005). Herbaceuticals: An overview for counselors. *Journal of counseling and development, 83,* 434–443.

Ingersoll, R. E., Bauer, A., & Burns, L. (2004). Children and psychotropic medication: What role should advocacy counseling play? *Journal of Counseling and Development, 82,* 337–343.

Inman, A. G. (2006). Supervisor multicultural competence and its relation to supervisory process and outcome. *Journal of Marital and Family Therapy, 32,* 73–85.

Irvin, J. E., Bowers, C. A., Dunn, M. E., & Wang, M. C. (1999). Efficacy of relapse prevention: A meta-analytic review. *Journal of Consulting and Clinical Psychology, 67,* 563–570.

Ivey, A. E., Ivey, M. B., & Simek-Morgan, L. (1993). *Counseling and psychotherapy: A multicultural perspective.* Boston: Allyn & Bacon.

Jackson, B., & Farrugia, D. (1997). Diagnosis and treatment of adults with attention-deficit/hyperactivity disorder. *Journal of Counseling and Development, 75,* 312–319.

Jacobson, N. (1995). The overselling of therapy. *The Family Therapy Network, 19,* 40–41.

Jacobson, N. S., Martell, C. R., & Dimidjian, S. (2001). Behavioral activation treatment for depression: Returning to contextual roots. *Clinical Psychology: Science and Practice, 8,* 255–270.

Jacobson, P. B., Bovbjerg, D. H., Schwartz, M. D., Hudis, C. A., Gilewski, T. A., & Norton, L. (1995). Conditioned emotional distress in women receiving chemotherapy for breast cancer. *Journal of Consulting and Clinical Psychology, 63,* 108–114.

Jakubowski, P., & Lange, A. J. (1978). *The assertive option: Your rights and responsibilities.* Champaign, IL: Research Press.

James, C. E. (1995). *Seeing ourselves: Exploring race, ethnicity and culture.* Toronto: Thompson Educational Publishing.

Jobes, D. A. (2000). Collaborating to prevent suicide: A clinical research perspective. *Suicide and Life-Threatening Behavior, 30,* 8–17.

Johnson, S. M. (2003). The revolution in couple therapy: A practitioner-scientist perspective. *Journal of Marital and Family Therapy, 29,* 365–376.

Joiner, T. E., Pettit, J. W., Perez, M., Burns, A. B.

Gencoz, T., Gencoz, F., et al. (2001). Can positive emotions influence problem-solving among suicidal adults? *Professional Psychology: Research and Practice, 32,* 507–512.

Joiner, T. E., Pettit, J. W., & Rudd, M. D. (2004). Is there a window of heightened suicide risk if patients gain energy in the context of continued depressive symptoms? *Professional Psychology: Research and Practice, 35,* 84–89.

Joiner, T. E., Sheldon, K. M., Williams, G., & Pettit, J. (2003). The integration of self-determination principles and scientifically informed treatments is the next tier. *Clinical Psychology: Science and Practice, 10,* 318–319.

Joiner, T. E., Voelz, Z. R., & Rudd, M. D. (2001). Problem-solving treatment may be better than treatment as usual for suicidal adults with comorbid depressive and anxiety disorders. *Professional Psychology: Research and Practice, 32,* 278–282.

Jones, D. R., Harrell, J. P., Morris-Prather, C. E., Thomas, J., & Omowale, N. (1996). Affective and physiological responses to racism: The roles of afrocentrism and mode of presentation. *Ethnicity and Disease, 6,* 109–122.

Jones, E. E., & Pulos, S. M. (1993). Comparing the process in psychodynamic and cognitive-behavioral therapies. *Journal of Consulting and Clinical Psychology, 61,* 306–316.

Jordan, K. (1998). The cultural experiences and identified needs of the ethnic minority supervisee in the context of Caucasian supervision. *Family Therapy, 25,* 181–187.

Joyce, A. S., Ogrodniczuk, J. S., Piper, W. E., & McCallum, M. (2003). The alliance as mediator of expectancy effects in short-term individual therapy. *Journal of Consulting and Clinical Psychology, 71,* 672–679.

Julien, R. M. (2001). *A primer of drug action: A concise nontechnical guide to the actions, uses and side effects of psychoactive drugs* (9th ed.). New York: Worth.

Jureidini, J. N., Doecke, C. J., Mansfield, P. R., Haby, M. M. Menkes, D. B., & Tonkin, A. L. (2004). Efficacy and safety of antidepressants for children and adolescents. *British Medical Journal, 328,* 879–883.

Kagan, J. (1989). Temperamental contributions to social behavior. *American Psychologist, 44,* 668–674.

Kagawa-Singer, M., & Kassim-Lakha, S. (2003). A strategy to reduce cross-cultural miscommunication and increase the likelihood of improving health outcomes. *Academic Medicine, 78,* 577–587.

Kaplan, J. A. (2004). The "good enough" fit: Psychoanalytic psychotherapy and psychoanalysis as culturally sensitive practice. *Clinical Social Work Journal, 32,* 51–59.

Karlsson, R. (2005). Ethnic matching between therapist and patient in psychotherapy: An overview of findings, together with methodological and conceptual issues. *Cultural Diversity and Ethnic Minority Psychology, 11,* 113–129.

Karno, M. P., & Longabaugh, R. (2005). Less directiveness by therapists improve drinking outcomes of reactant clients in alcohol treatment. *Journal of Consulting and Clinical Psychology, 73,* 262–267.

Kassaw, K., & Gabbard, G. O. (2002). Creating a psychodynamic formulation from a clinical evaluation. *American Journal of Psychiatry, 159,* 721–726.

Kazantzis, N., & Deane, F. (1999). Psychologists' use of homework assignments in clinical practice. *Professional Psychology: Research and Practice, 20,* 581–585.

Kazantzis, N., Lampropoulos, G. K., & Deane, F. P. (2005). A national survey of practicing psychologists' use and attitudes towards homework in psychotherapy. *Journal of Consulting and Clinical Psychology, 73,* 742–748.

Keltner, N. L., & Folks, D. G. (2001). *Psychotropic drugs* (3rd ed.). St. Louis, MO: Mosby.

Kemp, N. T., & Mallinckrodt, B. (1996). Impact of professional training on case conceptualization of clients with a disability. *Professional Psychology: Research and Practice, 27,* 378–385.

Kennard, B. D., Stewart, S. M., Hughes, J. L., Patel, P. G., & Emslie, G. J. (2006). Cognitions and depressive symptoms among ethnic minority adolescents. *Cultural Diversity and Ethnic Minority Psychology, 12,* 578–591.

Kenney, G. E. (1994). Multicultural investigation of

counseling expectations and preferences. *Journal of College Student Psychotherapy, 9,* 21–39.

Kernberg, O. (1976). *Object relations theory and clinical psychoanalysis.* Northvale, NJ: Aronson.

Kim, B. S. K., & Atkinson, D. R. (2002). Asian American client adherence to Asian cultural values, counselor expression of cultural values, counselor ethnicity, and career counseling process. *Journal of Counseling Psychology, 49,* 3–13.

Kim, N. S., & Ahn, W-K. (2002). Clinical psychologists' theory-based representations of mental disorders predict their diagnostic reasoning and memory. *Journal of Experimental Psychology: General, 131,* 451–476.

King, J. H., & Anderson, S. M. (2004). Therapeutic implications of pharmacotherapy: Current trends and ethical issues. *Journal of Counseling and Development, 82,* 329–336.

King, N. J., Eleonora, G., & Ollendick, T. H. (1998). Etiology of childhood phobias: Current status of Rachman's three pathways theory. *Behaviour Research and Therapy, 36,* 297–309.

King, R. N., & Koehler, D. J. (2000). Illusory correlations in graphological inference. *Journal of Experimental Psychology: Applied, 6,* 336–348.

Kirschenbaum, H., & Jourdan, A. (2005). The current status of Carl Rogers and the person-centered approach. *Psychotherapy: Theory, Research, Practice, Training, 42,* 37–51.

Kirsh, I., Moore, T. J., Scoboria, A., & Nichols, S. S. (2002). The emperor's new drugs: An analysis of antidepressant medication data submitted to the U.S. Food and Drug Administration. *Prevention & Treatment, 5,* Article 23. Retrieved on 06/01/06 from http://www.journals.apa.org/prevention/volume5/pre0050023a.html.

Kivlighan, D. M., Multon, K. D., & Patton, M. J. (2000). Insight and symptom reduction in time-limited psychoanalytic counseling. *Journal of Counseling Psychology, 47,* 50–58.

Kleespies, P. M. (1993). The stress of patient suicidal behavior: Implications for interns and training programs in psychology. *Professional Psychology: Research and Practice, 24,* 477–482.

Kleespies, P. M., Deleppo, J. D., Gallagher, P. L., & Niles, B. L. (1999). Managing suicidal emergencies: Recommendations for practitioners. *Professional Psychology: Research and Practice, 30,* 454–463.

Klein, M. (1975). *The psycho-analysis of children.* New York: Delta (Original work published in 1932).

Klein, M. H., Kolden, G. G., Michels, J. L., & Chisholm-Stockard, S. (2001). Congruence or genuineness. *Psychotherapy: Theory, Research, Practice, Training, 38,* 396–400.

Kleinman, A. (2004). Culture and depression. *New England Journal of Medicine, 351,* 951–953.

Klerman, G. L., Weissman, M. M., Rounsaville, B. J., & Chevron, E. S. (1984). *Interpersonal psychotherapy of depression.* New York: Basic Books.

Knoll, J. (2000). Use of no-suicide contracts by psychiatrists in Minnesota. *American Journal of Psychiatry, 157,* 1684–1686.

Knox, S., Burkard, A. W., Johnson, A. J., Suzuki, L. A., & Ponterotto, J. G. (2003). African American and European American therapists' experiences of addressing race in cross-racial psychotherapy dyads. *Journal of Counseling Psychology, 50,* 466–481.

Kohler, J. (2001, March 30). Therapists on trial in death of girl, 10. *Washington Post,* p. A19.

Kohut, H. (1971). *The analysis of the self.* New York: International Universities Press.

Kornstein, S. G., Schatzberg, A. F., Thase, M. E., Yonkers, K. A., McCullough, J. P., Keitner, G. I., et al. (2000). Gender differences in treatment response to sertaline versus imipramine in chronic depression. *American Journal of Psychiatry, 157,* 1445–1452.

Kort, B. (1997). Female therapist, male client: Challenging beliefs—a personal journey. *Women and Therapy, 20,* 97–100.

Kottler, J. A. (2000). *Nuts and bolts of helping.* Needham Heights, MA: Allyn & Bacon.

Kratochwill, T. R. (2002). Evidence-based interventions in school psychology: Thoughts on thoughtful commentary. *School Psychology Quarterly, 15,* 518–532.

Kremer, T. G., & Gesten, E. L. (1998). Confidentiality limits of managed care and client's willingness to self-disclose. *Professional Psychology: Research and Practice, 29,* 553–559.

Krieger, N., & Sidney, S. (1996). Racial discrimination and blood pressure: The CARDIA study of young Black and White adults. *American Journal of Public Health, 86,* 1370–1378.

Krupnick, J. L., Sotsky, S. M., Simmens, S., Moyer, J., Elkin, I., Watkins, J., et al. (1996). The role of the therapeutic alliance in psychotherapy pharmacological outcome: Findings in the National Institute of Mental Health Treatment of Depression Collaborative Research Program. *Journal of Consulting and Clinical Psychology, 64,* 532–539.

Kung, W. W. (2001). Consideration of cultural factors in working with Chinese American families with a mentally ill patient. *Families in Society, 82,* 97–107.

LaBrie, J. W., Lamb, T. F., Pedersen, E. R., & Quinlan, T. (2006). A group motivational interviewing intervention reduces drinking and alcohol-related consequences in adjudicated college students. *Journal of College Student Development, 47,* 267–280.

Ladany, N., Inman, A. G., Constantine, M. G., & Hofheinz, E. W. (1997). Supervisee multicultural case conceptualization ability and self-reported multicultural competence as functions of supervisee racial identity and supervisor focus. *Journal of Counseling Psychology, 44,* 284–293.

Lambert, M. J. (1992). Psychotherapy outcome research: Implications for integrative and eclectic theories. In J. C. Norcross & M. R. Goldfried (Eds.), *Handbook of psychotherapy integration* (pp. 94–129). New York: Basic Books.

Lambert, M. J., & Barley, D. E. (2001). Research summary on the therapeutic relationship and psychotherapy outcome. *Psychotherapy, 38,* 357–361.

Lampropoulos, G. K. (2000). Evolving psychotherapy integration: Eclectic selection and prescriptive applications of common factors in therapy. *Psychotherapy: Theory, Research, Practice, Training, 37,* 285–297.

Lang, A. J., & Craske, M. G. (2000). Panic and phobia. In John R. White and Arthur S. Freeman (Eds.), *Cognitive-behavioral group therapy: For specific problems and populations* (pp. 63–97). Washington, DC: American Psychological Association,

Langer, N. (1999). Culturally competent professionals in therapeutic alliances enhance patient compliance. *Journal of Health Care for the Poor and Underserved, 10,* 19–26.

La Roche, M. J. (2005). The cultural context and the psychotherapeutic process: Toward a culturally sensitive psychotherapy. *Journal of Psychotherapy Integration, 15,* 169–185.

La Roche, M. J., & Maxie, A. (2003). Ten considerations in addressing cultural differences in psychotherapy. *Professional Psychology: Research and Practice, 34,* 180–186.

Larson, C. A., & Carey, K. B. (1998). Caffeine: Brewing trouble in mental health settings? *Professional Psychology: Research and Practice, 29,* 373–376.

Lasser, K. E., Allen, P. D., Woolhandler, S. J., Himmelstein, D. U., Wolfe, S. M., & Bor, D. H. (2002). Timing of new black box warnings and withdrawals for prescription medications. *Journal of the American Medical Association, 287,* 2215–2220.

Laux, J. M. (2002). A primer on suicidality: Implications for counselors. *Journal of Counseling and Development, 80,* 380–383.

Lawson, D. (2003). Incidence, explanations and treatment of partner violence. *Journal of Counseling and Development, 81,* 19–32.

Lawson, W. B. (1996). The art and science of psychopharmacotherapy with African Americans. *The Mount Sinai Journal of Medicine, 63,* 301–305.

Lazarus, A. A. (1971). *Behavior therapy and beyond.* New York: McGraw-Hill.

Lazarus, A. A. (2000). Will reason prevail?: From classic psychoanalysis to new age therapy. *American Journal of Psychotherapy, 54,* 152–155.

Lecomte, T., & Lecomte, C. (2002). Toward uncovering robust principles of change inherent to cognitive-behavioral therapy for psychosis. *American Journal of Orthopsychiatry, 72,* 50–57.

Lee, C. C. (2006). *Multicultural issues in counseling: New approaches to diversity* (3d ed.). Washington, DC: American Psychological Association.

Lee, S. (1993). The prevalence and nature of lithium noncompliance among Chinese psychiatric patients in Hong Kong. *Journal of Nervous and Mental Diseases, 181,* 618–624.

Leichsenring, F. (2001). Comparative effects of short-term psychodynamic therapy and cognitive-behavioral therapy in depression: A meta-analysis. *Clinical Psychology Review, 21,* 401–419.

Leichsenring, F., & Leibing, E. (2003). The effectiveness of psychodynamic therapy and cognitive behavior therapy in the treatment of personality disorders: A meta-analysis. *American Journal of Psychiatry, 160,* 1223–1233.

Leuchter, A. F., Cook, I. A., Witte, E. A., Morgan, M., & Abrams, M. (2002). Changes in brain function of depressed subjects during treatment with placebo. *American Journal of Psychiatry, 159,* 122–129.

Leung, P., Cheung, K-F. M., & Stevenson, K. M. (1994). A strengths approach to ethnically sensitive practice for child protective service workers. *Child Welfare, 73,* 707–715.

Levant, R. F. (1996). The new psychology of men. *Professional psychology: Research and practice, 27,* 259–265.

Levine, S. B., Brown, G., Coleman, E., Cohen Kettenis, P., Hage, J. J., Van Maasdam, J., Petersen, M., et al. (1998). The standards of care for gender identity disorders (5th version). *International Journal of Transgenderism,* Vol. 2.

Lewinsohn, P. M. (1974). *A behavioral approach to depression.* In R. J. Friedman & M. M. Katz (Eds.). *The psychology of depression: Contemporary theory and research.* New York: Wiley

Li, L. C., & Kim, B. S. K. (2004). Effects of counseling style and client adherence to Asian cultural values on counseling process with Asian American college students. *Journal of Counseling Psychology, 51,* 158–167.

Liberman, R. P., Kopelowicz, A., & Young, A. S. (1994). Bio-behavioral treatment and rehabilitation of schizophrenia. *Behavior Therapy, 25,* 89–107.

Liem, J. H., & Pressler, E. J. (2005). Addressing relationship concerns in individual psychotherapy. *Journal of Psychotherapy Integration, 15,* 186–212.

Like, R. (1997). *Becoming culturally competent.* Newark, N. J.: Center for healthy families and cultural diversity, Department of Family Medicine, UMDNJ-Robert Wood Johnson Medical School.

Lilienfeld, S. O., Lynn, S. J., & Lohr, J. M. (2004). *Science and pseudoscience in clinical psychology.* New York: The Guilford Press.

Lin, K. M. (2001). Biological differences in depression and anxiety across race and ethnic groups. *Journal of Clinical Psychiatry, 62,* 13–19.

Lin, K. M., Miller, M. H., Poland, R. E., Nuccio, I., & Yamaguchi, M (1991). Ethnicity and family involvement in the treatment of schizophrenic patients. *Journal of Nervous and Mental Diseases, 179,* 631–633.

Lin, K. M., Poland, R. E., Anderson, D., & Lesser, I. M. (1996). Ethnopsychopharmacology and the treatment of PTSD. In A. J. Marsella, & M. J. Friedman (Eds.), *Ethnocultural aspects of posttraumatic stress disorder: Issues, research and clinical applications* (pp. 505–526). Washington, DC: American Psychological Association.

Lin, K. M., Poland, R. E. Nuccio, I., Matsuda, K., Hathuc, N., Su, T. P., et al. (1989). A longitudinal assessment of haloperidol dose and serum concentration in Asian and Caucasian schizophrenic patients. *American Journal of Psychiatry, 146,* 1307–1311.

Lin, Yii-Nii. (2002). The application of cognitive-behavioral therapy to counseling Chinese. *American Journal of Psychotherapy, 56,* 46–58.

Linehan, M. M. (1987). Dialectal behavioral therapy: A cognitive-behavioral approach to parasuicide. *Journal of Personality Disorders, 1,* 328–333.

Linehan, M. M. (1993a). *Cognitive-behavioral treatment for borderline personality.* New York: Guilford Press.

Linehan, M. M. (1993b). *Skills training manual for treating borderline personality disorder.* New York: Guilford Press.

Linehan, M. M. (1997). Validation and psychotherapy. In L. Greenberg (Ed.), *Empathy reconsidered: New directions in psychotherapy* (pp. 353–392). Washington, DC: American Psychological Association.

Linehan, M. M., Tutek, D., Heard, H., & Armstrong, H. (1994). Interpersonal outcome of cognitive-behavioral treatment of chronically suicidal borderline patients. *American Journal of Psychiatry, 151,* 1771–1776.

Li-Repac, D. (1980). Cultural influences on clinical

perception: A comparison between Caucasian and Chinese-American therapists. *Journal of Cross-Cultural Psychology, 11,* 327–342.

Littrell, J., & Ashford, J. B. (1995). Is it proper for psychologists to discuss medications with clients? *Professional Psychology: Research and Practice, 26,* 238–244.

Litwack, T. R. (2001). Actuarial versus clinical assessments of dangerousness. *Psychology, Public Policy and the Law, 7,* 409–443.

Liu, W. M., & Clay, D. L. (2002). Multicultural counseling competencies: Guidelines in working with children and adolescents. *Journal of Mental Health Counseling, 24,* 177–187.

Louw, F., & Straker, G. (2002). Borderline pathology: An integration of cognitive therapy and psychodynamic therapy. *Journal of Psychotherapy Integration, 12,* 190–217.

Luborsky, L. (1984). *Principles of psychoanalytic psychotherapy: A manual for supportive-expressive treatment.* New York: Basic Books.

Luborsky, L. (1997). The everyday clinical uses of the CCRT. In L. Luborsky & P. Crits-Christoph (Eds.), *Understanding transference: The core conflictual relationship theme method* (2nd ed., pp. 275–287). Washington, DC: American Psychological Association.

Luborsky, L., Barber, J. P., & Beutler, L. (1993). Introduction to the special section: A briefing on curative factors in dynamic psychotherapy. *Journal of Consulting and Clinical Psychology, 61,* 539–541.

Luborsky, L., Barber, J. P., Schaffler, P., & Cacciola, J. (1997). The narratives told during psychotherapy and the types of CCRTs within them. In L. Luborsky & P. Crits-Christoph (Eds.), *Understanding transference: The core conflictual relationship theme method* (2nd ed., pp. 135–150). Washington, DC: American Psychological Association.

Luborsky, L., & Crits-Christoph, P. (1997a). The early life of the idea for the core conflictual relationship theme method. In L. Luborsky & P. Crits-Christoph (Eds.), *Understanding transference: The core conflictual relationship theme method* (2nd ed., pp. 3–13). Washington, DC: American Psychological Association.

Luborsky, L., & Crits-Christoph, P. (1997b). *Under-standing transference: The core conflictual relationship theme method* (2nd ed., pp. 135–150). Washington, DC: American Psychological Association.

Luborsky, L., Diguer, L., Seligman, D. A., Rosenthal, R., Krause, E. D., Johnson, S., et al. (1999). The researcher's own therapy alliances: A "wild card" in comparisons of treatment efficacy. *Clinical Psychology: Science and Practice, 6,* 95–106.

Luoma, J. B., Martin, C. E., & Pearson, J. L. (2002). Contact with mental health and primary care providers before suicide: A review of the evidence. *American Journal of Psychiatry, 159,* 909–916.

Lynch, T. R., Morse, J. Q., Mendelson, T., & Robins, C. (2003). Dialectical behavior therapy for depressed older adults. *American Journal of Geriatric Psychiatry, 11,* 33–45.

Lyons, L., & Woods, P. (1992). The efficacy of rational-emotive therapy: A quantitative review of the outcome literature. *Clinical Psychology Review, 11,* 357–369.

Ma, S. H., & Teasdale, J. D. (2004). Mindfulness-based cognitive therapy for depression: Replication and exploration of differential relapse prevention effects. *Journal of Consulting and Clinical Psychology, 72,* 31–40.

Maas, P. (2001, Sep 9). The broken promise. *Parade Magazine,* 4–6.

MacDonald, D. A., & Friedman, H. L. (2002). Assessment of humanistic, transpersonal, and spiritual constructs: State of the science. *Journal of Humanistic Psychology, 42,* 102–125.

Mackay, H. C., Barkham, M., & Stiles, W. B. (1998). Staying with the feeling: An anger event in psychodynamic-interpersonal therapy. *Journal of Counseling Psychology, 45,* 279–289.

Mackay, H. C., Barkham, M., Stiles, W. B., & Goldfried, M. R. (2002). Patterns of client emotion in helpful sessions of cognitive-behavioral and psychodynamic interpersonal therapy. *Journal of Counseling Psychology, 49,* 376–380.

Magnavita, J. J. (1994). On the validity of psychoanalytic constructs in the 20th century. *Professional Psychology: Research and Practice, 25,* 198–199.

Mahler, M. (1968). *On human symbiosis and the vicissitudes of individuation.* New York: International Universities Press.

Mahler, M., Pine, F., & Bergman, A. (1975). *The psy-*

chological birth of the human infant. New York: Basic Books.

Mahoney, M. J. (1993). Introduction to special section: Theoretical developments in the cognitive therapies. *Journal of Consulting and Clinical Psychology, 61,* 187–193.

Malcolm, D. D. (1998). Another counselor educator's personal observations about the Rogerian approach and cross-cultural counseling. *ACES Spectrum, 58,* 12, 16.

Malik, M. L., Beutler, L. E., Alimohamed, S., Gallagher-Thompson, D., & Thompson, L. (2003). Are all cognitive therapies alike? A comparison of cognitive and noncognitive therapy: Process and implications for the application of empirically supported treatments. *Journal of Consulting and Clinical Psychology, 71,* 150–158.

Mallinckrodt, B. (1996). Change in working alliance, social support, and psychological symptoms in brief therapy. *Journal of Counseling Psychology, 43,* 448–455.

Mallinckrodt, B., Shigeoka, S., & Suzuki, L. A. (2005). Asian and Pacific Island American students' acculturation and etiology beliefs about typical counseling presenting problems. *Cultural Diversity and Ethnic Minority Psychology, 11,* 227–238.

Markowitz, J. C. (1998). *Interpersonal psychotherapy for dysthymic disorder.* Washington, DC: American Psychiatric Press.

Martin, S. (2001). Assessing women and their medications. *Monitor on Psychology, 46–47.*

Masterson, J. F. (2006). *The personality disorders through the lens of attachment theory and the neurobiologic development of the self: A clinical integration.* Ithaca, NY: Zeig, Tucker & Theisen.

Matthews, H. W. (1995) Racial, ethnic and gender differences in response to medicines. *Drug Metabolism and Drug Interactions, 12,* 77–91.

Mattox, R. J., & Hurt, D. J. (1992). Counselor pre-practicum: The impact of training on school counselor communication skills. *College Student Journal, 27,* 88–92.

Mayberg, H. S., Silva, J. A., Brannan, S. K., & Tekell, J. L.(2002). The functional neuroanatomy of the placebo effect. *American Journal of Psychiatry, 159,* 728–737.

Mayfield, W. A., & Kardash, C. A. M. (1999). Dif-

ferences in experienced and novice counselors' knowledge structures about clients: Implications for case conceptualization. *Journal of Counseling Psychology, 46,* 504–514.

McAdams, C. R., & Foster, V. A. (2000). Client suicide: Its frequency and impact on counselors. *Journal of Mental Health Counseling, 22,* 107–122.

McAuliffe, G. J., & Eriksen, K. P. (1999). Toward a constructivist and developmental identity for the counseling profession: The context-phase-stage style model. *Journal of Counseling and Development, 77,* 267–280.

McClure, E. B. Kubiszyn, T., & Kaslow, N. J. (2002). Advances in the diagnosis and treatment of childhood mood disorders. *Professional Psychology: Research and Practice, 33,* 125–134.

McCray, C. C. (1998). Ageism in the preclinical years. *Journal of the American Medical Association, 279,* 1035.

McDowell, T., Fang, S-R., Brownlee, K., Young, C. G., & Khanna, A. (2005). Transforming an MFT program: A model for enhancing diversity. *Journal of Marital and Family Therapy, 28,* 179–192.

McDowell, T., Ingoglia, L., Serizawa, T., Holland, C., et al. (2005). Raising multicultural awareness in family therapy through critical conversations. *Journal of Marital and Family Therapy, 31,* 399–412.

McGrath, M. E. (1987). Where did I go? *Schizophrenia: The experiences of patients and families.* Rockville, MD: National Institutes of Health.

McIssac, H., & Finn, C. (1999). Parents beyond conflict: A cognitive-restructuring model for high-conflict families in divorce. *Family and Conciliation Courts Review, 37,* 74–78.

McLaughlin, & Braun, K. L. (1998). Asian and Pacific Islander cultural values: Considerations for decision-making. *Health & Social Work, 23,* 116–126.

McPhatter, A. R. (1997). Cultural competence in child welfare: What is it? How do we achieve it? What happens without it? *Child Welfare, 76,* 255–278.

McQuaide, S. (1999). Using psychodynamic, cognitive-behavioral, and solution-focused questioning to co-construct a new narrative. *Clinical Social Work Journal, 27,* 339–353.

Medscape Neurology and Neurosurgery. (2004).

Tardive dystonia following antipsychotic treatment. Retrieved 11/14/2006 from http://www.medscape.com/viewarticle/489669.

Meichenbaum, D. (1993). Changing conceptions of cognitive behavior modification: Retrospect and prospect. *Journal of Consulting and Clinical Psychology, 61,* 202–204.

Meichenbaum, D. (2006). 35 years of working with suicidal patients: Lessons learned. *Canadian Psychology, 2005, 46,* 64–72.

Meier, S. T. (1999). Training the practitioner-scientist: Bridging case conceptualization, assessment, and intervention. *Counseling Psychologist, 27,* 846–869.

Melchert, T. P. (2007). Strengthening the scientific foundations of professional psychology: Time for the next steps. *Professional Psychology: Research and Practice, 38,* 34–43.

Melchert, T. P., & Patterson, M. M. (1999). Duty to warn and interventions with HIV-positive clients. *Professional Psychology: Research and Practice, 30,* 180–186.

Melfi, C., Croghan, T. W., Hanna, M. P., & Robinson, R. L. (2000). Racial variation in antidepressant treatment in a Medicaid population. *Journal of Clinical Psychiatry, 61,* 16–21.

Merta, R. J., Ponterotto, J. G., & Brown, R. D. (1992). Comparing the effectiveness of two directive styles in the academic counseling of foreign students. *Journal of Counseling Psychology, 39,* 214–218.

Messer, S. B. (2002). Empirically supported treatments: Cautionary notes. Medscape General Medicine. Retrieved 12/11/2005 from: http://www.medscape.com/viewarticle/445082

Meyer, W., III, W., Bockting, W., Cohen-Kettenis, P., Coleman, E., DiCeglie, D., Devor, H., et al. (February 2001). The standards of care for gender identity disorders (6th Version). Retrieved 12/14/2005 from http://www.symposion.com/ijt/soc_2001/index.htm.

Middleton, R., Arrendondo, P., & D'Andrea, M. (2000, Dec). The impact of Spanish-speaking newcomers in Alabama towns. *Counseling Today, 24.*

Miller, A. L., Glinski, J., Woodberry, K. A., Mitchell, A. G., & Indik, J. (2002). Family therapy and dialectical behavior therapy with adolescents. *American Journal of Psychotherapy, 56,* 568–584.

Miller, K. E. (2005). Association between illness and suicide risk in older adults. *American Family Physician, 71,* 1404–1405.

Miller, M. C., Jacobs, D. C., & Gutheil, T. G. (1998). Tailsman or taboo: The controversy of the suicide prevention contract. *Harvard Review of Psychiatry, 6,* 78–87.

Miller, W. R. (1983). Motivational interviewing with problem drinkers. *Behavioural Psychotherapy, 11,* 147–172.

Miller, W. R., & Rollnick, S. (2002). *Motivational interviewing (2nd ed.).* New York: Guilford Press.

Miller, W. R., Zweben, A., DiClemente, C. C., & Rychtarik, R. G. (1995). *Motivational enhancement therapy manual.* Rockville, MD: National Institute on Alcohol Abuse and Alcoholism.

Milrod, B., Leon, A. C., Busch, F., Rudden, M., Schwalberg, M., Clarkin, J., Aronson, A., et al. (2007). A randomized control clinical trial of psychoanalytic psychotherapy. *American Journal of Psychiatry, 164,* 265–272.

Mineka, S., & Zinbarg, R. (2006). A contemporary learning theory perspective on the etiology of anxiety disorders. *American Psychologist, 61,* 10–26.

Mio, J. S., & Iwamasa, G. (1993). To do, or not to do: That is the question for White cross-cultural researchers. *Counseling Psychologist, 21,* 197–212.

Miranda, J., & Cooper, L. A. (2004) Disparities in care for depression among primary care patients. *Journal of General Internal Medicine, 19,* 120–126.

Miranda, J., Green, B. L., Krepnick, J. L., Chung, J., Siddique, J., Belin, T., et al. (2006). One-year outcomes of a randomized clinical trial treating depression in low-income minority women. *Journal of Counseling and Clinical Psychology, 74,* 99–111.

Mischel, W. (1958). Preference for delayed reinforcement: An experimental study of a cultural observation. *Journal of Abnormal and Social Psychology, 56,* 57–61.

Mischoulon, D. (2002). The herbal anxiolytics kava and valerian for anxiety and insomnia. *Psychiatric Annals, 32,* 55–60.

Mishara, B. L. (2006). Cultural specificity and universality of suicide. *Crisis, 27,* 1–3.

Montuori, A., & Fahim, U. (2004). Cross-cultural encounter as an opportunity for personal growth. *Journal of Humanistic Psychology, 44,* 243–265.

Moradi, B., & Subich, L. M. (2004). Examining the moderating role of self-esteem in the link between experiences of perceived sexist events and psychological distress. *Journal of Counseling Psychology, 51,* 50–56.

Motschnig, R., & Nykl, L. (2003). Toward a cognitive-emotional model of Roger's person-centered approach. *Journal of Humanistic Psychology, 43,* 8–45.

Moyers, T. B., Miller, W. R., & Hendrickson, S. M. L. (2005). How does motivational interviewing work? Therapist interpersonal skill predicts client involvement within motivational interviewing sessions. *Journal of Consulting and Clinical Psychology, 75,* 590–598.

Muehlenkamp, J. J. (2006). Empirically supported treatments and general therapy guidelines for non-suicidal self-injury. *Journal of Mental Health Counseling, 28,* 166–185.

Munoz, R. F., Ying, Y. W., Bernal, G., Perez-Stable, J. L., Hargreaves, W. A., Miranda, J., et al. (1995). Prevention of depression with primary care patients: A randomized controlled trial. *American Journal of Community Psychology, 23,* 199–222.

Muran, J. C., Segal, Z. V., Samstag, L. W., & Crawford, C. E. (1994). Patient pretreatment interpersonal problems and therapeutic alliance in short-term cognitive therapy. *Journal of Consulting and Clinical Psychology, 62,* 185–190.

Murdock, N. L. (1991). Case conceptualization: Applying theory to individuals. *Counselor Education and Supervision, 30,* 355–365.

Myers, J. E., & Harper, M. C. (2004). Evidence-based effective practices with older adults. *Journal of Counseling and Development, 82,* 207–218.

Najavits, L. M., Ghinassi, F., Van Horn, A., Weiss, R. D., Siqueland, L., Frank, A., et al. (2004).

Psychotherapy: Theory, Research, Practice, Training, 41, 26–37.

Nathan, P. E. (1998). Practice guidelines: Not yet ideal. *American Psychologist, 53,* 290–299.

National Association of Social Workers. (2000). *Code of ethics of the National Association of Social Workers.* Washington, DC: Author.

National Institute of Mental Health. (2006a). Anxiety disorders. Retrieved 2/5/2007 from http://www.nimh.nih.gov/publicat/anxiety.cfm.

National Institute of Mental Health. (2006b). Borderline personality disorder: Raising questions, finding answers. Retrieved from www.nimh.nih.gov/publicat/bpd.cfm.

National Institute of Mental Health. (2006c). Results for sequenced treatment alternatives to relieve depression (STAR*D) study. Retrieved 8/21/2007 from www.nimh.nih.gov/healthinformation/stard.cfm.

National Institute of Mental Health. (2006d). Subsequent strategies for persistent depression yield modest results. Retrieved 8/21/2007 from www.nimh.nih.gov/press/stardphase3and4.cfm.

Neimeyer, R. A. (1993). An appraisal of constructivist psychotherapies. *Journal of Consulting and Clinical Psychology, 61,* 221–234.

Neimeyer, R. A. (2000). Suicide and hastened death: Toward a training agenda for counseling psychology. *Counseling Psychologist, 28,* 551–560.

Nelson, M. D., & Johnson, P. (1999). School counselors as supervisors: An integrated approach for supervising school counseling interns. *Counselor Education and Supervision, 39,* 89–100.

Nelson, M. L. (2002). An assessment-based model for counseling strategy selection. *Journal of Counseling and Development, 80,* 416–421.

Nelson, M. L., & Neufeldt, S. A. (1998). The pedagogy of counseling: A critical examination. *Counselor Education and Supervision, 38,* 70–88.

Ngo-Metzger, Q., Massagli, M. P., Clarridge, B. R., Manocchia, M., Davis, R. B., Iezzoni, L. I., et al. (2003). Linguistic and cultural barriers to care: Perspectives of Chinese and Vietnamese immigrants. *Journal of General Internal Medicine, 18,* 44–52.

Nielsen, S. L., Johnson, W. B., & Ridley, C. R. (2000).

Religiously sensitive rational emotive therapy: Theory, techniques, and brief excerpts from a case. *Professional Psychology: Research and Practice, 31,* 21–28.

Noonan, B. M., Gallor, S. M., Hensler-McGinnis, N. F., Fassinger, R. E., Wang, S., & Goodman, J. (2004). Challenges and success: A qualitative study of the career development of highly achieving women with physical and sensory disabilities. *Journal of Counseling Psychology, 51,* 68–80.

Norcross, J. C. (2000). Empirically supported therapeutic relationships: A Division 29 Task Force. *Psychotherapy Bulletin, 35,* 2–4.

Norcross, J. C. (2001). Purposes, processes, and products of the task force on empirically supported therapy relationships. *Psychotherapy, 38,* 345–356.

Norcross, J. C., Hedges, M., & Castle, P. H. (2002). Psychologists conducting psychotherapy in 2001: A study of the Division 29 membership. *Psychotherapy: Theory, Research, Practice, Training, 39,* 97–102.

Norcross, J. C., Hedges, M., & Prochaska, J. O. (2002). The face of 2010: A Delphi poll on the future of psychotherapy. *Professional Psychology: Research and Practice, 33,* 316–322.

Norcross, J. C., Prochaska, J. O., & Farber, J. A. (1993). Psychologists conducting psychotherapy: New findings and historical comparisons on the psychotherapy division membership. *Psychotherapy: Theory, Research, Practice, Training, 30,* 692–697.

Northcut, T. B. (2000). Constructing a place for religion and spirituality in psychodynamic practice. *Clinical Social Work Journal, 28,* 155–169.

Ogrodniczuk, J. S., & Piper, W. E. (1999). Use of transference interpretations in dynamically oriented individual psychotherapy for patients with personality disorders. *Journal of Personality Disorders, 13,* 297–311.

Ogrodniczuk, J. S., Piper, W. E., Joyce, A. S., & McCallum, M. (1999). Transference interpretations in short-term dynamic psychotherapy. *Journal of Nervous and Mental Disease, 187,* 571–578.

O'Hare, T. (1991). Evidence-based social work practice with mentally ill persons who abuse alcohol and other drugs. *Social Work in Mental Health, 1,* 43–62.

Oldham, J. M. (2006). Borderline personality disorder and suicidality. *American Journal of Psychiatry, 163,* 20–26.

Oordt, M. S., Jobes, D. A., Rudd, M. D., Fonseca, V. P., Runyan, C. N., Stea, J. B, et al. (2005). Development of a clinical guide to enhance care for suicidal patients. *Professional Psychology: Research and Practice, 36,* 208–218.

Organista, K. C. (2000). Latinos. In J. R. White & A. S. Freeman (Eds.), *Cognitive-behavioral group therapy: For specific problems and populations* (pp. 281–303). Washington, DC: American Psychological Association.

Organista, K. C., Muñoz, R. F., & Gonzalez, G. (1994). Cognitive-behavioral therapy for depression in low-income and minority medical outpatients: Description of a program and exploratory analyses. *Cognitive Therapy and Research, 18,* 241–259.

Osborn, C. J., Dean, E. P., & Petruzzi, M. L. (2004). Use of simulated multidisciplinary treatment teams and client actors to teach case conceptualization and treatment planning skills. *Counselor Education & Supervision, 44,* 121–134.

Osmo, R., & Rosen, A. (2002). Social workers' strategies for treatment hypothesis testing. *Social Work Research, 26,* 9–18.

Ost, L. G., & Hugdahl, K. (1981). Acquisition of phobias and anxiety response patterns in clinical patients. *Behaviour Research and Therapy, 19,* 439–447.

Oswald, L. M., Roache, J. D., & Rhoades, H. M. (1999) Predictors of individual differences in alprazolam self-medication. *Experimental and Clinical Psychopharmacology, 7,* 379–390.

Otto, R. K. (2000). Assessing and managing violence risk in outpatient settings. *Journal of Clinical Psychology, 56,* 1239–1262.

Owen, I. R. (1999). Exploring the similarities and differences between person-centered and psychodynamic therapy. *British Journal of Guidance and Counselling, 27,* 165–178.

Palmer, K. S. (2001, Sep 10). Younger women turn wrong way to escape abusive boyfriends. *USA Today,* p. A17.

Pancrazio, A. (2001, August 15). Old-world healers: Mexican folk cures find new believers. *The Bellingham Herald*, p. C1. (from the *Arizona Republic*).

Paris, J. (2005). Borderline personality disorder. *Canadian Medical Association, 172*, 1579–1583.

Patterson, C. H. (1996). Multicultural counseling: From diversity to universality. *Journal of Counseling and Development, 74*, 227–231.

Paulson, B. L., & Worth, M. (2002). Counseling for suicide: Client perspectives. *Journal of Counseling and Development, 80*, 86–93.

Pavlov, I. P. (1927). *Conditioned reflexes: An investigation of the physiological activity of the cerebral cortex* (G. V. Anrep trans. and ed.). London: Oxford University Press.

Pearson, Q. M. (2001). A case in clinical supervision: A framework for putting theory into practice. *Journal of Mental Health Counseling, 23*, 174–183.

Pedersen, P. B. (1991). Multiculturalism as a generic approach to counseling. *Journal of Counseling and Development, 70*, 6–12.

Pedersen, P. B. (1998). Culture-centered counselor education. *ACES Spectrum, 58*, 8–9.

Pepinsky, H. B., & Pepinsky, N. (1954). *Counseling theory and practice*. New York: Ronald Press.

Perls, F. (1969). *Gestalt therapy verbatim*. Lafayette, CA: Real Person Press.

Persons, J. B., Davidson, J., & Tompkins, M. A. (2001). *Essential components of cognitive-behavioral therapy for depression*. Washington, DC: American Psychological Association.

Persons, J. B., & Mikami, A. Y. (2002). Strategies for handling treatment failure successfully. *Psychotherapy: Theory, Research, Practice, Training, 39*, 139–151.

Peruzzi, N., & Bongar, B. (1999) Assessing risk for completed suicide in patients with major depressive disorder: Psychologists' view of critical factors. *Professional Psychology: Research and Practice, 30*, 576–580.

Peterman, L. M., & Dixon, C. J. (2003). Domestic violence between same-sex partners: Implications for counseling. *Journal of Counseling and Development, 81*, 40–47.

Piercy, F. P., Lipchik, E., & Kiser, D. (2000). Miller and de Shazer's article on "emotions in solution-focused therapy." *Family Process, 39*, 25–27.

Pikalov, A. (2003). American Psychiatric Association Practice Guidelines for the Treatment of Psychiatric Disorders Compendium 2002. *American Journal of Psychiatry, 160*, 1531–1532.

Piper, W. E., Joyce, A. S., McCallum, M., & Azim, H. F. (1993). Concentration and correspondence of transference interpretations in short-term psychotherapy. *Journal of Consulting and Clinical Psychology, 61*, 586–595.

Piper, W. E., Joyce, A. S., McCallum, M., & Azim, H. F. (1998). Interpretive and supportive forms of psychotherapy and patient personality variables. *Journal of Consulting and Clinical Psychology, 66*, 558–567.

Piper, W. E., McCallum, M., Joyce, A. S., Azim, H. F., & Ogrodniczuk, J. S. (1999). Follow-up findings for interpretive and supportive forms of psychotherapy and patient personality variables. *Journal of Consulting and Clinical Psychology, 67*, 267–273.

Polowy, C. I., & Gilbertson, J. (1997) Social workers and Subpoenas. From the world wide web, 6/27/03 www.naswnyc.org/e15.html

Pomerantz, A. M., & Handelsman, M. H. (2004) Informed consent revisited: An updated written question format. *Professional Psychology: Research and Practice, 35*, 201–205.

President's New Freedom Commission on Mental Health. (2003) Final report. DHHS Pub. No. SMA-03-3832. Rockville, MD: Department of Health and Human Services.

Prieto, L. R., & Scheel, K. R. (2002). Using case documentation to strengthen counselor trainees' case conceptualization skills. *Journal of Counseling and Development, 80*, 11–21.

Prochaska, J. O., & DiClemente, C. C. (1984). *The transtheoretical approach: Crossing the traditional boundaries of therapy*. Malabar, FL: Krieger

Prochaska, J. O., & Norcross, J. C. (2003). *Systems of psychotherapy: A transtheoretical analysis* (5th ed.). Pacific Grove, CA: Brooks/Cole.

Project Match Group. (1997). Matching alcoholism treatment to client heterogeneity: Project MATCH posttreatment drinking outcomes. *Journal of Studies on Alcohol, 58*, 7–29.

Project Match Group. (1998a). Matching alcoholism treatments to client heterogeneity: Project MATCH three-year drinking outcomes. *Alcoholism: Clinical and Experimental Research, 22,* 1300–1311.

Project Match Group. (1998b). Matching patients with alcohol disorders to treatments: Clinical implications from project MATCH. *Journal of Mental Health, 7,* 589–602.

Queener, J. E., & Martin, J. K. (2001). Providing culturally relevant mental health services: Collaboration between psychology and the African American church. *Journal of Black Psychology, 27,* 112–122.

Quick, E. (1998). Doing what works in brief and intermittent therapy. *Journal of Mental Health Counseling, 7,* 527–533.

Ramsey, S., Engler, P., & Stein, M. D. (2005). Alcohol use among depressed patients: The need for assessment and intervention. *Professional Psychology: Research and Practice, 36,* 203–207.

Randall, E. (2001). Existential therapy of panic disorder: A single system study. *Clinical Social Work Journal, 29,* 259–267.

Ravitz, P. (2004). The interpersonal fulcrum – Interpersonal therapy for the treatment of depression. *CPA Bulletin, 36,* 15–19.

Read, J., Agar, K., Barker-Collo, S., Davies, E., & Moskowitz, A. (2001). Assessing suicidality in adults: Integrating childhood trauma as a major risk factor. *Professional Psychology: Research and Practice, 30,* 367–372.

Reddy, M., Borum, R., Berglund, J., Vossekuil, B., Fein, R., & Modzelski, W. (2001). Evaluating risk for targeted violence in schools: Comparing risk assessment, threat assessment, and other approaches. *Psychology in the Schools, 38,* 157–172.

Resnicow, K., Dilorio, C., Soet, J. E., Borrelli, B., Hecht, J., & Ernst, D. (2002). Motivational interviewing in health promotion: It sounds like something is changing. *Health Psychology, 21,* 444–451.

Ribner, D. S., & Knei-Paz, C. (2002). Client's view of a successful helping relationship. *Social Work, 47,* 379–387.

Ridley, C. R., & Lingle, D. W. (1997). Cultural empathy in multicultural counseling. In P. B. Pedersen, J. D. Draguns, W. J. Lonner, & J. E. Trimble (Eds.), *Counseling across cultures* (4th Edition, pp. 21–46). Thousand Oaks, CA: Sage.

Rienzo, B. A., Button, J. W., Sheu, J-j., & Li, Y. (2006). The politics of sexual orientation issues in American schools. *Journal of School Health, 76,* 93–97.

Ritter, M. (2006, Sept. 17). Medical science pioneers win Lasker awards. *Sunday Gazette Mail,* p. 7A.

Rivas-Vazquez, R. A. (2001a). Antidepressants as first-line agents in the pharmacology of anxiety disorders. *Professional Psychology: Research and Practice, 32,* 101–104.

Rivas-Vazquez, R. A. (2001b). Reboxetine: Refocusing on the role of norepinephrine in the treatment of depression. *Professional Psychology: Research and Practice, 32,* 211–214.

Rivas-Vazquez, R. A. (2001c). St. John's wort (hypericum perforatum): Practical considerations based on the evidence. *Professional Psychology: Research and Practice, 32,* 329–332.

Rivas-Vazquez, R. A. (2001d). Understanding drug interactions. *Professional Psychology: Research and Practice, 32,* 543–547.

Rivas-Vazquez, R. A. (2001e). Ziprasidone: Pharmacological and clinical profile of the newest atypical antipsychotic. *Professional Psychology: Research and Practice, 32,* 662–665.

Rivas-Vazquez, R. A. (2003). Atomexetine: A selective norepinephrine reuptake inhibitor for the treatment of attention deficit-hyperactivity disorder. *Professional Psychology: Research and Practice, 34,* 666–669.

Rivas-Vazquez, R. A., & Blais, M. (1997). Serotonin reuptake inhibitors and atypical antidepressants: A review and update for psychologists. *Professional Psychology: Research and Practice, 28,* 526–536.

Rivas-Vazquez, R. A., Blais, M. A., Rey, G. J., & Rivas-Vazquez, A. A. (2001). A brief reminder about documenting the psychological consultation. *Professional Psychology: Research and Practice, 32,* 194–199.

Rivas-Vazquez, R. A., Johnson, S. L., Blais, M., & Rey, G. L. (1999). Serotonin reuptake inhibitor discontinuation syndrome: Understanding, recommendations and management for psychologists. *Professional Psychology: Research and Practice, 30,* 464–469.

Rivas-Vazquez, R. A., Johnson, S. L., Rey, G. L., & Blais, M. (2002). Current treatments for bipolar disorder: A review and update for the psychologist. *Professional Psychology: Research and Practice, 33,* 221–223.

Rivas-Vazquez, R. A., and Rey, J. (2002). Weight gain and metabolic distress associated with the atypical antipsychotics. *Professional Psychology: Research and Practice, 33,* 341–344.

Robbins, S. B. (1989). Role of contemporary psychoanalysis in counseling psychology. *Journal of Counseling Psychology, 36,* 267–278.

Roberts, D. D. (2000). Shorter term treatment of borderline personality disorder: A developmental, self-, and object relations approach. *Psychoanalytic Psychology, 17,* 106–127.

Robins, C. J., & Chapman, A. L. (2004). Dialectical behavior therapy: Current status, recent developments, and future direction. *Journal of Personality Disorders, 18,* 73–89.

Robins, C. J., & Hayes, A. M. (1993). An appraisal of cognitive therapy. *Journal of Consulting and Clinical Psychology, 61,* 205–214.

Robinson, T. L., & Howard-Hamilton, M. F. (2000). *The convergence of race, ethnicity, and gender.* Upper Saddle River, NJ: Prentice-Hall.

Roffers, T., Cooper, B., & Sultanoff, S. M. (1988). Can counselor trainees apply their skills in actual client interviews? *Journal of Counseling and Development, 66,* 385–388.

Rogers, C. R. (1942). *Counseling and psychotherapy.* Boston: Houghton Mifflin.

Rogers, C. R. (1957). The necessary and sufficient conditionings of therapeutic personality change. *Journal of Consulting Psychology, 21,* 95–103.

Rogers, C. R. (1961). *On becoming a person—A psychotherapist's view of psychotherapy.* London: Constable.

Rogers, C. R. (1975). Empathic: An unappreciated way of being. *The Counseling Psychologist, 5,* 2–10.

Rogers, C. R., & Dymond, R. F. (1954). *Psychotherapy and personality change.* Chicago: University of Chicago Press.

Rogers, C. R., & Sanford, R. C. (1985). Client-centered psychotherapy. In H. J. Kaplan & I. Sadock (Eds.), *Comprehensive textbook of psychiatry* (Vol. 2, pp. 1374–1388). Baltimore: William & Wilkins.

Rollnick, S., & Miller, W. R. (1995). What is motivational interviewing? *Behavioural and Cognitive Psychotherapy, 23,* 325–334.

Ronnestad, M. H., & Skovholt, T. M. (2001). Learning arenas for professional development: Retrospective accounts of senior psychotherapists. *Professional Psychology: Research and Practice, 32,* 181–187.

Roose, S. P. (2001). Men over 50: An endangered species. *Psychiatry Clinical Updates,* Medscape, Inc.

Rosenberg, J. (1999). Suicide prevention: An integrated training model using affective and action-based interventions. *Professional Psychology: Research and Practice, 30,* 83–87.

Rosenberger, E. W., & Hayes, J. A. (2002). Origins, consequences, and management of countertransference: A case study. *Journal of Counseling Psychology, 49,* 221–232.

Rossello, J., & Bernal, G. (1999). The efficacy of cognitive-behavioral and interpersonal treatments for depression in Puerto Rican adolescents. *Journal of Consulting and Clinical Psychology, 67,* 734–745.

Rubin, A., & Parrish, D. (2007). Views of evidence-based practice among faculty in master of social work programs: A national survey. *Research on Social Work Practice, 17,* 110–122.

Rudd, M. D., Joiner, T. E., Jobes, D. A., & King, C. A. (1999) The outpatient treatment of suicidality: An integration of science and recognition of its limitations. *Professional Psychology: Research and Practice, 30,* 437–446.

Rudman, L. A. (1998). Self-promotion as a risk factor for women: The costs and benefits of counter-stereotypical impression management. *Journal of Personality and Social Psychology, 74,* 629–645.

Ruiz, P. (Ed.). (2000). *Ethnicity and psychopharmacology.* Washington, DC: American Psychiatric Press.

Ruiz, P., Varner, R. V., Small, D. R., & Johnson, B. A. (1999). Ethnic differences in the neuroleptics treatment of schizophrenia. *Psychiatric Quarterly, 70,* 163–172.

Rupert, P. A., & Baird, K. A. (2004). Managed care and the independent practice of psychology. *Professional Psychology: Research and Practice, 35,* 185–193.

Ryan, V. L., & Gizynski, M. N. (1990). Behavior therapy in retrospect: Patients' feelings about their behavior therapies. *Journal of Consulting and Clinical Psychology, 37,* 1–9.

Sachse, R., & Elliott, R. (2002). Process-outcome research on humanistic therapy variables. In D. J. Cain & J. Seeman (Eds.), *Humanistic psychotherapies: Handbook of research and practice* (pp. 83–115). Washington, DC: American Psychological Association.

Safer, D. L., Telch, C. F., & Agras, W. S. (2001). Dialectical behavior therapy for bulimia nervosa. *American Journal of Psychiatry, 158,* 632–634.

Safran, J. D. (2002). Relational theory, constructivism, and psychotherapy integration: Commentary on Frank (2002). *Journal of Psychotherapy Integration, 12,* 294–301.

Safran, J. D., & Muran, J. C. (1996). The resolution of ruptures in the therapeutic alliance. *Journal of Consulting and Clinical Psychology, 64,* 447–458.

Safran, J. D., Muran, J. C., Samstag, L. W., & Stevens, C. (2001). Repairing alliance ruptures. *Psychotherapy: Theory, Research, Practice, Training, 38,* 406–412.

Safran, J. D., & Walker, L. K. (1991). The relative predictive validity of two therapeutic alliance measures in cognitive therapy. *Psychological Assessment: A Journal of Consulting and Clinical Psychology, 3,* 188–195.

Salyer, S. J. (1997, Feb 25). Virtual reality therapy shrinks fear of spiders away. *Bellingham Herald,* C1–2.

Sanderson, W. C. (2002). Are evidence-based psychological interventions practiced by clinicians in the field? *Medscape Mental Health, 7,* 1–3.

Sandhu, D. S. (1997). Psychocultural profiles of Asian and Pacific Islander Americans: Implications for counseling and psychotherapy. *Journal of Multicultural Counseling and Development, 25,* 7–22.

Sands, S. H. (2003). The subjugation of the body in eating disorders: A particularly female solution. *Psychoanalytic Psychology, 20,* 103–116.

Samuelson, S., & Campbell, C. D. (2005). Screening for domestic violence: Recommendations based on a practice survey. *Professional Psychology: Research and Practice, 36,* 276–282.

Satre, D. D., Knight, B. G., & David, S. (2006). Cognitive-behavioral interventions with older adults: Integrating clinical and gerontological research. *Professional Psychology: Research and Practice, 37,* 489–498.

Schachter, J. (2005). Contemporary American psychoanalysis: A profession?: Increasing the role of research in psychoanalysis. *Psychoanalytic Psychology, 22,* 473–492.

Schaefer, H. H. (1970). Self-injurious behavior: Shaping "head banging" in monkeys. *Journal of Applied Behavior Analysis, 3,* 111–116.

Scheel, M. J., Hanson, W. E., & Razzhavaikina, T. I. (2004). The process of recommending homework in psychotherapy: A review of therapist delivery methods, client acceptability, and factors that affect compliance. *Psychotherapy: Theory, Research, Practice, Training, 41,* 38–55.

Schmidt, N. B., & Woolaway-Bickel, K. (2000). The effects on treatment compliance on outcome in cognitive-behavioral therapy for panic disorder: Quality versus quantity. *Journal of Consulting and Clinical Psychology, 68,* 13–18.

Schneider, K. J. (1999). Clients deserve relationships, not merely "treatments." *American Psychologist, 54,* 206–207.

Schofield, W. (1964). *Psychotherapy: The purchase of friendship.* Englewood Cliffs, NJ: Prentice-Hall.

Schwartz, R. C. (2000). Suicidality in schizophrenia: Implications for the counseling profession. *Journal of Counseling and Development, 78,* 496–499.

Schwartzman, J. B., & Glaus, K. D. (2000). Depression and coronary heart disease in women: Implications for clinical practice and research. *Professional Psychology: Research and Practice, 31,* 48–57.

Seeley, K. M. (2004). Short-term intercultural psychotherapy: Ethnographic. *Social Work, 49,* 121–131.

Seem, S. R., & Johnson, E. (1998). Gender bias among counseling trainees: A study of case conceptualization. *Counselor Education and Supervision, 37,* 257–268.

Seeman, J. (2002). Looking back, looking ahead: A synthesis. In D. J. Cain (Ed.), *Humanistic psychotherapies: Handbook of research and practice* (pp. 617–636). Washington, DC: American Psychological Association.

Sexton, T. L. (2000). Reconstructing clinical training: In pursuit of evidence-based clinical training. *Counselor Education and Supervision, 39,* 218–227.

Sexton, T. L., & Whiston, S. C. (1991). A review of the empirical basis for counseling: Implications for practice and training. *Counselor Education and Supervision, 30,* 330–354.

Shadish, W. R., & Baldwin, S. A. (2003). Meta-analysis of MFT interventions. *Journal of Marital and Family Therapy, 29,* 547–560.

Shapiro, D. A., Rees, A., Barkham, M., Hardy, G., Reynolds, S., & Startup, M. (1995). Effects of treatment duration and severity of depression on the maintenance of gains after cognitive-behavioral and psychodynamic-interpersonal psychotherapy. *Journal of Consulting and Clinical Psychology, 63,* 378–387.

Shapiro, F. (1989). Efficacy of the eye movement desensitization procedure in the treatment of traumatic memories. *Journal of Traumatic Stress, 2,* 199–223.

Sharkin, B. S. (1995) Strains on confidentiality in college-student psychotherapy: Entangled therapeutic relationships, incidental encounters and third-party inquiries. *Professional Psychology: Research and Practice, 26,* 184–189.

Shin, S-M., Chow, C., Camacho-Gonsalves, T., Levy, R. J., Allen, I. E., & Leff, H. S. (2005). A meta-analytic review of racial-ethnic matching for African American and Caucasian American clients and clinicians. *Journal of Counseling Psychology, 52,* 45–56.

Shipman, K. L., Rossman, B. B., & West, J. (1999). Co-occurrence of spousal violence and child abuse: Conceptual implications. *Child Maltreatment, 4,* 93–102.

Shirk, S. R., & Karver, M. (2003). Prediction of treatment outcome from relationship variables in child and adolescent therapy: A meta-analytical review. *Journal of Consulting and Clinical Psychology, 71,* 452–464.

Shonfeld-Ringel, S. (2001). A re-conceptualization of the working alliance in cross-cultural practice with non-western clients: Integrating relational perspectives and multicultural theories. *Clinical Social Work, 29,* 53–63.

Silverstein, B. (2002). Gender differences in the prevalence of somatic versus pure depression: A replication. *American Journal of Psychiatry, 159,* 1051–1053.

Simon, C. C. (2002, Sept. 3). A change of mind: Thanks to managed care, evidence-based medical practice and change ideas about behavior, cognitive therapy is the talking cure of the moment. *The Washington Post, F01.*

Simon, R. I. (1999). The suicide prevention contract: Clinical, legal and risk management issues. *Journal of the American Academy of Psychiatry and the Law, 27,* 445–450.

Simon, R. I. (2006). Imminent suicide: The illusion of short-term prediction. *Suicide and Life-Threatening Behavior, 36,* 296–301.

Skinner, B. F. (1953). *Science and human behavior.* New York: Macmillan Free Press.

Smith, D. (2002). Guidance in treating ADHD. *Monitor on Psychology, 34–35.*

Smith, L. (2005). Psychotherapy, classism, and the poor: Conspicuous by their absence. *American Psychologist, 60,* 687–696.

Smith, N. G., & Ingram, K. M. (2004). Workplace heterosexism and adjustment among lesbian, gay, and bisexual individuals: The role of unsupported interactions. *Journal of Counseling Psychology, 51,* 57–67.

Sneed, J. R., Balestri, M., & Belfi, B. J. (2003). The use of dialectical behavior therapy strategies in the psychiatric emergency room. *Psychotherapy: Theory, Research, Practice, Training, 40,* 265–277.

Sommers-Flanagan, J., & Sommers-Flanagan, R. (1996). Efficacy of antidepressant medication with depressed youth: What psychologists should know. *Professional Psychology: Research and Practice, 27,* 145–153.

Speight, S. L., Myers, L. J., Cox, C. I., & Highlen, P. S. (1991). A redefinition of multicultural counseling. *Journal of Counseling and Development, 70,* 29–36.

Spengler, P. M., Strohmer, D. C., Dixon, D. N., & Shivy, V. A. (1995). A scientist-practitioner model of psychological assessment: Implications for training, practice, and research. *The Counseling Psychologist, 23,* 506–534.

Sperling, M. B., & Sack, A. (2002). Psychodynamics and managed care: The art of the impossible? *American Journal of Psychotherapy, 56,* 362–377.

Stalker, C. A., Levene, J. E., & Coady, N. F. (1999). Solution-focused brief therapy—one model fits all? *Families in Society, 80,* 468–477.

Steenbarger, B. N. (1993). A multicontextual model of counseling: Bridging brevity and diversity. *Journal of Counseling and Development, 72,* 8–15.

Stevens, L. (2003). Improving screening of women for violence: Basic guidelines for physicians. *Medscape, November 20, 2003,* http://www.medscape.com/viewprogram/2777_pnt, 12/2/2003.

Stevens, M. J., & Morris, S. J. (1995). A format for case conceptualization. *Counselor Education and Supervision, 35,* 82–94.

Stewart, A. E. (2004). Can knowledge of client birth order bias clinical judgment? *Journal of Counseling and Development, 82,* 167–176.

Stoltenberg, C. D., Pace, T. M., Kashubeck-West, S., Biever, J. L., et al. (2000). Training models in counseling psychology: Scientist-practitioner versus practitioner-scholar. *Counseling Psychologist, 28,* 622–640.

Straus, S. M., Bleumink, G. S., Dieleman, J. P., van der Lei, J., Jong, G. W., Kingma, J. H., et al. (2004). Antipsychotics and the risk of sudden cardiac death. *Archives of Internal Medicine, 164,* 1293–1297.

Stricker, G. (2003). Evidence-based practice: The wave of the past. *The Counseling Psychologist, 31,* 546–554.

Strumpfel, U., & Goldman, R. (2002). Contacting Gestalt Therapy. In D. J. Cain & J. Seeman (Eds). *Humanistic psychotherapies: Handbook of research and practice* (pp. 189–219). Washington, DC: American Psychological Association.

Stuart, S., & Robertson, M. (2003). *Interpersonal psychotherapy: A clinician's guide.* New York: Oxford University Press.

Sue, D. (1994). Incorporating cultural diversity in family therapy. *The Family Psychologist, 10,* 19–21.

Sue, D. (1997a). Counseling strategies for Chinese Americans. In C. C. Lee (Ed.), *Multicultural issues in counseling: New approaches to diversity* (2nd ed., pp. 173–187). Washington, DC: American Counseling Association.

Sue, D. (1997b). Multicultural training. *International Journal of Intercultural Relations, 21,* 175–193.

Sue, S., Fujino, D. C., Hu, L., Takeuchi, D. T., & Zane, N. W. S. (1991). Community mental health services for ethnic minority groups: A test of the cultural responsiveness hypothesis. *Journal of Consulting and Clinical Psychology, 59,* 533–540.

Sue, D., Ino, S., & Sue, D. M. (1983). Nonassertiveness of Asian-Americans: An inaccurate assumption? *Journal of Counseling Psychology, 30,* 581–588.

Sue, D., Sue, D. M., & Ino, S. (1990). Assertiveness and social anxiety in Chinese-American women. *Journal of Psychology, 124,* 155–164.

Sue, D. W., Ivey, A. E., & Pedersen, P. B. (1996). *A theory of multicultural counseling and therapy.* Pacific Grove, CA: Brooks/Cole Publishing Co.

Sue, D. W., & Sue, D. (2003). *Counseling the culturally different: Theory and practice* (4th ed.). New York: Wiley.

Sue, D. W., & Sue, D. (2008). *Counseling the culturally different: Theory and practice* (5th ed.). New York: Wiley.

Sundberg, N. D. (1981). Cross-cultural counseling and psychotherapy: A research overview. In A. J. Marsella & P. B. Pedersen (Eds.), *Cross-cultural counseling and psychotherapy.* New York: Pergamon Press.

Surgeon General's Call to Action to Prevent Suicide. (1999). Retrieved June 27, 2003 from the World Wide Web: http://sugeongeneral.gov/library/calltoaction/fact2.htm.

Svensson, B., & Hansson, L. (1999). Therapeutic alliance in cognitive therapy for schizophrenic and other long-term mentally ill patients: Development and relationship to outcome in an in-patient treatment programme. *Act Psychiatrica Scandinavica, 99,* 281–287.

Swartz-Kulstad, J. L., & Martin, W. E. Jr. (1999). Impact of culture and context on psychosocial adaptation: The cultural and contextual guide process. *Journal of Counseling and Development, 77,* 281–293.

Swindle Jr., R., Heller, K., Pescosolido, B., & Kikuzawa. (2000). Responses to nervous breakdowns in America over a 40-year period: Mental health policy implications. *American Psychologist, 55*, 740–749.

Tanner, L. (2006, Mar 17). Study: Drugs for kids unproven. *Bellingham Herald*, B4.

Taylor, S., Thordarson, D. S., Maxwell, L., Fedoroff, I. C., Lovell, K., & Ogrodniczuk, J. (2003). Comparative efficacy, speed, and adverse effects of three PTSD treatments: Exposure therapy, EMDR, and relaxation training. *Journal of Consulting and Clinical Psychology, 71*, 330–338.

Teasdale, J. D., Segal, Z. V., Williams, J. M. G., Ridgeway, V. A., Soulsby, J. M., & Lau, M. A. (2000). Prevention of relapse/recurrence in major depression by mindfulness-based cognitive therapy. *Journal of Consulting and Clinical Psychology, 68*, 615–623.

Tervalon, M. (2003). Components of culture in health for medical students' education. *Academic Medicine, 78*, 570–576.

Teusch, L., Bohme, H., Finke, J., & Gastpar, M. (2001). Effects of client-centered psychotherapy for personality disorders alone and in combination with psychopharmacological treatment. *Psychotherapy and Psychosomatics, 70*, 328–336.

Thompson, L. W., Powers, D. V., Coon, D. W., Takagi, K., McKibbin, C., & Gallagher-Thompson, D. (2000). In J. R. White & A. S. Freeman (Eds.), *Cognitive-behavioral group therapy: For specific problems and populations* (pp. 235–261). Washington, DC: American Psychological Association.

Thompson Sanders, V. L., & Alexander, H. (2006). Therapists' race and African American clients' reaction to therapy. *Psychotherapy: Theory, Research, Practice, Training, 43*, 99–110.

Thorndike, E. L. (1911). *Animal intelligence.* New Jersey: Transaction Publishers.

Tischler, C. L., Gordon, L. B., & Landry-Meyer, L. (2000). Managing the violent patient: A guide for psychologists and mental health professionals. *Professional Psychology: Research and Practice, 31*, 34–41.

Tobin, J. J., & Friedman, J. (1983). Spirits, shamans, and nightmare death: Survivor stress in a Hmong refugee. *American Journal of Orthopsychiatry, 53*, 439–448.

Todd, J., & Bohart, A. C. (1999). *Foundations of clinical and counseling psychology.* New York: Addison Wesley Longman.

Trierweiler, S. J., Muroff, J. R., Jackson, J. S., Neighbors, H. W., & Munday, C. (2005). Clinician race, situational attributions, and diagnosis of mood versus schizophrenia disorders. *Cultural Diversity and Ethnic Minority Psychology, 11*, 351–364.

Truscott, D., Evans, J., & Mansell, S. (1995). Outpatient psychotherapy and dangerous clients: A model for clinical decision-making. *Professional Psychology: Research and Practice, 26*, 484–490.

Tryer, K., Catalan, J., Schmidt, U., Dent, J., Tats, P., Thorton, S., et al. (1999) Manual-assisted cognitive behavioural therapy (MACT): A randomized controlled trial of brief intervention with bibliotherapy in the treatment of recurrent self-harm. *Psychological Medicine, 29*, 19–25.

Turner, R. M. (2000). Naturalistic evaluation of dialectical behavior therapy-oriented treatment for borderline personality disorder. *Cognitive and Behavioral Practice, 7*, 413–419.

Ukens, C. (1999). Chain drug stores seek regulatory relief from pharmacy boards. *Drug Topics, 22*, 143–145.

U.S. Census Bureau. (2000). *Data highlights.* Retrieved 10/14/2003 from http://www.census .gov.

U.S. Census Bureau. (2002). Poverty and income reports. Washington, DC: U. S. Government Printing Office.

U.S. Census Bureau. (2004). *The foreign-born population in the United States: 2003.* Washington, DC: U.S. Government Printing Office.

U.S. Census Bureau. (2005). *Population projections.* Washington, DC: U. S. Government Printing Office.

U.S. Census Bureau. (2006b). *65+ in the United States: 2005.* Washington, DC: U. S. Government Printing Office.

U.S. Department of Health and Human Services. (1998). *The national elder abuse incidence study.* Washington, DC: U. S. Government Printing Office.

U.S. Department of Health and Human Services. (2001). *Mental Health: Culture, race, and ethnicity—A supplement to mental health: A report of the*

Surgeon General—Executive summary. Rockville, MD: U.S. Department of Health and Human Services.

Valenstein, M., Copeland, L. A., Own, R., Blow, F. C., & Visnic, S. (2001). Adherence assessments and the use of depot antipsychotics in patients with schizophrenia. *Journal of Clinical Psychiatry, 62,* 545–554.

Vallis, M. T. (1998). When the going gets tough: Cognitive therapy for the severely disturbed. In C. Perris & P. D. McGorry (Eds.), *Cognitive psychotherapy of psychotic and personality disorders: Handbook of theory and practice* (pp. 37–62). Chichester, England: Wiley.

VandeCreek, L., & Knapp, S. (2000). Risk-management and life-threatening patient behaviors. *Journal of Clinical Psychology, 56,* 1335–1351.

Vasilaki, E. I., Hosier, S. G., & Cox, W. M. (2006). The efficacy of motivational interviewing as a brief intervention for excessive drinking: A meta-analytic review. *Alcohol and Alcoholism, 41,* 328–335.

Vatcher, C.-A., & Bogo, M. (2001). The feminist/emotionally focused therapy practice model: An integrated approach for couple therapy. *Journal of Marital and Family Therapy, 27,* 69–84.

Vedantam, S. (2004, Sep 24). FAD suppressed antidepressant risks, panel says. *Houston Chronicle,* p. 12.

Vitiello, B., Riddle, M. A., Greenhill, L. L., March, J. S. Levine, J., Schacher, R. J., et al. (2003) How can we improve the assessment of safety in child and adolescent pharmacology? *Journal of the American Academy of Child and Adolescent Psychiatry, 42,* 634–641.

Vontress, C. E. (1998). The courage to be an existential counselor: An interview of Clemmont E. Vontress. *Journal of Mental Health Counseling, 20,* 1–12.

Vontress, C. E., Johnson, J. A., & Epp, L. R. (1999). *Cross-cultural counseling: A casebook.* Alexandria, VA: American Counseling Association.

Wachtel, P. L. (2002). Psychoanalysis and the disenfranchised: From therapy to justice. *Psychoanalytic Psychology, 19,* 199–215.

Wagner, A. K., Zhang, F., Soumerai, S. B., Walker, A. M., Gurwitz, J. H., Glynn, R. J., et al. (2004). Benzodiazepine use and hip fracture in the elderly: Who is at greatest risk? *Archives of Internal Medicine, 164,* 1567.

Wagner, A. W. (2005). A behavioral approach to the case of Ms. S. *Journal of Psychotherapy Integration, 15,* 101–114.

Walsh, R. (2004). What is good psychotherapy. *Journal of Humanistic Psychology, 44,* 455–467.

Walsh, R. A., & McElwain, B. (2002). Existential psychotherapies. In D. J. Cain & J. Seeman (Eds.), *Humanistic psychotherapies: Handbook of research and practice* (pp. 253–278). Washington, DC: American Psychological Association.

Wampold, B. E. (2001). *The great psychotherapy debate: Models, methods, and findings.* Mahwah, NJ: Erlbaum.

Want, V., Parham, T. A., Baker, R. C., & Sherman, M. (2004). African American students' ratings of Caucasian and African American counselors varying in racial consciousness. *Cultural Diversity and Ethnic Minority Psychology, 10,* 123–136.

Ward, E. C. (2005). Keeping it real: A grounded theory study of African American clients engaging in counseling at a community mental health agency. *Journal of Counseling Psychology, 52,* 471–481.

Watson, J. B., & Raynor, R. (1920). Conditioned emotional responses. *Journal of Experimental Psychology, 3,* 1–14.

Watson, J. C. (2002). Re-visioning empathy. In D. J. Cain & J. Seeman (Eds.), *Humanistic psychotherapies: handbook of research and practice* (pp. 445–471). Washington, DC: American Psychological Association.

Watson, J. C., Gordon, L. B., Stermac, L., Kalogerakos, F., & Steckley, P. (2003). Comparing the effectiveness of process-experiential with cognitive-behavioral psychotherapy in the treatment of depression. *Journal of Consulting and Clinical Psychology, 71,* 773–781.

Watts, R. E., & Pietrzak, D. (2000). Adlerian "encouragement" and the therapeutic process of solution-focused brief therapy. *Journal of Counseling and Development, 78,* 442–447.

Webster, C. D., Douglas, K. S., Eaves, D., & Hart, S. D. (1997). *HCR-20: Assessing risk for violence* (Version 2). Burnaby BC: Mental Health, Law and Policy Institute, Simon Frazier University.

Weinberger, J. (2002). Short paper, large impact: Rosenzweig's influence on the common factor movement. *Journal of Psychotherapy Integration, 12,* 67–76.

Weinrach, S. G. (2003). Much ado about multiculturalism, part 4. *Counseling Today* (January): 31.

Weinrach, S. G., & Thomas, K. R. (1998). Diversity-sensitive counseling today: A postmodern clash of values. *Journal of Counseling and Development, 76,* 115–122.

Weiss, A. (2001). The no-suicide contract: Possibilities and pitfalls. *American Journal of Psychotherapy, 55,* 414–419.

Weissman, M. M. (2007). Cognitive therapy and interpersonal psychotherapy: 30 years later. *American Journal of Psychiatry, 164,* 693–696.

Westefeld, J. S., Range, L. M. Rogers, J. R., Maples, M. R., Bromley, J. L., & Alcorn, J. (2000). Suicide: An overview. *Counseling Psychologist. 28,* 445–510.

Westen, D., Novotny, C. M., & Thompson-Brenner, H. (2004). The empirical status of empirically supported psychotherapies: Assumptions, findings, and reporting in controlled clinical trials. *Psychological Bulletin, 130,* 631–663.

Wetchler, J. L., & Fisher, B. L. (1991). A prepracticum course for beginning marriage and family therapy students. *The Clinical Supervisor, 9,* 171–180.

Wheelock, I. (2000). The value of a psychodynamic approach in the managed care setting. *American Journal of Psychotherapy, 54,* 204–215.

Whelton, W. J. (2004). Emotional processes in psychotherapy: Evidence across therapeutic modalities. *Clinical Psychology and Psychotherapy, 11,* 58–71.

Whiston, S. C., & Coker, J. K. (2000). Reconstructing clinical training: Implications from research. *Counselor Education and Supervision, 39,* 228–253.

White, K. P. (2000). Psychology and complementary and alternative medicine. *Professional Psychology: Research and Practice, 31,* 671–681.

Whittingdon, C. J., Kendall, T., Fonagy, P., Cottrell, D., Cotgrove, A., & Boddington, E. (2004). Selective serotonin reuptake inhibitors in childhood depression: Systematic review of published versus unpublished data. *Lancet, 363,* 1335, 1341–1345.

Wiggins, J. G., & Cummings, N. A. (1998). National study of the experience of psychologists with psychotropic medication and psychotherapy. *Professional Psychology: Research and Practice, 29,* 549–552.

Williams, G. C., Rodin, G. C., Ryan, R. M., Grolnick, W. L., & Deci, E. L. (1998). Autonomous regulation and long-term medication adherence in adult outpatients. *Health Psychology, 17,* 269–276.

Wisch, A. F., & Mahalik, J. R. (1999). Male therapists' clinical bias: Influence of client gender roles and therapist gender role conflict. *Journal of Counseling Psychology, 46,* 51–60.

Wolkenstein, B. H., & Sterman, L. (1998). Unmet needs of older women in a clinic population: The discovery of the possible long-term sequelae of domestic violence. *Professional Psychology: Research and Practice, 29,* 341–348.

Wolpe, J. (1958). *Psychotherapy by reciprocal inhibition.* Stanford, CA: Stanford University Press.

Wong, E. C., Kim, B. S. K., Zane, N. W. S., Kim, I. J., & Huang, J. S. (2003). Examining culturally based variables associated with ethnicity: Influences on credibility perceptions of empirically supported interventions. *Cultural Diversity and Ethnic Minority Psychology, 9,* 88–96.

Woodard, V. S., & Lin, Y-N. (1999). Designing a prepracticum for counselor education programs. *Counselor Education and Supervision, 39,* 134–145.

Woody, R. H. (1999) Domestic violations of confidentiality. *Professional Psychology: Research and Practice, 30,* 607–610.

Woody, S. R., & Sanderson, W. C. (1998). Manuals for empirically supported treatments: 1998 update. *Clinical Psychologist, 51,* 17–21.

Wszola, B. A., Newell, K. M., & Sprague, R. L. (2001). Risk factors for tardive dyskinesia in a large population of youth and adults. *Experimental and Clinical Psychopharmacology, 9,* 285–296.

Yalom, I. D. (1980). *Existential psychotherapy.* New York: Basic Books.

Yapko, M. D. (1994). Suggestibility and repressed

memories of abuse: A survey of psychotherapists' beliefs. *American Journal of Clinical Hypnosis, 36,* 163–171.

Yedidia, T. (2005). Immigrant therapists' unresolved identity problems and countertransference. *Clinical Social Work Journal, 33,* 159–171.

Yeung, A., Chang, D., Gresham, R. L., Nierenberg, A. A., & Fava, M. (2004). Illness beliefs of depressed Chinese American patients in primary care. *Journal of Nervous and Mental Disease, 192,* 324–327.

Yonkers, K. A., Kando, K. C., Cole, J. O., & Blumenthal, S. (1992). Gender differences in pharmacokinetics and pharmacodynamics of psychotropic medication. *American Journal of Psychiatry, 150,* 678–679.

Yoshihama, M. (2002). Battered women's coping strategies and psychological distress: Differences by immigration status. *American Journal of Community Psychology, 30,* 429–452.

Young, J. E. (2005). Schema-focused cognitive therapy and the case of Ms. S. *Journal of Psychotherapy Integration, 15,* 115–126.

Young, M., Read, J., Barker-Collo, & Harrison. (2001). Evaluating and overcoming barrier to taking abuse histories. *Professional Psychology: Research and Practice, 32,* 407–414.

Ziguras, S. J., Klimidis, S. Lambert, T. J., & Jackson, A. C. (2001). Determinants of anti-psychotic medication compliance in a multicultural population. *Community Mental Health Journal, 37,* 273–283.

Zlotnick, C., Johnson, S. L., Miller, I. W., Pearlstein, T., & Howard, M. (2001). Postpartum depression in women receiving public assistance: Pilot study of an interpersonal-therapy–oriented group intervention. *American Journal of Psychiatry, 158,* 638–641.

Zuroff, D. C., & Blatt, S. J. (2006). The therapeutic relationship in the brief treatment of depression: Contributions to clinical improvement and enhanced adaptive capabilities. *Journal of Consulting and Clinical Psychology, 74,* 130–140.

Zuroff, D. C., Blatt, S. J., Sotsky, S. M., Krupnick, J. L., Martin, D. J., Sanislow, C. A., et al. (2000). Relation of therapeutic alliance and perfectionism to outcome in brief outpatient treatment of depression. *Journal of Consulting and Clinical Psychology, 68,* 114–124.

Author Index

421

Subject Index